(Post)Socialist Transformation of Primary Schools

Jiří Zounek • Oto Polouček • Michal Šimáně

(Post)Socialist Transformation of Primary Schools

Processes, Stories and Challenges
in the Czech Republic

 Springer

Jiří Zounek 🆔
Department of Educational Sciences
Masaryk University, Faculty of Arts
Brno, Czech Republic

Michal Šimáně 🆔
Department of Social Sciences
Mendel University in Brno
Brno, Czech Republic

Oto Polouček 🆔
Department of Educational Sciences,
Department of European Ethnology,
Faculty of Arts
Masaryk University
Brno, Czech Republic

ISBN 978-3-031-58767-2   ISBN 978-3-031-58768-9   (eBook)
https://doi.org/10.1007/978-3-031-58768-9

This work was supported by Czech Science Foundation

This Springer imprint is published by the registered company Springer Nature Switzerland AG
The registered company address is: Gewerbestrasse 11, 6330 Cham, Switzerland

Paper in this product is recyclable.

Preface

This book focuses on Czech primary schools after the fall of the communist regime in 1989, a chapter in time that holds a special position in historical-pedagogical topics. For some readers, the period of the late 1980s and early 1990s may not be 'history' because they lived in the given period and remember much of it, and some events might seem to have happened 'a few weeks ago'. For some, it may be a sensitive period of their lives in which they experienced both good and bad times. Other readers may perceive this period as a regular historical theme because they were born in the 1990s or later.

For us as historians, this period is a great challenge because the history of the transformation of schools after 1989 remains unknown in many ways. It is a challenge for us in terms of both content and methodology. The transformation of the post-socialist school system cannot be fully understood without knowledge of the broader historical contexts and developments of the school system and society in Czechoslovakia and Europe throughout virtually the entire twentieth century. For this reason, this book contains a rather extensive section focused on the history of the Czechoslovak school system in the last century with an emphasis on the second half of the century. The research of transformation is also a challenge in terms of methodology. It might seem that a topic 'only' a few decades old could be researched on the basis of a huge amount of contemporary documents. This is only partially true. Many archival documents are currently unavailable or still await processing. Some documents are probably irretrievably lost because the period of revolution was not very amenable to storing documents in archives. In our research, we therefore used a mixed historical-pedagogical research design, combining an oral history method with the study of contemporary sources. The oral history method provided us with unique insights into the lives and behaviour of the direct participants in the transformation as well as into the period just before it of late socialism. Oral history broadens the base of our sources and allows us to engage the human dimension in historical topics. The book thus processes the topic in a unique way, linking general historical frameworks with the history of everyday life of post-socialist schools and the everyday lives of their school heads, teachers, and parents.

This book is the result of several years of the authors' collaborations on research projects that focused on the history of socialist and post-socialist primary school systems. In writing the book, our primary goals were to acquire new scientific insights on the transformation and to broaden and deepen the existing expert knowledge on the topic in many ways. The methodology used enabled us to show the often-hidden processes of transformation, thereby leading to a better understanding of the various mechanisms of change in the post-revolutionary years. Our results can aid in understanding the development of Czech primary schools, including the successes and failures of post-1995 reforms. Findings from the research can serve as important sources of information for education policy, teacher educators, current initiators of changes in the school system, and the wider professional public. The results of the research can contribute to the international debate on the shaping of primary school systems as well as on the life and profession of teachers (not only) in post-socialist countries. The insights into the mechanisms and processes of un/successful reforms or innovations in the reality of schools and into the behaviour of the main participants in the course of these changes may be of particular interest to the reader.

We build on the conviction that the period of socialism, and particularly of post-socialism, is of key importance for the historical experience of individuals and the entire society of the second half of the twentieth century in Czechoslovakia and in many European countries. Indeed, even today, we should not underestimate the various forms of the 'heritage' of the difficult period of the second half of the twentieth century in these countries, in reference to people's memories and especially to their thinking about contemporary society, politics, culture, science, education, school systems, and life, and in reference to the prospects of the near or distant future.

In writing this book, we had yet another goal in mind: to preserve the memory of a very complex and contradictory period in the school system of a European country that is simultaneously extremely interesting and inspiring. This memory forces consideration of the processes of the transformation of schools in general and about the roles of school policy; it also inspires reflections on the influence of reforms on the everyday life of schools and teachers, on the roles the different levels of management can play, on the possible results of unprepared reforms of the school system, on the ways in which various innovations are perceived by ordinary teachers, on the reasons teachers have for being cautious about accepting changes, and on the ways in which parents enter the life of schools. In the course of reading of our book, readers will discover which aspects of the topic will be the most central or interesting for them.

We would like for this book to be an inspiration for further (similar) research in other countries as well, as time is unfortunately running out and the numbers of eyewitnesses of various important events of the twentieth century school systems are dwindling. We would also be happy if our book was useful to readers who are interested in the problems of contemporary history (of the school system), whether they are researchers, teachers, students, people interested in modern history, or even the general public, and not only in 'post-socialist countries'.

Brno, Czech Republic   Jiří Zounek
March 2024

Oto Polouček

Michal Šimáně

Acknowledgments

First, we would like to thank our families and friends, without whose support and especially patience we would never have been able to finish this book.

We would also like to thank our colleagues and co-workers from the Department of Educational Sciences and the Department of European Ethnology at the Faculty of Arts of Masaryk University for their help.

Our book could not have been written without the help of many archivists and librarians, or without the help of our students. Special thanks go to all the eyewitnesses who cooperated with us. Many of them sacrificed a lot of their time to the interviews and to tracking down various contemporary documents or they recommended other eyewitnesses to us.

We want to thank Jonáš Lasák and Anne Johnson for their indispensable assistance with the linguistic aspects of the text, reviews, and proofreading.

Last but not least, we thank the reviewers who helped us with their comments, valuable advice, and feedback.

This publication was created in the course of the research project Post-socialistická transformace základních škol—procesy, příběhy, dilemata (Post-Socialist Transformation of Primary Schools—Processes, Stories, Dilemmas) funded by the Czech Science Foundation (project number 20-11275S). We are hereby grateful for this support.

Contents

1 Introduction   1
   Bibliography 30

Part I   Contexts of Czechoslovakian School System Development

2 **From the Habsburg Monarchy to the Czechoslovak**
   Republic: Education in Historical Context. 37
   2.1   Education Since the Eighteenth Century 37
   2.2   Interwar Czechoslovakia (1918–1938) 40
   2.3   Interwar Education: A Period of Many
         (Un)successful Reforms. 42
   2.4   Schooling During World War II 45
   Bibliography 47

3 **From Stalinism to the Prague Spring—Education**
   in Complicated Times 51
   3.1   The Forms of Postwar Reconstruction (1945–1953) 52
   3.2   Stabilization of the Communist Regime and the Period
         of Hope (1953–1968). 55
   3.3   Prague Spring 1968 56
   3.4   Postwar School System—Between Two Totalitarian Systems 58
   3.5   A Period of Chaotic Changes in the 1950s 62
   3.6   Socialism with a Human Face in Schools 64
   3.7   Teachers and Schools After August 1968 67
   3.8   Ideological Hardening After 1969: The Advent
         of 'Normalization' and Ideological Education 70
   Bibliography 73

**4   Schools and Teachers Two Decades Before the Fall
     of the Communist Regime**   77
    4.1   Normalization in Czechoslovakia (1969–1989)   78
    4.2   Normalization in Education: The Way Back   83
    4.3   A Look Inside a Socialist Teacher's Workshop   88
    4.4   Aids and Textbooks in a Socialist School   90
    4.5   Teachers' Life Outside Work, or Teachers Shall
          Not Live by School Alone   97
    4.6   Perestroika and the Debate on School System Reforms   103
    Bibliography   110

Part II   Schools and Teachers in the Period of Changes

**5   Transforming the Education System: A Difficult Return
     to Democratic Europe**   117
    5.1   Broader Contexts of Transformation: Between Ideology,
          Chaos, and Freedom.   117
    5.2   Legislative Framework of Reforms: (Only) Partial Changes.   121
    5.3   Expert Discussions on the School System Reforms After 1989 . . .   125
    5.4   Schools and Economic Problems of Transformation.   130
    5.5   Comparison of the Transformation of the School
          System with Neighbouring Post-Socialist Countries.   135
    Bibliography   138

**6   Schools: Everyday Life in the Period of Post-Socialist
     Transformation**   143
    6.1   Schools on the Threshold of a New Era.   143
    6.2   Staffing Changes in Schools   150
    6.3   New School Management   161
    6.4   Educational Offices: The Backbone of Primary Schools.   164
    6.5   Municipality as the Founder of the School   168
    6.6   School Autonomy—Hopes and Disappointments   171
    Bibliography   177

7   Schools in a Network of (External) Relationships   179
    7.1   People Involved in School Life and the Transformation
          of Relationships Between Them   180
    7.2   Small-Town Schools and the Founding of Multi-year
          Grammar Schools.   185
    7.3   Large Urban Schools and the Reverberations
          of Late Socialist Building   191
    7.4   Schools and Social Inequalities in Society   195
    7.5   The Functional Rural Community and Its Impact
          on School Life   200
    7.6   Transformation of School Inspection After 1989   204
    Bibliography   208

8   Teachers: Various Life Stories and Perspectives 213
      8.1   Generations 213
      8.2   Karel's Story 215
      8.3   František's Story 220
      8.4   Olga's Story 224
      8.5   Vlasta's Story 231
      8.6   Life Stories in the Context of Time 238
      Bibliography 240

9   Learning and Teaching: The Legacy of the Socialist
      Era and New Challenges 243
      9.1   On Teaching and Learning 243
      9.2   The Revolution in Schools (That Didn't Happen) 246
      9.3   Textbooks: New Possibilities and the Free Market 250
      9.4   Aids and Equipment in Schools – A Good Basis
             of a Socialist School. 253
      9.5   Computers in Primary Schools: The First Shy Steps. 255
      9.6   Foreign Language Teaching: Clear Direction, Difficult
             Implementation 258
      9.7   Further Teacher Education: The Old System Has
             to Be Abolished, But What Next? 260
      9.8   Looking Back at the Interviews 262
      Bibliography 264

Conclusion 267

Index 279

About the Authors

Jiří Zounek (1973) works as Associate Professor in the Department of Educational Sciences at the Faculty of Arts at Masaryk University (Czech Republic). For a long time, he has been focusing on the history of Czech pedagogy and school systems in the twentieth century and at the same time on the use of digital technologies in education. In the past ten years, he has been the grantee or a project partner in several research and development projects. Between 2017 and 2019, he was the main researcher for the research project entitled *Digital Technologies in Everyday Lives and Learning of Students* (Czech Science Foundation, 17-06152S). Between 2014 and 2016, he was the grantee of the research project entitled *Everyday Life of Basic Schools in the Normalization Period as Seen by Teachers: Applying Oral History to Research in History of Contemporary Education* (Czech Science Foundation, 14-05926S). He was the main researcher for the follow-up project *Post-Socialist Transformation of Czech Primary Schools: Processes, Stories, Dilemmas* (Czech Science Foundation, 20-11275S).

He has (co-)authored books about ICT in primary schools, teachers and technology, mobile technologies in education, and e-learning. He is the main author of *Life and Learning of Digital Teens: Adolescents and Digital Technology in the Czech Republic* (Springer, 2022). He has (co-)authored books about the history of Czech primary schools in communist Czechoslovakia. He has published the results of his work in scientific journals and at international conferences. He is a member of the Czech Oral History Association and a member of Czech Association of Educational Research (member of European Educational Research Association). He is also a member of the SAB (Science Advisory Board of the Vice-Rector for Research) at Masaryk University. More information at http://zounek.cz/ and https://www.muni.cz/en/people/1752-jiri-zounek.

Oto Polouček (1990) works as Assistant Professor in the Department of European Ethnology at the Faculty of Arts at Masaryk University in Brno. He focuses primarily on the transformations of the Czech countryside in the second half of the twentieth century with an emphasis on the period of late socialism and post-socialist transformation. He is also interested in the contemporary countryside and the influence of memory and identity on the sustainability of life of rural communities. He considers the study of everyday life, forms of socialization, and the quality of life of people in the countryside. He is interested in the perspectives of people at the periphery and their situation in the contemporary world. He is the author of the book *Grannies at the Big Beat Party: The Social Life in the Late-Socialist Moravian Countryside* (2020). Between 2020 and 2023, he collaborated on the project *Post-Socialist Transformation of Czech Primary Schools: Processes, Stories, Dilemmas* (Czech Science Foundation, 20-11275S). In 2023, he worked in a local organizing committee for the World Congress of the SIEF (International Society for Ethnology and Folklore), of which he is a member. More information at https://www.muni.cz/en/people/361772-oto-poloucek.

Michal Šimáně (1982) works as the Head of the Department of Social Sciences and as Deputy Director of the Institute of Lifelong Learning at Mendel University in Brno (Czech Republic). His primary long-term focus has been on the history of pedagogy and school systems in the nineteenth and twentieth century and on the problems of vocational education. Between 2019 and 2022, he was the main researcher on a research project entitled *Secondary Technical School in Socialist Czechoslovakia from the History of the Everyday Life Point of View: Oral History Interviews with Teachers* (Czech Science Foundation, 19-24776S). Between 2014 and 2016, during his doctoral studies, he was a member of the research team on the project *Everyday Life of Basic Schools in the Normalization Period as Seen by Teachers: Applying Oral History to Research in the History of Contemporary Education* (Czech Science Foundation, 14-05926S).

He is the author or co-author of several books on the history of Czechoslovak school system in the interwar period and in the socialist period. These include monographs entitled *Czech Minority Education in the Czechoslovak Republic: To the Everyday Life of Primary Schools in Political District Ústí nad Labem* (2019) and *Normal Life in Not So Normal Times: Primary Schools and Their Teachers (Not Only) During the So-Called Normalization Period* (2017).

He regularly publishes the results of his research in scientific journals and at international conferences. He is a member of the Czech Oral History Association, the Czech Association of Educational Research, and the International Standing Conference for the History of Education. He is also a member of editorial boards for several academic journals (e.g., History: Sources and People or Discourse and Communication for Sustainable Education). More information at https://uvis.mendelu.cz/26370-Lide-na-MENDELU?osoba=71953.

List of Abbreviations

BOZP	Occupational health and safety
CEE	Central Eastern Europe
CSK	Czechoslovak crown (currency)
CZK	Czech crown (currency)
ČMOS PŠ	Czech and Moravian Trade Union of Workers in Education
ČNR	Czech National Council
ČŠI	Czech School Inspection
ČSSD	Czech Social Democratic Party
ČSR	Czech Socialist Republic
ČSSR	Czechoslovak Socialist Republic
JZD	Unified Agricultural Cooperative
KSČ	Communist Party of Czechoslovakia
MEYS	Ministry of Youth, Education and Sports
NATO	North Atlantic Treaty Organization
NEMES	Independent Interdisciplinary Group
ODS	Civic Democratic Party
OECD	Organisation for Economic Co-operation and Development
PE	Physical education
SRPŠ	Associations of parents and friends of schools
SSR	Slovak Socialist Republic
StB	State Security Service
USSR	Union of Soviet Socialist Republics
ÚV KSČ	Central Committee of the Communist Party of Czechoslovakia
V4	Visegrad Four
ZVS	Military service

Chapter 1
Introduction

Abstract This introduction presents the theme of the book in the context of the history of Czechoslovakia and later the Czech Republic, and also in an international context. It focuses on the theoretical bases and key concepts used in the book: post-socialist transformation, contemporary history, everyday life history, and microhistory. The second part of this introduction describes the methodology and the course of the research project leading to the results presented in the book. The conclusion provides an outline of the organization of the book and its chapters.

Keywords Czechoslovakia · History · Education · Post-socialist transformation · Research · Methodology · Oral history · Archive

The main topics of this book are the everyday life and transformations of primary schools in Czechoslovakia (now the Czech Republic) during the period of late socialism and especially during the post-socialist transformation. The book focuses on the last two decades of the twentieth century, with the centre of its focus in the period from 1989 to 1999, the first and largely 'spontaneous' period of the transformation of primary schools and, ultimately, of the entire school and education system.

Our book is based on research of the broader contexts of the development of education in Czechoslovakia, specifically since the establishment of the Czechoslovak Republic in 1918 through the period of enforcement of communist education after the communist coup in 1948 to the Velvet Revolution in 1989. The culture and everyday life of schools at the end of the twentieth century were necessarily influenced by previous educational developments. After 1989, for example, discussions arose about a return to the model of education from the First Czechoslovak Republic (1918–1938); this became the basis for the school reform at that time. Socialism and socialist education then formed an important historical framework. Teachers and school heads had lived and received their own education during this period, and a significant portion of them also worked in unified socialist schools for a large part of their careers. Moreover, the problems of the school system and the ideas about possible reforms after 1989 were related to the periods of enforcing perestroika and glasnost in Eastern Europe in the late 1980s (Polouček &

© Masaryk University, Faculty of Arts, Registration no. 00216224,
VAT ID: CZ00216224 2024
J. Zounek et al., *(Post)Socialist Transformation of Primary Schools*,
https://doi.org/10.1007/978-3-031-58768-9_1

Zounek, 2021). The book thus also focuses on the period of 'normalization' (1969–1989), with an emphasis on the 1980s and the fall of the communist government.

The eyewitnesses in the book relate their memories to the past, but they also thematize their current problems and needs, which naturally shape their view of the past as presented in oral history interviews (Yow, 2005; McAdams et al., 1996). Even though the focal point of our interest is delimited by the first decade of school transformation after 1989, we can by no means ignore the broader context and the previous and subsequent developments.

The book focuses on the Czechoslovak or Czech school system, but it places the findings in a broader international context of school system transformation in other (post)socialist countries of Central and Eastern Europe, including Poland, Hungary, Latvia, and the former German Democratic Republic.

The book is based on the historical-pedagogical research of the authors (Polouček & Zounek, 2021; Zounek & Polouček, 2021), which used an oral history method (Abrams, 2016) that provided unique data on the transformation of the everyday life of schools and on the life and work of key participants in the transformation, including teachers and headteachers and other people involved in education, including former school inspectors, officials at the Ministry of Education, and officials in regional educational authorities.[1]

We researched available contemporary documents from the field of education policy, scientific journals for teachers, and relevant legislation. School chronicles and other archived records on the work of schools and teachers also represented an important resource. We made an effort to combine different approaches to history and research methods in order to gain the most comprehensive understanding of the issues (Iggers, 2002). We describe our methodology in more detail later in this chapter.

In the course of working on this book, we built on our earlier research (Zounek, 1996; Zounek & Vichrová, 2008), especially concerning primary schools in Czechoslovakia during the period of normalization (Zounek et al., 2016, 2017a, b, c, d, 2018). We present some of those results in this book. In our previous research, we focused on the problems of primary schools in the second half of the last century; we also examined the history of secondary vocational schools (Šimáně & Kamanová, 2020, 2021; Šimáně, 2021).

In our previous research, we explored the rural social transformations in the period of late socialism, emphasizing socialization and social life while including

---

[1] Educational authorities (Školské úřady) were established in Czechoslovakia on the basis of the Czech National Council Act No. 564/1990 Coll. on State Administration and Self-Government in Education as budgetary organizations for an indefinite period of time. The authority was managed directly by the Ministry of Education, and its activities were defined by the aforementioned Act, by the implementing regulations, and by the statute approved by the Minister of Education.

The funding of regional education (primary and nursery schools, secondary schools, etc.) was one of the most important functions of the educational authorities. The authority allocated funds for salaries, textbooks, and school supplies. At the request of a school or of teaching workers, it provided methodological assistance to its workers regarding labour relations and salary issues.

the important role that educational institutions and youth organizations play in the lives of rural residents (Polouček, 2019, 2020a, b).

This book can be seen as the conclusion of one stage of our efforts aimed at understanding socialist society and the school system, in which we used similar theoretical starting points, including in particular the intersections of microhistory, the history of everyday life, and social anthropology (Dülmen, 2002; Geertz, 2000). In terms of methodology, this stage concerned gathering oral histories combined with studying contemporary documents of various natures and provenance.

All of our research, and ultimately this book, are based on the conviction that the periods of socialism and post-socialism[2] are of crucial importance for the historical experience of individuals and of the entire society in the second half of the twentieth century in the former Czechoslovakia and in the European countries sometimes referred to as 'Eastern bloc' countries, including Poland, Hungary, Romania, and Bulgaria.

The political, economic, and social changes that Czechoslovakia underwent at the end of the 1980s and beginning of the 1990s were so fundamental and deeply affecting for all fields of life for individuals and for the entire society that they can be considered one of the most important milestones in modern history. The events of 17 November 1989 marked the quick and non-violent fall of a totalitarian power; at the same time, they initiated the foundation of a pluralistic democratic system and the formation of civic society. The economic field underwent extensive restructuring and the privatization of the economy, which had been exclusively state-owned before 1989. These processes were connected to a liberalization of business and commerce and the deregulation of prices and the job market. Other post-socialist countries underwent similar changes (Holmes, 1997; Saxonberg, 2001; Kenney, 2002; Walterová & Greger, 2006; Berend, 2009; Holý, 2010; McDermott, 2015; Vaněk & Mücke, 2016). However, the situation in Czechoslovakia was distinctive because the country ceased to exist at the end of 1992: the Czech Republic and the Slovak Republic became successor independent states (Rychlík, 2012).

Fundamental changes in the field of schooling and education took place in Czechoslovakia and later in the Czech Republic in this context. In this book, we focus on describing and explaining the changes in the education policy, school legislation, and the organization and structure of the school system. For example, the opportunity to gain autonomy in all important areas of operation, accompanied by changes in objectives, content, and teaching methods, was a significant change in the management of primary schools. The teaching profession and the external

---

[2] In this book, we use the terms 'socialism' and 'post-socialism', although the countries of Central and Eastern Europe during the Cold War era are often referred to as communist countries (especially internationally). In the Central European region, these terms are typically used interchangeably. In Czechoslovakia, the term socialism, or more precisely state socialism, represents a better definition of the political and economic organization of Czechoslovakia and has been established in the professional community. The country ruled by the Communist Party of Czechoslovakia had a monopoly in terms of a centrally planned economy as well as in politics and ideology, but the (utopian) ideas of communism were never achieved. We focus on the state ideology in more detail in subsequent chapters (Rychlík, 2020).

relations of schools underwent a transformation. All of these topics are captured in the book, both from the traditional perspective of official resources and from the perspectives of immediate eyewitnesses to these processes. The post-socialist transformation is also associated with the opening of imaginary social scissors and the asymmetric development of different regions (Bernard et al., 2018; Pospěch, 2021; Prokop, 2022). We therefore pay attention to the social context of the development of individual regions, including the differences between urban and rural schools and the development of schools in prosperous and declining regions. The latest research in the field of contemporary history[3] pointed out a number of connections between (technocratic) late socialism and (neo-liberal) post-socialism (Kopeček, 2019; McDermott, 2015; Rákosník et al., 2018). These phenomena can be observed in the field of education as well. In this book, we show that many changes and problems were connected with attempts at school reforms from the period of perestroika in the late 1980s.

Processes of pedagogical transformation are among the key themes of our book. We note how teachers processed changes in their work during the transformation and the reasons for their eventual resistance to these changes. We monitor how the teachers navigated the selection and use of new textbooks and teaching aids, including the offer of digital technologies. The relationships between teachers and students and the relationships between teachers and parents are at the centre of our interest. We also focus on the dilemmas teachers faced in their work and in their personal lives as a result of the transformation. We provide information about the first contacts with foreign ('Western') schools, educational institutions, and experts.

At this point, we could end the basic introduction of the topic. However, we believe that it is necessary to introduce the individual key terms at least briefly and to set them in the broader context of the topic and the book as a whole. In the following paragraphs, we therefore introduce the basic key terms used in this book. We then move on to describe the research design and methodology of the project. In the final part, we outline the organization of the book and the contents of each chapter.

In connection to the topic of the book, the reader may automatically consider the concept of a *post-socialist transformation* and the question of how it can actually be understood. This concept encompasses delimitation in terms of both time and content. In terms of time, there is no clear delimitation of the post-socialist transformation, whether we are referring to the transformation of Czechoslovak or Czech society, economy, or culture. Similarly, there is no precise delimitation of the period

---

[3] The area of interest of contemporary history is usually delimited by the period of the recent past, which is distinctive because of the presence of a large number of living eyewitnesses, which resonates in communicative memory and has a strong relationship to the present; it thus becomes a subject of political debate. The temporal delimitation of the period of contemporary history varies for that reason. In Czechia, 1938—which was the year of the Munich Agreement and the beginning of the German occupation of Czechoslovakia before World War II—is now usually considered the milestone for the study of contemporary history. The Institute for Contemporary History at the Academy of Sciences now defines its area of interest using that milestone. However, the definition of contemporary history may vary in geographical terms (Institute of Contemporary History, 2022, cf. Gildea & Simonin, 2008; Niethammer, 2012).

of transformation in the field of education. It is clear that fundamental, rapid, and visible reforms took place in all areas of societal life immediately after the Velvet Revolution started on 17 November 1989. This is where the actual beginning of transformation in Czechoslovakia and later in the Czech Republic took place. However, the end of the transformation is rather difficult to delimit because the transformation processes progressed at different speeds in different regions. It is similar in the field of education. Although we can identify a point in time that marked the notional beginning of a new stage in the development of the Czech school system, there is no clearly determinable point in time that could be defini- tively described as the end of the transformation. In our book, we consider 1999, the year when work began on the '*White paper*', the first modern strategic document of Czech education policy, to be the end of the transformation (Kotásek, 2001). Thus began a phase of systemic preparation for a fundamental reform of the school sys- tem and education policy at the national level. This phase culminated with the adop- tion of the first democratic 'Education Act' in 2004 (Act 561/2004 Coll., on Pre-School, Basic, Secondary, Tertiary Professional and Other Education). Before 2004, primary and secondary education were regulated by the 'socialist' Education Act of 1984, which was amended many times during its existence in the post- revolutionary period. We must emphasize that 1999 is a delimitation only for the purposes of our book and research. In the book, this delimitation serves mainly for the sake of clarity and for reader orientation in time. We fully understand that this period of time cannot be studied and understood without the context of previous and subsequent developments or without the socio-historical context. Therefore, we do not see our delimitation as the only possible one; the post-socialist period can be viewed in different ways, including those that reject any periodization in the field of transformation of the educational system (Fig. 1.1).

In the context of education, the actual concept of *transformation* can be under- stood as 'a complex long-term process of transformation of the societal model in which the social needs, demands and expectations associated with education are changing fundamentally while respecting the societal, group and individual

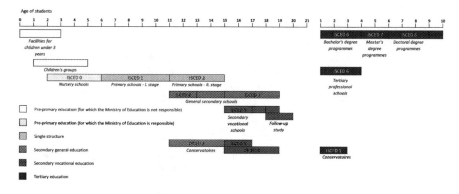

Fig. 1.1 School system in the Czech Republic. (Adapted from Eurydice n.d.)

interests' (Walterová & Greger, 2006, p. 20). This term has been adopted to describe the changes in Czechoslovakia and in Eastern and Central Europe (Chankseliani & Silova, 2018). However, in a broader sense, transformation tends to be a product of a society-wide acceptance of the need for change rather than its initiative. The need for change arose from the Velvet Revolution. At this time, a large part of society identified itself with the ideals thematized by the protest movement formed after 17 November 1989 and previously promoted by the anti-communist opposition. These included demands for the democratization of society and for freedom of speech. The pressure for a transition to a market economy also intensified gradually. However, few people imagined a fundamental departure from state socialism in November 1989. Rather, a large part of society hoped for a kind of 'middle ground' that would preserve the gains of socialism, such as free education and health care, and that would bring Western prosperity and quality of services (Krapfl, 2013). However, the inefficiency of the centrally planned economy, dissatisfaction with supply shortages, the inferior quality of products and services, and the catastrophic state of the environment provided a fertile ground for ideas of a radical transition to a market economy, following a neoliberal model inspired by the Anglo-Saxon environment (especially Thatcher's Britain). In Czechoslovakia, the finance minister of the first post-Soviet government, Václav Klaus (later the prime minister and subsequently the president of the Czech Republic) was the leading pioneer of this idea of a free market, minimal state regulations, and low taxes. The Slovak representatives, however, preferred a more cautious approach to reforms. This differing approach eventually became one of the causes of the Czechoslovak federation break-up.[4]

According to Bauman (1994), the spirit of the post-1989 era and the strong interest of the revolutionary elites in change were crucial for the post-socialist transformation. According to Ther (2016), 'transformation is generally understood as a change in the political and economic system and its social impacts' (p. 25). Across many scientific disciplines, the term has been widely adopted as a denotation of the process of transition from dictatorship to democracy or from a planned to a market economy, with 1989 being symbolically perceived as 'year zero'.[5] Although the

---

[4]The assertion of the neoliberal free market model in post-communist countries is sometimes referred to as the Washington Consensus, because it was strongly supported by supranational and US institutions including the World Bank, International Monetary Fund, and US Treasury. These institutions recommended a model of transition to a market economy according to the ten prescriptions written by economist John Williamson in 1989. These included an emphasis on a balanced state budget, financial liberalization, privatization of state-owned enterprises, and the removal of barriers to foreign investment (Berend, 2009; Ther, 2016). These ideas were shared by politicians such as Václav Klaus and Polish Finance Minister Leszek Balcerowicz.

[5]The concept of 'year zero' has been made very problematic by recent research in the field of contemporary history. In the expert environment of late socialism, the questions of various forms of economic transformation were already studied and considered in the 1980s. This was also true in the field of education. In the field of economics, it is not possible to speak of an 'equal starting line', since both the representatives of the nomenclature elites and people experienced in trading within the rampant grey economy (i.e., those with the appropriate economic and social capital) subsequently benefited the most from the post-socialist transformation (Kopeček, 2019).

definition of transformation can undoubtedly be applied to other periods of social change as well (e.g. the revolutionary period at the end of the eighteenth century), Ther (2016) emphasized that the particular characteristics of different historical phases make the term hard to define without reference to a specific period. That is why we also do not write about transformation in general, but rather about the specific post-socialist transformation of the countries of Central and Eastern Europe.

The development of education and the school system after 1989 has been the subject of a number of studies and books, written at varying time intervals and contributing to the reflection on changes since then. Czech authors include Kotásek (1996), Koucký (1996), Čerych (1995, 1999), Spilková (1997), Walterová (2004), Greger (2011), and Moree (2013). These works have focused on various aspects of transformation, such as transformations in school organization, changes in curriculum, and the political context of changes in education; they have also focused in detail on the transformation of specific schools.

The topic of post-socialist transformation in Czechoslovakia has also been addressed by foreign authors, some of whom have compared the transformation processes in Czechoslovakia with other post-socialist countries (von Kopp, 1992; Mitter, 2003; Perry, 2005).

Studies describing ongoing changes and studies offering a theoretical reflection on changes in the region were of interest to transnational organizations that even initiated some of the studies. In the field of education, studies have been supported by the Council of Europe (Bîrzea, 1994), the OECD (Čerych, 1996), and the World Bank (Berryman, 2000; Fiszbein, 2001). These studies mainly concern analyses of the key principles and processes of the transformation of education and the school system in the context of the transformation of society.

Thus, more than 30 years after the Velvet Revolution, knowledge has been gathered and presented of the basic developmental tendencies and trends of the post-socialist transformation of the school system. It is clear from the cited studies that a number of changes related to organization, structure, content, and pedagogy were adopted. A question remains of whether and how the changes were actually implemented and how they affected the real situation in schools.

That is why the study of the *everyday life of schools* forms a basic starting point for identifying the reflections of the transformations directly in schools. The everyday life refers to the regular 'ordinary' form of school life. Specifically, it refers to the way in which the teachers taught and spent their free time, how their regular routine or daily programme changed or did not change, and what life in the classrooms or teacher's rooms looked like.

In the study of everyday life, we draw inspiration both from pedagogical research of the school environment (Lawn & Grosvenor, 2005; Silova et al., 2018) and from the principles of research of the *history of the everyday life* in historiography (Certeau, 1984; Dülmen, 2002; Lüdtke, 1995). This fuels our efforts to uncover the often hidden or less visible rules of everyday life and routine actions of individuals as well as groups of ordinary people. In this regard, we operate near anthropology and ethnology, which provide many interesting suggestions to history (Isaac, 1994; Schnepel, 1999; Stone, 1979). Through ethnology, referred to by Isaac (1994) as the treasure trove of history, understanding of the various cultures of the world and a reconstruction of different mentalities is achieved; anthropology primarily provides history with a detailed analysis of an individual event and of its anchoring in the broader context. The convergence of history with ethnology and anthropology has led to the creation of historical anthropology, which, according to Medick (2001), focuses on topics such as family and kinship, birth and death, ritual, and mentality. The study of mentalities, the norms and ideas about the world shaped by the social environment, is crucial for understanding the impacts of transformation on the lives of schools and teachers.

Therefore, the representation of transformation in resources of central provenance is not the only focal point of our interest. We do not focus simply on the 'grand narrative' of the primary education transformations; we are particularly interested in the image of the transformation in the memories of direct participants and sources of local provenance, linked with the everyday routines anchored in the contemporary and local context. We also try to capture the ways of perception, the world of emotions, and the subjective feelings of people who do not always act rationally (Dülmen, 2002).

At this level of consideration, we approach 'microhistory' (Ginzburg, 1993), which can be understood as a historical approach that focuses on an intensive analysis of narrowly delimited phenomena such as a rural society, a group of families, or specific individuals almost as if they were under a magnifying glass (Ginzburg & Poni in Nodl, 2004). Figuratively speaking, this concerns replacing the view through a telescope with a view through a microscope (Burke in Čechura, 1994). Thus, it is possible to interpret 'small histories', without which large events seem incomprehensible, on the example of a single location and its population. Systematic research on a single village or an entire region can thus contribute to a better understanding of the past within the everyday life (Grulich, 2001).

Microhistorical research is often based on 'small facts' that tend to be neglected in archival sources (cf. Szijártó, 2002; Brooks et al., 2008). In connection with this, Lenderová et al. (2009) wrote about the 'new' reading of sources. Traditional historical sources such as school registers, class catalogues, inspection reports, etc. are researched from a different perspective, comparable to reading 'between the lines'. A well-studied source may thereby give different testimonies than those found by other methods. Indeed, these examples of sources, used primarily in quantitatively oriented historical research, may contain information overlooked or left unused (e.g. information about students' parents or their social status, or teachers' character traits). This is connected to studying people's actions at the individual level, monitoring the local conditions or contexts that led to their actions, and monitoring the meanings attributed to the studied phenomena by the individuals. It is because of this approach that we can achieve the interconnectedness of cultural, social, economic, and power moments (i.e., the global perspective) with the context of people's everyday lives in the monitored past (Medick, 2001).

On the basis of these insights, we can then build a microhistorical view of the history of the post-socialist transformation. In doing so, we understand microhistory neither as a set of procedures or methods verifying macrohistorical rules or general history, nor as their opposite (Ginzburg & Poni, 1979). We understand microhistory and macrohistory as mutually complementary approaches to understanding and researching history with the goal of describing and explaining past events and processes as comprehensively as possible. In our case, this concerns on one hand the transformations of the Czech society, economy, (school) politics, and school system management, and on the other hand the processes of transformation within schools in the lives and work of teachers and school heads taking place in a particular socio-historical context.

This book is the result of a research project that aimed to explore and comprehensively describe the everyday life of primary schools and changes to that life in the period of post-socialist transformation. In this part of the chapter, we discuss in more detail our research methodology, which combined several research methods. The research took place largely during the COVID-19 pandemic, which meant increased demands on the flexibility of the researchers and the deployment and use of individual data collection methods.

We must at least briefly describe our previous project. This project was of fundamental importance to the current research, in terms of both methodology and substance. It was the first project to use an oral history method to research contemporary history in educational sciences in the Czech Republic. The project was entitled *Everyday life of basic schools in the normalization period as seen by teachers. Applying oral history to research in history of contemporary education.* It was conducted between 2014 and 2016 (Zounek et al., 2017a, 2018).[6]

In the field of methodology, research has shown that it is especially useful to use a 'mixed design' in researching the contemporary history of the school system, i.e., to combine the possibilities of oral history and research of teachers' life stories with the study of historical sources and archival research. Our research focused on the teachers' everyday life (microhistory) and the operation of primary schools during the period of normalization in Czechoslovakia (roughly 1968–1989), but also on learning the general historical context and the history of socialist education (macrohistory). This approach allowed us to get to know the given topic more comprehensively and to understand and interpret new findings in a broader context that provided a solid framework for this rather sensitive topic. This framework protected us from perceiving contemporary history, especially the period between 1948 and 1989, in only black and white, or from simplifying or even vulgarizing certain topics. In this case, we have to keep in mind that we were focusing on education under an authoritarian regime, in which teachers were perceived, among other things, as instruments for spreading ideology, and that many of the eyewitnesses are still alive today.

In terms of methodology, we have tested the advantages and limitations of all the research methods we used in the project. We have partially expanded the oral history method towards a greater sensitivity to issues from the field of education, the teaching profession, teaching, (school) politics, the functioning of schools, and

---

[6] The cited works have been published in English and provide information about the methodology and partial results of the project.

teachers' extracurricular activities. One issue was that the eyewitnesses did not talk about the daily routines in their work, about teaching in the classroom, or about relationships with colleagues or parents, because they considered these topics so ordinary as to not be worth mentioning. Therefore, we adapted the preparation for the oral history interviews, the order of questions, and the manner of formulating questions directed specifically to the profession of teacher or school head. Reflecting on the conducted interviews was very useful, since it helped us in the subsequent interviews. The eyewitnesses' reactions to questions regarding sensitive topics, mainly politics or ideology and their influence on the work of a teacher, but also various events from personal life represented an example of methodological challenges in these interviews. The oral history method proved to be a very effective tool for data collection in our research. Its potential is emphasized especially in connection to the fact that (historical) source material from before 1989 is still unavailable in Czech archives for many reasons (see below for more details).

In the field of historical-pedagogical research theory, we have created a new classification of historical sources that reflects the role of digital technologies in historical-pedagogical research and in the field of archiving of historical documents.

The previous research project brought many new findings about the socialist school system between 1968 and 1989, but also about the 1950s and 1960s, when the communist authorities' interventions into education were fundamental and also probably the most dramatic, as they often negated previous national developments in order to bring the Czechoslovak school system closer to the Soviet one: the professional foundations of the reforms were lacking and political reasons clearly prevailed. Some of our findings from the project were related to the 'post-socialist' school system of the 1990s. It turned out that this type of research, focused on the everyday life, contributed to explaining some of the phenomena and processes of the transformation of the Czech school system after 1989. In this respect, our previous research raised quite a lot of new questions and challenges. These then became the basis for the research of the post-socialist transformation.

The results of the previous project are comprehensively presented in the book *Normal life in not so normal times. Primary schools and their teachers (not only) during the so-called normalization period* (Zounek et al., 2017b) which was published in Czech. The second main result is the book *Socialist primary school as seen by eyewitnesses: Probing teachers' life in the South Moravian Region* (Zounek et al., 2017c), which presents selected interviews and contemporary documents (also published in Czech).

In our research we have built on the aforementioned project, and we have also divided the research strategy into two mutually overlapping phases.

The first phase of the research project consisted of a detailed study of the post-socialist transformation from the perspective of historiography, pedagogy, political science, economics, and sociology. The entire research was based on Czech and foreign scientific resources, primarily on educational and general legislation, contemporary proposals for school system reform, statistical information of the development of the school system in Czechoslovakia in the 1980s and 1990s, journals for teachers, and other relevant resources with the aim of creating a comprehensive historical framework for the investigated problems. We cite the individual resources with specific topics in the appropriate chapters.

The research of contemporary sources or documents stored in archives[7] represented an important part of our research (McCulloch, 2004). A number of sources are available on the transformation of the school system and education; these have been published either officially or for the needs of the Ministry of Education and include statistical information on the number of schools, teachers, or students in a certain time period; legislation; proposals regarding the school system reform by various independent groups and associations; first international comparative studies. These documents are stored in libraries in which they are relatively accessible for research purposes. However, the previous research (Zounek et al., 2015a, b) showed that the availability of archived documents from the field of education is often limited. One of the main reasons for this unavailability is that they have not yet been professionally processed. The inaccessibility of sources for the period after 1989 is also due to the corresponding legislation. According to Act No. 499/2004 Coll., on Archiving and Records Management and on Amendments to Certain Acts, archival materials younger than 30 years are not accessible for viewing. In addition, according to archivists from the Moravian Provincial Archives (one of the largest archives in the Czech Republic), the collections from the field of education will not be processed in the next few years (e-mail communication between J. Zounek and a specialist at the archive). Archival materials may contain sensitive personal data of individuals who are still alive, which is another reason research is not possible in many of the collections.

As part of our research, we visited a number of archives to gain insights into the research topic and to determine whether the availability of sources is truly limited. We conducted our research in various institutions at the regional level and also at the national level, as we were interested in the topic of general/systemic transformations of the school system after 1989. In the following chapters, we provide exact citations of the sources we obtained in specific archives. Within this chapter, we just want to mention that we visited the National Archives of the Czech Republic,[8] the Slovak National Archives in Bratislava (this archive contains sources such as archival materials on school system management from the period of socialist Czechoslovakia as well as from the post-socialist period prior to the dissolution of the federation in 1993), the Moravian Provincial Archives[9] (visited as part of the previous research), the Archives of the Academy of Sciences of the Czech Republic (school system analyses were written in this institution even before 1989), and the Brno City Archives (archival materials from schools in Brno and materials used in their management). Furthermore, we reviewed sources available in several state

---

[7] Basic information on archives in the Czech Republic are available in English here: https://www. mvcr.cz/mvcren/article/introduction.aspx

[8] Basic information on the archive is available in English here: https://www.nacr.cz/en/about-us/ basic-information

[9] Basic information on the Moravian Provincial Archives is available in English here: https://portal. ehri-project.eu/institutions/cz-002230

district archives that form a part of the Moravian Provincial Archives (see table below) and collect archival materials of district and local provenance. In all the archives, we experienced a friendly approach and a great level of assistance from the scientific workers. The archives differ in the level of processing of their individual collections and in the amount and types of sources they hold. This determines the availability of resources for researchers. For example, we had opportunities to study the archival collection of the Government of the Czech Republic in the National Archives, the archival collection of the Czechoslovak Ministry of Education (documents from 1987 to 1991, which concerned matters of primary education in Czechoslovakia, i.e., its organization, teaching of subjects, and curricula), and the collection of the Department of Education of the Regional National Committee of the South Moravian Region in the Moravian Provincial Archive (devoted to the issues of education and its development in the entire region in the period before 1989). In the district archives, we had the opportunity to study the meetings of local school authorities and the school system as well as school chronicles, annual reports of individual schools, records of teacher meetings in schools, inspection reports, and reports on the extracurricular activities of schools, teachers, and students. In some cases, there were also photographs or student works available, and even teaching materials or aids (Harvey, 2009) (Table 1.1).

In the research of written contemporary (archival) documents, we used selected methods of historical research (Claus & Marriott, 2013). One was the direct method, which involves obtaining historical facts by directly studying the information source (Zounek & Šimáně, 2014). In this case, we took advantage of the fact that most of the documents from the post-socialist transformation period were written as part of the processes of the time and directly provide information about these processes. As a part of the direct method, we used content analysis techniques to capture the content and themes of the document (Krippendorff, 2019; Dobson & Ziemann, 2009). We were also interested in the intended audience of the document (which could

Table 1.1 Sources in regional archives

Brno City Archive	Collections of 12 schools: part. 12 school chronicles from 8 schools, 8 record books from pedagogical board meetings from 4 schools, school work plans and school work analyses from 3 schools. Inspection reports from one school
State District Archive of Brno-Country District in Rajhrad	11 school chronicles from the collections of 10 schools
State District Archive in Zlín	17 school chronicles from the collections of 15 schools, collection of the Department of Education of District National Committee—i.e., records from meetings of the school committee, circulars
State District Archive Znojmo	Collections of 8 schools: 5 school chronicles from 4 schools, annual reports from one school, materials for rehabilitation of a teacher and a competition for a school head from one school. Inspection reports from the collection of District National Committee.
Documents stored in schools	One chronicle (Hodonín district)

influence its content or the degree of open criticism, for example), what topics it addressed, and whether it was focused on a certain region or on the Czech Republic as a whole. We also used the statistical method, which is used in research of the quantitative aspects of historical phenomena or processes (Zounek & Šimáně, 2014). While mapping the general framework of the transformation, we also analysed quantitative data such as the number of primary schools in a given region and the numbers of students and teachers, and changes in these numbers in the late 1980s and early 1990s. Most of the documents containing statistical data on the school system were stored in libraries. The results of this part of the research helped create a general (interpretive) framework for the entire research project and provided the research team with some of the background information needed for preparing their own empirical research, such as interview topics.

The second phase of the research project was an empirical investigation based on the oral history method, which we see—in agreement with Vaněk and Mücke—as 'a series of sophisticated but constantly evolving and self-refining procedures through which the researcher … reaches new findings on the basis of oral accounts of persons who participated in or witnessed a certain event, process or period, which the researcher investigates, or persons whose individual experiences, attitudes and opinions may enrich the researcher's knowledge of themselves or of the investigated problem in general' (2015, p. 14; see also Abrams, 2016). This method played several roles in our research:

(a) It was the method that demonstrated the most appropriate and effective way to obtain and use orally communicated information and to subsequently analyse and interpret it.
(b) It represented an application of the science on sources (when seeking respondents, it is necessary to assess their information competence, credibility, etc., from the outset).
(c) It was a specific kind of heuristics. Our 'sources' were eyewitnesses to the event[10] (teachers and school heads) who had to be located, and information about the past in accordance with the focus of the research had to be obtained from them by means of an interview.

In some cases, we supplemented the oral history method with the 'think aloud' technique (Branch, 2013), which we adapted for the needs of the project based on our experience of using it in previous research (Zounek et al., 2017b). In our case, the eyewitnesses might have used teaching materials prepared by themselves or other similar teaching material or other documents of a personal or professional nature during the interview. They might also have offered photos of classes or of some event in the life of the school. During the interview, the eyewitness then

---

[10] In our book, we use the terms 'eyewitness', 'narrator', and 'respondent' as synonyms to refer to the research participants with whom we conducted oral history interviews. We are aware that in the fields of history of education and educational sciences, the term 'respondent' is typically used. By contrast, in the historical sciences and in the field of oral history, the term 'narrator' is used more frequently.

explained the circumstances of the material's creation, its purpose, practical use, etc. This technique contributed to a deeper understanding of many of the researched topics and also served to 'jog the memory' or 'start' the narrative. In describing some of the materials, the eyewitnesses became more open and spoke without much inhibition.

In our research, we conducted 45 oral history interviews with 36 narrators, and the respondents were mainly teachers and school heads who were working in primary schools during the post-socialist transformation. Throughout the entire research, eight eyewitnesses declined to be interviewed. Suitable narrators were sought and contacted through our contacts: co-workers in schools, colleagues, and acquaintances. This method was chosen because of the higher chance of gaining the trust of potential narrators (Thompson & Bornat, 2017). The issues of socialism and post-socialism in relation to the school system can be perceived as sensitive due to the ideologization of the school system before 1989, and a guarantee of the reliability of the interviewers was important for many narrators. Potential respondents who declined to be interviewed (although there were few) were generally among those who had often already been approached using the snowball sampling method that we used. This method relies on a narrators we have already spoken to providing us with additional contacts of other potential narrators.

We guaranteed the degree of representativeness of the sample of respondents by approaching teachers from diverse sources and using different contacts (both professional and private), thus managing to obtain interviews with teachers from all corners of the South Moravian Region. A few interviews were also conducted through targeted contacting of a school head without prior cooperation or recommendation.

A detailed overview of our respondents is provided in the following table. In this table, we provide pseudonyms, primarily for ethical reasons. Throughout our research, we anonymized the names of towns and villages and the personal information of the eyewitnesses, as well as details about other people and places (including the names of schools, villages, and towns) mentioned by the eyewitnesses in the interviews.[11] For towns, villages, and other settlements, we do not use the name of the place, but always describe it so that it sufficiently is clear where the phenomena described by the eyewitness happened (Table 1.2).

We focused our search for respondents on the territory of the former South Moravian Region (according to the 1960 legislation), which was one of the largest regions of Czechoslovakia. It is a relatively representative region, characterized—like the rest of the country—by high territorial diversity and fragmentation (the Czech Republic currently has 6250 independent self-governing municipalities) (Kučerová et al., 2019). The South Moravian Region has a large city, several district towns, smaller rural towns, and larger and smaller villages. The rural area is also diverse: there are suburban villages benefitting from the arrival of new residents and

[11] All parts of this research project were conducted in compliance with the legislation of the Czech Republic and the ethics codes of the Czech Educational Sciences and Research, the Czech Oral History Association, and Masaryk University.

Table 1.2 Characteristics of respondents

Pseudonym	Sex	Year of birth	Job title[a]	Teaching qualification (teachers in the second stage of primary schools)	Location	Number of interviews
Adam	Man	1956	Director of an educational authority		District town	1
Alena	Woman	1933	Teacher in the first and second stage of primary school	Music education, German	Rural	1
Antonín	Man	1963	Teacher in the second stage of primary school	Czech, Music education	Rural	2
Barbora	Woman	1957	Teacher in the second stage of primary school, school head	Czech	Rural	1
Blanka	Woman	1937	Teacher in the first stage of primary school		Large city	1
Ctirada	Woman	1937	Teacher in the second stage, then grammar school, school inspection	Czech	Large city	2
Dana	Woman	1943	Teacher in the first stage of primary school		Small city	2
Eliška	Woman	1958	Lawyer working in education		Large city	1
Eva	Woman	1944	Teacher in the second stage of primary school	Mathematics	District town	1
František	Man	1944	Teacher in the second stage of primary school, school head	Biology, geography	District town	1
Gabriela	Woman	1944	Teacher in the first stage of primary school, school head		Rural	1
Helena	Woman	1958	Teacher in the second stage of primary school, school head	Czech	Rural	1
Hynek	Man	1946	Teacher in the second stage of primary school, deputy school head	Natural history, physical education	District town	1

(continued)

Table 1.2 (continued)

Pseudonym	Sex	Year of birth	Job title[a]	Teaching qualification (teachers in the second stage of primary schools)	Location	Number of interviews
Irma	Woman	1948	Teacher in the second stage of primary school	Czech, English	Large city	2
Jana	Woman	1950	Teacher in the second stage of primary school	German, Russian	Large city	2
Jaroslava	Woman	1960	Teacher in the first stage of primary school		Small city	1
Karolína	Woman	1950	Teacher in the second stage of primary school	History, English	Small city	1
Kryštof	Man	1960	Teacher in the second stage of primary school, school head	Mathematics, physics	Rural	1
Libor	Man	1960	Teacher in the second stage of primary school, left the school system in the 1990s	Mathematics, physics	Rural	1
Ludmila	Woman	1952	Teacher in the first stage of primary school, school head, then teacher in multi-year grammar school		Rural suburban	3
Michal	Man	1960	Teacher in the second stage of primary school + multi-year grammar school	Mathematics	Rural suburban	1
Miroslava	Woman	1952	Department of education at the city council		Large city	1
Naděžda	Woman	1952	School inspection		Large city	1
Nina	Woman	1960	Teacher in the first stage of primary school		Rural	1
Olga	Woman	1953	Teacher in the second stage of primary school	Physical education, German	District town	2

(continued)

Table 1.2 (continued)

Pseudonym	Sex	Year of birth	Job title[a]	Teaching qualification (teachers in the second stage of primary schools)	Location	Number of interviews
Pavla	Woman	1952	School head, school for children with special needs		Rural	1
Petra	Woman	1960	Teacher in the second stage of primary school	Russian; switched to German after 1989	District town	1
Radka	Woman	1953	Teacher in the second stage of primary school	Physical education, mathematics	Rural	1
Soňa	Woman	1954	Teacher in the second stage of primary school	Geography, physical education	Large city	1
Stanislava	Woman	1960	Teacher in the first and second stage of primary school, deputy school head	English	Rural	1
Tereza	Woman	1955	Teacher in the second stage of primary school, school head	Natural history, chemistry	Large city	1
Tomáš	Man	1961	Teacher in the second stage of primary school	Czech, history	Rural suburban	1
Václav	Man	1955	Educational authority		District town	1
Valerie	Woman	1956	Ministry of Education		Prague	1
Vlasta	Woman	1961	Teacher in the second stage of primary school	Mathematics, physics, industrial arts, physical education	Rural suburban	2
Zdeněk	Man	1956	Teacher in the first stage of primary school, school head		Large city	1

[a]In the first stage of primary schools (1–4/5 grade, ISCED 1 / ISCED 100), the teachers have a general specialization; the teachers in the second stage (5/6–8/9 grade, ISCED 2 / ISCED 244) specialize in specific subjects (see also https://eurydice.eacea.ec.europa.eu/national-education-systems/czech-republic/czech-republic). As we state later in the book, the number of grades in the individual stages of Czech schools kept changing in the second half of the twentieth century.

Fig. 1.2 Czech regions and districts in 1989. The grey area denotes our research area

remote depopulating villages in the borderlands and in the hilly parts of the region. There are both industrial and agricultural areas in the region, and the social situation, the sources of livelihood,[12] and the level of religiosity of the inhabitants[13] vary. Since the forced removal of the German population after World War II, the Czech lands have been fairly homogeneous in terms of nationality (unlike Slovakia with a significant Hungarian minority) (cf. Frank, 2020; Czech Statistical Office, 2021a). This was also the case in the South Moravian Region (Fig. 1.2).

All interviews were recorded on a dictaphone and subsequently transcribed. Each interview was accompanied by an 'interview protocol' in which we captured the identifying data about the interview (date, duration of the interview, name of the person conducting the interview, and place of the interview). The protocol primarily contained a description of the course of the interview, including the respondent's non-verbal expressions, notes on topics not covered or not exhausted in the

---

[12] The South Moravian Region has both industrial and agricultural areas. In traditional coal mining areas, the industry declined after 1989; other areas underwent a successful transformation and are developing.

[13] The Czech Republic is generally considered to have a low level of religiosity for various historical reasons, including the fifteenth century reformation (Hussite movement) and its suppression, the perception of the Catholic Church as an ally of the Austro-Hungarian monarchy, which was viewed rather negatively in Czechoslovakia especially in the interwar period, and the strong suppression of religiosity by the communist authorities. However, the South Moravian Region, especially some of its rural areas, is associated with relatively higher levels of religiosity than other regions of the Czech Republic (Spousta, 2002; Chorvát et al., 2019; Czech Statistical Office, 2021b).

interview, and a description of any unusual events. Each respondent signed an informed consent form regarding their participation in the research. This form included the contact information of the researcher, and, more importantly, basic information about the research as well as the narrator's rights as a research participant. At the end of the informed consent form, a blank space was included for individual requests related to the interview and research (e.g., sending a link to a published article or specific requests beyond anonymization).

We typically conducted one interview with each respondent, sometimes a second interview if necessary, and only rarely a third one.[14] The first interview or the first part of the interview (if only one interview was conducted) was a biographical narrative in which the respondent was encouraged by the researcher to speak freely with minimal interventions on part of the interviewer. If there were two interviews, the initial interview was transcribed and analysed in order to prepare for the second interview. If there was just one interview, the interviewer took notes during the narrative to prepare for the second part of the interview. The second part of the interview was already a 'research dialogue' between the researcher and the respondent, in which themes or events from the first interview (or its introductory part) were to be discussed in order to clarify/explain any ambiguities, to acquire more detailed information about important topics, or to expand the knowledge of the topic with additional circumstances, etc. Interviewers always entered the interviews prepared with topics or frameworks that each of the narrators were asked about. As the interviews progressed, the topics were augmented and refined based on the transcripts and analyses of previous interviews. This was all done in research team meetings (Fig. 1.3).

The data collected (interviews) were analysed in several ways. The first analytical procedures were based on research on the teachers' life stories (Goodson, 2008). These procedures aimed to organize the material into simple short stories. This was a type of open coding focused on the chronological sequence of events. Other procedures were also based on open coding but focused more on themes in the narrative (content analysis). Subsequent categorizations of the resulting codes revealed all the themes that were relevant in relation to our topic. We used open coding because it made it possible to capture even completely new topics in the data. In the next steps, we used other data analysis techniques such as the 'laying out the cards' technique and thematic coding. We combined these techniques with narrative analysis (Goodson & Gill, 2011; Bold, 2012) focused on the structure of the narrative. Using all these methods, we followed both chronological and thematic lines. In this way, we are able to describe and explain the life and profession of the teacher (even before 1989, but especially in the period of transformation). As regards the technical component of our work, the analyses were performed in Atlas.ti 8.

---

[14]We decided on the need for a second interview after the transcription and first analysis of the interview; we also took into consideration the course of the interview and the willingness of the respondent, etc. In many cases, it was not worth asking for a second interview because, for example, the information provided had started to repeat at the end of the first interview.

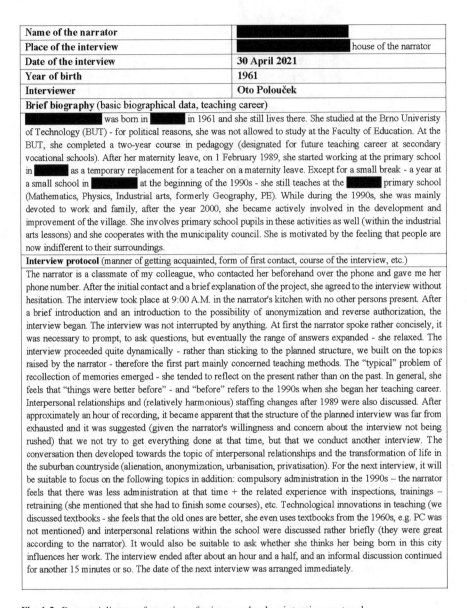

Name of the narrator	▮▮▮▮▮▮▮▮▮▮
Place of the interview	▮▮▮▮▮▮▮▮▮▮▮ house of the narrator
Date of the interview	30 April 2021
Year of birth	1961
Interviewer	Oto Polouček

Brief biography (basic biographical data, teaching career)

▮▮▮▮▮▮▮▮ was born in ▮▮▮▮ in 1961 and she still lives there. She studied at the Brno Univeristy of Technology (BUT) - for political reasons, she was not allowed to study at the Faculty of Education. At the BUT, she completed a two-year course in pedagogy (designated for future teaching career at secondary vocational schools). After her maternity leave, on 1 February 1989, she started working at the primary school in ▮▮▮▮▮ as a temporary replacement for a teacher on a maternity leave. Except for a small break - a year at a small school in ▮▮▮▮▮▮ at the beginning of the 1990s - she still teaches at the ▮▮▮▮ primary school (Mathematics, Physics, Industrial arts, formerly Geography, PE). While during the 1990s, she was mainly devoted to work and family, after the year 2000, she became actively involved in the development and improvement of the village. She involves primary school pupils in these activities as well (within the industrial arts lessons) and she cooperates with the municipality council. She is motivated by the feeling that people are now indifferent to their surroundings.

Interview protocol (manner of getting acquainted, form of first contact, course of the interview, etc.)

The narrator is a classmate of my colleague, who contacted her beforehand over the phone and gave me her phone number. After the initial contact and a brief explanation of the project, she agreed to the interview without hesitation. The interview took place at 9:00 A.M. in the narrator's kitchen with no other persons present. After a brief introduction and an introduction to the possibility of anonymization and reverse authorization, the interview began. The interview was not interrupted by anything. At first the narrator spoke rather concisely, it was necessary to prompt, to ask questions, but eventually the range of answers expanded - she relaxed. The interview proceeded quite dynamically - rather than sticking to the planned structure, we built on the topics raised by the narrator - therefore the first part mainly concerned teaching methods. The "typical" problem of recollection of memories emerged - she tended to reflect on the present rather than on the past. In general, she feels that "things were better before" - and "before" refers to the 1990s when she began her teaching career. Interpersonal relationships and (relatively harmonious) staffing changes after 1989 were also discussed. After approximately an hour of recording, it became apparent that the structure of the planned interview was far from exhausted and it was suggested (given the narrator's willingness and concern about the interview not being rushed) that we not try to get everything done at that time, but that we conduct another interview. The conversation then developed towards the topic of interpersonal relationships and the transformation of life in the suburban countryside (alienation, anonymization, urbanisation, privatisation). For the next interview, it will be suitable to focus on the following topics in addition: compulsory administration in the 1990s – the narrator feels that there was less administration at that time + the related experience with inspections, trainings – retraining (she mentioned that she had to finish some courses), etc. Technological innovations in teaching (we discussed textbooks - she feels that the old ones are better, she even uses textbooks from the 1960s, e.g. PC was not mentioned) and interpersonal relations within the school were discussed rather briefly (they were great according to the narrator). It would also be suitable to ask whether she thinks her being born in this city influences her work. The interview ended after about an hour and a half, and an informal discussion continued for another 15 minutes or so. The date of the next interview was arranged immediately.

Fig. 1.3 Post-socialist transformation of primary schools—interview protocol

The oral history method and the research of written documents were complemented by research of visual and material objects collected from the respondents.

The visual and material objects collected or created by the narrators (photographs, yearbooks, journals, their preparations for teaching or even textbooks) not only form silent witnesses to the past but also support the narrators' recollections. Doing so helps to create a more comprehensive picture of the school environment and its culture (Meda & Viñao, 2017; Dávila et al., 2017). In addition, tangible artefacts can reinforce and make a more visible professional identity and, more broadly, could increase the sense of belonging to the school and community. Narrators' approaches to preserving these objects vary naturally. Some collect and make them available for study, while others dispose of them. Motivation to keep may be higher when tangible objects document the narrator's achievement. For example, one narrator brought a sports yearbook documenting her students' competition successes to a café meeting. In another case, we could examine the narrator's creations, specifically self-made teaching aids. However, it cannot be overlooked that our research took place in a live setting. Indeed, these objects did not merely represent the "archaeology of school materialities" (Yanes-Cabrera & Escolano Benito, 2017, p. 267) but were evaluated by our narrators in the context of contemporary experiences. Indeed, many of these objects are still in use today. Some narrators showed us proven assignments in old discarded textbooks that they still use in their teaching. Similarly, their own older teaching aids are still part of their teaching.

We tried to ensure the credibility of the research by a careful selection of respondents. We meet the transferability criterion by accurately documenting all of the research, including a description of the limitations of the research that we considered, particularly the methodology used). We meet the reliability criterion through the consistency of questions and an accurate transcription of recordings.

During oral history research, it is necessary to take into consideration a number of circumstances that can be perceived as weaknesses of this method and that were the subject of scepticism by some historians when it was established (Grele, 2003; Vaněk & Mücke, 2015).[15] We show that these 'weaknesses' can actually be seen as strengths of oral history.

The question of memory (and forgetting) is the first sensitive issue. As our research has also shown, memories can be highly selective and distorted; the teachers' descriptions of the past were often inherently idealized and nostalgic in the interviews. On the other hand, the form of recollection can show us what is essential for those teachers, what legacy the period of transition brings to the present day, and what images are held in their memory.

The influence of the environment teachers have lived and are living today cannot be overlooked. Teachers' memories form part of the memory of a specific professional group that shares traditional narratives, perspectives or ideas about the good practice among themselves. Teachers' memories are also part of a broader complex of school memory, which is shaped by the perspectives of other actors—students, parents, and community members—as well as by the culture of remembering school in general and the images of school in the national discourse (Meda & Viñao, 2017).

---

[15] A number of methodological manuals have been published that deal with various aspects of conducting oral history interviews. The factors that may influence the course of the interview as well as ethical issues were discussed in great detail by Yow (2005). Thompson and Bornat (2017) placed oral history research in a broader context of studies of memories. A set of texts considering oral history from the perspective of various topics and cultural backgrounds was compiled by Perks and Thomson (2003). Richie (2003) offered a practical guide aimed at general audiences.

By their very nature, oral history interviews are a representation of the present day, and they are strongly influenced by the current situation. Although the teachers talked about the past, the contents of their memories were more or less permeated by their current perspectives, frames of mind, health, and overall satisfaction with their own lives. For the teachers who still teach, the current situation in the school system played a role, and, predictably, they were more likely to thematize those aspects of the transformation that affected the current school system.

However, the strength of oral history lies in the fact that the interviewer has a direct influence on the form of the interview, can set the agenda, influence the manner of narration, and records the context of emergence and the factors that may have influenced the interview. In this way, oral history research differs from an analysis of written sources, which were admittedly created in the investigated period, but can often only provide a vague idea about the context in which they were written (Portelli, 2003). We can think critically about who wrote the material in question and for whom (and through this consideration, for example, estimate the degree of self-censorship of the writer), but the degree of 'reliability' must be conceptualized as critically for written sources as for oral histories.

Factors that influence the content of an oral history narrative include, first and foremost, the persona of the interviewer, i.e., their gender, age, manners, and degree of interference in the interview (Yow, 2005). It should be emphasised that there is no 'ideal' or 'only correct' combination. For example, our research involved extensive interviews between two men with a relatively small age difference of about 10 or 15 years; many shared topics and experiences, including the interest in education, may have contributed to mutual trust. There were also interviews between a younger interviewer and significantly older women. The assumption that the interviewer, born after 1989, was not familiar with many details of (post) socialist school life and therefore needed the environment explained to him in detail may have played a positive role.

Perhaps the dynamics of the interview, the ability to create a 'relaxed' atmosphere and to establish a mutual trust, matter even more than the persona of the interviewer. The narrators were of course different. Some were helpful from the very initial contact; others were more reserved at first and needed more time to start feeling relaxed during the interview. The interviewers themselves may have anticipated the quality of the interview based on the initial (phone, email) contact. However, there were several times when the impression from the initial contact was deceptive. We met some very helpful narrators who turned out not to be the best storytellers; others seemed reserved at first but subsequently talked in a convivial atmosphere for almost 3 h.

Each narrator is different. Some are natural storytellers and the interviewer hardly had to interject; other interviews were more of a dialogue with frequent input and questions from the interviewer. In general, teachers are narrators who are used to communicating and talking to people, who are careful about their cultivated speech, and who had relatively high expectations of the interviewers and their level of preparedness and erudition. They highly valued that the interviewers were representatives of an institution with a good reputation and were appropriately educated[16]; many saw the opportunity to give an interview as an honour. However, it should be emphasized that the teachers who were willing to be interviewed were predominantly those who were proud of their profession, who were motivated, and who had a positive attitude towards it.

The location in which the interview took place may have had a major influence on its form. Some narrators immediately invited us to their homes, which seems to be the best option. This is an environment in which they feel relaxed, and it can stimulate further reminiscing, for example, by looking at photographs or documents related to the teaching practice –the oldest narrators in particular looked up such materials in the course of their own preparation for the interview. Younger narrators tended to invite us to the schools where they worked. The advantage of this location is that this is also the narrator's 'own' environment; the disadvantage is a risk of more frequent interruption. The younger narrators who invited us to their workplace significantly often related to their professional present, for which the environment gave them many cues. Other narrators invited us to a café—although the setting was less suitable, we conducted some good quality interviews in the quiet surroundings of a cosy café. However, excessive noise and large numbers of people also affected the interviews negatively as neither the narrator nor the interviewer felt comfortable. By contrast, the interviewer's workplace provided a quiet environment. A disadvantage in the position of power has to be taken into consideration in such cases, since the narrator entered an environment 'controlled' by the interviewer. However, because of the peace and quiet and the reputation of the (university) institution (which, admittedly, might have made the narrators worried about 'disappointing'), we managed to record some good quality interviews at the interviewers' workplace. In our research, the narrator generally chose the interview location and the interviewer adapted.

The length and content of the interviews varied. For time reasons, some narrators were able to give us 'only' less than an hour and their interviews mainly concerned education; others were not limited by time and talked at length about their personal lives as well. However, the length of an interview is not necessarily indicative of its quality. Some teachers showed competence in getting to the heart of the matter in a few brief sentences; others enjoyed telling stories that were not always directly related to education. Other teachers also got to very sensitive topics during their interviews, sharing traumatic experiences in their working lives or considering the question of their own work performance during the socialist period. Many of the older teachers were still coming to terms with the fact that they had to teach in the name of ideology before 1989 or to judge their students according to

their parents' behaviour and life (e.g. their relationship with the communist authorities, their class background, and their religion). In this way, they could fundamentally influence the future fate of their students, specifically their options for

---

[16]Teachers, like other experts, rate the erudition of an interviewer highly, which may distinguish them from narrators from working-class backgrounds who may be put off by an interviewer's excessive erudition. A certain degree of adaptability to various environments is thus a prerequisite for using the oral history method (cf. Krátká et al., 2018; Vaněk & Mücke, 2015).

further studies. Some narrators were willing to talk very openly about these issues, to formulate their position, and some may have felt the need to defend themselves. It is important to bear in mind that an oral history interview may not only serve the function for the narrators of telling their story: for some of them, it may have been the first opportunity to organize their thoughts, reflect on their past, and talk to someone about their life. Thus, the interview can be somewhat therapeutic (cf. Thompson & Bornat, 2017; Vaněk & Mücke, 2015). In this regard, interviewers should be prepared to play the role of a certain (professional) support, they should be willing to listen to often very painful or sensitive narratives and be able to respond with empathy. Conducting oral history interviews is by no means 'mere' data collection.

This is also why the collaboration with the narrators does not end with the interview but continues further. We are bound by codes of ethics, and also by our own interest in continuing to use the interview in collaboration with the narrator. As we have already indicated, we strictly anonymized all interviews, including locations. Some narrators directly requested the anonymization; others did not. A few narrators even emphasized that they did not mind appearing under their own name. Others requested that they be provided with ongoing information about how the interviews are used. The narrators are able to contact the members of the research team at any time.

The COVID-19 pandemic, which broke out shortly after the beginning of the project (in March 2020), had a significant impact on our research. There were closures of primary schools and restrictions on the free movement of people. We were unable to conduct interviews with eyewitnesses working in schools or even with eyewitnesses who had already retired. The retired respondents were particularly afraid of disease transmission and therefore did not want to meet us in person, which was completely understandable. Interviews via digital technologies (MS Teams, ZOOM) were not possible because most of the (older) eyewitnesses did not use these technologies. Moreover, online interviews could negatively affect the quality of the data, as they limit the opportunities to observe non-verbal reactions of the eyewitnesses during the interview, for example. As we are investigating a sensitive period that could have profoundly affected the lives of many teachers, building trust with the eyewitnesses was very important to us. Face-to-face contact helped to get more 'in depth' on some topics, so we did not elect to use interviews via online technologies. A telephone interview would have been completely inappropriate for our purposes.

Therefore, we conducted only eleven interviews with eight eyewitnesses in 2020. We consider this to be the maximum under the given conditions. We took advantage of the times when restrictions on movement, meetings, etc. imposed by the government of the Czech Republic were relaxed. The actual conduct of the interviews required preparation and setting up a suitable date with the narrator, which was a time-consuming activity, because we always adapted to the free time of the eyewitnesses.

The archives were also closed or open only on a limited basis for a part of 2020. This presented a rather large obstacle to the research and made it virtually impossible in some months. Furthermore, travelling to Slovakia was restricted, which was a problem because we planned to do a part of our research in the Slovak National Archives. The level of digitization of archival collections' lists varies significantly among Czech archives. Therefore, we were able to search through the archival collections on the Internet only to a limited extent. Digitized sources for our research were practically non-existent in the archives.

The situation was similar in 2021, especially in the spring. We were unable to start conducting the interviews before May 2021, when the pandemic situation and especially the willingness of the eyewitnesses to meet with the researchers allowed it. We could not begin any more systematic and more intensive data collection (either interviews or research of archival materials) until the autumn of 2021, at which time the access to archives was still limited.

All of these constraints represented significant obstacles to the progress of the project research. The progress of the research thus required changes in the workflow, but not in the research strategy or data collection methods. The research generally required a relatively high level of flexibility from the research team members, both in terms of time and workflow.

In connection with the COVID-19 pandemic, we must also mention one methodological issue related to the actual conduct of the oral history interviews with survivors. That is to say, the pandemic affected people's lives very significantly, and not only in terms of restricting people's movements and meetings or closing schools or other institutions. In a number of families, people became very seriously ill and there were even deaths of family members. Media reports about the increasing numbers of infected people, the rapid spread of disease, and the situation in hospitals were quite dramatic in some places. All of this certainly influenced our interviews in terms of their preparation and course and in terms of the attitudes and opinions of many of the eyewitnesses. In fact, the interviews with the eyewitnesses quite predictably reflected the situation in general as well as their personal experience of the situation. Some commented directly on the pandemic; others compared their life experiences with the time of the pandemic. Many teachers commented on the weeks of the online teaching that was going on in primary schools at that time. In a number of cases, the pandemic situation greatly influenced the opening parts of the interviews and the building of trust with the eyewitness. We return to this issue repeatedly in the subsequent chapters, working with the data from the oral history interviews. For our research, it is very important to keep in mind during the analysis and interpretations that the interviews took place at an extraordinary time.

The book has two main parts. In the first part, 'Contexts of Czechoslovak School System Development', we briefly present the history of Czechoslovakia, but we primarily describe and explain the modern developments and transformations of the school system. This part of the book shows the broader historical context of our research, as we also introduce the reader to key milestones and events in Czechoslovak history that had an impact on the school system and education levels. Within this section, we describe the interwar Czechoslovak school system in some detail. This is particularly important because after the Velvet Revolution in 1989, inspiration for school system reform was sought from other times, especially this period, as the interwar school system was among the most advanced in Europe. In the first part of the book, however, we focus mainly on the period after 1948, when the Communist Party took power in Czechoslovakia and started a forty-year social-ist school system, during which most of our research respondents lived and studied, and some even worked at primary schools. The socialist school system shaped sev-eral generations of people and was among the important components of the state at that time. After the collapse of the communist regime, a number of changes occurred in the school system, although a number of continuities between the socialist and the democratic school system were still visible after 1989. At the end of the first part of the book, we focus on the late socialist primary school system and the teachers' work in the late 1980s.

The second part of the book, 'Schools and Teachers in a Period of Changes' presents the main results of our research. We focus on the school system transfor-mation in Czechoslovakia after 1989, on the changes in schools in a broader con-text, and on the everyday life and work of teachers. This approach allows us to show the schools and the people involved in a rather detailed way, as we were able to capture the main historical events as well as the everyday life of a teacher in differ-ent environments and schools. In this part of the book, we follow the reforms, inno-vations, hopes, and expectations associated with democratic developments in Czechoslovakia after 1989 as well as the disillusionments and disappointments brought about by the post-socialist transformation, and not just in the school system.

The following paragraphs present the focus of the individual chapters.

The book opens with a Chap. 2 titled 'From the Habsburg Monarchy to the Czechoslovak Republic: Education in Historical Context'. The foundations of the primary school system in the Habsburg Monarchy were laid at the end of the eigh-teenth century, and the issue of education became a matter of state concern. This chapter maps the history from the reign of Maria Theresa to the formation of an independent Czechoslovakia in 1918, and then to the interwar and war period (up until 1945). We briefly describe the general history to show the (international) polit-ical context and the key economic characteristics of the time. We note the legislation and present the primary school system and its development and reforms, including proposed changes that were not implemented. We also mention the issues of minor-ity education, teacher education, co-education, the changing role of the church in the school system, and changes in the content of education.

The next Chap. 3, titled 'From Stalinism to the Prague Spring—Education in Complicated Times (1945–1968)', presents the history of Czechoslovakia from the end of World War II to the end of the 1960s. The post-war years were associated with hopes for a free life and the general development of the country. These hopes were extinguished in 1948, when the Communist Party of Czechoslovakia took over all power and the building of a socialist (totalitarian) state, and the country simulta-neously became a satellite of the Soviet Union. The chapter goes on to describe the 1960s in Czechoslovakia, when the regime relaxed and changes occurred in many areas of life. The reforms culminated in the 'Prague Spring', which ended with the invasion of the Red Army and other Warsaw Pact troops in 1968. We focus on the period of 'normalization', i.e. a return to the status before the reform movement, brought about by the presence of the occupational forces. In the field of education and the school system, a 'Sovietization' occurred in the 1950s, resulting in many deformations and unprepared reforms aimed at bringing the school system closer to that of the Soviet Union. The chapter describes specific laws as well as ideological influences in the school system, including the specific impacts of the interventions into the school system and into the lives of teachers and students. In the 1960s, schools and teachers had both regained more freedom for their work. This period ended after 1968, when staffing purges took place in schools and the onset of normalization was accompanied by the return of ideological pressure.

The next Chap. 4 is titled 'Schools and Teachers Two Decades Before the Fall of the Communist Regime', and it deals with the period of 1969–1989. We focus on the process of normalization and on how Czechoslovak society slowly fell into a state of lethargy and taciturnity. We explain the deteriorating economic situation. The communist government tried to 'calm' the population with pro-social and pro-family policies as well as with tolerance for people's escape into private life. In the text, we introduce perestroika and glasnost, initiated by Mikhail Gorbachev. The Czechoslovak government showed little willingness to follow this new course. Adherence to ideological dogmas brought continuously increasing stagnation and it brought the country to the brink of economic collapse in the late 1980s. The main part of the chapter is devoted to the school system, especially to primary schools and primary school teachers. We map the topic in a macro-historical perspective, describing the key education laws, presenting critical analyses of the state of the school system and of the limited education reforms. These could not go beyond the ideologically conditioned concept of the unified school until November 1989. We also focus on the everyday life of teachers, looking into the 'workshop' of socialist teachers and their lesson plans, tools, and textbooks. Teachers' out-of-school life and how they spent their free time are important topics in this chapter. We also discuss the topic of the political education of teachers. The text is based on research of contemporary sources and on interviews with teachers who taught in primary schools at the time.

The second part of the book opens with the Chap. 5 'Transforming the Education System: A Difficult Return to Democratic Europe', which introduces the reader to the broader context of the transformation of the Czech education system after 1989 with an emphasis on the primary school system. We briefly introduce the political and economic development of Czechoslovakia after the fall of the communist government in 1989. We then describe the process of transition to a market economy and the dissolution of Czechoslovakia in 1993, when two separate states, the Czech Republic and the Slovak Republic, were established. In this chapter, we focus primarily on the situation in the Czech Republic by presenting the fundamental reforms of the education system. We explain the actual reforms and the specific changes in legislation that formed the background for the changes in the Czech school system. We then focus attention on expert discussions and educational system reform proposals. Although these largely remained in the realm of ideas and intentions, they are important for understanding the reform considerations of the time. We describe the fundamental problems of the Czech school system, connected primarily to the complicated economic situation of the country undergoing transformation. The chapter concludes with a brief introduction of the developments and reforms of the school systems in neighbouring post-communist countries, which we compare to the situation in the Czech Republic.

The book continues with the Chap. 6 titled 'Schools: Everyday Life in the Period of Post-Socialist Transformation', in which we shift our attention to the life of primary schools and their changes. The first years after the Velvet Revolution were characterized by vigorous change, experimentation, and the search for possible ways to reform school management and administration.

In this chapter, we show that the resistance to rules and excessive bureaucracy and the desire for freedom formed the dominant image of early 1990s schools that is present in the memory of teachers. The neo-liberal turn also brought a high appreciation for responsibility, as reflected in the self-governance (autonomy) of schools. However, this brought the people involved in school life completely new responsibilities, rules, and challenges.

Sensitive topics included changes in school management and the first competitive selections for new school heads; these selections were initially conducted without clear rules. At the end of the chapter, we focus on the relationships between schools and the educational offices that were supposed to manage the schools and that were a part of the school management reform. Cooperation with the municipalities that became the school founders then became a new challenge for schools. The quality of the relationship between the municipality and the school could significantly influence the atmosphere in the school and the education conditions.

In the Chap. 7 titled 'Schools in a Network of (External) Relationships', we map the (interpersonal) relations as well as the environment or location in which the school is situated. In the introductory part of the chapter, we focus on students, parents, and teachers. The narrators' perspectives of the developments and transformations of relationships among the different people involved during the post-socialist transformation is at the centre of our focus. We mention the topic of (economic) transformations of society based on neo-liberalism, the development of private enterprise and individualism with regard to changes in parental behaviour, and the transformation of parent relationships with teachers. The lack of preparedness of teachers for the transformation of their position after 1989 and the challenges in the perception of parents as partners of the school is mentioned.

We focus on the life of schools in different environments and locations, specifically in small and large towns as well as rural areas. We monitor schools that were considered to be of high quality in the 1990s and those that faced a number of challenges. The stories of the schools are connected on two levels: continuities from the socialist period (for example, insufficient school capacities) and the need to face new and often unexpected challenges (for example, the rise of social inequalities after 1989). The chapter also describes the competitive relationship between primary schools and the newly established multi-year grammar schools. Finally, we turn our attention to an important external factor in the life of schools: the School Inspectorate. The School Inspectorate had to overcome a poor reputation, which can be seen as a legacy of the communist government; at the same time, it was dealing with problems stemming from the new network of relationships for schools after 1989.

The Chap. 8 'Teachers: Various Life Stories and Perspectives' focuses on the life stories of teachers of several generations who were both witnesses and direct participants in the post-socialist transformation of the primary school system in Czechoslovakia at different stages of their careers. Our aim is to get to know the lives of specific teachers and also to complement the knowledge about the transformation of the school system with the views and experiences of specific eyewitnesses. In studying the life stories of teachers, we had to include the period before 1989 and the socialist school system, as this often had a significant impact on the life and the work of teachers.

Although it is not possible to generalize the stories of teachers, they can be used to show how diverse everyday reality was before 1989 and in the period of post-socialist transformation, both in schools and outside of them. It is important to understand the personal lives of teachers and their approach to life. We focus on the working and the non-working lives of teachers, the possibilities of aligning work and private life, including the sensitive issue of the (insufficient) financial remuneration of the teaching profession. Teachers' life stories show how complex the paths of post-socialist society and the school system were.

The book concludes with a Chap. 9 titled 'Learning and Teaching: The Legacy of the Socialist Era and New Challenges', which focuses more specifically on teaching and learning in primary schools, but also on school equipment, including teaching aids and even computers in the first decade after the fall of the communist regime. From the perspective of the teachers/eyewitnesses, we primarily observe the changes in teaching or educational content, followed by the radical changes in foreign language teaching and in the quality and concepts of 'traditional' textbooks (published before 1989), as well as new ones, often distributed by private publishers. The range of teaching aids gradually expanded. Teachers faced many dilemmas in these areas. The chapter shows how the teachers perceived the post-1989 period, as they acquired enormous freedom in their work and teaching practically from 1 day to the next. For many teachers, it was not easy to cope with the challenges brought by the post-socialist transformation. For example, some eyewitnesses positively evaluated the uniformity of textbooks and their contents before 1989. The Velvet Revolution represented, among other things, the end of some established institutions (e.g. in the field of further teacher education); the narrators evaluated this change negatively. The chapter describes the initially lacklustre role of the Ministry of Education and the School Inspectorate in the field of pedagogical innovations. To some extent, the chapter breaks down the prevailing narrative of fundamental and rapid changes in schools and the entirely new opportunities brought about by the post-communist era. Our research shows that in fact, many changes or innovations were introduced slowly and gradually, and their acceptance depended on the teachers themselves and on the support of the school head or the school's founder.

Bibliography

Abrams, L. (2016). *Oral history theory* (2nd ed.). Taylor & Francis Group.

Bauman, Z. (1994). A revolution in the theory of revolution. *International Political Science Review, 15*, 15–24.

Berend, I. T. (2009). *From the soviet bloc to the European Union*. Cambridge University Press.

Bernard, J., Kostelecký, T., Mikešová, R., Šafr, J., Trlifajová, L., & Hurrle, J. (2018). *Nic se tady neděje…: životní podmínky na periferním venkově* [Nothing happens here…: living conditions in the peripheral rural areas]. Sociologické nakladatelství (SLON).

Berryman, S. E. (2000). *Hidden challenges to education systems in transition economies*. The World Bank.

Bîrzea, C. (1994). *Educational policies of countries in transition*. Council of Europe Press.

Brooks, J. F., DeCorse, C. R. N., & Walton, J. (2008). *Small worlds. Method, meaning, & narrative in microhistory*. School for Advanced Research Press.

Bold, C. (2012). *Using narrative in research*. SAGE.

Branch, J. L. (2013). The trouble with think alouds: Generating data using concurrent verbal protocols. In *Proceedings of the Annual Conference of CAIS / Actes Du congrès Annuel De l'ACSI*. https://doi.org/10.29173/cais8

Claus, P., & Marriott, J. (2013). *History: An introduction to theory, method and practice*. Routledge.

Czech Statistical Office. (2021a). *Census: Ethnicity*. https://www.czso.cz/csu/scitani2021/ethnicity

Czech Statistical Office. (2021b). *Census: Religion*. https://www.czso.cz/csu/scitani2021/religious-beliefs

Certeau, M. (1984). *The practice of everyday life*. University of California Press.

Čechura, J. (1994). Mikrohistorie - nová perspektiva dějepisectví konce tisíciletí? [Microhistory - a new perspective of historiography at the end of the millennium?]. *Dějiny a současnost, 1*(16), 2–5.

Čerych, L. (1995). Educational reforms in central and Eastern Europe. *European Journal of Education, 30*(4), 423–435.

Čerych, L. (1996). *Zprávy o národní politice ve vzdělávání: Česká republika* [Reports on National Educational Policy: the Czech Republic]. Ústav pro informace ve vzdělávání.

Čerych, L. (1999). General report on the symposium "educational reforms in central and Eastern Europe: Processes and outcomes". *European Education, 31*(2), 5–38.

Dávila, P., Naya, L. M., & Zabaleta, I. (2017). Memory and yearbooks: An analysis of their structure and evolution in religious schools in 20th century Spain. In C. Yanes-Carera, J. Meda, & A. Viñao (Eds.), *School memories: New trends in the history of education* (pp. 65–79). Springer. https://doi.org/10.1007/978-3-319-44063-7

Dobson, M., & Ziemann, B. (Eds.). (2009). *Reading primary sources: The interpretation of texts from nineteenth- and twentieth-century history*. Taylor & Francis Group.

Dülmen, R. (2002). *Historická antropologie: vývoj, problémy, úkoly* [Historical anthropology: Development, issues, tasks]. Dokořán.

Eurydice. (n.d.). *Česká republika: Overview* [Czech Repubic: Overview]. https://eacea.ec.europa.eu/national-policies/eurydice/content/czech-republic_cs

Fiszbein, A. (2001). *Decentralizing education in transition societies: Case studies from central and Eastern Europe*. The World Bank.

Frank, L. (2020). Trends in demography and migration in the Czech Republic. In P. Tálas & A. Etl (Eds.), *Demography and migration in central and Eastern Europe* (pp. 45–63). Dialóg Campus.

Gildea, R., & Simonin, A. (Eds.). (2008). *Writing contemporary history*. Hodder Education.

Ginzburg, C., & Poni, C. (1979). Il nome et il come: Scambio ineguale e mercato storiografico. *Quderni storici, 14*(40), 181–190.

Ginzburg, C. (1993). Zwei oder drei Dinge, die ich von ihr weiss. *Historische Antropologie, 1*(2), 169–192.

Goodson, I. (2008). *Investigating the Teacher's life and work*. Sense Publishers.

Goodson, I., & Gill, S. (2011). *Narrative pedagogy: Life history and learning*. Peter Lang.

Geertz, C. (2000). *Local knowledge: Further essays in interpretive anthropology.* Basic books.

Greger, D. (2011). Dvacet let českého školství optikou teorií změny vzdělávání v post-socialistických zemích [Twenty years of Czech education as viewed through the theory of change of education in post-socialist countries]. *Orbis scholae, 5*(1), 9–22.

Grele, R. J. (2003). Movement without aim: Methodological and theoretical problems in oral history. In R. Perks & A. Thomson (Eds.), *The oral history reader* (pp. 38–52). Routledge.

Grulich, J. (2001). Zkoumání maličkostí. Okolnosti vzniku a významu mikrohistorie. *Český časopis historický, 3*(99), 519–547.

Harvey, K. (Ed.). (2009). *History and material culture: A student's guide to approaching alternative sources.* Taylor & Francis Group.

Holmes, L. (1997). *Post-communism: An introduction.* Polity Press.

Holý, L. (2010). *Malý český člověk a skvělý český národ: národní identita a postkomunistická transformace společnosti* [Little Czech and the great Czech nation: national identity and post-communist social transformation]. Sociologické nakladatelství.

Chankseliani, M., & Silova, I. (Eds.). (2018). *Comparing post-socialist transformations: Purposes, policies, and practices in education.* Symposium Books.

Chorvát, I., Šafr, J., Hofreiter, R., Patočková, V., Paulíček, M., & Zeman, M. (2019). *Volný čas, společnost, kultura: Česko – Slovensko* [Leisure, Society and Culture in The Czech Republic and Slovakia]. Sociologické nakladatelství (SLON).

Iggers, G. (2002). *Dějepisectví ve 20. století: od vědecké objektivity k postmoderní výzvě* [Historiography in the 20th century: From scientific objectivity to postmodern challenge]. Lidové noviny.

Isaac, R. (1994). Geschichte und Anthropologie – oder: Macht und (Be-)Deutung. *Historische Antropologie, 2*(1), 107–130.

Institute of contemporary history. (2022). About us. https://www.usd.cas.cz/en/about-us

Kenney, P. (2002). *A carnival of revolution: Central Europe 1989.* Princeton University Press.

Kopeček, M. (2019). *Architekti dlouhé změny. Expertní kořeny postsocialismu v Československu* [Architects of long changes: expert roots of post-socialism in Czechoslovakia]. Argo.

Koucký, J. (1996). Školské reformy ve společenských proměnách: střední Evropa v období transformace [School reforms in social changes: Central Europe in the transformation period]. In J. Hendrichová, L. Čerych, & J. Kotásek (Eds.), *Reformy školství ve střední a východní Evropě. Průběh a výsledky* [Education reforms in Central and Eastern Europe. Progress and results]. (pp. 15–38). ÚIV.

Kotásek, J. (1996). Struktura a organizace sekundárního školství ve střední a východní Evropě [Structure and organisation of secondary education in Central and Eastern Europe]. In J. Hendrichová, L. Čerych, & J. Kotásek. *Reformy školství ve střední a východní Evropě. Průběh a výsledky* [Education reforms in Central and Eastern Europe. Progress and results] (pp. 39–59). ÚIV.

Kotásek, J. (Ed.). (2001). *National Programme for the Development of Education in the Czech Republic: White Paper.* https://planipolis.iiep.unesco.org/en/2001/national-programme-development-education-czech-republic-white-paper-5687

Krapfl, J. (2013). *Revolution with a human face: politics, culture, and community in Czechoslovakia, 1989–1992.* Cornell University Press.

Krátká, L., Wohlmuth Markupová, J., & Vaněk, M. (2018). *(K)lidová věda?: proměny a konstanty v práci i životě vědců a vědkyň v letech 1968–2008* [Peaceful/people science?: Changes and constants in the work and life of scientists in 1968–2008]. Fakulta humanitních studií Univerzity Karlovy.

Krippendorff, K. (2019). *Content analysis: An introduction to its methodology.* Sage.

Kučerová, S. R., Trnková, K., & Meyer, P. (2019). Changing structures and the role of education in the development of the educational system in Czechia. In J. Holger, C. Kramer, & P. Meusburger (Eds.), *Geographies of schooling* (pp. 125–144). Springer. https://doi.org/10.1007/978-3-030-18799-6

Lawn, M., & Grosvenor, I. (Eds.). (2005). *Materialities of schooling: Design, technology, objects, routines.* Symposium Books.

Lenderová, M., Jiránek, T., & Macková, M. (2009). Z dějin české každodennosti. *Život v 19. století* [From the history of Czech everyday life. Life in the 19th century]. Univerzita Karlova.

Lüdtke, A. (Ed.). (1995). *The history of everyday life: Reconstructing historical experiences and ways of life*. Princeton University Press.

McAdams, D. P., Hoffman, B. J., Mansfield, E. D., & Day, R. (1996). Themes of agency and communion in significant autobiographical scenes. *Journal of Personality, 64*(2), 339–377.

McCulloch, G. (2004). *Documentary research in education, history and the social sciences*. Taylor & Francis Group.

McDermott, K. (2015). *Communist Czechoslovakia, 1945–89: A political and social history*. Macmillan Education.

Meda, J., & Viñao, A. (2017). School memory: Historiographical balance and heuristics perspectives. In C. Yanes-Carera, J. Meda, & A. Viñao (Eds.), *School memories: New trends in the history of education* (pp. 1–9). Springer. https://doi.org/10.1007/978-3-319-44063-7

Medick, H. (2001). Quo vadis Historische Anthropologie? Geschichtsforschung zwischen Historischer Kulturwissenschaft und Mikro-Historie. *Historische Antropologie, 9*(1), 78–92.

Mitter, W. (2003). A decade of transformation: Educational policies in Central and Eastern Europe. *International Review of Education, 49*(1–2), 75–96.

Moree, D. (2013). *Učitelé na vlnách transformace: kultura školy před rokem 1989 a po něm* [Teachers in the period of transformation: School culture before and after 1989]. Karolinum.

Niethammer, L. (2012). *Memory and history: Essays in contemporary history*. Peter Lang.

Nodl, M, (2004). Mikrohistorie a historická antropologie [Microhistory and historical anthropology]. *Dějiny-teorie-kritika* (2), 237–253.

Perks, R., & Thomson, A. (Eds.). (2003). *The oral history reader*. Routledge.

Perry, L. B. (2005) The seeing and the seen: Contrasting perspectives of post-communist Czech schooling. *Compare: A Journal of Comparative and International Education, 35*(3), 265–283.

Polouček, O. (2019). Dance parties and the symbolic construction of communities in the era of late socialism in Czechoslovakia. *Národopisná revue, 29*(5), 18–28.

Polouček O. (2020a). *Babičky na bigbítu: Společenský život na moravském venkově pozdního socialismu* [Grannies at the big beat party: The social life in the late socialist Moravian countryside]. Masarykova univerzita.

Polouček, O. (2020b). Kontinuity v období „revolučních proměn" a „soumraku selského stavu": příspěvek ke studiu života na venkově v socialistickém Československu [Continuities in the period of 'revolutionary changes' and the 'dusk of the peasant status': Contribution to the study of rural life in socialist Czechoslovakia]. *Slovenský národopis / Slovak Ethnology, 68*(1), 29–46. https://doi.org/10.2478/se-2020-0002.

Polouček, O., & Zounek, J. (2021). Vzdělávací systém a československá verze přestavby (1987–1989): Analýza, kritika a návrhy na reformy v kontextu ideologie a krize [Education and the Czechoslovak form of perestroika (1987–1989): Analysis, criticism, and planned reforms in the context of ideology and crisis]. *Studia paedagogica, 26*(3), 83–108. https://doi.org/10.5817/SP2021-3-4

Portelli, A. (2003). What makes oral history different. In R. Perks & A. Thomson (Eds.), *The oral history reader* (pp. 63–74). Routledge.

Pospěch, P. (2021). *Neznámá společnost: pohledy na současné Česko*. Host.

Prokop, D. (2022). *Slepé skvrny: o chudobě, vzdělávání, populismu a dalších výzvách české společnosti* [Blind spots: on poverty, education, populism and other challenges of Czech society]. Host.

Rákosník, J., Spurný, M., & Štaif, J. (2018). *Milníky moderních českých dějin: krize konsenzu a legitimity v letech 1848–1989* [Milestones of modern Czech history: The crisis of consensus and legitimacy in the years 1848–1989]. Argo.

Richie, D. A. (2003). *Oral history: A practical guide*. Oxford University Press.

Rychlík, J. (2012). *Rozdělení Československa: 1989–1992* [Partition of Czechoslovakia: 1989–1992]. Vyšehrad.

Rychlík, J. (2020). *Československo v období socialismu: 1945-1989* [Czechoslovakia in the era of Socialism: 1945–1989]. Vyšehrad.

Saxonberg, S. (2001). *The fall: A comparative study of the end of communism in Czechoslovakia, East Germany, Hungary and Poland.* Harwood Academic Publishers.

Silova, I., Piattoeva, N., & Millei, Z. (Eds.). (2018). *Childhood and schooling in (post)socialist societies: Memories of everyday life.* Palgrave Macmillan. https://doi.org/10.1007/978-3-319-62791-5

Schnepel, B. (1999). Ethnologie und Geschichte. Stationen der Standortbestimmung in der britischen 'Social Anthropology'. *Historische Antropologie, 7*(1), 109–128.

Spilková, V. (1997). *Proměny primární školy a vzdělávání učitelů v historicko-srovnávací perspektivě* [The development of primary schools and teacher training from historical-comparative perspective]. Pedagogická fakulta Univerzity Karlovy.

Spousta, J. (2002). Changes in religious values in The Czech Republic. *Sociologický časopis / Czech Sociological Review, 38*(3), 345–364. https://doi.org/10.13060/00380288.2002.38.3.06

Stone, L. (1979). The revival of narrative: Reflections on a new old history. *Past and Present, 85*(1), 3–24.

Szijártó, I. (2002). Four arguments for microhistory. *Rethinking History, 2*(6), 209–215.

Šimáně, M., & Kamanová, L. (2020). Přijímací řízení na středních odborných školách v období socialistického Československa [The admission procedure at secondary vocational schools in socialist Czechoslovakia]. *Studia Paedagogica, 25*(3), 69–101. https://doi.org/10.5817/SP2020-3-3

Šimáně, M., & Kamanová, L. (2021). Developing of the secondary technical schools in Czechoslovakia under the influence of the Soviet Union in 1948–1959. *History: Sources and People, 24,* 276–281.

Šimáně, M. (2021). Střední odborné školství v Československu v letech 1945–1953 [Secondary vocational education in Czechoslovakia in the years 1945–1953]. In P. Adamec & M. Šimáně (Eds.), *Vybrané kapitoly soudobých témat odborného vzdělávání [Selected chapters of contemporary vocational education topics]* (pp. 10–29). Powerprint.

Ther, P. (2016). *Europe since 1989: A history.* Princeton University Press.

Thompson, P., & Bornat, J. (2017). *The voice of the past: Oral history.* Oxford University Press.

Vaněk, M., & Mücke, P. (2015). *Třetí strana trojúhelníku: Teorie a praxe orální historie* [The third side of a triangle: Theory and practice of Oral history]. Univerzita Karlova v Praze, nakladatelství Karolinum.

Vaněk, M., & Mücke, P. (2016). *Velvet revolutions: An oral history of Czech society.* Oxford University Press.

von Kopp, B. (1992). The Eastern European revolution and education in Czechoslovakia. *Comparative Education Review, 36*(1), 101–113.

Walterová, E. (2004). *Úloha školy v rozvoji vzdělanosti (1. Díl)* [The role of school in the development of education (Part 1)]. Paido.

Walterová, E., & Greger, D. (2006). Transformace vzdělávacích systémů zemí visegrádské skupiny: srovnávací analýza [Transformation of educational systems of Visegrad countries: Comparative analysis]. *Orbis scholae, 1*(1), 13–29.

Yanes-Cabrera, C., & Escolano Benito, A. (2017). Archaeology of memory and school culture: Materialities and "immaterialities" of school. In C. Yanes-Carera, J. Meda, & A. Viñao (Eds.), *School memories: New trends in the history of education* (pp. 263–270). Springer. https://doi.org/10.1007/978-3-319-44063-7

Yow, V. R. (2005). *Recording oral history: A guide for the humanities and social sciences.* AltaMira.

Zounek, J. (1996). Filozofická fakulta Masarykovy univerzity v letech 1948–1949. [Faculty of Arts of Masaryk University in 1948–1949]. *Časopis Matice moravské, 115*(2), 299–312.

Zounek, J., & Poloucek, O. (2021). Každodenní život venkovskych zakladnich škol na jižni Moravě během postsocialistické transformace [Everyday life of rural elementary schools in South Moravia during the post-socialist transformation]. *Národopisný věstník, 80*(2), 31–50.

Zounek, J., & Šimaně, M. (2014). *Úvod do studia dějin pedagogiky a školství: kapitoly z metodologie historicko-pedagogického výzkumu* [An introduction to the study of history of pedagogy and educational system: Chapters from the historical-pedagogical research history]. Masarykova univerzita.

Zounek, J., & Vichrová, M. (2008). Der Wissenschaftler und Pädagoge in den totalitären Regimen des 20. Jahrhunderts in der Tschechoslowakei. In A. Pehnke (Ed.), *Widerständige sächsische Schulreformer im Visier stalinischer Politik (1945–1959)* (pp. 216–228). Peter Lang GmbH, Internationaler Verlag der Wissenschaften.

Zounek, J., Knotová, D., & Šimáně, M. (2015a). Výzkum soudobých dějin pedagogiky a školství: k metodologickým otázkám historicko-pedagogického výzkumu [The research of contemporary history of education (To the issue of historical-pedagogical research)]. *Studia Paedagogica, 20*(3), 89–112. https://doi.org/10.5817/SP2015-3-6

Zounek, J., Šimáně, M., & Knotová, D. (2015b). Dějiny socialistického školství: terra inkognita historicko pedagogického výzkumu? K problematice zdrojů poznání minulosti [The history of socialist education: Terra incognita of historical-pedagogical research? To the issue of the sources of the past]. *Pedagogická orientace, 25*(3), 319–344. https://doi.org/10.5817/PedOr2015-3-319

Zounek, J., Šimáně, M., & Knotová, D. (2016). Cesta k učitelství v socialistickém Československu pohledem pamětníků [The Path to Teaching in Socialist Czechoslovakia as Seen by Witnesses]. *Studia paedagogica, 21*(3), 131–159. https://doi.org/10.5817/SP2016-3-7

Zounek, J., Šimáně, M., & Knotová, D. (2017a). Primary school teachers as a tool of secularization of society in communist Czechoslovakia. *History of Education: Journal of the History of Education Society, 46*(4), 480–497. https://doi.org/10.1080/0046760X.2016.1276970

Zounek, J. Šimáně, M., & Knotová, D. (2017b). *Normální život v nenormální době. Základní školy a jejich učitelé (nejen) v období normalizace* [Normal life in not so normal times. Primary schools and their teachers (not only) during the so-called normalization period]. Wolters Kluwer.

Zounek, J., Šimáně, M., & Knotová, D. (2017c). *Socialistická základní škola pohledem pamětníků. Sonda do života učitelů v Jihomoravském kraji* [Socialist primary school as seen by eyewitnesses: Probing teachers' life in the South Moravia region]. Wolters Kluwer.

Zounek, J., Knotová, D., & Šimáně, M. (2017d). Život Karla – příběh učitele v socialistickém Československu [Karel's Life – the Story of a Teacher in Socialist Czechoslovakia]. *Orbis scholae, 11*(1), 31–52. https://doi.org/10.14712/23363177.2018.56

Zounek, J., Šimáně, M., & Knotová, D. (2018). 'You have betrayed us for a little dirty money!' The Prague Spring as seen by primary school teachers. *Paedagogica Historica. International Journal of the History of Education, 54*(3), 320–337. https://doi.org/10.1080/0030923 0.2017.1394884

Part I
Contexts of Czechoslovakian School System Development

Chapter 2
From the Habsburg Monarchy to the Czechoslovak Republic: Education in Historical Context

Abstract The chapter presents Czechoslovakia and its school system in historical context. The foundations of a system of elementary education were established under the Habsburg monarchy at the end of the eighteenth century, and the matter of education also became a matter of state. The text follows the history from the reign of Maria Theresa to the establishment of an independent Czechoslovakia in 1918 and then the interwar and war periods. The authors briefly describe the general history of a particular period, showing the (international) political context and presenting key economic characteristics of the time. They then place the levels of education, education itself, and the school system in a historical framework. They take note of the laws and present the system of elementary education, including its development and reforms as well as changes that could not be implemented. The authors note the problems of minority education, mixed-sex education, the education of teachers, the changing role of the church in education, and changes in the content of education.

Keywords Czechoslovakia · History of the eighteenth to twentieth century · School system · Elementary education · Reforms · World war II

2.1 Education Since the Eighteenth Century

The Czech Republic is a country situated in the centre of Europe. An abbreviated name, Czechia, is also used internationally. The Czech Republic was originally a part of Czechoslovakia; since 1993, it has been an independent state (the dissolution of Czechoslovakia will be discussed in more detail below).

As early as in the fourth century BC, the Bohemian Basin was inhabited by Celtic Boii tribes, after whom the territory was named Boiohaemum, or Bohemia in

© Masaryk University, Faculty of Arts, Registration no. 00216224,
VAT ID: CZ00216224 2024
J. Zounek et al., *(Post)Socialist Transformation of Primary Schools*,
https://doi.org/10.1007/978-3-031-58768-9_2

Latin.[1] The land of its main historical territories (Bohemia, Moravia, and Silesia[2]) has remained essentially unchanged since the Middle Ages; from the sixteenth century onward, the lands of the Bohemian Crown were a part of the Habsburg Monarchy. The reform of the school system, carried out under the rule of Maria Theresa in 1774, was an important event in the history of education in the Habsburg monarchy, and thus in the history of the Czech lands as well. Because of this reform, a fixed organization of elementary education was introduced in the territory of Bohemia for the first time, even though it only introduced a 'general teaching obligation', and not compulsory schooling. In other words, parents were not forced to send their children to school, which would have been an issue especially during seasonal work and in other cases in which parents needed help with the household (Rýdl, 2006; O'Brian, 1970; Melton, 2003).

Although Maria Theresa expected German to be the main teaching language in these schools, in practice, because of the lack of qualified teachers, it was common for other languages to be used as well. The Czech lands were no exception in this respect. This was also one reason that the development of this system of elementary education also later helped the process of national awareness among the Czech population (Mitter, 2004).

The reform of 1849, which established eight-year grammar schools, was an important milestone in the history of secondary education. The main purpose of the grammar schools was to provide higher general education; they were divided into lower and higher stages. The grammar school was officially seen as a preparation for university studies. Grammar school studies were newly concluded with a Matura exam (school-leaving examination), which allowed the graduates to continue their studies at a university (see also Entwurf der Organisation..., 1849). Six-year 'Realschule' (science and technology-oriented schools), which had the status of secondary schools, were established as well. This began the differentiation of secondary schools into humanities and technical schools (Cohen, 1996; Melton, 2003; Cvrček, 2020).

The year 1869 was also of great importance for elementary education. Two years after the establishment of the Austro-Hungarian Empire, a new school law, called 'Hasner's Law', was adopted. Hasner's Law brought many very positive changes, resulting in a significant expansion of the national level of education and in the effective elimination of illiteracy in the Czech lands (Šafránek, 1897, 1918). The introduction of eight-year compulsory schooling for children from the age of six might be the most significant provision of Hasner's Law. In contrast to previous decades, any non-compliance with compulsory schooling was punished severely,

---

[1] In general historical overviews and in the history of school systems in the Czech territory, in this and other chapters, we build on the sources listed at the end of the chapter. We cite directly in the text only those sources that provide a specific piece of information, or if the citation is required by the context of the interpretation.

[2] The terms 'Czech lands' and 'Lands of the Bohemian Crown' are also used; these terms are used mainly in a historical-geographical context. In their narrower definition, they align almost entirely with the territory of today's Czech Republic.

and the Law did not allow any exemptions (for example, because of seasonal works in the fields). The Law also removed church supervision over schools, as from this point, church officials were only allowed to teach religion as one of the compulsory subjects (Překlad zákonníka…, 1869).

The structure of the elementary school system itself also underwent fundamental changes. The original 'Trivialschule', 'Hauptschule', and 'Normalschule' established under Maria Theresa were replaced by 'Volksschule' and 'Bürgerschule'. The compulsory schooling could be completed in several ways at these schools. The students could complete the full 8 years at a Volksschule. However, this closed their path to further studies. From this type of school, students could not continue to any secondary school and therefore not to any university. Another option was to complete the first 5 years of a Volksschule and then transfer to a 'Bürgerschule', at which the students studied for another 3 years. After completing the first 5 years of a Volksschule, students could also continue to one of the 'lower secondary schools'. Continuing at one of the lower secondary schools was the only way the students could attempt to pass the Matura exam and thus also the only possibility to continue studying at a university (Šimáně, 2019). The lower secondary schools represented the very lower stages of grammar schools and also other types of schools, such as Realschule. This created a very complicated system of schools and educational paths that were not mutually compatible. In addition, there were differences in the availability of schools in urban and rural areas (Table 2.1).

In larger towns, the Volksschule were divided into girls' and boys' schools, a division that disappeared many decades later; the curricula were otherwise uniform as in this respect, the school system did not distinguish between girls and boys. The Volksschule became schools for all children, not only for the upper classes.

In 1883, an amendment to the law was issued that once again provided exemptions from compulsory schooling for students in the last 2 years of compulsory schooling especially to secure seasonal work, and it was even possible to conclude the compulsory schooling after 6 years. The amendment thus essentially confirmed the prevailing practices of the time, especially in rural areas. The influence of the church on schools increased again (Zákonník říšský, 1883; Cibulka et al., 2021).

Despite all the twists and turns, the quality of education gradually improved during the nineteenth and early twentieth century. The achieved level of education of the population also increased, which allowed the people to better cope with the changing economic, commercial, social, and political conditions.

Table 2.1 School system and compulsory schooling

	Compulsory schooling									
Age	6–7	7–8	8–9	9–10	10–11	11–12	12–13	13–14	14–19	19 and older
Grade	1	2	3	4	5	6	7	8		
School type	Volksschule									
	Volksschule					Bürgerschule				
	Volksschule					Secondary schools				University studies

2.2   Interwar Czechoslovakia (1918–1938)

Independent Czechoslovakia was established on 28 October 1918, i.e., at the end of World War I. The newly established republic followed the Austro-Hungarian rule of law and administrative structure. This continuity was ensured by the hastily pre-pared Act No. 11/1918 Coll., commonly referred to as the 'Reception Norm', which stipulated that 'all existing provincial and imperial laws and regulations remain in force'. This prevented a legal vacuum and possible chaos just after the establish-ment of a new state, when no new legislation existed yet. It was not until February 1920 that the Constitutional Charter of the Czechoslovak Republic[3] (hereafter referred to as the Constitution), modelled after the American and French constitu-tions, was adopted. The constitution created a republican form of state, defined the legislative, executive, and judicial powers, and established the rights of national minorities, freedom of religion, and universal and equal suffrage for women. The legislative power was represented by a bicameral parliament (the Chamber of Deputies and the Senate); the executive power consisted of the government and the president. From 1918 to 1938, Czechoslovakia was a pluralist democracy, which was somewhat of an exception in the Central European region.

The idea of a Czechoslovak nation ('Czechoslovakism'), which was anchored in the 1920 Constitution, was an important aspect of the Czechoslovak Republic between 1918 and 1938. This political or cultural-political concept was created pri-marily so that a new state entity could be asserted in the aftermath of World War I and the collapse of Austria-Hungary. The largely artificial project created a single Czechoslovak nation-state that recognized the minority nations living on its terri-tory (Hudek et al., 2019).

The Germans were the largest national minority in Czechoslovakia (23% of the Czechoslovakian population), followed by the Hungarian minority in southern Slovakia and southern Carpathian Ruthenia (6%), by the Russians and Rusyns (3%), and by the Polish minority (0.75% of the Czechoslovakian population). Approximately 1% of the Czechoslovak population was declared to be of Jewish ethnicity (Tóth et al., 2012; Kořalka, 1998).

Promoting the ideas of the Czechoslovak nation went hand in hand with defining the nation against the heritage of the multi-ethnic Habsburg monarchy. This was reflected in the rejection of monarchism, which led to the abolition of noble titles and was an argument for a land reform that took some assets away from the nobility, especially forests and farmland. The rejection of the monarchy was also reflected in the attitude towards the Catholic Church, which, according to the contemporary narrative, embodied everything Habsburg and Austrian. Thus, in the name of reformist traditions (the legacy of Jan Hus and the Hussite movement), a new Czechoslovak Hussite Church was created, and the part of the population that iden-tified with the ideas of the new republic (often civil servants, teachers, etc.) inclined

---

[3]Two names—the Republic of Czechoslovakia and the Czechoslovak Republic—were used for this new state. We use these names in this book as well.

to it. The anti-Catholic ideas that labelled the period of Counter-Reformation as the 'Dark Ages' constituted one of the narratives of the nineteenth century Czech movement centred around the ideas of national identification. The roots of the relative success of the communist regime's anti-religious policy can thus be seen in the reform movement, in the Czech national revival, and also in the ideas of the First Czechoslovak Republic (compared to Poland, for example). This is also where to find the roots of the secular character and low religiosity of contemporary Czech society. This still influences the character of Czech education, in which the churches have only a marginal influence.

From an economic point of view, the Czechoslovak Republic can be characterized as an industrial-agrarian state. However, there was a difference between the industrial Czech territories with relatively advanced agriculture and the predominantly agrarian Slovakia with low agricultural productivity. Immediately after the establishment of the state, Czechoslovak governments tried to reduce these differences; the less developed areas of the state received investments to promote industrial and agricultural production. For the same reasons, the intelligentsia, civil servants, engineers, as well as doctors and police officers left the Czech lands for Slovakia and Carpathian Ruthenia.[4]

In the first decade after World War I, Czechoslovakia mostly went through a period of economic boom. The main industrial branches included mechanical engineering, metallurgy, food processing industry, textile, and clothing industry. The Baťa shoe factories in Zlín can be seen as an example of the successful growth of the Czechoslovak economy. The Baťa company also represented an example of successful expansion abroad. Already in the first months after the establishment of Czechoslovakia, the National Assembly adopted an eight-hour working day and a system of social legislation.

From the beginning of its existence, Czechoslovakia oriented its foreign policy towards the Western powers, especially France. It became a founding member of the League of Nations based in Geneva (1920). At the beginning of the 1930s, Czechoslovakia was a stable state with a functioning parliamentary democracy, an advanced economy, and a relatively high standard of living by Central European standards. The symptoms of the world economic crisis that began in the United States in the autumn of 1929 started to be felt in Czechoslovakia in 1930. The Czechoslovak economy was strongly export-oriented, which further amplified the crisis. It was first felt in agriculture, then it spread to industry, and, at the same time, unemployment rates began to rise sharply. The increasingly deteriorating social situation of the unemployed led to protest actions and their radicalization, which was escalated by a violent repression of demonstrations. The crisis also hit small artisans and tradespeople very hard, and a general decline of the Czechoslovak economy occurred. The crisis afflicted the intelligentsia as well, whose employment

---

[4]Carpathian Ruthenia was one of the self-governing territories within the First Czechoslovak Republic between 1919 and 1939; the territory was attached to Czechoslovakia after the dissolution of Hungary. It was then ceded to the Soviet Union in 1945. It is now a territory located in the Ukrainian Zakarpattia Oblast (region).

numbers were reduced through layoffs and early retirement and whose wages were cut. In Czechoslovakia, the economic crisis gradually began to subside in the mid-1930s, when production recovered and the unemployment rate decreased. However, it was not until 1938 that the Czechoslovak economy reached the level before the outbreak of the crisis in 1929 (Klápště & Šedivý, 2019).

The economic crisis fuelled tensions between the Czechoslovak and German populations of the republic. The border areas ('Sudetenland'), which were populated predominantly by the German population, were hit the hardest. Out of the five hundred thousand unemployed in Czechoslovakia in 1932, four hundred thousand lived in the territory of Sudetenland (Glassl, 1995; Jaworski, 1991). At the same time, the threat to Czechoslovakia from neighbouring Germany, where the Nazis had seized the power in early 1933, was also growing. This created both international and intranational tensions, which resulted in German claims to Czechoslovak territories inhabited by a predominantly German population. These claims against Czechoslovakia were explained to the world public as a partial correction of the Versailles Treaty, which had set too harsh conditions for Germany after World War I (Zückert, 2007).

The First Czechoslovak Republic ended with the signing of the Munich Agreement on 29 September 1938. A conference of powers was held in Munich to decide the future fate of Czechoslovakia without the participation of any Czechoslovak representatives. Germany (Adolf Hitler), Great Britain (Neville Chamberlain), France (Édouard Daladier), and Italy (Benito Mussolini) signed an agreement accepting all German demands. Thus, in early October 1938, Czechoslovakia had to cede all the border territories demanded by Germany, with a further course of action to be determined in relation to Poland and Hungary.

2.3 Interwar Education: A Period of Many (Un) successful Reforms

In Czechoslovakia, the school system was perceived as one of the key attributes of the development and functioning of the state during the interwar period, and considerable resources were spent on its development and expansion. Although it built on the previous period a more extensive reform was planned to better correspond with the needs of the new state. The first partial changes were adopted shortly after the establishment of Czechoslovakia. They concerned primarily those provisions of the Austro-Hungarian legislation that were in direct conflict with the new state system based on democratic principles and liberalism. For example, between 1919 and 1922, the celibacy of female teachers that had been introduced by Hasner's Law in 1869 was abolished. Female teachers were put on generally equal footing with men in terms of both law and service. Girls were allowed to study at universities and mixed-sex education was introduced in secondary schools and Bürgerschule. The church lost its influence over the educational curriculum and staffing matters in the field of education. Only the teaching of religion remained under its control. This was a compulsory subject, but parents could opt their children out of it. The compulsory subject of civics was newly introduced, as the education of responsible democratic citizens was one of the main aims of the interwar Czechoslovak school system and education. The subject was supposed to provide basic knowledge about the Czechoslovak state, about systems of government, and about economic, sociopolitical, and cultural issues. At the same time, the subject was supposed to lead the students to a republican education and to a propensity to democracy, love for the nation, mutual tolerance, respect, and love. However, these were only partial measures and adjustments that did not fundamentally affect the school system or school education.

The first post-World War I years were characterized by many reform efforts in which individual teachers or even teacher organizations or associations participated. These reforms usually did not have a broader theoretical basis and were of a rather local character, although in many respects they drew on global reform pedagogy.[5] For example, they were driven by the desire to transform the inner life of the school or the relationship between the teacher and the students. The expected 'great' reform of the school system never came in the period of the First Czechoslovak Republic. Although various discussions on the subject were held between Czech experts and university professors from the mid-1920s onwards, the proposals discussed were never realized. This was partly due to dealing with other 'current' problems such as the economic crisis and the deteriorating international situation, especially the threat from Nazi Germany.

As a result, many legislative norms from the Austro-Hungarian period were in force in the school system for the entire interwar period. This was also true for the

---

[5] Other European countries also sought to reform their schools and entire school systems (including school policy). For example, in Austria, as in Czechoslovakia, the laws of the monarchy were adopted, and the newly established republic adapted them to the changed circumstances. Changes were then made to the school system in the 1920s and 1930s, including the division of competences in the field of education at the national level and at the level of the individual federal states, and reforms of primary and secondary schools, including reforms of teaching methods. Otto Glöckel (1874–1935) was a prominent figure in the Austrian reform movement. In Germany, too, the school system underwent a number of changes, many of which were inspired by reform pedagogy, especially during the Weimar Republic. As in other countries, the questions of the unified school and its form, mixed-sex education and the availability of education to all children were discussed, the influence of the church on teaching was limited, the education of teachers at universities was another important matter, and many other changes were implemented. Contributing to the building of the republic was among the general aims of education. After the end of the Weimar Republic, the German education system once again became authoritarian, militant, and nationalistic, as it had been before 1919. A similar situation prevailed in other European countries' school systems, particularly in those that emerged as a result of World War I, like Czechoslovakia. Although many years have passed since then, there has not yet been a substantial comparative study of the development of school systems in these countries (Oelkers, 2020). From 1918 onwards, school systems were being built in Poland and Hungary, but also in the Balkans and the Baltic States, and with similar intentions to Czechoslovakia. They each take into account the local political, social, cultural, and other specificities of the country (see e.g. Gyuris, 2019; Jamrożek, 2018; Oelkers, 2020).

complicated system of elementary education with Volksschule and Bürgerschule, although several efforts and proposals for a unified school emerged. It was still only possible to attempt to pass the Matura exam and thus to have the possibility of studying at university after transferring from a Volksschule to one of the 'lower secondary schools' (multi-year grammar schools). Grammar schools continued to transform throughout the twentieth century. However, the interwar form of the (multi-year) grammar schools was a model/template on which the reform efforts were based even after 1989. The education of elementary school teachers did not change fundamentally in the interwar period. Elementary school teachers only received a secondary education, which they could supplement with further education, including at private schools or in special courses. From the mid-nineteenth century onwards, only secondary school teachers were educated at universities.

During the First Republic, a more significant development took place, primarily in Slovakia. Until 1918, the Hungarian language and the school system of the former Hungarian empire dominated in Slovakia, and the school system had to be completely rebuilt. This was one reason so many Czech teachers and university professors moved to Slovakia. The situation in Slovakia gradually began to change from the 1930s onwards, when the first wave of newly educated Slovak intelligentsia came into the picture. For example, public libraries were established through the development and support of the school system. In addition to Czech and Slovak schools, the state also supported minority schools, mainly German, followed by Hungarian and Polish schools (Kudláčová, 2016).

Charles University was founded in 1348. During the First Czechoslovak Republic, other Czechoslovak universities were established. Masaryk University in Brno was founded in 1919. In the same year, the first ever university was founded in Slovakia: Comenius University in Bratislava. Two technical universities based in Prague and Brno were also important institutions of tertiary education. All these universities contributed significantly to the further development of many scientific disciplines and have in many respects equalled similar institutions abroad in terms of quality and standards.

The main consequence of the Munich Agreement, concluded at the end of September 1938, was the territorial truncation of Czechoslovakia, the associated end of the First Republic and the establishment of the 'Second Czechoslovak Republic'. The Czechoslovak alliance system, built since 1918 and oriented towards France and Great Britain, collapsed as well. At the end of November 1938, the National Assembly of the Czechoslovak Republic adopted constitutional laws on the autonomy of Slovakia and Carpathian Ruthenia. The official name of the state was changed to Czecho-Slovakia. In March 1939, an independent Slovak State was established. During its short existence, the Second Czechoslovak Republic was effectively at the mercy of neighbouring Nazi Germany, and it also continuously and increasingly moved towards an authoritarian regime ('authoritarian democracy'). The short life of this state was finally ended by the beginning of German occupation on 15 March 1939.

2.4 Schooling During World War II

From 15 March 1939, the Czech lands were occupied by the German army and the Nazis established a 'Protectorate of Bohemia and Moravia'. The Protectorate was to be 'autonomous and self-governing' within the German Reich, but it could only exercise its rights 'in accordance with the political, military and economic needs of the Reich'.

For the duration of the war, the occupiers were particularly interested in making the widest possible economic use of the Czech industry and agriculture. Moreover, the Protectorate of Bohemia and Moravia was also to serve as a pool of labour force for German economy. Similarly to other Nazi-dominated countries, the Jewish population was systematically murdered in the Protectorate. The Nazis acted in a similar way against the Roma.

Brutal terror was also directed against all active opponents of the occupation. The Nazis regarded the Czech intelligentsia as particularly dangerous to their intentions. After student protests and their brutal suppression (leading to the death of student Jan Opletal), Czech universities were closed on 17 November 1939.[6] Therefore, the only Protectorate universities were the German Charles University in Prague and the German technical universities in Prague and Brno. There were also radical changes in the secondary and primary school systems. The educational system in primary and secondary schools was to be adapted to the German Reich's system of education. For this reason, the Volksschule was shortened to 4 years and the Bürgerschule was in turn extended by 1 year to a total of 4 years. Classification was also adapted to the German educational system. Attempts at the Germanization of the school system during the Protectorate of Bohemia and Moravia were also apparent in the restriction of studies in primary and secondary schools. For example, according to the 1941 reform, only 35% of students from the fourth year at Volksschule could advance to Bürgerschule, regardless of their school results, and a mere 5% could advance to secondary schools. The rest, about 60% of the children, had to stay in Volksschule and complete their compulsory eight-year schooling at these schools (Bosák, 1969). In the Protectorate, various types of Czech secondary schools were gradually restricted, not only reducing the number of students admitted—some schools, for example, were not allowed to admit girls.

The educational curriculum was also changed, of course. Beginning in primary schools, all students had to learn German, and it was forbidden to teach about a number of topics and characters from the Czech history and culture. The aim of the Protectorate school system was to educate Czech youth to be loyal to the German Reich and the national socialist ideology. The aim was therefore to 're-educate' the

---

[6] 17 November was later declared International Student Day. Fifty years later, it once again played a significant role in Czech history. The violent police crackdown on students who commemorated the closure of universities in Prague on 17 November 1989 triggered the fall of the communist government. This event constitutes a crucial moment linked to the theme of our book. We therefore focus on it in the following chapters as well.

youth to be obedient and cooperative in the building of the Nazi 'New Europe'. Teachers were subjected to political, linguistic, and racial vetting. Those who failed this vetting had to leave the profession and were eventually persecuted even further. Good knowledge of German was compulsory. German schools of various types usually received advantages over Czech schools and the number of German schools was increased. In 1942, a new umbrella organization called the Board of Trustees for the Education of Youth in Bohemia and Moravia was founded, and the targeted out-of-school education of Czech youth within the meaning of Nazi ideas was supposed to be its main activity (Fig. 2.1).

A resistance movement fought against the Nazi occupation and for the restoration of Czechoslovakia both at home and abroad, but there were also cases of collaboration with the Nazis. For Czechoslovakia, it is rather difficult to quantify the human and material losses. The number of its citizens who perished between 1939 and 1945 is estimated at between 340,000 and 370,000. By far the largest portion of this number were the Czechoslovak Jews who were victims of the Holocaust (Rothkirchen, 2005). The victory of the anti-Hitler coalition in World War II made the restoration of the Czechoslovak state possible. The restored state simultaneously came within the sphere of power of the Soviet Union.

Protectorate of Bohemia and Moravia (1939-1945)

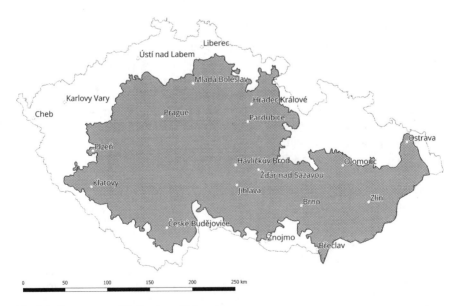

Fig. 2.1 Protectorate of Bohemia and Moravia

Bibliography

Bosák, F. (1969). *Česká škola v době nacistického útlaku: příspěvek k dějinám českého školství od Mnichova do osvobození* [Czechoslovak school in the time of Nazi oppression: a contribution to the history of Czechoslovak school system from the Munich agreement to liberation]. Státní pedagogické nakladatelství.

Cibulka, P., Kladiwa, P., Pokludová, A., Popelka, P., & Řepa, M. (2021). *Čas změny: moravský a slezský venkov od zrušení poddanství po Velkou válku* [A time of change: The Moravian and Silesian countryside from the abolition of serfdom to the great war]. Masarykův ústav a Archiv AV ČR.

Cohen, G. B. (1996). *Education and middle-class Society in Imperial Austria. 1848–1918.* Purdue University Press.

Cvrček, T. (2020). *Schooling under control: The origins of public education in imperial Austria 1769–1869.* Mohr Siebeck.

Entwurf der Organisation der Gymnasien und Realschulen in Oesterreich. (1849). Ministerium des Cultus und Unterrichts. https://www.digitale-sammlungen.de/de/view/bsb10679180?page=5

Franc, M., Halířová, M., Knapík, J., Lenderová, M., Maur, E., Nodl, M., & Rýdl, K. (2021). *Velké dějiny zemí Koruny České. Tematická řada. Dětství* [The great history of the lands of the Czech crown. Thematic series. Childhood]. Paseka.

Gebhart, J., & Kuklík, J. (2007). *Velké dějiny zemí Koruny české* (Svazek XV.b, 1938–1945) [The great history of the lands of the Czech crown. Volume XV.b, 1938–1945]. Paseka.

Glassl, H. (1995). Pokus multinárodního řešení. Bylo Československo vzornou demokracií? [An attempt at a multinational solution. Was Czechoslovakia a model democracy?]. In *Češi a Němci – historická tabu* [Czechs and Germans – historical taboos] (pp. 127–132). Prago Media.

Gyuris, F. (2019). Ideology, spatial planning, and rural schools: From interwar to communist Hungary. In H. Jahnke, C. Kramer, & P. Meusburger (Eds.), *Geographies of schooling. Knowledge and space* (pp. 97–124). Springer. https://doi.org/10.1007/978-3-030-18799-6

Hudek, A., Kopeček, M., & Mervart, J. (Eds.). (2019). *Čecho/slovakismus* [Czecho/Slovakism]. NLN.

Jamrożek, W. (2018). The educational practice and thought of the second Polish Republic on the 90th anniversary of regaining Independence. *Biuletyn Historii Wychowania, 38*(1), 301–307. https://doi.org/10.14746/bhw.2018.38.38

Jaworski, R. (1991). The German minorities in Poland and Czechoslovakia in the interwar period. In P. Smith (Ed.), *Ethnic groups in international relations. Comparative studies on Goverments and non-dominant ethnic groups in Europe 1850–1940* (pp. 169–185). New York University Press.

Kárník, Z. (2000). *České země v éře První republiky (1918–1938)* (Díl první, Vznik, budování a zlatá léta republiky (1918–1929) [Czech lands in the era of the First republic (1918–1938) (Volume One, Establishment, building and golden years of the republic (1918–1929)]. Libri.

Kárník, Z. (2002). *České země v éře První republiky (1918–1938)* (Díl druhý, Československo a České země v krizi a v ohrožení (1930–1935) [Czech lands in the era of the First republic (1918–1938) (Volume Two, Czechoslovakia and the Czech lands in crisis and under threat (1930–1935)]. Libri.

Kárník, Z. (2003). *České země v éře První republiky (1918–1938)* (Díl třetí, O přežití a o život (1936–1938) [Czech lands in the era of the First republic (1918–1938) (Volume Three, For survival and for life (1936–1938)]. Libri.

Kárník, Z. (2018). *České země v éře První republiky* (Druhé vydání) [Czech lands in the era of the First republic]. Libri.

Kasper, T., & Kasperová, D. (2020). *"Nová škola" v meziválečném Československu ve Zlíně: ideje, aktéři, místa* [The "New School" in interwar Czechoslovakia in Zlín: ideas, actors, places]. Academia.

Kasper, T., Kasperová, D., & Pánková, M. (Eds.). (2018). *"Národní" školství za první Československé republiky* ["National" schooling in the First Czechoslovak Republic]. Academia.

Klápště, J., & Šedivý, I. (Eds.). (2019). *Dějiny Česka* [History of Czechia]. NLN.

Kořalka, J. (1998). Menšinový status jako východisko z nouze [Minority status as a way out of distress]. In J. Havránek et al. (Eds.), *Stereotypy a symboly* [Stereotypes and symbols] (pp. 111–133). Institut základů vzdělanosti UK.

Kudláčová, B. (Ed.). (2016). *Pedagogické myslenie, školstvo a vzdelávánie na Slovensku v letech 1918–1945* [Pedagogical thinking, school system and education in Slovakia 1918–1945]. Trnavská univerzita v Trnavě.

Mann, E. (2014). *School for Barbarian. Education under Nazis*. Dover Publications.

Melton, J. V. H. (2003). *Absolutism and the eighteenth-century origins of compulsory schooling in Prussia and Austria*. Cambridge University Press.

Mitter, W. (2004). Das deutschsprachige Schulwesen auf dem Territorium der heutigen Tschechischen Republik von der Allgemeinen Schulordnung (Maria Theresias) bis 1938. In *Mezinárodní konference Všeobecné vzdělávání pro všechny* [International conference on General education for all] (pp. 24–31). Pedagogické muzeum J. A. Komenského.

O'Brian, G. (1970). Maria Theresa's attempt to educate an empire. *Paedagogica Historica, 10*(3), 542–565.

Oelkers, J. (2020). Authoritarianism and education in the interwar period: A history and its renewal. *Paedagogica Historica, 56*(5), 572–586. https://doi.org/10.1080/00309230.2020.1825497

Pine, L. (2010). Education in Nazi Germany. .

Potočárová, M. (2021). School and education objectives of the interwar period in the 1st Czechoslovak republic. *Polska Myśl Pedagogiczna, 7*, 349–364. https://doi.org/10.446 7/24504564PMP.21.019.13949

Překlad Zákonníka říšského vydaný pro království české [Translation of the Reich Code published for the Kingdom of Bohemia]. (1869). Místodržitelská tiskárna.

Rothkirchen, L. (2005). *The Jews of Bohemia and Moravia: Facing the holocaust*. University of Nebraska Press and Yad Vashem.

Rýdl, K. (2006). Historický vývoj českého vzdělávání do roku 1989 [Historical development of Czechoslovak education until 1989]. In J. Kalous & A. Veselý (Eds.), *Vzdělávací politika České republiky v globálním kontextu* [Educational policy of the Czech Republic in a global context] (pp. 7–22). Karolinum.

Šafránek, J. (1897). *Vývoj soustavy obecného školství v Království českém od roku 1769–1895* [Development of the system of general education in the Kingdom of Bohemia from 1769–1895]. F. Kytka.

Šafránek, J. (1918). *Školy české. Obraz jejich vývoje a osudů. II. svazek. R. 1848–1913* [Czech Schools. A depiction of their development and fate. Volume II. Year 1848–1913]. Matice česká.

Šimáně, M. (2019). *České menšinové školství v Československé republice: ke každodennosti obecních škol v politickém okresu Ústí nad Labem* [Czech minority education in the Czechoslovak republic. To the everyday life of primary schools in political district Ústí nad Labem]. Masarykova univerzita.

Tenorth, H.-E. (2000). *Geschichte der Erziehung: Einführung in die Grundzüge ihrer neuzeitlichen Entwicklung* (Grundlagentexte Pädagogik). Juventa.

Tóth, A., Novotný, L., & Stehlík, M. (2012). *Národnostní menšiny v Československu 1918–1938: od státu národního ke státu národnostnímu?* [National minorities in Czechoslovakia 1918–1938: from a national state to a state of nationalities?]. Univerzita Karlova.

Vykoupil, L. (2000). *Slovník českých dějin* [A dictionary of Czech History]. Julius Zirkus.

Zahra, T. (2008a). *Kidnapped souls. National Indifference and the Battle for children in the bohemian lands, 1900–1948*. Cornell University Press.

Zahra, T. (2008b). The "minority problem" and National Classification in the French and Czechoslovak borderlands. *Contemporary European History, 17*(2), 137–165.

Zákonník říšský pro království a země v radě říšské zastoupené [The Reich Code for the kingdoms and countries represented in the Reich Council]. (1883). Císařské a královské tiskárny dvorské a státní.

Zückert, M. (2007). Vom Aktivismus zur Staatsnegation? Die Sudetendeutschen zwischen Staatsakzeptanz, regional-nationalistischer Bewegungund dem national sozialistischen Deutschland. In P. Haslinger & J. von Puttkamer (Eds.), *Staat, Loyalität und Minderheiten in Ostmittel- und Südosteuropa 1918–1941* (pp. 69–98). R. Oldenbourg Verlag.

Chapter 3
From Stalinism to the Prague Spring— Education in Complicated Times

Abstract This chapter presents the history of Czechoslovakia from the end of World War II to the end of the 1960s. The postwar years were associated with hopes for a free life and the general development of the country. These hopes were extinguished in 1948 when the Communist Party of Czechoslovakia (Komunistická strana Československa, KSČ) fully assumed power and started building a socialist (totalitarian) state and a satellite of the Soviet Union. The next part of the chapter describes Czechoslovakia in the 1960s when the regime relaxed and changes took place in many aspects of life. The reforms culminated in the 'Prague Spring', which ended with the invasion of the Warsaw Pact troops in 1968.

In the field of education and in the school system, the 'Sovietization' of education occurred in the 1950s, which resulted in many deformations and unprepared reforms aimed at bringing the school system closer to that of the Soviet Union. The chapter describes laws as well as ideological influences in the school system, including the specific impacts of the interventions into the school system and into the lives of teachers and students. In the 1960s, teachers regained more freedom for their work. This period was brought to an end after 1968, when staffing purges took place in schools and the onset of normalization in schools was once again accompanied by ideological pressure.

Keywords Czechoslovakia 1945–1968 · Communist Party · Prague spring · Sovietization · Socialism · Ideology · School system · Primary education · Schools · Teacher · Legislation

© Masaryk University, Faculty of Arts, Registration no. 00216224,
VAT ID: CZ00216224 2024
J. Zounek et al., *(Post)Socialist Transformation of Primary Schools*,
https://doi.org/10.1007/978-3-031-58768-9_3

3.1   The Forms of Postwar Reconstruction (1945–1953)

The restored Czechoslovak Republic differed significantly from the 1918–1938 Republic in terms of political, economic, and national direction.[1] At the beginning of April 1945, the government published the Košice government programme,[2] which brought significant changes to the Czechoslovak political structure. Political competition now took place within the closed system of the National Front, which included four political parties in the Czech lands (the Communist, National Socialist, Social Democratic, and People's parties) and two in Slovakia (the Democratic and Communist parties). The renewal of the Agrarian Party, the strongest political entity in interwar Czechoslovakia, was not allowed.[3] The Košice government programme determined the foreign political and military orientation of Czechoslovakia towards the Soviet Union (also referred to as the Union of Soviet Socialist Republics, abbreviated USSR), and it included the punishment of collaborators and traitors from the period of Nazi occupation and the confiscation of German and Hungarian property. National committees (Národní výbory) were to be the new authorities of state power. The programme presumed equal rights for Czechs and Slovaks. At that time, Czechoslovakia was led by the government of the 'National Front of Czechs and Slovaks' with social democrat Zdeněk Fierlinger as the prime minister. The Communists assumed important positions in this government, gaining, for example, the Ministries of the Interior, Agriculture, and Information.

Until the convention of the Provisional National Assembly on 28 October 1945, legislative activity in Czechoslovakia was carried out through Presidential Decrees. On the basis of these decrees and other measures, the nationalization of banks, insurance companies, key industries, and other industrial plants with more than five hundred employees took place in October 1945. In addition to the nationalized sector, the private sector and artisanal small-scale production continued to function in the Czechoslovak economy. The confiscation of land owned by Germans, Hungarians, and collaborators, which was then allocated to interested parties at a low price, represented a major change in ownership and social structure of the postwar republic.[4]

---

[1] In general historical overviews and in the history of the school systems in the Czech territory, in this and other chapters, we build on the sources listed after the chapter. We cite directly in the text only those sources that provide a specific piece of information or a date, or if the citation is required by the context of the interpretation.

[2] The government programme was named after the town in which it was announced: the Slovak town of Košice. Its content was negotiated at the Moscow talks in March 1945. The draft of the programme was submitted by the Communists; representatives of democratic parties were only able to make partial changes to it.

[3] In the 1930s, this party was quite close to German fascism, and it did not oppose the Munich Agreement in any fundamental way. During World War II, some of the party's leaders were even regarded as leading Czech collaborators with the Nazis.

[4] A more detailed overview of the history of Slovakia from the end of the Second World War to 1989 is given in book Two sides of the same coin: Examples of free and unfree education in Slovakia during the period of socialism (Kudláčová, 2023).

After World War II, the national composition of Czechoslovakia changed significantly. The displacement of the German population, which took place mainly between 1945 and 1947, was the biggest intervention. Immediately after the end of the war, a number of excesses and crimes were committed against the German population during the 'wild' displacement before August 1945. An organized displacement of the German population from the Czechoslovak Republic, which was approved by the Allied Powers at the Potsdam Conference in August 1945, was then carried out, mainly in 1946.

The experience of the German occupation, the disillusionment with the 'Munich betrayal' of the Western Allies (Kocian, 2018), and the experience of the Great Depression and the reflection on the need to rebuild the republic all led to a significant part of the republic's population having increased sympathies for the Soviet Union and the KSČ. The KSČ was able to strongly benefit particularly from anti-German sentiments in its ideology.[5]

The Communist Party won the parliamentary elections in 1946 and seized absolute power in the state in February 1948. For Czechoslovakia, the events of February 1948 marked the assumption of totalitarian power by the KSČ, or rather by its leadership. After February 1948, there was a large-scale purge in the state apparatus, the economy, social organizations, science, culture, and the school system. At that time, the pluralist parliamentary system became a de facto formality.

The National Assembly passed laws that had previously been prepared and approved by the Communist leadership. The judicial system ceased to function as an independent branch of state power and the mass media became instruments of propaganda.

There were also major changes in the field of culture oriented almost exclusively towards the socialist culture and the programme of 'socialist realism' in art. The culture was dominated by a single ideology: dogmatically understood Marxism-Leninism. Everything that contradicted this orientation had to be removed. Hitherto independent artistic and cultural associations were dissolved and centralized institutions were created in their place. Cultural ties with Western countries were almost completely severed, and the organization of Czechoslovak science was rebuilt according to the USSR model. Many characters from Czechoslovak science and culture were silenced or imprisoned for many years, or they emigrated.

Czechoslovakia's foreign and domestic policy became totally dependent on the USSR. Czechoslovakia became a solid part of the Soviet power bloc in Central and Eastern Europe. It was a member of both the economic Council for Mutual Economic Assistance (established in 1949) and the military-political Warsaw Pact (established in 1955). Between 1949 and 1956, advisers sent from the USSR intervened directly or indirectly in nearly all areas of Czechoslovak society.

The economic development after February 1948 was characterized by the almost complete destruction of the private sector. The management of the economy was

---

[5] Bílek and Lupták (2014) refer to the period of 1945–1948 as a hybrid, as the political regime combined democratic principles from the times of the First Republic with the non-democratic principles typical after February 1948.

carried out from a single centre and according to a central plan, with political objectives usually taking precedence over economic ones. The economy was managed by a vast bureaucratic apparatus led by the State Planning Office and by means of five-year economic plans, the first of which was launched in 1949.

Particular emphasis was placed on the development of heavy industry, based mainly on the military needs of the entire Soviet bloc. The strong focus on heavy engineering resulted in a lagging behind of the consumer industry and services, and it had an adverse effect on the living standards of the population and on the environment.

After February 1948, a land reform was carried out that limited land ownership to 50 ha per individual and mandated the 'compulsory sale' of lands above this limit. This can be seen as a special form of expropriation in return for compensation, although compensation was often not provided. Soon after the communist assumption of power, preparations for the collectivization of agriculture were also made, once again following the Soviet model.[6] In February 1949, the Act on *Unified Agricultural Cooperatives* (Jednotná zemědělská družstva, JZD) was adopted, launching the first wave of collectivization. The next phase of this early 1950s campaign was accompanied by harsh political and economic pressure on farmers, who were to be forced to join the JZDs. Particularly the larger owners of farmland, who constituted the main obstacle to collectivization according to the communist regime, were the targets of often brutal judicial and extra-judicial persecution.

Although the communist assumption of absolute power in Czechoslovakia in February 1948 was relatively smooth, forces remained in Czechoslovak society that rejected the transition to the totalitarian system of a single political party. A wave of repressions and other adverse circumstances prevented the emergence of more widespread anti-communist resistance in Czechoslovakia. Individual underground groups were usually quickly discovered by the State Security. With the aim of enforcing absolute control over society, the consolidation of the communist regime in Czechoslovakia was accompanied by widespread persecution of its real and perceived and potential opponents. Especially in the period from 1948 to 1953, these repressions were particularly brutal and affected a large number of people. Former high-ranking officials of non-communist political parties were victims of political trials. The Catholic Church, especially high-ranking church dignitaries, religious orders, and Catholic intellectuals were the target of repressions (this topic is discussed in more detail later in this chapter).

---

[6] In Czechoslovakia, collectivization was a process of transforming individual private farming into collective farming initiated and managed by the KSČ according to the Soviet model. The main phase of the expropriation of agricultural production and its merger of cooperative and state enterprises took place at the end of the 1940s and during the 1950s. This process destroyed an entire social stratum—private farmers, which formed an important pillar of society at the time. The collectivization also had a major impact on the lives of people living in rural areas as it disrupted traditional social ties and cultural practices (Jech, 2008).

3.2 Stabilization of the Communist Regime and the Period of Hope (1953–1968)

The relaxation of conditions in the USSR after Stalin's death in 1953 led to partial changes in Czechoslovakia as well. In June 1953, Czechoslovakia underwent a monetary reform, which brought about an exchange of cash and deposits in the ratio from 5:1 to 50:1; at the same time, rationing[7] was terminated and uniform retail prices were introduced. For the majority of the population, these measures meant an increase in living costs and a substantial devaluation of savings. The monetary reform fundamentally shook the credibility of the KSČ government, even among those social groups that had supported it. That is to say, even the relatively well-paid class of workers and miners lost a considerable part of their savings. In connection with this, manifestations of mass discontent were seen in many locations (Šlouf, 2021).

As a result of these events and the pressure from the new leaders of the USSR, the KSČ leadership announced a 'new course' in September 1953. In its assessment of the previous development, KSČ admitted certain mistakes and shortcomings in the application of its policies; the economy became more focused on the production of consumer goods and there were reductions in retail prices, salary increases, and adjustments in agricultural policy. There was also some relaxation of the system of repressions.

Adoption of the new socialist constitution, approved by the National Assembly in July 1960, was supposed to be a formal confirmation of the strength of the communist regime and the irreversible changes in Czechoslovakia. This constitution contained an article on the 'leading role of the Communist Party in the society'. It also effectively eliminated the powers of the Slovak autonomous authorities. A new name for the state was adopted: Czechoslovak Socialist Republic (Československá socialistická republika, hereinafter also CSSR). The amnesties of most political prisoners in 1960 and 1962 were a sign of positive development, but only a few of them were rehabilitated in the 1960s.

The economy remained the weakness of the regime. The system of a centrally planned economy, based primarily on the development of heavy industry, allowed for neither a flexible response to the needs of the population nor an introduction of the necessary technological changes. Industrial products were losing the ability to compete on foreign markets and the national income and per capita income were decreasing.

Under these circumstances, the KSČ leadership had to allow a discussion about the future direction of the Czechoslovak economy, the basic problem of which was determined to be an inefficient management system. Reformist economists developed a project of economic reform that would combine socialist planning with the

---

[7]The rationing was an administrative measure that determined how many basic necessities each inhabitant was allowed to purchase. It covered the basic life necessities: food, fuel, clothing, tobacco products, soap, etc. It was used during the war and, in Czechoslovakia, even after the war.

functioning of market mechanisms. After 1965, the implementation of this reform encountered serious obstacles. It became increasingly apparent that its consistent implementation would only be possible with a simultaneous democratization of the political system.

In the 1960s, Czechoslovak society underwent a series of changes. The power monopoly of the KSČ remained, but the way it was exercised shifted. The role of the National Assembly and the authorities of the state administration grew. The harshness of the Criminal Act was toned down and the first rehabilitation of victims from the 1950s took place, although these mostly only concerned prominent Communist Party functionaries. A new generation that was less connected to the past practices of the totalitarian regime and that was more open to other approaches and ideas entered political and economic life. Czechoslovak science and culture were awakening, and the interrupted contacts with the West began to be re-established. The 1958 World Exhibition in Brussels was a great success for Czechoslovakia.[8]

Despite the disapproval of party ideologues, other elements of the Western youth lifestyle infiltrated Czechoslovakia as well. More extensive opportunities for travelling to the West allowed many young people to compare the realities of life, which often led to a deepening of their critical attitudes. A number of magazines and student societies, which became open platforms for the exchange of ideas, were established at universities.

Czechoslovak culture became an important phenomenon of the 1960s. It manifested the strong influence of a new generation of artists who were no longer willing to be bound by the schemes of 'socialist realism' and demanded and practically exercised creative freedom.

Remarkable works were produced in Czechoslovak cinema at this time. Representatives of the 'Czechoslovak New Wave' included directors such as Miloš Forman and Jiří Menzel.

Czech and Slovak literature experienced a very busy period. The works of authors who had written books even before World War II, including Jaroslav Seifert, who won the Nobel Prize for literature (in 1984), as well as the works of the younger literary generation, such as Josef Škvorecký and Milan Kundera, were popular with readers. The writers probably most clearly perceived the strong contrast between the established relatively free artistic space and the little-changing political system.

3.3   Prague Spring 1968

The desire for change in Czechoslovak society resulted in widespread criticism of the KSČ leadership. A reformist wing gradually formed within the Communist Party. This wing sought economic reform and democratization of society, but under

---

[8] More information about the Expo 58 exhibition, also known as the 1958 Brussels World's Fair, is available here: https://en.wikipedia.org/wiki/Expo_58

the leadership and control of the KSČ. Zdeněk Mlynář, Ota Šik, and Alexander Dubček were among the leaders of this reformist trend in the KSČ.

In January 1968, Antonín Novotný was dismissed from the position of First Secretary of the Central Committee of the KSČ, and the previous First Secretary of the Central Committee of the Communist Party of Slovakia, Alexander Dubček, was elected in his place.

The media began to report without censorship and events originally limited to the KSČ leadership acquired a society-wide dimension. The barriers that had prevented discussion about the pressing problems of the past and present also fell. The legacy of democratic traditions was revived. Civil society was awakening. Representatives of churches came forward with demands for the creation of a space for a free religious life and for a fair organization of relations with the state. In Slovakia, attention was focused on the assertion of its equal status within the Czechoslovak state, which was achieved in October 1968 when the law on federation was adopted.

The Soviet leadership, headed by Leonid Brezhnev, the supreme leader of the Communist Party of the Soviet Union, watched the reform process in Czechoslovakia with growing unease. It feared that the weakening of the totalitarian political system in the CSSR would lead to similar developments in other states of the Soviet power bloc and ultimately threaten the Soviet Union's control over Central and Eastern Europe. The Soviet political concept—referred to as the Brezhnev Doctrine— according to which the 'defense of socialism' in one country was a common concern of all Warsaw Pact states, significantly limited the sovereignty of the individual members of the Soviet bloc. The fact that no Soviet troops were stationed in Czechoslovakia (unlike the other Warsaw Pact states) added to the anxiety of Soviet officials.

The escalation of Soviet pressure occurred during a meeting of the Czechoslovak and Soviet delegations at the turn of July and August 1968. Despite some partial concessions, the Czechoslovak leadership refused to radically change its political line, which was confirmed during the meeting of the delegations of Communist parties of the Soviet bloc in Bratislava at the beginning of August 1968. In this situation, the representatives of the USSR and of other Warsaw Pact states stopped relying on changing the situation in Czechoslovakia through 'internal' means and unambiguously focused on preparing their military intervention. This was legitimized by a request for help against the 'counter-revolution' in Czechoslovakia, signed by representatives of a conservative pro-Soviet group within the KSČ leadership. This 'invitation letter' was handed over to Soviet representatives during the Bratislava meeting.

On 20 August 1968, USSR troops and smaller units from Hungary, Poland, the German Democratic Republic, and Bulgaria crossed the border into Czechoslovakia. The Czechoslovak army, several times weaker and deployed mainly in the western part of the republic, did not resist in the hopeless military situation, followed the instructions of the President of the Republic, and let the invading forces capture the territory of the state.

A mass civil resistance of the Czechoslovak public against the invasion was organized by the media, which the interventionists failed to silence. Despite the non-violent nature of these protests, over 90 Czechoslovak citizens died and several hundred were injured in the first days after 21 August 1968 (Pauer, 1995).

The 'Moscow Protocol', which can be described as a unilateral dictate by the Soviet leadership, was crucial for the development of Czechoslovakia after August 1968. Czechoslovak representatives adopted the document after rather dramatic events, especially in response to threats from Soviet representatives about the possibility of escalation of the conflict into a civil war or the introduction of military administration in Czechoslovakia. This document contained commitments by the Czechoslovak party to stop the activities of 'anti-socialist' organizations, to establish control over the media, and to dismiss a number of functionaries unacceptable to the Soviet party.

The Moscow Protocol was the first to use the word 'normalization', which was later adopted to refer to the subsequent twenty-year period of Czechoslovakia's development. In October 1968, the National Assembly passed a law on the residence of Soviet troops in the Czechoslovak territory.

In November 1968, university youth protested the emerging 'normalization', i.e. the restoration of the mechanisms of the totalitarian regime, with a three-day occupation strike. However, an atmosphere of disillusionment and resignation gradually began to permeate most Czechoslovak society.

3.4   Postwar School System—Between Two Totalitarian Systems

The postwar reconstruction and development of the school system followed the Košice government programme.[9] The question of the future direction of Czechoslovakia was unambiguously connected to the Soviet Union. The cooperation concerned political and economic matters as well as cultural and educational ones. In the Košice government programme, the school system was the topic of the fifteenth chapter, which stated that schools would be purged of Nazi collaborators and that all textbooks published during the period of Nazi occupation would also be removed. All German and Hungarian universities were to be closed and a restoration of Czech universities was expected. The students who had been forbidden to study during the occupation were to be allowed to return to the Czech schools as soon as possible and to finish their education.

Removal of views critical of the Soviet Union from textbooks and the unambiguous preference for the Russian language within the hierarchy of foreign language

---

[9]The Košice government programme is available (in Czech) in digital form on the website of National Archives of the Czech Republic: https://www.nacr.cz/wp-content/uploads/2021/04/labyrint-1945-Kosicky-vladni-program.pdf

teaching were typical features of the implementation of the Košice government pro-gramme and the early cooperation with the USSR in Czechoslovak primary schools (Fawn, 2000; Nevers, 2003; Vorlíček, 2004).

The Manifesto Congress/Assembly of Czech Teachers (Manifestační sjezd českého učitelstva), which took place in July 1945, was a significant event for the school system. Among other things, the congress reopened the discussion about uni-fied schools, a very important topic that remained unresolved from the prewar period. *Presidential Decree No. 132 of 27 October 1945 on Teacher Education*, which introduced university education at pedagogical and other university faculties for teachers of all types and stages of schools (Presidential Decree, 1945) was another important milestone in the postwar history of the school system. On the basis of this decree, in 1946, universities established pedagogical faculties that com-bined both pedagogical and didactic preparation and professional preparation, i.e. the study of a given subject (e.g. mathematics, physical education, and Russian).

In addition, 1948 marked the beginning of what was, with only slight exaggera-tion, another new era for education. Relatively soon after the February 1948 coup d'état, a new Education Act, a significant milestone in the history of Czechoslovak school system, was adopted. The fact that it was adopted with virtually no say from the supporters of other approaches or concepts (i.e. those from the non-communist camp) in the process of drafting the 1948 Act can be considered a significant draw-back. From another point of view, it was a standard that introduced a unified school system for the first time. The complicated system of elementary education (described in previous chapters) was eliminated. Therefore, every citizen was able to advance through the school system without any dead endspreventing progression to the next stage of the school system. At the same time, the right of all citizens to an education was guaranteed. The school system was nationalized, meaning the end of all private and alternative schools, and the 1948 Act included a limitation on the number of students in a class. Compulsory education was free. Some experts in the field of education saw a contradiction in this law in that it reflected traditions and modern trends but was strongly influenced by the approaches and principles of the emerging communist dictatorship, not giving much space to democratic school development (Walterová, 2004). The honorific 'comrade teacher' was introduced, and the terms socialist (later communist) school and education began to be used. The Communist Party gradually assumed a decisive role in the field of education and made decisions on practically all relevant events in the form of conclusions or resolutions put into practice through various (legislative) standards and regulations.

During this period, the KSČ completely uncritically imitated the school system of the Soviet Union without regard for the real needs of Czechoslovak society. Soviet methods and templates were promoted and introduced regardless of their applicability in Czechoslovak conditions. One example of this trend was the inte-gration of schools into accomplishing political and economic tasks, which led to a change in the entire school system. The Lány action (Lánská akce)' of 1949, which aimed at getting boys to choose mining jobs after leaving school, is another example.[10] Alongside this, there was also the 'village teachers' movement', within which the teachers were to support collectivization of agriculture; teachers were even expected to urge farmers to join the Unified Agricultural Cooperatives.

The creation of a completely atheist society based on the ideas of Marxism-Leninism was a goal of the KSČ (Madsen, 2014; Müller & Neundorf, 2012).[11] This meant a society in which religious faith had no justification, because, according to the socialist opinion of the time, religion represented the opium of the people and it was a sign of human decadence and backwardness (Balík & Hanuš, 2013). The KSČ faced a very difficult task, as 75% of its members reported belonging to a religion before 1948 and 90% of the KSČ voters were religious (Kaplan, 1990; Kaplan, 1993). To some extent, this situation affected the future relations between the Czechoslovak state and the individual churches and also predetermined the search for a means of everyday coexistence. After 1948, the communist leadership sought to integrate the individual churches into its power-political system, to limit their ties with foreign countries (especially the Vatican), and to create a national church community that would serve the regime's goals (Cuhra, 1999; Kaplan, 2001).

To this end, the communist regime passed several 'church laws' in 1949.[12] In compliance, the State Office for Church Affairs and subordinate authorities at the regional and district levels were established.[13] The new office was headed by a minister appointed by the president of the republic, and the branches at the regional and district levels were headed by church secretaries. The powers and all of the property of the individual churches and religious societies that operated in the territory of Czechoslovakia were transferred to this office (Cuhra, 1999).[14] The office supervised the operation of these churches and it was responsible for developing standards in church and religious matters. The issuance of church laws was accompanied by a wave of persecutory crackdowns, and the communist government used the same tools as in the fight against political opponents of the regime. Male religious orders and the Greek Catholic Church were destroyed in a series of ecclesiastical show trials, many bishops and monks were removed or interned, and the church press, religious literature, and church ceremonies were restricted.

---

[10] The Lány action was a plan of a nationwide organized recruitment of labour, especially of young people, for apprenticeships in heavy industry such as mining and metallurgy. It concerned the recruitment itself and it later also included a construction of vocational schools and miners' housing (boarding schools).

[11] At this time, the situation in Central and South-Eastern Europe was very similar. A communist regime had been established everywhere. The relationship between the state and the religious churches and sects differed. In some countries (e.g. Poland, Slovenia, and Croatia), strong identification with the Catholic Church persevered as a result of historical circumstances and traditions. In other countries, including Albania and especially Czechoslovakia, attempts were made to remove religion from the life of society altogether.

[12] This is a series of Acts No. 217–223 of 1949 that regulated the affairs of churches and religious societies in Czechoslovakia.

[13] In 1956, it was transformed into the Secretariat for Religious Affairs under the Ministry of Education and Culture, which was subordinated to the Office of the Prime Minister in the 1970s.

[14] Sixteen non-Catholic churches and religious societies operated in Czechoslovakia.

In everyday life, the public practice of religious faith became a reliable tool for attracting problems in life or even making it impossible to find a job in many professions. Teaching was among the professions that were inherently connected with atheism. The Communist Party continued the traditions of the Austro-Hungarian Empire, in which Czechoslovak teachers were the leading carriers of the idea of removing the influence of religion upon public and private life. This was also a reason for the relatively unproblematic takeover of Czechoslovak schools by the totalitarian regime after 1948 (Balík & Hanuš, 2013).

In the early 1950s, a change of opinion on the teaching of religion occurred. Religion was a compulsory subject until the 1952/1953 school year. The 1953 Decree of the Ministry of Education, Science and Arts brought a new regulation. It introduced the teaching of religion only as an optional subject in primary schools. Instruction was to take place only in schools; it was not allowed, for example, in rectories. Registration for the lessons was deliberately complicated by the fact that parents had to register their children using a special form at the beginning of each school year. When doing so, they were reminded by the school administration that the religion lessons were optional and voluntary. In some cases, school heads demanded that the parents sign the form in person in the school heads' office. This provided them with some opportunity to pressure the parents to withdraw their request. Indeed, many teachers made personal commitments that no student from their class would sign up for religion lessons. Many school heads even hid the applications for religion lessons during the first days of school, claiming that they did not have them, or scheduled the lessons in the evening hours. The school heads' motivation to enroll as few children as possible into the religion lessons was also due to external circumstances, not just inner communist beliefs. The number of children enrolled in religion lessons was a measure of the success or failure of atheization. This data was taken into consideration when school heads were evaluated by their superiors (Zounek, Šimáně, & Knotová, 2017c). A careful accounting of the students who attended religion lessons also served as a tool to monitor which families continued to live a religious life.

By 1954, the KSČ had managed to completely cripple all religious life in Czechoslovakia with its interventions. And it did so in such a way that by the mid-1950s, the Communist Party had ceased to see churches and religious societies as a serious danger. The situation was so secure for the party that there was no need to take further measures. This did not mean that the totalitarian regime dropped the issue from its consideration. From 1953 until the end of the communist regime in 1989, religion lessons never again appeared in the curricula of primary schools, and they were controlled only by special regulations of the State Office for Church Affairs or the Ministry of Education. In that way, the school system of communist Czechoslovakia had achieved a complete secularization after 1953.

3.5   A Period of Chaotic Changes in the 1950s

The Education Act of 1953 (Act No. 31/1953 Coll.) can literally be considered a disaster for the development of Czechoslovak education. It was preceded by a rather harsh and ideological criticism of schools as well as of the prewar (democratic) developments in pedagogy. The 1953 Act is an example of the uncritical approximation of Czechoslovak school system to the school system of the Soviet Union—the 'Sovietization' of the school system (Crampton, 1997; Kaplan & Paleček, 2008; Vorlíček, 2004). The 1953 Act lacked a professional basis and even interrupted the previous development by abolishing the 1948 Act that had been in force for barely 5 years. The 1953 Act created eleven-year secondary schools that provided basic general education in the first 8 years and offered higher general education in the last 3 years that prepared students primarily for university studies. In this way, compulsory schooling was shortened to 8 years and grammar schools were completely eliminated.

Overburdening of students was one of the consequences of this 'reform', as the shortening of compulsory schooling was not accompanied by an adequate reduction in the content of the curriculum. Textbooks suffered from serious didactic shortcomings and the ideological infiltration of the content was very high. Polytechnic education[15] was favoured at the expense of humanities, etc. One of the effects of the 1953 Act was an increased percentage of students who failed some subjects or did not even complete the first 8 years of the secondary school. This situation was criticized by many experts, including the pro-regime ones. Positive aspects of the 1953 Act included the further expansion of the school network and the increased chances of obtaining a secondary education. At the same time, the number of classes increased significantly and the average number of students per teacher or class in primary schools decreased, and these ratios continued to decrease over the following years (Jelínková & Smolka, 1989).

There were rather fundamental changes in the education of primary school teachers. In 1953, pedagogical faculties were dissolved just 7 years after their establishment. Four-year pedagogical grammar schools were established at which teachers at kindergartens and the national schools (first stage of primary schools) began to be educated. This was a step back to the situation from the interwar period (for more

---

[15] The polytechnic teaching (also referred to as polytechnic education) was supposed to introduce the students to the basic principles of all types of production and to teach them how to use manufacturing tools. Czechoslovak pedagogues adopted most of the ideas about the implementation of polytechnic teaching from the Soviet Union. The polytechnic education was supposed to support the introduction of new socialist production. Mathematics, physics, chemistry, natural history and geography were considered the core subjects of a polytechnic education. These subjects were evaluated as having the greatest potential to implement polytechnic education. Excursions to manufacturing plants, laboratory works, work in the school garden, work in technical workshops, etc. were also to be part of the curriculum. The principles of polytechnic teaching/education permeated other subjects (humanities) taught in schools.

see e.g. Šimáně 2014, 2010), as the education of some teachers returned to a mere secondary school level.

The efforts to allow more students to study was one of the proclaimed reasons for this transformation. More importantly, the reform of teacher education was not based on justified expert foundations; it was driven by a series of ill-considered (and unprepared) regulations and administrative interventions that resulted in the gradual decline in the level of teacher education. The 1953 Act designated three new types of schools for teacher education: four-year secondary pedagogical schools, two-year pedagogical colleges, and four-year pedagogical universities.[16]

The 1953 Act created a rather unclear and complex system of teacher education and the duration of pedagogical studies was shortened at the two-year pedagogical colleges[17]: many graduates completed their studies at the young age of 19. The length of studies at this type of school was shortened and the content was also mechanically reduced, offering a concrete example of the reduction in the quality of teacher education.

Narrators' recollections bring a lesser-known problem to light. One of the teachers we spoke with in our previous research stated: 'Well, and I also had the education for one to five [1st to 5th grade], but because there were few qualified teachers at that time, they put me right to the second stage and I could choose. So I taught various subjects, but I chose mathematics and art' (Zounek et al., 2016, p. 144). Although this teacher was not qualified to teach subjects at the second stage of the school, she was permitted to choose any subject and teach it without a proper education. This teacher's recollection can be seen as an example of what may have negatively affected the quality of teaching in the 1950s. Teaching by unqualified teachers went hand in hand with the shortage of teachers. In the context of the ill-considered and chaotic changes in the 1950s, it is clear that the chosen (unprofessional) solutions and the actual course of changes only contributed to recurring problems. Thus, the measures taken often had no effect, as the subsequent rapid succession of changes incidentally suggests (Zounek et al., 2016).

In 1959, as a part of another reform, four-year pedagogical institutes were established in all regions of Czechoslovakia, while the previous types of pedagogical schools were dissolved. After only 2 years of operation of these institutes, the lack of clarity of the entire concept became apparent. The problems lay primarily in the unpolished content of the studies and the unclear legal status of these schools. The pedagogical institutes were dissolved 1964, after about 5 years of existence. Most of the institutes were converted into pedagogical faculties with four-year study programmes. Those that were located in regional towns were incorporated into the local university affiliations.

In the university education, the 1950 Act can be described as a turning point, as it was the first of its kind in Czechoslovak history (some legislative regulations

---

[16] Pedagogical universities, which were not part of the universities, educated secondary school teachers in a four-year programme.

[17] They educated teachers of the second stage of primary school.

focused on university education had been in force for 50 years or more, i.e. since the time of the Habsburg monarchy). But the 1950 Act brought fundamental changes to the life of universities. The centralization of administration was strengthened significantly, and the traditional autonomy of universities was abolished completely. The internal organization also underwent changes, as the law was 'inspired' in many aspects by the Soviet model. It should be noted that changes at universities had been taking place since 1948, with the 'purge of public and political life of the enemies of the people's democratic establishment and reaction'. To put it simply, democratically minded teachers and students as well as opponents of the regime had to leave the faculties or universities. However, it is important to remember that after 1948, there were more types of purges, not only exclusively politically motivated ones. A 're-examination' of the academic record of university students was another type of purge. This was a mass action that affected virtually all students in the country. Everything was done under the political supervision of the power structures of the time, which also controlled the life of individual faculties. Because of the 'meticulous' work of the politically vetted disciplinary committees and subcommittees, and because many students voluntarily left their studies, the numbers of expelled students were relatively high. In many cases, it was not the political views, but rather the failure to complete or fulfil study obligations that was the reason for termination (Zounek, 1996).

The university education gradually started to include the study of 'social sciences', and later Marxism-Leninism, which can be considered a key part of the ideological education of future teachers and of almost all university students, who could hardly avoid it.

Each graduate had their own cadre record and their job placement after graduation was decided by a committee (consisting of the dean, the head of the department, a KSČ member, and other representatives of various organizations). On the basis of the committee's decision, each graduate received a 'job offer' and was obligated to start the designated job (school) no later than 1 month after graduation. This was the 'placement of workers' within which the graduates, in this case teachers, were not free to choose their employer. This measure was only abolished in the mid-1960s (Rychlík, 2020).

3.6 Socialism with a Human Face in Schools

A new round of changes in the education policy of the Czechoslovak state (i.e. the KSČ) occurred in the late 1950s. Nikita Khrushchev's condemnation of the Stalinist regime and of Stalin's cult of personality at the 20th Congress of the Communist Party of the Soviet Union in 1956 brought about a certain relaxation of measures in Czechoslovakia. In Czechoslovakia, the late 1950s and early 1960s were characterized by a gradual abandonment of the blind imitation of the Soviet Union and a gradual orientation towards the real needs of Czechoslovak society. The need for change was found to be particularly urgent in the economic activities of the state;

over time, the needs manifested themselves in other areas of Czechoslovak society as well, and the school system was no exception. This did not mean an abandonment of communist ideals, as proven by the formulation of the mission of Czechoslovak schools in the new Education Act of 1960. According to the 1960 Act, schools were to 'educate the youth and workers in the spirit of scientific worldview, Marxism-Leninism ... enthusiastic builders of communism' (Act No. 186, 1960). Similarly, the document *The Concept of Nine-Year Primary School and its Curriculum* (*Pojetí* ..., 1960) stated that 'from an early age, children should be taught to work and live in a communist manner and to strive to adopt the principles of communist morality in their nature' (p. 4).

In practice, the unfortunate consequences of the 1953 Act became apparent quite early, and the continuation of this state of affairs was no longer sustainable. Thus, the 1960 Act once again extended the compulsory schooling to 9 years and the school system was expanded to include new types of schools (e.g. art schools, music schools, and dance schools). Studying while working was also considered to be of great importance, and secondary schools for workers were established. The 1960 Act almost seemed to foreshadow the liberal spirit of the 1960s, which was reflected in a much more favourable environment for school development.

During this period, theory and research of the pedagogical profession began to develop and attention was paid to the quality of education. In 1966, a new Act on university education was released (Act No. 19, 1966) that represented a rather liberal norm, on the basis of which traditional degrees for university graduates that had been abolished in the 1950s were returned and the universities were allowed to cooperate with (Western) foreign institutions. The reform of the lower stages of schools re-entered the discussion, and a reflection on the existing developments in the school system, cautiously acknowledging that many mistakes were made in the postwar period, was an important part of these debates.

The *Akční program KSČ* [Action Programme of the KSČ] of April 1968 formulated attempts to involve the wider public in the political issues of the state. According to the programme, even though the leading role in the administration of the state was still played by the KSČ, the KSČ newly wanted to advance its goals through persuasion rather than coercion. Science, art, and culture were no longer to be completely subordinated to the KSČ and the state. Marxism-Leninism was to lose its monopolistic ideological position in the life of the entire society and in the school system as well.

Archival documents provide an idea of the situation in primary education. According to the Regional Committee of the Communist Party of the South Moravian Region, in the mid-1960s, the regional leadership of the KSČ tended to process educational documents coming from the Central Committee of the KSČ with a delay of up to half a year, which was a previously completely unthinkable procedure.[18] Witnesses also recalled that fewer and fewer documents from the

---

[18] Archive fond G 593 KSČ JmK (1969). *Analysis of Activities and Developments at Schools of the 1st and 2nd Cycle 1965–1969*. Moravian Provincial Archive, Brno, p. 1. Unless otherwise stated,

higher authorities arrived at the schools. It can be assumed that regional and district school authorities 'filtered' documents and regulations coming from the central party authorities and they themselves decided which ones to send on to individual schools regardless of the orders from the superior (and party) authorities. This particular form of autonomy represents a completely new element in the totalitarian state and can be perceived as a specific manifestation of the Prague Spring. In the early 1960s, such a procedure would have been impossible (Zounek et al., 2018).

The cited archival source further revealed that these documents truly no longer emphasized the ideological side of upbringing and education: 'Terms such as communist education or upbringing towards socialist patriotism and internationalism are omitted. Most of the space is devoted to the modernization of the process of teaching.'[19] In view of the relaxation of the regime, the representatives of the Regional Committee of the KSČ were explicitly refraining from promoting communist ideology in upbringing and education; because of the same practices throughout the country, the situation was similar in other regions of Czechoslovakia. Under the influence of these events, the Ministry of Education and the regional authorities gradually began to essentially ignore the orders of the central (party) authorities, further relaxing the life in schools and the work of teachers.

During the spring of 1968, the influence of the KSČ in schools was practically completely suppressed. This is proven by an archival document: 'During the spring of 1968, the neglect of the Party's influence on cadre policy already manifested itself. The dislocation[20] neglected the ideological and political needs and job openings were to be filled only via a selection procedure without the influence of the party. Opponents to the politics of the time were being gradually eliminated from party activity.'[21] Thus, the selection of teachers was no longer so strictly influenced by the KSČ, and teachers who did not want to be a part of the new trend, i.e. the supporters of the 'old order' or representatives of the pro-Soviet political line, left the schools.

According to witnesses, enthusiasm for the change in the social situation dominated some schools (Zounek et al., 2018). In the new freer atmosphere, the many years of uncritical orientation towards the Soviet Union were replaced by a return to the traditions of the first Czechoslovak Republic. There were even cases of open rejection of Soviet models. This was also reflected in educational and schooling activities. Ideological decorations disappeared from the schools and the lessons once again included previously taboo topics describing, for example, the prewar democratic republic. Sections that uncritically praised the developments of the Soviet Union or the positives of the communist regime were excised from many teaching materials.

---

when referring to archival documents, these are always unpublished sources kept in the given institution (available to researchers).

[19] Ibid.

[20] Dislocation meant placement of teachers in schools, filling positions.

[21] Archive fond G 593 KSČ JmK (1969). *Analysis of Activity*, p. 5.

Open enthusiasm for the relaxation of the regime did not prevail in all schools. It was not entirely unusual for school heads to forbid any discussion about the political situation in schools.

A different situation may have arisen in some rural schools. The distance from larger cities (the centres of reform) may have influenced the course of the Prague Spring at these schools to some extent, as one narrator's recollections suggest: 'Political reasons and such things … we didn't know these. We were people from rural mudholes. Let them say whatever they will, that was a Prague thing' (Zounek et al., 2018, p. 328). This may indicate a lesser known or perhaps less mentioned point. Indeed, the reforms of the time were not unambiguously supported across the country, and the situation in rural areas in particular may have been different from the generally communicated enthusiasm for reforms, even those of the school system. The very diverse experiences with the course of the Prague Spring in schools (and not only the rural ones) show that the different approaches may not have been just a matter of lack of information, but rather a belief that the former regime was the only right one, or that the Prague Spring reforms were subverting Czechoslovakia (Zounek et al., 2018).

In connection with the relaxation of the communist regime in Czechoslovakia during the 1960s, reformist communists tended to interpret religion more favourably than the official communist line wished. In general terms, this manifested itself in the preparation of a series of changes that raised many hopes among religious believers. The personnel changes in the management of the Office for Church Affairs, the amnesty for many members of the clergy, the cancellation of the internment of clergy, and the resumption of operation of the Greek Catholic Church or religious orders represented visible examples of this trend.

In the field of education, some of the existing regulations on religion lessons were relaxed. Applications for religion lessons were no longer accepted by school heads but by clergy. Religion lessons could now take place outside of school institutions. After a long period of time, religious teachers who had previously concealed their faith could attend churches without the threat of punishment.

3.7   Teachers and Schools After August 1968

Teachers themselves perceived the events of August 1968 in many different ways. Apart from the understandable disillusionment with the behaviour of the Soviet Union and other socialist countries, they mentioned fears about the uncertain future. In August 1968, teachers found themselves in the position of having to start preparing lessons in a completely unclear political situation (the school year started at the beginning of September, about 2 weeks after the invasion of the troops). They did not know whether they could continue the trend set by the events of the Prague Spring or if they should, for the sake of 'safety', re-adapt the teaching to the conditions prevailing before the Prague Spring. There were some completely purposeful changes of opinion, with supporters of the Prague Spring reforms quickly becoming its critics and turning into supporters of the incoming regime almost 'overnight'. Such behaviour can be labelled in various ways, but it could have been a completely pragmatic strategy, or s 'survival' strategy leading to the preservation of the position of a school head or a teacher or other positions in the school system or school administration (Vaněk, 2007). Similar rapid changes of opinion were common in many other professions as people tried to avoid trouble or even recrimination. It was possible for a person to face trial and even imprisonment for attacking the principles of socialist schools or for spreading anti-Soviet propaganda (Zounek et al., 2017a).

In the following months, steps were taken under the supervision of the Soviet Union to gradually consolidate the regime (i.e., the return to the 'normal state' before the reforms began), which in fact meant silencing and removal of reform advocates, restoration of censorship, banning of many political movements, and renewed persecution of churches and religious societies. Together with these steps, the leadership of the KSČ was replaced and the member base was gradually 'purged'. The 'purge' of the 'right-wing elements or opportunists', as the Communists denoted both the supporters of the reforms and the opposition, was a characteristic and completely fundamental phenomenon of the first years of normalization. Supporters of the Prague Spring and the authors and supporters of reforms were removed from the state sector and more visible professions. Even a publicly declared opposition to the invasion of the Warsaw Pact troops was a reason for expulsion from the party or forced resignation from one's job. The teaching profession was considered a visible profession by the KSČ. It is therefore not surprising that 'purges' based on 'interviews' took place at schools.[22]

The first personnel changes in the field of education began in the governing authorities at the level of regions and districts. Subsequently, school heads and teachers who had been members of the KSČ were vetted. 'Non-party members' and members of other political parties were vetted at the same time. For school heads, the evaluation of school inspectors was particularly important. However, even in contemporary documents of the KSČ, it can be seen that the information obtained in this way was often problematic. The following quote provides evidence: 'It is a great hindrance, and it does not always inspire confidence in the eyes of school workers that in some districts, the evaluations are carried out 'from the bottom up', i.e., the school heads are evaluated by inspectors whose evaluation has not yet begun, and some of them will even be replaced in the school authorities after their work has been evaluated.'[23] The purges very quickly gained speed, leading to much confusion and ambiguity in the ranks of the 'normalizers'. It is clear that this was a mishandled process at the beginning, but it was refined as the Communists

---

[22] Archive fond Secretariat of the Ministry, Ministry of Education Fond 1967–1992 (1971). *Report on the Overall Results of the Professional Evaluation of School Staff and Personnel Measures for Purposes of the Purging and Political Strengthening of School Administration Authorities*. National Archives, Prague.

[23] Archive fond G 593 KSČ JmK. *Evaluation of the Current State of Consolidation in Schools of the 1st and 2nd Cycle*. Moravian Provincial Archive, Brno, p. 6.

gradually consolidated their power. As a result of systematic vetting, nearly 30% of school heads in the South Moravian Region were fired.[24]

While the school heads were vetted by school inspectors, the teachers appeared before 'interview committees' consisting of three to four members. Usually, the previously 'vetted' school head of the school in question was the chair of the committee. The remaining members were representatives of various communist and school administration authorities. These were always individuals who had been approved by the relevant party authority or the ideological committee of the district committee of the KSČ.[25] In connection with the vetting, some witnesses recalled the composition of the vetting committees, which were dominated by older people. Importantly, the core of the opponents to the Prague Spring consisted mainly of older generations of KSČ members, around whom middle-aged pragmatists connected to the power apparatus assembled. In short, these were people who had lost their bearings in the freer environment of the Prague Spring. They missed the totalitarian clarity and harshness of the government (Bárta & Kural, 1993; Zounek et al., 2018).

The actual work of the vetting committees had several steps. First, the committee evaluated oral information from colleagues or the public about each teacher, then it moved to written information and records, such as information from the previous workplace, CVs and CV supplements, analyses of records from class visitations and records from educational activities, extracurricular activities, and any comments from party bodies. The vetting committees had a great variety of material at their disposal that became the basis for the actual interview with teachers. In some cases, the course of the vetting process could be quite heated and stressful, as some settling of accounts could occur. The opposite situation also occurred, during which efforts were made to ensure that the interview was conducted calmly and that no excesses arose. The school head's position as chair of the committee was the key, as the school head could affect the final verdict of the committee greatly and thus intervene quite significantly in the personal and professional life of the vetted teacher (Zounek et al., 2017a).

At the end of the vetting, the committee formulated a conclusion: 'keep at the current workplace', 'keep in the current position', etc. The committee also formulated sanctions or punishments. Through the decisions of the committee, the regime could punish the teacher financially. Apart from the denial of homeroom teacher duties (which meant bonuses to regular salary), this variant of punishment included denial of raises or a prohibition to teach beyond the basic teaching duty (hours

---

[24] Archive fond G 593 KSČ JmK. *Analysis of Activities and Developments at Schools of the 1st and 2nd Cycle 1965–1969.* Moravian Provincial Archive, Brno, p. 14.

[25] Archive fond G 593 KSČ JmK. *Final Report on the Implementation of Government Resolution No. 213/70 in the South Moravian Region.* Moravian Provincial Archive, p. 82. Brno; Fond G 593 KSČ JmK. *Instructions for Completion of the Purge in the Composition of the Apparatuses in the Organizations Directly Controlled by the Departments of Education of the KNV, NV of the Cities of Prague, Pilsen, Brno, and Ostrava and the ONV.* Moravian Provincial Archive, Brno, p. 2.

worked above this duty were paid extra).[26] In addition to these milder financial penalties, teachers could be transferred from their original workplace to another (more distant) school, often involving a difficult and time-consuming commute, also a type of punishment. In the most extreme cases, the teacher's employment could be terminated.[27] The individual punishments could be combined in various ways: a teacher could be transferred to another school and be financially penalized. In addition to these punishments, awards and honorary titles from the Prague Spring period were also being taken away from their recipients. People who received awards between 1968 and 1969 were vetted particularly closely.[28]

The termination of employment was a very sensitive and unpleasant matter even for the totalitarian regime. Teachers defended their rights in court[29] and the power apparatus had to prepare thoroughly for these cases. This suggests that the regime felt somewhat threatened, and moreover, that the nature of power was already different from the Stalinist period of the 1950s, in which human rights and the rule of law were often trampled upon.

3.8 Ideological Hardening After 1969: The Advent of 'Normalization' and Ideological Education

In parallel with the course of the 'interviews', the leaders of the KSČ began to prepare more organized interventions into the ideological 'education' of teachers. The primary attention was to be paid to the teachers and their activities, which were to be performed in the spirit of Marxist-Leninist ideas.[30] On the basis of these demands, a new (political-educational) education of teachers[31] and school workers was

---

[26] Archive fond Secretariat of the Ministry, Fond of the Ministry of Education 1967–1992. *Overview of Cadre Changes by Categories of Pedagogical Workers in Schools of the 1st and 2nd Cycle in the CSR.* National Archives, Prague.

[27] Ibid.

[28] Archive fond Secretariat of the Ministry, Ministry of Education Fond 1967–1992 (1971). *Report on the Overall Results of the Professional Evaluation of School Staff and Personnel Measures for Purposes of the Purging and Political Strengthening of School Administration Authorities.* National Archives, Prague, p. 5.

[29] Archive fond G 593 KSČ JMK. *Report on the Overall Results of the Political and Expert Evaluation of Consolidation (Future Cadre Plan), the Consolidation Process and the Achieved Results of the Educational Work in Schools and Educational Institutions of the 1st and 2nd Cycle.* Moravian Provincial Archive, Brno, p. 190. The document does not indicate the extent to which these teachers were successful. It merely states that the courts always complied with the legal standards in these cases.

[30] Archive fond G 593 KSČ JmK. *Evaluation of the Current State of Consolidation in Schools of the 1st and 2nd Cycle.* Moravian Provincial Archive, Brno, p. 1.

[31] The pedagogical education also included political preparation. The perception of the teacher as the main agent of the ideological education of future generations was so fundamental for the regime of the time that even the admission procedure was conducted according to the rules set

planned. This education was to primarily include the problems of patriotism of the time (especially the solidarity with the socialist establishment of the Czechoslovak Republic), internationalism (orientated exclusively towards the Soviet Union and other socialist countries), and the leading role of the KSČ. Special attention was to be paid to Russian and social sciences teachers, who were to bear the bulk of the ideological work in teaching. In December 1969, the Ministry of Education even issued guidelines for teachers regarding the mandatory study of Marxism-Leninism, and, at the same time, identified the basic works of the classic authors of Marxism-Leninism that were to be studied.[32]

The ideological consolidation concerned the education of teachers and it was also reflected in the everyday life of schools, especially in the teachers' work in the classrooms. The teachers were to take special care to educate students in traditional friendship towards the Soviet Union.[33] The emphasis on these educational goals is not surprising. From the point of view of the ruling party, in the new political climate, it was an absolutely necessary measure to encourage students to foster warm relations with the Soviet Union, since these relations were severely damaged for many of their parents by the August invasion. For this purpose, teachers compiled educational plans and cooperated with various communist organizations such as the Pioneer Organization of the Socialist Youth Union.[34] The concrete results of their work were to manifested in the decoration of classrooms, the neatness of bulletin boards, and in participation in work brigades on the maintenance of school equipment, school playgrounds, and the schools' surroundings, for example. Significant anniversaries and holidays were celebrated in appropriate measures for these educational goals.[35] Specific examples of a return to the period before the Prague Spring

---

during the height of Stalinism. The content of pedagogical studies inseparably included a professional (subject teaching) and pedagogical component, and also a political part. This specifically meant that in every year of the four-year study programme, there was at least one subject that was supposed to imprint the minds of future teachers with a chapter of communist ideology. The subject Foundations of Marxism-Leninism, which was included in the state final exams, was a typical example of this practice.

[32] Archive fond Ministry Secretariat, Ministry of Education 1967–1992. *Analysis of Some of the Current Problems in the Field of Education– Submission to the Bureau of the ÚV KSČ.* National Archives, Prague, p. 32.

[33] Records of Meetings of the Commission for Education and Culture. Archive fond R 149 KSČ-MV Brno 1949–1989. *The Condition of Political and Cadre Consolidation, Level of Political and Educational Work at Schools of the 1st and 2nd Cycle Managed by the National committee of the City of Brno.* Brno City Archives, Brno.

[34] The Pioneer Organization (Pionýrská organizace) of the Socialist Youth Union (Socialistický svaz mládeže) was a mass leisure organization for children and youth between the ages of six and fifteen run by the ruling KSČ. The education in Pioneers was conducted in the spirit of Marxism-Leninism. The Pioneers were raised towards socialist patriotism and admiration for the Soviet Union. In the period of normalization, the educational system emphasized the development of children through games and competitions that were ideologically and politically motivated (Knapik, 2022).

[35] For example, the anniversary of the Great October Socialist Revolution, the anniversary of the birth of Lenin, Army Day, and Press Day.

were that ideologically oriented bulletin boards were created and open discussions of the democratic ideals of the Czechoslovak First Republic were not allowed. In addition, the teachers remembered that the fulfilment rate of educational (ideological) goals was closely monitored by school inspectors. One teacher we spoke to during our previous research remembered: 'They, I mean inspectors, when they were doing class visits, it's true that they monitored those educational goals … we had to keep praising the Soviet Union and the army … they were all ears if you would say it or not' (Zounek et al., 2018, p. 334). Although the teachers were strictly policed in this matter, these situations were not necessarily stressful for the teachers and the policing may have been merely formal.

The inspection of 'proper' educational activities in schools was not carried out exclusively by inspectors, but also by colleagues who did not hesitate to report 'slips' to their superiors. The consequences of such vetting among teachers thus led to a deterioration of the climate and collegial relations in schools. In particular, it affected trust between colleagues and what could and could not be said openly. The working climate was complicated in some schools in the early years of normalization and there was mutual distrust, uncertainty, and even suspicion (Zounek et al., 2018).

Criticisms reported by a colleague to superiors could represent a rather serious problem that could end in professional disaster and termination of employment. The reason for termination was recorded in the teacher's personal file, which each teacher had to submit at the next workplace. A negative evaluation made any further work in education impossible. Some witnesses saw the evaluations in the personal files as a means of putting pressure on teachers, who thus had practically no choice: either they could remain a teacher, doing the work they liked and submitting to the regime, or they could leave the school system and with a bad evaluation (Zounek et al., 2017a).

The state's church policy also returned to 'normal' after 1969. During the first years of normalization, the regime issued several legal standards with which it was returning to the original church laws adopted in the late 1940s and early 1950s. The transition back to the old 'order' was accompanied by personnel purges in the administration of the church departments of the ministry and in the ranks of bishops and monks.

The atheistic influence on young people was a KSČ priority until the mid-1980s. Universal education of young people on the basis of Marxist-Leninist foundations was its goal. In order to prevent the communist youth from being influenced by any church, the KSČ also tried to make maximum use of their free time. Atheist-oriented programs were broadcast on television (weekend programs for young people) and the organization of celebrations and tourist sports meetings on important church holidays were means of atheization.

At the same time, secret and—from the point of view of the state administration—illegal religion lessons were organized in private apartments, or these lessons were hidden under the activities of various leisure organizations or interest groups, such as the tourist club or the young firefighters' club (Cuhra, 2006). Thus, some children received a religious education, but they were not allowed to talk about it publicly. The concealment of religious beliefs may have affected the mental and moral development of religious children. Many religious children were taught not to express their true beliefs in public during the communist period in order not to be penalized by the state apparatus. According to Gruner and Kluchert (2001), they developed a 'double morality' typical of life in totalitarian/authoritarian regimes (Kudláčová, 2023). Hlavinková (2007) even referred to this condition in a totalitarian society as 'social schizophrenia'. A gradual change in this field was only noticeable in the later 1980s with the change in the geopolitical situation related to Mikhail Gorbachev's perestroika.

Bibliography

Act No. 31/1953 Coll. on the School System and Teacher Education (Education Act). (1953). https://www.psp.cz/sqw/sbirka.sqw?cz=31&r=1953

Act No. 186/1960 Coll. on the System of Upbringing and Education (Education Act). (1960). https://www.psp.cz/sqw/sbirka.sqw?cz=186&r=1960

Act No. 19/1966 Coll. on Universities. (1966). https://www.psp.cz/sqw/sbirka.sqw?cz=19&r=1966

Balík, S., & Hanuš, J. (2013). *Katolická církev v Československu 1945–1989* [Catholic Church in Czechoslovakia 1945–1989]. Centrum pro studium demokracie a kultury.

Bárta, M., & Kural, V. (1993). *Československo roku 1968* (2. díl, Počátky normalizace) [Czechoslovakia in 1968 (Volume 2, The beginnings of normalization)]. Parta.

Bílek, J., & Lupták, Ľ. (2014). Československo 1945–1948: Případ hybridního režimu? [Czechoslovakia 1945–1948: A case of hybrid regime?]. *Středoevropské politické studie, 16*(2–3), 188–213. https://doi.org/10.5817/CEPSR.2014.23.188

Bracke, M. (2007). *Which socialism, whose détente?: West European communism and the Czechoslovak crisis, 1968.* CEU Press.

Crampton, R. J. (1997). *Eastern Europe in the twentieth century – and after.* Routledge.

Cuhra, J. (1999). Církevní politika KSČ a státu v letech 1969–1972 [Church Policy of the KSČ and the state in 1969–1972]. Ústav pro soudobé dějiny AV ČR.

Cuhra, J. (2006). *České země v evropských dějinách* (Díl čtvrtý, Od roku 1918) [Czech Lands in European History (Volume Four, Since 1918)]. Paseka.

Cuhra, J., Černá, M., Devátá, M., Hermann, T., & Kourová, P. (2020). *Pojetí a prosazování komunistické výchovy v Československu 1948–1989* [The Concept and Promotion of Communist Education in Czechoslovakia 1948–1989]. Ústav pro soudobé dějiny AV ČR.

De Nevers, R. (2003). *Comrades no more: The seeds of political change in Eastern Europe.* The MIT Press.

Fawn, R. (2000). *The Czech Republic: A nation of velvet.* Routledge.

Gruner, P., & Kluchert, G. (2001). Erziehungsabsichten und Sozialisationseffekte. Die Schule der SBZ und frühen DDR zwischen politischer Instrumentalisierung und institutioneller Eigenlogik. *Zeitschrift für Pädagogik, 47*(6), 859–868.

Heißig, K., Hoffmann, R. J., & Kittel, M. (Eds.). (2010). *Odsun – die Vertreibung der Sudetendeutschen: Dokumentation zu Ursachen, Planung und Realisierung einer „ethnischen Säuberung" in der Mitte Europas 1848/49–1945/46* (Band 2, Von der Errichtung des "Protektorats Böhmen und Mähren" im März 1939 bis zum offiziellen Abschluß der Vertreibung Ende 1946). Sudetendeutsches Archiv.

Heitlinger, A. (2006). *In the shadows of the holocaust & communism: Czech and Slovak jews: Since 1945.* Transaction.

Hlavinková, L. (2007). Socialismus jako sekularizovaná společnost: Být věřícím v době socialismu-případová studie [Socialism as a secularized society: Being religious during socialism-a case study]. In T. Bubík, & H. Hoffmann (Eds.), *Náboženství a politika* [Religion and politics]. (pp. 62–71). Pantheon.

Immerman, R. H., & Goedde, P. (Eds.). (2016). *The Oxford handbook of the cold war*. Oxford University Press.

Jech, K. (2008). *Kolektivizace a vyhánění sedláků z půdy* [Collectivization and driving farmers off the land.]. Vyšehrad.

Jelínková, V., & Smolka, R. (1989). *Základní školství v ČSSR a některé trendy jeho vývoje od roku 1921* [Primary education in Czechoslovakia and some trends of its development since 1921]. Ústav školských informací.

Judt, T. (2005). *Postwar: A history of Europe since 1945*. Penguin Books.

Kalinová, L. (2007). *Společenské proměny v čase socialistického experimentu: k sociálním dějinám v letech 1945–1969* [Social transformations in the time of the socialist experiment: Towards social history in 1945–1969]. Academia.

Kaplan, K. (1984). *Das verhängnisvolle Bündnis: Unterwanderung, Gleichschaltung und Vernichtung der Tschechoslowakischen Sozialdemokratie 1944–1954*. Pol-Verlag.

Kaplan, K. (1986a). *Die politischen Prozesse in der Tschechoslowakei 1948–1954*. R. Oldenbourg.

Kaplan, K. (1986b). *The overcoming of the regime crisis after Stalins death in Czechoslovakia Poland and Hungary*. Index.

Kaplan, K. (1987). *The short march: The communist takeover in Czechoslovakia: 1945–1948*. C. Hurst.

Kaplan, K. (1990). *Staat und Kirche in der Tschechoslowakei: die kommunistische Kirchenpolitik in den Jahren 1948–1952*. R. Oldenbourg.

Kaplan, K. (1993). *Stát a církev v Československu v letech 1948–1953* [State and Church in Czechoslovakia in 1948–1953]. Doplněk.

Kaplan, K. (2001). *Těžká cesta: spor Československa s Vatikánem 1963–1973* [The hard road: The Czechoslovakia-Vatican dispute 1963–1973]. Centrum pro studium demokracie a kultury.

Kaplan, K. (2004). *Československo v poválečné Evropě* [Czechoslovakia in Postwar Europe]. Karolinum.

Kaplan, K., & Paleček, P. (2008). *Komunistický režim a politické procesy v Československu* [The communist regime and political processes in Czechoslovakia]. Barrister & Principal.

Kavan, J. (2008). Czechoslovakia 1968: Revolt or reform? 1968—A year of hope and non-understanding. *Critique, 36*(2), 289–301. https://doi.org/10.1080/03017600802185415

Klimke, M., Pekelder, J., & Scharloth, J. (Eds.). (2011). *Between Prague spring and French may: Opposition and revolt in Europe, 1960–1980*. Berghahn Books.

Knapík, J. (2022). *Pionýři, malované děti? Pionýrská organizace ČSM a dětský kolektiv (1949–1968)* [Pioneers, beautiful children? The Pioneer Organization of the Czechoslovak Youth Union and the children collective (1949–1968)]. NLN.

Kocian, J. (2018). Československo mezi dvěma totalitami (1945–1948) [Czechoslovakia between two totalitarian regimes (1945–1948)]. In J. Pánek & O. Tůma (Eds.), *Dějiny českých zemí* [History of the Czech lands] (pp. 475–502). Karolinum.

Kudláčová, B. (Ed.). (2019). *Pedagogické myslenie, školstvo a vzdelávanie na Slovensku v rokoch 1945–1989* [Pedagogical thinking, schooling and education in Slovakia between 1945–1989]. Typi Universitatis Tyrnaviensis.

Kudláčová, B. (Ed.). (2023). *Two sides of the same coin: Examples of free and unfree education in Slovakia during the period of socialism*. Peter Lang.

Kural, V. (1993). *Československo roku 1968* (1. díl, Obrodný proces) [Czechoslovakia in 1968 (Volume 1, Revival Process)]. Parta.

Kusin, V. V. (2002). *The intellectual origins of the Prague spring: The development of reformist ideas in Czechoslovakia 1956–1967*. Cambridge University Press.

Madsen, R. (2014). Religion under Communism. In S. A. Smith (Ed.), *The Oxford handbook of the history of communism* (pp. 585–601). Oxford University Press.

McDermott, K. (2015). *Communist Czechoslovakia, 1945–89: A political and social history.* Macmillan Education.

Müller, T., & Neudorf, A. (2012). The role of the state in the repression and revival of religiosity in Central Eastern Europe. *Social Forces, 91*(2), 559–582. https://doi.org/10.1093/sf/sos142

Pauer, J. (1995). *Prag 1968: Der Einmarsch des Warschauer Paktes: Hintergründe, Planung, Durchführung.* Edition Temmen.

Pehe, J. (Ed.). (1988). *The Prague spring: A mixed legacy.* Freedom House.

Pelikán, J. (Ed.). (1971). *The secret Vysočany congress: Proceedings and documents of the extraordinary fourteenth congress of the communist party of Czechoslovakia, 22. August 1968.* Allen Lane the Penguin Press.

Pernes, J. (2022). *Velké dějiny zemí Koruny české* (Svazek XVII., 1948–1956) [Great history of the lands of the bohemian crown (Volume XVII., 1948–1956)]. Paseka.

Pojetí základní devítileté školy a učební plán této školy [The Concept of the Nine-Year Primary School and the Curriculum of This School]. (1960). Státní pedagogické nakladatelství.

Presidential Decree No. 132 of 27 October 1945 on Teacher Education. (1945). https://www.aspi.cz/products/lawText/1/12040/0/2/dekret-c-132-1945-sb-o-vzdelani-ucitelstva

Průcha, V. (2009). *Hospodářské a sociální dějiny Československa 1918–1992* (II. díl, Období 1945–1992) [Economic and social history of Czechoslovakia 1918–1992 (Volume II, Period 1945–1992)]. Doplněk.

Renner, H. (1989). *A history of Czechoslovakia since 1945.* Routledge.

Rokovský, J. (2018). Košický vládní program. Na cestě sovětizace Československa [The Košice government Programme. On the way to Sovietization of Czechoslovakia.] In J. Kalous, & P. Zeman (Eds.), *1945: konec války a obnova Československa* [1945: The end of the war and restoration of Czechoslovakia] (pp. 158–165). Ústav pro studium totalitních režimů.

Rychlík, J. (2020). *Československo v období socialismu: 1945–1989* [Czechoslovakia in the Period of Socialism: 1945–1989]. Vyšehrad.

Schwartz, H. (1969). *Prague's 200 days: The struggle for democracy in Czechoslovakia.* Pall Mall.

Segert, D. (2008). An unexpected Dawn: The Prague spring and the mechanism of change in state socialism. *Debatte: Journal of Contemporary Central and Eastern Europe, 16*(2), 203–211. https://doi.org/10.1080/09651560802318754

Šimáně, M. (2010). K problematice zřizování českých menšinových obecných škol na Ústecku v letech 1867–1918 [On the Problems of Establishing Czech Minority Volksschule in Ústí nad Labem in 1867–1918]. *E-Pedagogium, 10*(4), 83–92. https://doi.org/10.5507/epd.2010.058

Šimáně, M. (2014). Učitelé menšinových škol pohledem dějin každodennosti [Minority school teachers through the eyes of history of everydayness]. *Studia paedagogica, 19*(3), 89–122. https://doi.org/10.5817/SP2014-3-6

Skilling, H. G. (1976). *Czechoslovakia's interrupted revolution.* Princeton University Press.

Šlouf, J. (2021). *Praha v červnu 1953: dělnická revolta proti měnové reformě, vyjednávání v továrnách a strukturální proměna dělnické třídy* [Prague in June 1953: The Workers' revolt against monetary reform, negotiations in factories and structural transformation of the working class]. Academia.

Smith, S. A. (Ed.). (2014). *The Oxford handbook of the history of communism.* Oxford University Press.

Szalontai, B. (2008). Show trials. In R. Dijk, W. Glenn Gray, S. Savranskaya, J. Suri, & Q. Zhai (Eds.), *Encyclopedia of the cold war* (pp. 783–786). Routledge.

Vaněk, M. (2007). Jsem dělník a kdo je víc? Sonda do života příslušníků dělnických profesí v socialistickém Československu [I am a worker, and who is more? A probe into the lives of workers in socialist Czechoslovakia.]. In M. Vaněk (Ed.), *Obyčejní lidé–?!: pohled do života tzv. mlčící většiny: životopisná vyprávění příslušníků dělnických profesí a inteligence* [Ordinary people–?!: a Glimpse into the lives of the so-called silent majority: Biographical narratives of members of the working Professions and Intelligentsia] (p. 472–528). Academia.

Vorlíček, Ch. (2004). České školství v letech 1945–2000 [Czech school system between 1945–2000]. In E. Walterová (Ed.), *Česká pedagogika: Proměny a výzvy: Sborník k životnímu jubileu profesora Jiřího Kotáska* [Czech pedagogy: Transformations and challenges: Collection for the Jubilee of Professor Jiří Kotásek] (p. 119–176). Pedagogická fakulta Univerzity Karlovy.

Walterová, E. (2004). *Úloha školy v rozvoji vzdělanosti* [The Role of School in the Development of Education]. Paido.

Williams, K. (1997). *The Prague spring and its aftermath: Czechoslovak politics, 1968–1970.* Cambridge University Press.

Zounek, J. (1996). Filozofická fakulta Masarykovy univerzity v letech 1948–1949 [Faculty of Arts of Masaryk University in 1948–1949]. *Časopis Matice moravské, 2*(115), 299–312.

Zounek, J., Šimáně, M., & Knotová, D. (2016). Cesta k učitelství v socialistickém Československu pohledem pamětníků [The journey to teacher profession in socialist Czechoslovakia as seen by eyewitnesses]. *Studia paedagogica, 21*(3), 131–159. https://doi.org/10.5817/SP2016-3-7

Zounek, J. Šimáně, M., & Knotová, D. (2017a). *Normální život v nenormální době. Základní školy a jejich učitelé (nejen) v období normalizace* [Normal life in not so Normal times. Primary schools and their teachers (not only) during the so-called normalization period]. Wolters Kluwer.

Zounek, J., Šimáně, M., & Knotová, D. (2017b). Socialistická základní škola pohledem pamětníků. *Sonda do života učitelů v Jihomoravském kraji* [Socialist primary school as seen by eyewitnesses: Probing teachers' life in the South Moravia region]. Wolters Kluwer.

Zounek, J., Šimáně, M., & Knotová, D. (2017c). Primary school teachers as a tool of secularization of Society in Communist Czechoslovakia. *History of Education: Journal of the History of Education Society, 46*(4), 480–497. https://doi.org/10.1080/0046760X.2016.1276970

Zounek, J., Šimáně, M., & Knotová, D. (2018). "You have betrayed us for a little dirty money!" the Prague spring as seen by primary school teachers. *Paedagogica Historica, 54*(3), 320–337. https://doi.org/10.1080/00309230.2017.1394884

Chapter 4
Schools and Teachers Two Decades Before the Fall of the Communist Regime

Abstract This chapter focuses on the period between 1969 and 1989. Attention is paid to the onset of 'normalization' after the invasion of the Warsaw Pact troops, to how Czechoslovak society slowly fell into a state of lethargy and closedpmindedness, and to the deteriorating economic situation. The communist government tried to 'calm' the population by implementing pro-social and pro-family policies and by tolerating people's escape into private life. The perestroika and glasnost initiated by Mikhail Gorbachev are presented in the text. However, the Czechoslovak government showed little willingness to follow this new course.

The main part of the chapter is devoted to the school system, particularly primary schools and teachers. The topic is mapped from a macro-historical perspective, describing the key education acts and presenting critical analyses of the state of the school system and the limited possibilities for educational reforms, which were not able to go beyond the ideologically conditioned concept of a unified school until November 1989. We pay attention primarily to the everyday life of teachers, looking into the 'workshop' of a socialist teacher, including his lesson planning, tools, and textbooks. Teachers' out-of-school life and free time activities are also an important topic. The political education of teachers is briefly considered.

Keywords Czechoslovakia 1969–1989 · Communist Party · Perestroika · Legislation · Primary Education · Schools · Teacher · Teaching · Free time

© Masaryk University, Faculty of Arts, Registration no. 00216224,
VAT ID: CZ00216224 2024
J. Zounek et al., *(Post)Socialist Transformation of Primary Schools*,
https://doi.org/10.1007/978-3-031-58768-9_4

4.1   Normalization in Czechoslovakia (1969–1989)

The events of 21 August 1968 connected to the invasion of Czechoslovakia by Warsaw Pact troops represented a considerable disappointment for Czechoslovak society.[1] Initially, many people were determined to clearly oppose the destruction of the process of democratization. In the year after the invasion, there were manifestations of civil discontent in Czechoslovakia.

Already at the time of the Prague Spring, the relationship between Czechs and Slovaks was quite important. In October 1968, a federative state structure was enacted, thus creating the Czech and Slovak Socialist Republics (CSR and SSR). This overcame the asymmetrical state-law structure of Czechoslovakia that had existed since 1945. However, in the conditions of the oncoming normalization, the federation represented a virtually hollow or formalized institution, as all decision-making powers were concentrated in the hands of the Central Committee (Ústřední výbor, ÚV) of the Communist Party of Czechoslovakia (Komunistická strana Československa, KSČ). The principle of centralism in state administration continued.

At the end of September 1969, the ÚV KSČ met and reconsidered and effectively condemned the developments of 1968, removing Alexander Dubček and other reform supporters from the leadership of the Communist Party of Czechoslovakia. At the same time, many reform supporters were expelled from the communist party. The KSČ defined the invasion as 'fraternal international aid'. The September session of the ÚV KSČ effectively meant the beginning of the 'normalization' process, as the process of returning to the status prior to the reform period of the Prague Spring was called. The beginning of normalization was characterized by widespread purges, which mainly took the form of terminating KSČ memberships and were also reflected in layoffs. They affected a large part of society—especially the cultural, scientific, and economic sectors.

At the beginning of 1970, major purges within the ÚV KSČ began. Immediately afterwards, 'vetting' within the KSČ started. This was not limited to communist party members; it extended to the entire Czechoslovak society. The vetting followed in several successive waves and consisted of a mass replacement of Communist Party member cards. Only those who signed up to the normalization policy of the KSČ received new communist party member cards; others lost their party membership and were removed from the members' list. The most visible supporters of the Prague Spring were immediately expelled from the party. The expulsion constituted a 'more serious' handicap than being removed from the list and usually led to further political persecutions. This could include surveillance by the secret police and loss of employment. Indeed, the expelled KSČ members were considered the

---

[1] In general historical overviews and in the history of school systems in the Czech territory, in this and other chapters, we build on the sources listed after the chapter. We cite directly in the text only those sources that provide a specific piece of information or if the citation is required by the context of the interpretation.

greatest threat to the party. The post-August persecutions in combination with the invasion caused another wave of mass emigration, as in 1948. The purges and mass layoffs, affecting particularly the educated and intellectual populations in the scientific, educational, and cultural sectors, contributed to the overall stagnation of the country and its economy, and to the reduction of the quality of life in all aspects. Experts and intellectuals often left their jobs to take positions as unskilled workers; they were replaced by people who were often less educated, inadequately skilled, or less capable, but loyal to the normalising authorities. The loss of the elites damaged the society for the next 20 years.

By the early 1970s, Czechoslovak society had definitively lost hope for any continuation of the reforms of the spring of 1968, and it slowly slipped into a state of lethargy and closed-mindedness. The 'normalization' period is characterized by an escape of a large part of the population into private life and by a resignation from public life. This was subliminally encouraged by the KSČ government under the motto of looking for 'peace to work'. Favouring a private life reduces the risk that citizens will engage in activities that threaten the ruling regime. The idealized image of a private life in a 'developed socialist society' was subliminally conveyed—for example, through increasingly popular television series (Bren, 2010).

Security forces regained their crucial role in the power structure. The police, called the National Security Corps relied on many collaborators to maintain order, including the Auxiliary Guard of Public Security, People's Militias,[2] and local KSČ organizations. Social control was also ubiquitous, with communist party members in particular being called upon to keep a close watch and report anything suspicious in their surroundings. Activities potentially threatening the normalization regime itself were then in the crosshairs of the secret police. The secret police also focused on monitoring of the supporters of the reformist faction of 1968 to a large extent. Once again, KSČ membership became an important aspect for more important jobs or for possible career advancement. This negative trend manifested itself in the society throughout the entire 1970s and 1980s.

For the majority of non-party members (the 'passive zone of the population'), public manifestations of approval of the regime continued to be mandatory. These

---

[2] The Auxiliary Guard of Public Security was an organization that helped maintain public order in Czechoslovakia from about the 1950s until 1990. In their free time, members of the Auxiliary Guard of Public Security actively helped the security authorities free of charge. In the language of the time, this was a form of direct citizen participation in the protection of public order (see Decree…, 1962). Public Security was the regular police force of the Czechoslovak Socialist Republic, created in 1945.

The People's Militias were established as an armed guard of industrial enterprises as early as in February 1948. Gradually, they became an armed force of the Czechoslovak Socialist Republic directly subordinated to the KSČ leadership. Military exercises with the army and the police were organised for People's Militias members. The People's Militias were deployed together with the Public Security and the army against demonstrators and other 'anti-socialist elements'. The People's Militia's position was never anchored in law. They were dissolved in December 1989, when they had over eighty thousand members (Bašta, 2008).

primarily included participation in May Day parades,[3] ideological trainings, factory meetings, and, last but not least, mandatory 'voter turnout'. However, unlike in the 1950s, there was no longer so much emphasis on intervention in the privacy of the population. Not even the normalization government lived under the illusion that people actually believed in the ideology. Therefore, manifestations became 'mere' performative expressions of loyalty (Krakovský, 2020). The image of each individual was built on the basis of cadre record, i.e. a mixture of ideological phrases and subjective observations as well as various statements from informants and unsupported statements from co-workers or neighbours. The majority of the population was practically prevented from travelling to the countries of the capitalist bloc.

Some people reacted to these conditions with passivity and resignation to public engagement; many people sought activities outside the public space, often withdrawing into a personal zone. For example, this trend took the form of weekend trips to cottages or summer houses (Schindler-Wisten, 2017), at which the real world of real socialism became something distant for a short period of time.

In their policies, the representatives of the normalization powers tried to gain the loyalty of the population by at least satisfying their basic life needs. First of all, a rather generous pro-social and pro-family policy was implemented in the early 1970s. It was possible to obtain various newlywed loans and new flats were being built. At that time, this mainly concerned building extensive housing developments of panel buildings on the outskirts of large cities, often without any respect for the natural and cultural heritage of the area. Together with the coming of age of strong post-war generations, this led to an increase in birth rates, which was reflected in schools exceeding their capacity (Kalinová, 2012; Kopeček, 2019). The KSČ also promoted an orientation towards consumption. This mainly concerned the availability of cheap food, and, to a lesser extent, consumer goods, which was how the regime prevented manifestations of discontent. The 'shadow' (grey) economy became widespread, i.e. under-the-counter sales, bribery, and other negative phenomena (economic crime) generally associated with the poor functioning of the 'socialist economy'.[4] Other negative phenomena within the macroeconomic sector included the increasing indebtedness of the KSČ to advanced capitalist countries, particularly visible from the early 1980s onward, when the currency reserves (loans) were invested almost exclusively towards consumption of the population.

---

[3] Labour Day or May Day is the international workers' holiday, celebrated on May 1 since 1890. It was the most important holiday of the communist regime. The state propaganda described it as a celebration of labour and the working class. May Day was a public holiday. On this day, mass May Day parades were organized in all towns and villages, and the participation of students, and local factory workers was compulsory.

[4] The grey economy was created and evolved because 'the official economy was unable to satisfy the demand for the required goods and services on the one hand and it did not provide enough opportunities for people to exercise their skills and earn adequate legal wages on the other hand. This was caused by the ownership by state and excessive centralisation. The imbalance between supply and demand reinforced the chances of the shadow economy. It is difficult to quantify the extent of the shadow economy. For 1989 Czechoslovakia, some authors indicate that it accounted for 6% of GDP' (Bálek, 2007, p. 48)

In 1975, a Conference on Security and Cooperation in Europe was held in Helsinki. Thirty-two countries including Czechoslovakia participated. A section on respect for all human and civil rights, which the CSSR committed to uphold by signing, was one of the outcomes of the conference. The reality within the state did not correspond with this at all.

Opposition groups reacted to this. In January 1977, a declaration by a group called Charter 77 was issued, calling on the normalization regime to respect human and civil rights (precisely in accordance with the provisions of the Helsinki Conference) and to allow open democratic debate in society (Prečan, 1990). The signatories of the Declaration of Charter 77 included individuals of various political and social orientations: Vaclav Havel, who later became the first post-communist president, as well as reformist communists and other cultural and scientific figures.

The Czechoslovak communist regime continued to rigidly adhere to the line based on '*Poučení z krizového vývoje* [Lessons from the Crisis Development][5]' and considered any reforms, even the most minor, extremely dangerous. However, the threat to its stability came from the least expected place: the USSR. In March 1985, Mikhail S. Gorbachev became the General Secretary of the central committee of the Communist Party of the Soviet Union and launched a completely new policy. The 'glasnost' (openness) and, above all, the initiation of the process of 'perestroika' (literally: restructuring) were its main features. Gorbachev was clearly aware of the complicated economic situation of the USSR and its lagging behind the advanced 'capitalist' world. The USSR had been able to keep up with the 'West' (and even surpass it in many respects) only in the field of technologies related to the arms and space industries.

Gorbachev certainly did not intend to dismantle the Eastern bloc, but rather to strengthen and 'rejuvenate' the socialist system of government by launching economic and political reforms. He made no secret of the fact that he found considerable inspiration for his policies in the reforms of the Czechoslovak Prague Spring of 1968.

However, glasnost and political relaxation, including the abandonment of the 'Brezhnev Doctrine', caused a stir within the USSR and its satellites, which, after a certain phase, could hardly be set right without the use of force, meaning the military and/or the security forces. The Czechoslovak normalizers showed little willingness to take on this new course set by Gorbachev, as it was all too reminiscent of what they had opposed in 1968.

However, the KSČ could not completely resist the application (at least formally) of the new pro-reform policy. At the beginning of 1987, the document *Principles of Perestroika of the Economic Mechanism in CSSR* (Štrougal & Jakeš, 1987) was published, and these principles became the basic starting point for the

---

[5] The Lessons from the Crisis Development in the Party and Society after the 13th Congress of the KSČ was a document approved by the ÚV KSČ in December 1970. In the document, the regime officially described and interpreted the events of the Prague Spring and the intervention of Warsaw Pact troops. It basically states that Czechoslovakia was in crisis since January 1968 and the coming of Warsaw Pact troops was a case of fraternal aid.

reconstruction of Czechoslovakia. As the title implies, the reforms were primarily aimed at the economic sector, but it was clear that the changes would also affect the power structures (Pullmann, 2012). Some members of the KSČ leadership considered perestroika a Soviet specificity that could not be consistently applied to the Czechoslovak conditions. The situation did not change significantly even after Gorbachev's visit to Prague in April 1987, a visit that the Czechoslovak public associated with hopes of promoting greater democratization. Nevertheless, glasnost also emerged in Czechoslovakia on a limited scale. For example, articles about rising juvenile delinquency or poor supply appeared in the press. However, glasnost was seen mainly on a performative level. Expressions such as 'decentralization' or 'democratization' appeared in the public space, and the lagging national economy was criticized, but nothing actually improved. The attempt to 'colonize' the language of perestroika while in fact clinging to the established principles did not work very well for KSČ. Public discontent grew precisely because the problems the public felt were also reported in the party press (Green, 2014; McDermott, 2015; Polouček & Zounek, 2021).

On 21 August 1988, the twentieth anniversary of the Warsaw Pact troops' invasion of Czechoslovakia, the first major anti-regime demonstration since 1969 took place in Prague. Other demonstrations took place on 28 October 1988, the 70th anniversary of the founding of Czechoslovakia. The security forces cracked down hard on the participants in these demonstrations. A manifesto entitled *Několik vět* [A Few Sentences], published at the end of June 1989 and signed by several thousand people in a short period of time, became a clear expression of the dissatisfaction with the previous developments (Urban, 2010). For example, the manifesto demanded accelerated democratization, freedom of speech, and the release of political prisoners. On 21 August 1989, another demonstration took place in Prague, and it was again dispersed by the police. This time, it was also attended by foreign activists from Hungary and Poland, where, unlike the Czechoslovakia, the process of liberalization and democratization was already under way (Burakowski et al., 2021).

The fall of the Berlin Wall (9 November 1989), which had been the symbol of the divided Europe, further reinforced the impression of the unsustainability of the existing conditions in Czechoslovak society. The normalization regime had been weakened and was in fact already quite isolated within the Eastern bloc, except for Romania and Bulgaria. Nevertheless, the regime prepared for further clashes with its opponents.[6] In this respect, it considered Human Rights Day on 10 December 1989 to be a particularly dangerous date.

The beginning of a fundamental break and the end of the KSČ's rule in Czechoslovakia came on 17 November 1989, on the 60th anniversary of the Nazi closure of Czech universities. On this occasion, a permitted student rally was held in Prague's Albertov district to commemorate Jan Opletal.[7] The students

---

[6] The regime's basic ideological dogma was still based on the beginning of normalization, i. e. the early 1970s.

[7] Jan Opletal (1914–1939) was a student at the Faculty of Medicine of Charles University who was fatally wounded during an anti-Nazi demonstration on 28 October 1939.

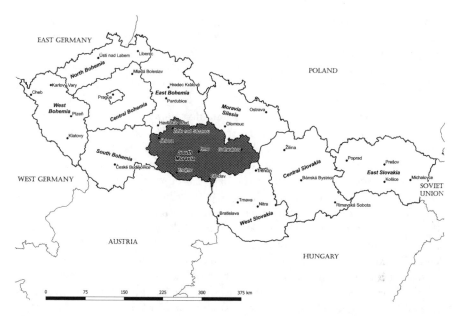

Fig. 4.1 Czechoslovak regions in 1989. The grey area denotes our research area

subsequently set off on a march through the city, but clashed with security forces who wanted to prevent the march from continuing towards the city centre. That morning, the KSČ leadership had issued instructions for the security forces to avoid any possible forceful intervention, if possible (Tomek, 2019). The brutality against the students provoked a violent reaction. University students went on strike; they were subsequently joined by actors, and soon the protests spread 'uncontrollably' across the country (Fig. 4.1).[8]

4.2 Normalization in Education: The Way Back

For the Czechoslovak school system, as for many other fields of Czechoslovak life, the onset of normalization after August 1968 meant a return to the previous practices, i.e. to the state before the reform movement. The KSČ's efforts to achieve this state of affairs led to a new round of purges among the pedagogical workers and to a modification of the content of education. Once again, schools were seen as a bulwark of socialism, and cadre evaluations of students and teachers reappeared and gradually turned stricter. At the same time, discussions about reforms and hints of progressive trends in the school system concept were stifled (Walterová, 2004).

---

[8] The course of the Velvet Revolution will be discussed later.

At the beginning of the 1970s, principles for the development of the school system were once again prepared by the KSČ. In 1973, the need to introduce a compulsory, universal, polytechnic, ten-year secondary education for all youth was formulated. This was followed by the publication of a comprehensive programme (1976) and then by a codification of the changes in the form of a constitutional law (1978).

The comprehensive programme was entitled *Further Development of the Czechoslovak Education System* (*Další rozvoj...*, 1976) and it was supposed to ensure democratization in the school system and to bring about innovations in in accordance with the educational demands in the socialist society. At the same time, the programme created a basis for the legislative changes that took place in 1978. In June 1978, the Act on Measures in the System of Primary and Secondary Schools] (No. 63/1978 Coll.) was published, and it extended the compulsory schooling to 10 years and to secondary school. Completion of the eight-year primary school,[9] newly mandated by law, did not constitute the end of compulsory schooling; students still had to complete 2 years of secondary school. Primary school consisted of a first stage encompassing the first to fourth grade and a second stage encompassing fifth to eighth grade. This level of school was intended to provide the basics of general polytechnic education and to prepare students for further studies.

The definition of primary school in this law is rather interesting. It is clear in which areas the school was to be the mainstay of the regime. Section 4.2 states that primary school 'provides for intellectual education, education towards a scientific world view, political education, education towards socialist patriotism and proletarian internationalism, moral, labour, aesthetic, physical, and defence education of students.'[10] The Act also refers to nine-year primary schools at which nine-year compulsory schooling was in force. This gradually ended and was finally abolished in 1984.

The 1978 Act also mentions an educational counselling service in institutions, which was to provide schools, students, and parents with advice on issues related to the raising and education of children and young people as well as on the choice of further educational careers. The Act presumed cooperation between primary schools and the Pioneer Organization (Pionýrská organizace). This organization was an important assistant in the ideological education of students, as it was particularly

---

[9] For example, the benefits of shortening the first stage of primary school had already been verified by research in the first half of the 1970s and therefore it was not a purely politically motivated change, as it had been in Czechoslovakia in the 1950s.

[10] At the same time, this citation is also an example of contemporary (formal) language. For example a passage speaks of education towards a scientific worldview, of political education, and especially of education towards socialist patriotism and proletarian internationalism. Practically the same phrases can be found in various contexts, almost 'obligatorily' in many, if not all, legislative documents, books, and studies on education from the period of normalization (more examples are included in this chapter). In most cases these are just phrases. As the Russian-American anthropologist Alexei Yurchak writes, ideological language had only a performative function in the period of late socialism—it did not carry real meaning and had to be used mechanically to maintain the status quo (Yurchak, 2006).

involved in education outside of the classroom. Membership was not explicitly compulsory. However, it was formally important because it was included in the recommendations for secondary schools and universities. Such recommendations were written by the schools (homeroom teachers) for each student. Non-membership could be a problem, because it could give the impression of a lack of support for the communist government and thus cause the status of inadvisability to further studies.

Act No. 29/1984 Coll. On the System of Primary and Secondary Schools, in force from September 1984, was the last law in the period of socialist school. This Act retained the ten-year compulsory schooling, and the structure of the eight-year primary school remained unchanged as well. According to Sect. 4.3, Czech or Slovak was the language of instruction. For the first time since 1945, citizens of German nationality were listed among the nationalities entitled to being taught in their native language. The Act belatedly responded to trends in developed countries that had introduced similar changes in previous decades. For example, in primary and secondary schools, conditions for the development of exceptionally gifted students were to be created. Classes or schools with extended teaching of certain subjects (e.g. foreign languages, mathematics) could be established, and the Act also allowed exceptionally gifted students to finish primary school earlier than in 8 years.[11]

There were also changes in the training of future pedagogues. Even though the system of pedagogical education survived the turbulent period of the Prague Spring and the beginnings of the normalization process, with future teachers being prepared for their profession primarily at the pedagogical faculties, the normalization period saw significant changes in the content of this education towards the strengthening of socialist ideals. During the Prague Spring (and for several years before it), socialist ideas were being pushed aside to make space for dealing with professional pedagogical issues. According to the Resolution of the Fourteenth Congress of the KSČ in 1971, the young generation was supposed to be prepared for life in compliance with the programme of socialist development, in the spirit of the Marxist-Leninist worldview, socialist ethics, socialist patriotism, and proletarian internationalism (Rezoluce…, 1971). Candidates for the teaching profession were thoroughly vetted professionally and in terms of their political beliefs, family background, etc. Their activities were checked and evaluated regularly. The KSČ characterized teachers as public political workers, actively promoting the policies of the KSČ (Further Development, 1976). Teachers even committed themselves to this duty by taking an oath: 'I promise to always work in the interest of the working class and to implement the policy of the Communist Party of Czechoslovakia […] I will, according to the principles of communist education, cultivate in students […] love for the socialist homeland […] educate in the spirit of the Marxist-Leninist worldview' (Code of practice…, 1985). Teachers were supposed to fulfil the demands of the ruling party within their education practice and also in their personal private life

---

[11] In our book, we focus on state primary education. The issue of unofficial forms of education before 1989 (e.g. within the framework of dissent) is beyond the scope of this book. This topic is dealt with e.g. by Kudláčová (2023).

through their attitudes and actions or their participation in the public life of society (ibid).[12] In some situations, the signing of this oath was used as means of coercing the teachers, because in the event of any disobedience to orders or attempts to 'do something differently', the teacher was reminded that they had signed 'something'. Teachers' fear of losing their jobs stemmed from this as well (Zounek et al., 2016).

The normalization powers were also concerned with the students of pedagogical faculties who studied at the end of the 1960s. These were graduates from the period of the Prague Spring, whose final exams did not have to include questions on Marxism-Leninism, for example. Therefore, these graduates were to be under the constant supervision of school authorities who particularly monitored their political development.[13]

Participation in the 'Ideological Political Teacher Education' was a common part of the everyday life of teachers and school heads during the period of normalization.[14] As the following remark by a former teacher shows, this training concerned all teachers, both members and non-members of the KSČ: 'All of us teachers had to go there, for party education. Ordinary teachers!' (Zounek et al., 2017a, p. 93).[15] Our interviewees reported that the Ideological Political Teacher Education was organized by teachers/KSČ members who worked in the schools: 'It was everywhere, in all the schools. It just came from the top... they didn't call special lecturers for it; these were party members from the school who just prepared some of the topics, but I don't know what was there anymore and we had to take some tests at the end of it, so they tested us' (Zounek et al., 2017a, p. 93). The activity of the 'lecturers' consisted of ideological work in the form of speeches[16] and also of verification in the form of a final assessment of the listeners' knowledge. The training

---

[12] We focus on the teachers' non-working lives in more detail in the next part of this chapter.

[13] Fond B 338, Department of Education of the South Moravian Regional National Committee (1971). *Principles for the Work of Schools and Education Institutions of the South Moravian Regional National Committee for the 1971/72 School Year*. Moravian Land Archive, Brno.

[14] For leading workers or 'cadre reserves', it was even compulsory to complete the 'Evening University of Marxism-Leninism'. This was organised by the KSČ committees outside of school (Hradecká & Koudelka, 1998).

[15] In this part, we supplement the text with citations from interviews with teachers from a book previously published in Czech: Zounek, J. Šimáně, M., & Knotová, D. (2017a). *Normální život v nenormální době. Základní školy a jejich učitelé (nejen) v období normalizace* [Normal Life in Not So Normal Times. Primary Schools and Their Teachers (not only) During the Normalization Period]. Wolters Kluwer. Oral history interviews with teachers were focused mainly on primary schools and the school system in Czechoslovakia in the 1969–1989 period. By contrast, the interviews that form the bases of the other chapters of this book focused mainly on the post-socialist transformation of schools.

[16] The form of such political trainings in the South Moravian Region was recorded, for example, in the *Draft Supplement to the Guidelines on the Ideological and Political Training of Teachers and Other Educational Workers in the 1979/1980 School Year*. The individual seminars focused, for example, on the contemporary issues of the development of Czechoslovak socialist society, the basics of Marxism-Leninism, the party's economic policy, and the basic issues of the worldview education. Fond B 338, South Moravian Regional National Committe Brno (1980). Moravian Provincial Archives.

sessions might have caused some anxiety in the teachers about the consequences of failure at the final assessment. However, the teachers' recollections provide a different picture. For example, as one narrator laughingly described: 'We had compulsory training, … every month, it was scheduled… and at the end of that school year, there were… these exams… but of course we hardly knew any of it' (Zounek et al., 2017a, p. 94). The amusement with which the narrator recalled these situations suggests that for many, it was a matter of meeting formal requirements without any personal engagement. This was on the part of the audience and, presumably, also on the part of the lecturers. This was suggested by another narrator's recollections focused on the course of these training sessions: 'Every Monday, we had to have some kind of political training. Or not really every Monday, (…) once every three weeks. Now everybody had to prepare some of the gibberish that we had to give a lecture about… I don't know, Marxism, Leninism, what we studied in school. And everybody had to make a contribution. Nobody liked it, nobody was listening, the staff room was full, but we always had to come forward and say something like that.' Another former primary school teacher told a similar story: 'We used to spend most of the time, when no one from the administration was there, correcting the notebooks' (Zounek et al., 2017a, p. 94). Other teachers (including KSČ members) read, crocheted, knitted, or even slept during these training sessions. For our interviewees, the trainings and the ideological proclamations of the lecturers were hollow, uninteresting, and perceived as a necessary evil to be endured. It is not surprising, then, that they created space for their own activities during these training sessions.

Interestingly, the KSČ leadership was well aware of this reality. In fact, it responded to the situation regarding the political education of teachers in one of its documents. In this document, it admitted that 'the system of further teacher education lacks a more coordinated management, concentration on the main forms of study, and a relationship to other actions carried out mainly along the lines of the party and the trade unions. There are also shortcomings in direct political work with teachers and in cadre and staffing work'.[17] Steps to remedy the situation were also included in the text: 'In the political work, deeper and more systematic interest in working with teachers on the part of higher state and party authorities would be particularly desirable, and in lower authorities, the same applies to a more frequent personal contact with teachers' (ibid). Even greater and closer cooperation between teachers and representatives of party authorities was supposed to be the solution to this problem. However, the emphasis on political education gradually declined during the 1980s. According to Kohnová (1999), the ideological component of education was gradually pushed into the background at the expense of addressing the professional and methodological aspects of teacher education for the needs of the school.

---

[17] Fond Ideological Commission of the ÚV KSČ 1969–1971 (1971). *The 1971 Report on the Development, Problems and Prospects of Czechoslovak Education*. National Archives of the Czech Republic, p. 22.

4.3   A Look Inside a Socialist Teacher's Workshop

Before 1989, there was a unified school system in Czechoslovakia. Schools and the school system were centrally managed, and virtually everything was uniform and planned in detail. The everyday life of the schools and the work of the teachers corresponded to this. The recollections of one of the teachers clearly illustrated this: 'The school administration drew up a framework plan, the subject departments[18] were given tasks which they incorporated into their plans. The plans were drawn up by the month. Great care was taken to fulfil the curricula, which were unified, because the schools were unified, the textbooks were unified' (Zounek et al., 2017a, p. 96). The 'uniformity' is confirmed by the Further Development of the Czechoslovak Education System (1976) document, which stated that 'within the territory of the Czechoslovak Socialist Republic, schools of the same stage and specialization work according to unified curricula and unified syllabi and textbooks respecting national peculiarities' (p. 4).

Planning (together with unification) was one of the important characteristics of the socialist society and its economy. The 'five-year plans' (Žídek, 2019), within the frame of which the entire economy of the country was precisely organized, are particularly well-known.[19] However, these plans often did not correspond with reality or were based on decades-old methodologies. In such cases, the plans were then implemented only 'on paper' and it is clear that they were far from always being followed (Vykoukal et al., 2000). In terms of the implementation of plans, the school system was in a situation similar to that of other areas of the economy, as our narrator recalls: 'At every school, there were plans that had to be fulfilled, (…) then it was being cheated, we copied it, paraphrased it, because it was burdensome for us, because I would write down that on the twentieth of September I would be done with reviewing, and if something came up, I didn't make it' (Zounek et al., 2017a, p. 96). It is clear from the citation that curricula were planned exactly by the lesson and teachers had to follow these plans. This made any 'official' improvisation or modification of the curriculum with regard to the specifics of a particular class virtually impossible. However, the citation also suggests that teachers circumvented the non-functioning plans in order to tailor teaching to the realities of the given class (although the options were very limited). Admittedly, such teacher practices cannot be generalized based solely on our research. Naturally, it can be assumed that many teachers were comfortable with the exact plans, as they did not have to take any

---

[18] The subject departments at schools brought together teachers of the same or related subjects (e.g. sciences, languages, etc.) who cooperated in the methodology and didactics of teaching, coordinating their activities in the pedagogical and educational fields.

[19] A five-year plan was an economic plan of the centrally planned economy over a five-year period, first introduced in the Soviet Union and then used in other Eastern bloc countries as well. The planned economy was introduced in Czechoslovakia after World War II. For the KSČ, the introduction of five-year plans was an absolutely essential element of the new order. The state propaganda claimed that the five-year plans were the best for increasing living standards and the efficiency of the economy. However, this planning was in fact inflexible and inefficient.

personal initiative and just followed the plan. However, the quality of such teaching is questionable.

Quite predictably, interviews with teachers revealed that some parts of the teacher's job are important all the time, regardless of the historical, social, or political context in which they take place. Lesson planning proved to be such a part. This topic resonated strongly in many of the interviews, with former teachers talking about how the lesson planning was quite a demanding activity, especially for novice teachers. After a certain period of time, more experienced teachers did not plan their lessons as thoroughly or in as much detail, and reused previously prepared plans and materials repeatedly, even several years in a row. Such practices were kept by experienced teachers, but also by those who did not care very much about the pedagogical and didactic issues of lesson planning and just routinely taught the same content every year, and even at the same time (as prescribed by the plan). Other respondents innovated their lesson plans continuously: 'Well, so I prepared every day because I couldn't imagine using the plan from last year. I just consider every class is different, every year you progress to some place, so I could never reuse the same plan in my life' (Zounek et al., 2017a, p. 97). The teachers' recollections suggest that they had some freedom in this area and thus could work according to their pedagogical beliefs. However, we have to realize at this point that in many areas, new knowledge was slow or more or less delayed in entering the teaching in the countries 'behind the Iron Curtain' because of their isolation from the Western world and the 'Western' science of the time. So, from this point of view, the lesson plans could indeed have remained more or less up-to-date for several years.

However, the content of the lesson plan was important. Here, the situation could have been somewhat different. Contemporary didactics textbooks (e.g. Hladílek, 1984) contain quite detailed descriptions of what the teacher had to think about during the lesson planning and what the plan depended on (among other things, it mentions the teacher's experience or the specifics of the subject), as well as recommendations on specific elements the plan should contain. The date, the topic and objective of the lesson, the structure of the lesson and the methodological procedure, the aids, the educational elements, and the testing were considered important elements. In many ways, these are still appropriate recommendations for teachers. However, in a school during normalization, an educational objective was virtually synonymous with a political objective. This was aptly described by a former teacher: 'Every plan had to include—an educational goal, or rather a political goal, something to educate towards. Imagine the equations in mathematics... I don't know, I always wondered about that... You can't imagine, it was a nuisance. But it wasn't the school head pestering us, he did not invent it, it was a general one, general atmosphere that everything had to go as ordered. I, we always said to ourselves: the party [meaning the KSČ—authors' note] must check on us even during our lesson planning' (Zounek et al., 2017a, p. 98). Other narrators recalled that they fulfilled the political goal in mathematics by calculating the number of tanks in the socialist bloc, etc. in mathematic exercises.

The checking of lesson plans, with the eyewitnesses mentioning various experiences, was one of the important themes in the interviews. The recollections show that the plans were mainly checked by the school head: 'At that time, it was a duty. The school head would call, it was not a regular thing. But maybe once, twice a week, or in two weeks, he would call, "You, you, you, bring the plans," So, so we would bring the plans there' (Zounek et al., 2017a, p. 98). In addition, the school heads could check the plans for the current lesson as well as the plans for previous lessons. However, the novice teachers were by no means the only ones checked. For example, a 'less than great' lesson during a previous classroom observation could be a reason for checking the plans of experienced teachers.[20] The school head would call the teacher after a short period of time to see if and what lesson planning had been made for that day. This was far from always being an inspection of the ideological aspect of the plans; the motive for the inspection could be the quality of teaching.

The inspections were often very detailed, especially those by the school inspection. it was checking in terms of whether the actual lesson plan contained all the prescribed points and whether the teacher actually followed them in instruction: 'They compared what you taught and what you had written. Sometimes I had a plan that was worthless, and they praised me and did not even want to see the plan' (Zounek et al., 2017a, p. 99). It is clear from the excerpt that the individual inspector mattered, and probably other factors also influenced the final teacher score. Probably the same exact rules and criteria were not always followed even in this case. However, if the inspection found a problem, it reproached the teacher and informed the school administration of the discovered problems. The school administration drew conclusions from such findings and discussed them with the individual teachers, which could sometimes be quite unpleasant. Memories of inspections in socialist schools vary. At the same time, the inspectors could be far from being incompetent persons who frightened teachers. Some of our narrators recalled inspectors who, while sharing the 'party line', were otherwise experts in their field and did their best to help the schools and teachers. This did not mean that they were not strict or afraid to point out mistakes. It cannot be unequivocally said that 'socialist' inspection was always only a necessary 'evil'.

4.4   Aids and Textbooks in a Socialist School

Aids and textbooks are an important topic in the work of teachers because they co-shape teaching and have a significant influence on its course and on student learning and results. This is probably also the reason this topic arose quite often in our interviews. Uniformity was characteristic for this field as well, as one former teacher put it: '(…) the textbooks were of one type, nationwide, no selection, so we would teach by the same textbooks' (Zounek et al., 2017a, p. 100). The problems of textbooks

---

[20] Classroom observation is a visit to a lesson in order to determine the state and quality of the teaching. It is carried out by school inspectors and school heads for inspection purposes.

and other school supplies was defined in detail in the early 1970s by the *Directive on the Free Provision of Textbooks and School Supplies* (Směrnice…, 1972), which contained a description of the scope of the provision of free textbooks and school supplies, in other words, what textbooks would be provided free of charge and to which students. The period of use of some textbooks was also defined. For example, at the first stage of primary school, the selected textbooks were to have a shelf life of 4 years; the minimum period of use for textbooks at the second stage was set at 2 years. School supplies were to be ordered for the entire year, with the school head being responsible for purchasing. The National Committees that managed the schools then confirmed the order, paid for it, and arranged for delivery. There were precise financial limits on the purchase of school supplies. In addition, an average financial standard for school supplies per student per school year was determined and attached to the cited directive. According to our eyewitness, it was often not easy for schools to have enough money for everything they needed. Even some well-to-do schools could not afford to buy more expensive aids. From the point of view of official documents, the system did not allow for much 'creativity' or flexibility, but our narrators also related varied experiences in this respect.

The respondents Could be easily divided into two groups based on how equipped their school was. Some taught in a well-equipped school; others in a poorly equipped school. One of the respondents described a well-equipped school: 'Well there was quite a lot of the aids, we had the slide projectors, we had various maps, there was quite a lot of aids. I am not complaining' (Zounek et al., 2017a, p. 100). In their memories, former teachers sometimes compared the situation before and after 1989: 'No, we had the aids we needed, so we just like the school mostly bought us… if I had to make an aid, like write something on paper yeah, or a concentration game, yeah, we did that ourselves, of course. The kinds of concentration games like those that are now common in English or German, so that was not so common then, that's clear, no discussion' (Zounek et al., 2017a, p. 100–101). There are two interesting notes in the citation. Teachers in the well-equipped school also created aids themselves, even if they were only some minor or specific aids. The self-production of aids is another important topic related to the socialist school system and is a rather specific example of the creativity of the teachers. The creativity was motivated by the desire to improve their own teaching by creating didactic materials or aids 'tailored' to a given class, but also by the scarcity and very limited supply of aids. The second point mentioned in the citation is that the school purchased everything the teachers needed, if it was within the school's means. This is the difference between a well-equipped school and a poorly equipped school, judging by the respondents in our research. There may be many reasons for these differences. One narrator expressed a difference that could be called the human factor: 'Well, it depended on how clever the school head was, how he was able to just get the money, and once he got the money, he came in and said, "Well, what do you need? Write it down…." Well, I wrote down what I needed the most and he tried to just make sure that every teacher got a certain part, not that he would give one teacher all of it. So over the years, it worked out nicely' (Zounek et al., 2017a, p. 100). This suggests that even in the era of central planning, there were ways and means to equip schools well. The eyewitness did not mention whether this was possible because the school head was a KSČ member or if he had acquaintances in the 'right' places (and thus had unofficial advantages). The interviews show that in some cases, a partner industrial enterprise helped. However, in the interviews, some narrators captured another form of the 'human factor' that was typical of the socialist era: DIY ('do-it-yourself'). With the scarcity of many different goods and the low quality of many products, the DIY approach was one way for families to improve their house or flat or repair their car (for a more detailed account, see e.g. Mlčoch, 2014). The situation was similar in some schools: 'And we had a deputy school head there at that time, and he was handy, so he would make furniture, so he made school desks, so a classroom was made for chemistry, for biology, gas was installed, water was installed to that chemistry classroom, so we were kind of a model school at times' (Zounek et al., 2017a, p. 101). The deputy was apparently not able to make and equip entire classrooms 'at home', but this story can be seen as a good example of the school system at that time, when it was very difficult to get many different things (aids, furniture) and it was not possible to buy anything from abroad (except from socialist countries, in which case, of course, the quality of the products was often an low). Self-help was then sometimes the only solution to difficult situations (not only) in the field of school equipment.

Within our research, we cannot generalize in any way, but the narrators mentioned that schools in rural areas tended to be poorly equipped, as the following excerpt shows: '(…) an old village school, there weren't many aids, so what could you do? So no technology, no…, so chalk and blackboard. The best I could do was to do experiments in front of them, I mean, to demonstrate, and the kids basically just had a twelve-volt connection in one single desk so they could do circuits and so on. Well, we made do with what we had.' The same narrator went on to describe her experience quite eloquently in the interview: '(…) we were trying to get the aids, everything, with interest. But this was a lost era, a lost time' (Zounek et al., 2017a, p. 101–102). In some cases, practically the whole family helped with manufacturing aids. A former teacher described her approach in the following way: 'I did everything myself, and my husband helped me too, I didn't see it as a burden, I saw it as my job and I liked it' (Zounek et al., 2017a, p. 102). Thus, making aids became a part of family life. It is interesting to note the different assessments of the female respondents of our research, although both perceived making aids as part of their work and admitted interest. The first of the former teachers stated that it was 'lost time',[21] whereas the second did not perceive this activity as a burden. This shows how differently the contemporary reality of socialist education can be perceived in retrospect.

The acquisition or purchase of textbooks and teaching aids was another topic that emerged as important in the interviews. Although it was an era of central planning

---

[21] The narrator herself stated that she tried to get the aids with interest, yet it was lost time for her. This can be understood as her trying to improve her teaching as much as possible, but the effort and time spent could perhaps have been used in a different and more effective way. The term 'lost time' can be seen as a rather apt description of the life of a part of society at that time.

and unified curricula and textbooks, the experiences vary. All schools received textbooks free of charge according to the number of students. One narrator said: 'The advantage was that all that time the children had textbooks, supplies, everything for free. So the first graders, when they came to school, had their textbooks, crayons, watercolours, notebooks ready on their desks, well, so I think at that time, on one hand they were happy that they all had the same things, and on the other hand, the parents were happy that after all, a certain sum of money was saved' (Zounek et al., 2017a, p. 102). Aids, textbooks, and other teaching supplies could also be bought with prizes won by the schools in various competitions. According to the *Organizational Guidelines for Nine-Year Primary Schools* (Organizační směrnice…, 1972), it was also possible to sell products made during lessons in school workshops and produce from the school garden. The money raised could then be used by the schools, for example, to improve their (technical) equipment.

The quality of textbooks and teaching materials was a major issue in socialist education. We captured a variety of experiences and opinions in memories, but negative evaluations tended to prevail. The necessity for teachers to create their own aids might not have been due only to scarcity, but also to the quality of available materials or textbooks: 'The textbooks were crazy back in the day too. In the 80s… I can't tell you exactly. But it was such a mess just… That I just closed the textbook like that after about 2 months, and I said, I'm not going to teach according to that' (Zounek et al., 2017a, p. 103). Some teachers then used their own materials to teach, perhaps using only certain exercises or tasks from the textbook. The respondents described a lack of teaching aids and good quality textbooks even for the strongly preferred foreign language, Russian.

Far from all of our respondents were explicitly critical of textbooks. One former teacher described her experience as follows: 'The textbooks were perfect, because they were simple, friendly. And what extra work we did, we did also because there was actually a unified curriculum in the textbook. You're going to teach the kids this, this, and that in that year, we went through it, and we made aids on top of it and made the lessons more varied' (Zounek et al., 2017a, p. 103). Furthermore, the respondent noted in the interview that some textbooks of today are 'oversaturated with information'; moreover, today's students have many other available sources of information, and it is therefore very difficult to find time for other activities or to cope with the flood of information. Other eyewitnesses were satisfied with the textbooks and that is why they taught by them for up to 20 years, and these were the very same textbooks according to their own words. In this case, we can once again ask how much this was routine work and how much it was quality teaching. The question of the 'immutability' of textbooks that have been used in schools for such a long time is interesting. The timeliness of the information contained in the textbooks is related to this question. However, the research method we chose does not allow us to answer these or similar questions and these problems are beyond the scope of our research. In addition, regarding the textbooks, we can only conclude that the isolation of Czechoslovakia at that time created virtually no demand for regularly updated textbooks. Moreover, because of their own creativity, teachers supplemented many of the teaching materials themselves and thus 'updated' the textbooks in a way. The situation was all the more interesting after 1989, when the textbook market opened up and private and foreign publishers entered the market. For many teachers, the possibility and even necessity to choose a textbook represented a completely new and rather difficult problem.

The topic of classroom teaching itself is very important for the history of education, as it is at the heart of teachers' work, and the oral history method is probably the only way to gain a deeper insight into the processes of teaching during the period of normalization. The research has produced interesting results in this regard, but also certain 'disappointments' that can be considered one of the important methodological findings of our research. The interviews clearly showed that the course of everyday teaching was far from being one of the main themes, even though we directed some of our questions to instruction and the work of teachers. Our research thus reveals a weakness of data collection through interview. It is difficult to talk about the routine or the everydayness (Nosková, 2014). We believe this to be one of the main reasons this category is relatively under-saturated. The response of one former teacher to a question about teaching and its course may be indicative: 'Have you never taught?' The narrator was somewhat taken aback by a question about the teaching process; it was not obvious to her why the researcher was asking such an obvious question. The fact that many respondents had been retired for a long time and the details of everyday practice are just one of many topics in the back of their memories, in which specific elements and practices of teaching had lost their importance, may be another reason. The eyewitnesses who still teach today tended to talk more about the current teaching or to compare teaching in different periods: before 1989, in the 1990s, and now.

This is perhaps the reason suggested by one of our respondents in her interview: 'The teaching was, I would say, as it usually goes today, in the end it depended on the teachers, how many aids they had, in what way they taught. If there was no classroom observation by the school head, nobody would interfere and tell me what to do' (Zounek et al., 2017a, p. 104). Some eyewitnesses did not see anything special or fundamentally different about the topic and form of teaching during the normalization period in comparison to the current reality in schools (roughly the reality between 2015–2022, when the interviews took place), while the schools actually differed in many ways. The end of the citation in which the respondent mentioned a certain form of autonomy in instruction is interesting for us as the eyewitnesses described to us in what detail everything was planned and checked. However, the formality of complying with some regulations was also mentioned in the interviews. The sentence: 'If there was no classroom observation by the school head, nobody would interfere and tell me what to do' can lead back to a reflection on the formality of many regulations, but also on the fact that the everyday reality in the classroom was not and could not be managed according to a uniform model or unified in detail. It is necessary to take into consideration that the differences between schools may have been quite large.

In the interviews, many narrators mentioned the traditional structure of the lesson, which began with repetition, then followed with testing and/or an explanation of new subject matter and a possible application of the new knowledge or a repetition of the new knowledge. Unsurprisingly, the eyewitnesses described different approaches to lessons in different subjects; history and Czech differed from mathematics and physics lessons. Many eyewitnesses mentioned motivation in their interviews, as the teacher tried to get the students interested in learning, not only to make them enjoy learning, but to make her enjoy it as well. One respondent assessed the situation of the time in a very interesting way: '(…) students' independent work was not encouraged, students' creative work was not encouraged, they were not encouraged to participate in the explanation of the material; at that time, the teachers were just starting to learn to do this' (Zounek et al., 2017a, p. 106). The 1960 document *The Concept of the Nine-Year Primary School and the Curriculum of This School* asserted that 'the education of active, creative people is the aim of communist education' (*Pojetí…*, 1960, p. 4), and therefore, methods and forms of work that encouraged and developed students' activeness were to be applied. Sixteen years later, the document *Further Development of the Czechoslovak Education System* (1976) stated that 'in contrast to the previous traditional teaching, focused on verbal acquisition and mechanical reproduction of the subject matter, the focus of the education work of the primary school lies in the continuous development of students' activity and creativity' (p. 32). On the one hand, there are official documents, precise planning and checking, and the formality of many regulations; on the other hand, there is the reality, which is described very diversely by the eyewitnesses. From the relative autonomy in lessons and the traditional structure of the lesson to the need for motivation and to the observation that the promotion of creativity was still being learned by the teachers.

Assessment and grading are integral and important parts of teaching. The eyewitnesses used a variety of methods, from assessing student activity in class to tests and examinations and to final exams and essays. One respondent described an elaborate system that connected lesson planning to an overview of individual student grades: 'In addition, I used to write who to test and then the resulting grade in the lesson planning notebook. So it didn't happen to me that I had some grades in my notebook and I wouldn't know if they were from six months ago or from a month ago. I would flip through my notebook, and I would know I needed to test that student because he was only tested once and he wasn't tested recently, from the new material' (Zounek et al., 2017a, p. 106). It is necessary to reiterate that the respondent experiences are purely individual. Some recalled having as many as forty or forty-two students in their classroom, which is evidence of overcrowded classrooms. This state of affairs probably prevented innovations in teaching and forced the teachers to stick to a routine structure. Frontal teaching or mass testing of knowledge was probably an effective solution to the given situation.

Former teachers recalled the meeting day, which was Monday, and they also talked about how long each meeting lasted and how much time meetings and conferences generally took up. The number and length of meetings may have depended on how active the school and its teachers were. Such a working day often ended after seven o'clock in the evening. 'The meetings were gruelling because of the different characters of the meetings (…). Those meetings were not for an hour or two, but they were maybe for five hours. I really remember going home at maybe seven,

seven-thirty in the evening' (Zounek et al., 2017a, p. 108). The eyewitnesses did not question the importance of some meetings for the school operation, such as grading meetings or regular 'operational' meetings.

The document *Instructions to Organizational Guidelines for Nine-Year Primary Schools* (1972) is quite clear about the planning and organization of the meetings of the pedagogical board. These meetings were to be held no more than six times during the school year. The first meeting was to be concerned with the organization of the new school year, the other four meetings were to deal with the assessment and grading of students. At the meetings of the pedagogical board, the participants could additionally discuss serious questions regarding the educational work both in and out of school, issues regarding student health, and measures to improve the pedagogical and methodological work of the school. The meetings were convened by the school head and were not supposed to take more than 3 h. The document stated that administrative and economic problems regarding the school's operation were to be discussed at operational meetings, not at the pedagogical board meetings.

The 'public meetings of the KSČ', which were organized in municipalities and in schools and which were compulsory for all members of the teaching staff, i.e. not only for KSČ members, can be regarded as a kind of symbol of socialist Czechoslovakia. A young teacher at the time, Břetislav (a party member), 'hit the wall' in an interesting manner: '(…) me as a young guy, uninformed as to what can and cannot be said, then you would say something, so almost from that leadership you were like "and tomorrow you will be disciplined, because you are not supposed to say this, that, or the other…" Simply put, at that time, it was restricted, like what could be said, what could not be said, what we could say here. That was just a time when even in our family, and I think in most families, you would speak differently than you would speak at work' (Zounek et al., 2017a, p. 110). Here, the eyewitness aptly described the situation at school party meetings, as well as the 'double morality' (speaking differently at home and in public) that was one of the distinctive characteristics of normalization (Kluchert & Gruner, 2001). It is worth mentioning that even KSČ members had to be careful to keep their questions and opinions inside the defined field of permissible discussion topics.

As part of our research, we asked about a typical day at school. Unfortunately, we did not gain much insight into this topic from the interviews, only snippets or partial information. However, one eyewitness described an interesting daily routine: '(…) there was really already a sort of a routine of being ready for hallway duty at 7:15 a.m. What I didn't like was that the school didn't really open until 7:45 a.m. We as teachers were allowed to enter earlier, but the kids who came early had to stand outside, and that bothered me even then. The other thing is that there was a strict regime, they changed into slippers, the janitor checked it, there wasn't that much freedom for the kids to run to school and to talk in the locker room or run together in the hallway for a while or something. There was hallway duty and everybody had to go to class. It was a bit like, you can't say 'military regime', but some kind of regime in a Pioneer camp… We had to, even if we started teaching at nine, we had to get to school at eight o'clock, that's a given, because if someone was absent, they would need a substitute' (Zounek et al., 2017a, p. 111). There was a fairly precise guideline for the organization of the normal school day, which provides a general insight into the prescribed organization of the normal day. *The Instructions to Organizational Guidelines for Nine-Year Primary Schools* (1972) sets out the 'principles of the pedagogical and hygienic regime'. According to the document, classes began between 7:45 and 8:15 a.m., depending on local conditions, and the lunch break could not be shorter than 60 minutes. Afternoon classes had to end at 6 p.m. at the latest. Probably the most interesting piece of information concerned Wednesday afternoon, which was to be used for rest; therefore, no afternoon classes were to be scheduled for that afternoon and teachers were not to assign homework. However, the eyewitnesses did not mention this regulation at all in the interviews.

4.5 Teachers' Life Outside Work, or Teachers Shall Not Live by School Alone

Teachers' life outside work, including how they spent their free time, reflected the social and economic development in post-war Czechoslovakia. Our narrators were a homogeneous group in terms of their profession. However, in terms of the period in which they studied and worked, they represent two groups that differ mainly in their emphasis on active life and social engagement, as reflected in their private worlds outside of work. The first group consists of the oldest narrators who began their professional careers in the 1950s, and the second group consists of teachers entering practice in the following decades. In this section, we somewhat interrupt the line of our explanation by following the theme of teachers' lives outside of work from the 1950s onwards. We briefly describe the contemporary context and the major political and economic changes since 1948.

The everyday life outside of school and the living conditions of teachers were fundamentally affected by the gradual approximation of Czechoslovakia to the Soviet Union as the great role model. The communist party had announced the first five-year plan in 1949 (1949–1953). The plan focused on arms and heavy and mining industries, the collectivization of agriculture began, and political processes were set in motion (Kalinová, 2007; Kaplan, 2004; Kaplan & Paleček, 2008; McDermott, 2015). All of these events affected the lives of our narrators. For example, Jiřina recalled: 'My husband (…) was my college sweetheart; when he was a student, he was in some resistance collective, he was locked up for 4 years as a political prisoner, but I married him anyway.' Interestingly, this fact did not translate into her later professional life. Moreover, the narrator did not emphasize her husband's imprisonment in her subsequent account of her professional career in any way.

The preference for industries, especially in the 1950s, brought feminization to the school system. Teaching became a typically female profession (Václavíková-Helšusová, 2007). Men left for more physically demanding professions in industry, which were also better paid than the profession of a teacher. Although the communist government advocated a policy of economic egalitarianism and the differences in salaries were small, the 'blue-collar professions' had more favourable salary conditions. 'Moving to a position in the lower management of a company meant a decrease in salary for a skilled blue-collar worker' (Knapík & Franc, 2011, p. 24). The salary conditions set in such a way greatly promoted feminization of some fields. It is clear from the respondents' recollections that women teachers' earnings constituted a smaller part of the family budget. If both spouses were teachers in the families of our narrators, they tended to belong to families with a lower living standard. This affected the opportunities for private activities and the amount and the ways of spending free time.

Apart from the relatively low salary, some of our respondents recalled another significant phenomenon accompanying the everyday life in their memories—a noticeable lack of consumer goods. 'There was nothing, nothing available at all, everything was given against vouchers (…) you had to wait, for example, they were supposed to deliver goods to the shoe store, so we waited there—my mother, my sister, and I—and everyone got, got some shoes, yes, but nobody asked what size they were. Then people exchanged them amongst themselves, so I got shoes, I don't know, men's forty-two (…), it was really hard, there was nothing at all' (Zounek et al., 2017a, p. 114). The lack of consumer goods can be considered a characteristic of the 1950s and early 1960s. The unrealistic third five-year plan, in the first half of the 1960s, made the economic situation even more problematic. It resulted in serious problems in energy and many other sectors of Czechoslovak industry. All of this also led to supply shortages. Many basic daily consumer goods were in short supply, such as consumer electronics, household appliances, and cars. The quality of goods was also very problematic (Kalinová, 2007).

Despite these economic difficulties, there was a general increase in the living standard during the 1960s. Everyday life was impacted by many restrictions, but some social 'certainties' were guaranteed. These included work and remuneration for it, the possibility of obtaining free company or state housing, and the provision of interest-free loans (Knapík & Franc, 2011). Teacher salaries also rose. More housing construction began and infrastructure and both public and individual transport was developing.

The issue of housing was one of the most prominent themes in our respondents' narratives in relation to their out-of-work life. Young teachers did not have enough money to afford their own housing and, moreover, flats were scarce. Even though they could get a municipal (state) flat free of charge, the quality could be very poor (dampness, leaking roofs, mice infestation, etc.).

However, in the following decades, housing construction brought a much higher quality of accommodation than in the previous period (Hubatová-Vacková & Říha, 2018). One of the narrators recalled moving to a new flat that had been built for teachers in the village: 'There were two semi-detached houses, so we moved into the one, it was a very nice flat, big, sunny, at the end of the village, big living room, big bedroom, kitchen, hall, bathroom, cellars, laundry room, garden, front garden. It was a very nice flat, really' (Zounek et al., 2017a, p. 115).

The issue of housing was also connected with transportation to work. A number of our respondents mentioned in their recollections that it was not uncommon for them to have a complicated daily commute to schools from their homes. Mass transport was not yet properly developed or very frequent, and teachers did not have cars. Therefore, they often had to walk to work. This problem persisted over several postwar decades. Transportation to schools in rural areas in particular was very difficult. The situation was particularly difficult for those teachers who already had children of their own. The following recollection may serve as proof: 'In the morning, I had to take the bus and the tram and there I dropped her off (daughter at the nursery— authors' note), then I took the trolleybus (…) there I changed to the bus and vice versa again in the afternoon. So it was terribly complicated' (Zounek et al., 2017a, p. 116).

Thus, our respondents' recollections show that in addition to their pedagogical duties, teachers had to deal with a number of issues outside of work that affected their lives (the aforementioned housing issues, problems with commuting to work and the connected commute time). It was not until the late 1960s and early 1970s that some improvements occurred in a number of pressing issues. Seemingly paradoxically, this occurred during a new round of consolidation of the socialist regime; this was part of the politics. A resignation to participation in public life, a resignation to questions regarding the observance of human rights, etc. was the payment for social certainties.

Teachers were required to be socially and politically engaged. This requirement manifested itself as it did for other citizens: for example, as pressure to participate in May Day parades and to have memberships in various organizations or directly in the KSČ, which was often a precondition for career advancement.

Many teachers became important youth movement organizers, founding and leading clubs of various organizations, such as the Czechoslovak Youth Union (Československý svaz mládeže) and/or Pioneers. In this context, it is interesting to note that many of our eyewitnesses carried out these activities with enthusiasm. Many were happy to participate in various forms of collective life, regardless of their experience with the communist regime. Even though some sources pointed out that the notion of spontaneous enthusiasm for Pioneers was an illusion (e.g. Knapík & Franc, 2011), in the recollections of our narrators it is hardly described thus. One narrator represents a typical young teacher of this decade: 'I really wanted to, I was already doing something in the union organization at that time (…), I helped to lead a Pioneer group. Well, I liked working with children' (Zounek et al., 2017a, p. 117).

The Pioneer organization was another element of the ideological education of the emerging socialist generation, which was not to be burdened by the 'legacy of capitalism'. 'Thus the work of the Pioneer organization and the schools complement each other and form a single process of socialist education of pioneers and students' (Lebeda, 1956, p. 726). The aim was to educate a 'socialist man' who would be committed to the socialist motherland and have a socialist attitude to work. Education in a collective was the basic element of this effort. Young teachers became important promoters and organizers of this education. This activity was also organized during the holidays and the Pioneer leaders (often teachers) started to go to camps with the children. The camps thus ensured childcare and the organization of free time, especially during the summer holidays.

The concept of Pioneer work changed in the 1960s and was no longer primarily organized by the schools. However, local Pioneer groups remained in schools, and many of our narrators continued to lead them. One of them recalls: 'Well, since we didn't have children (…) I was at school from dawn till dusk. In the morning I taught, in the afternoon we had these Pioneers' (Zounek et al., 2017a, p. 118). Memories framed as 'I was a young teacher, I didn't have children yet' appeared in other interviews: young female teachers were willing to sacrifice their free time to school. Some added that when they had their own children, their attitude changed in this respect. Other teachers recalled that once their own children were a little older, they would bring them to various out-of-school events.

Teachers who started teaching in the early 1970s recalled that it also was a duty of theirs to lead Pioneer organizations. This was due to an acute shortage of leaders. Because of the political events of 1968–1969, the Czechoslovak Youth organization and Pioneer were abolished. Instead, a new structure of a single youth organization controlled by the KSČ was established. Once again, the Communists exercised supervision and centralization of the leisure and interest activities of the young people. Thus, the Socialist Youth Union (Socialistický svaz mládeže) was newly established and the Pioneer Organization became a part of it. The aim was to create a mass organization. Pioneer groups were revived in primary schools. The Pioneer Organization had the maximum political and material support, and a network of professional (paid) group leaders was gradually built up. In each school, the role of group leaders primarily fell to the students of pedagogical fields of study. Therefore, teachers were no longer obliged to lead Pioneer groups in the 1980s. Some respondents remember the activities of the Pioneer organization in a good way and the contemporary ideology is completely absent from their recollections.

In addition to Pioneer groups, various interest clubs, once again led by teachers, also formed in schools. Apart from satisfying the interests of the children, these interest clubs were intended to influence the direction of their future careers. Teachers devoted their free time to these activities, very often even on weekends at the expense of the time they could spend with their families. The focuses of interest clubs kept transforming during the period of socialism. For example, Knapík (2014) stated that in the 1950s, technical, cultivation, and breeding clubs were mainly supported by the state authorities. In the following period, mainly technical, science, sports, and aesthetic-educational clubs or clubs focused on specific interests (e.g. photography, chess) operated in schools.

The accounts of our narrators show that they did not find the work connected to running the clubs bothersome. They took it as a standard addition to their work, and many enjoyed doing it. 'It was kind of a given that every one of those teachers would run some kind of a club… I didn't have to, but I could. I liked it' (Zounek et al., 2017a, p. 119). However, running the clubs was demanding in terms of time and organization. 'Mere' public recognition and respect for the results of the pedagogical work were often the only reward.

Individual work in temporary jobs, most often in agriculture (typically potato picking or beet thinning) was a common part of the social engagement of teachers and others. This form of social engagement was typical for the teachers during their pedagogical studies and it also became an integral part of their professional careers. The respondents recalled them with some enthusiasm: 'We really grew up with those temporary jobs… we were always going somewhere to help, but with such joy to get something done' (Zounek et al., 2017a, p. 120). The attitude of one teacher illustrated the real atmosphere. The social engagement was not only expected but necessary. There was a shortage of labour and the necessary mechanization in agriculture, especially in the 1950s. Teachers in rural areas had to take part in many temporary jobs that were not related to their profession. There was a shortage of workers in agriculture as a result of collectivization and teachers were still a welcome workforce in the first half of the 1960s. In many interviews, the narrators mentioned the youthful enthusiasm and passion for activities that helped develop the state and its economy. Many did not perceive the ideological or propaganda contexts at all.

The social engagement was also manifested in the fact that teachers actively supported diverse (municipal) cultural activities and organized activities of various kinds in the villages in which they taught. This could involve the founding and running of a traditional dances club in which teachers, parents, and students worked together. Teachers did these activities voluntarily, often initiating and preparing them themselves. The narrators were active and sociable people, and also young at the time, so they were probably satisfying a natural need for sharing and peer group experiences in this way. This is not to say that the older teachers did not participate in activities of this type.

In addition to these activities, a number of teachers were involved in various organizations in their non-working life, such as the Czechoslovak Red Cross, Svazarm,[22] the Women's Union, and the Union of Physical Education and Sport. This diverse range of teachers' social engagement activities reflects both the complicated period in which our eyewitnesses lived and their personal interests, which, given the limited possibilities and opportunities of the time, often could not be satisfied in any other way.

Free time is an important part of life today, and it was similarly significant for our eyewitnesses. It is a time in which the free choice of activities is important (Knotová, 2011). Non-utilitarian activities that liberate a person from routine or patterned habits are typical for such time. Free time is an area of life that complements work time and bound time (Dumazedier, 1966). For our narrators, the separation of these three domains was sometimes not clear. Many of their activities were liminal. That is, although they were performed in free time, they were also part of working time (i.e., for teachers, this concerns pedagogical work in non-work time). For our narrators, these were typically leading interest clubs, going to camps, and leading Pioneer groups. These activities were among the semi-voluntary activities that were partly based on a voluntary choice, but at the same time conditioned by a connection to the profession (Dumazedier, 1966). Semi-voluntary activities usually included caring

---

[22] Svazarm, a shortcut for Svaz pro spolupráci s armádou (Union for Cooperation with the Army), was a Czechoslovak conscription organization established in 1951 according to the Soviet model.

for the household, children, livestock, and garden (Duffková, 2003). Given the predominance of women in our sample of eyewitnesses, care for the children and household and housework were among their typical activities during nonworking hours. Regardless of gender, then, gardening and tending to the livestock were common and popular.

The narrators' typical workday usually started at school around 7.30 a.m. and ended usually between 2 and 3 p.m., followed by various socially engaged activities, then there was childcare and household chores, and the evening was often dedicated to preparation for school, including correcting tests. There was little free time. Families helped some of our narrators with their preparations for school in the evening. For example, they even made teaching aids together. Women in particular recall the time-consuming nature of the profession, which was a limiting factor for leisure activities and which also complicated care for children and household and housework.

Some of the eyewitnesses maintained very close relations with their parents, even though they had families of their own. Family was very important to them. Teachers coming from rural areas regularly helped their parents handle the household and the livestock on their days off. One of our narrators recounted: 'I packed up the children, did laundry, ironed, and we went to his family (the father's - authors' note). There he had fields, meadows, so we went to work.' Strong family relations were also confirmed by another narrator: 'I had parents, my husband had parents (…) and they had big gardens. So our Saturday and Sunday trips were there because we went to help them.' To a certain extent, this allowed families to self-supply with produce (fruits and vegetables) that were scarce on the market, or to raise funds in this way as well. A former teacher recalls these activities: 'We tended to do other things than just school, of course that includes the vineyard (…) and because there was not much money, as it were, so it was no problem to plant ten ares of cucumbers (…) because when we sold the cucumbers and for thirty crowns, there was a chicken, which was of course very welcome' (Zounek et al., 2017a, p. 120).

The free weekends and especially the holidays brought much more free time. However, many of the teachers' free days were spent at events with the children they led in interest clubs or Pioneers. These included participating in various competitions, performances, and races or leading camps. Some teachers volunteered to attend various educational courses during the holidays.

In the mid-1960s, some of our narrators were among the people who very much liked to travel abroad in their free time. The travel was made possible by the easing of the political climate and also by the development of public transport (trains, buses) and individual motoring. People would travel to other socialist bloc countries, most often to the Soviet Union, German Democratic Republic, and Hungary. People began to go on holiday to the warm seas in Yugoslavia, Bulgaria, and Romania. They did not travel with a travel agency, but typically travelled individually in their own cars. In addition to travelling to 'friendly socialist countries', there were also those among our teachers who managed to overcome the bureaucratic barriers that made it difficult to travel to 'capitalist foreign countries'.

However, travelling outside of socialist countries was very rare among our eye-witnesses, with typical travel opportunities described by one teacher: 'We asked for permission several times, for example, to go to Yugoslavia to the sea, because people would go (…). But it was no earlier than in '87 when I went to Yugoslavia back then, I got, I don't know what it was called, I guess an allowance, but when I asked I think ten times before that, I didn't get it' (Zounek et al., 2017a, p. 120).[23]

Many of our narrators living in cities were also among those who were 'struck' by the cottage and summer house culture. This trend was particularly visible after the 1970s. It was brought about by an increase in the standard of living; teachers had plenty of free time and sufficient financial resources. Problematic commuting was no longer an obstacle, as the traffic infrastructure and state-subsidised rail and bus services were sufficiently developed. Car ownership was also more common.

As Duffková (2003) added, the political framework in the period of normalization gave going to the cottage or summer house a specific subtext; it was difficult to interfere with the privacy of the cottage from the outside; people could replace the problematic lack of self-realization in their professions and occupations with self-fulfilling DIY and gardening at the cottage in their free time while also satisfying the need to own something of their own. The narrators emphasized the importance of stays at the cottage, which brought them a slowing down and relaxation in their hectic way of life and allowed them to be free from the demands of their profession. One of the former teachers illustrated this succinctly: 'We had a cottage and I was happy and I was always studying something, so I was tired, so I was happy at that cottage' (Zounek et al., 2017a, p. 125).

4.6   Perestroika and the Debate on School System Reforms

In the last part of this chapter, we shift again to the general history of Czechoslovakia and the school system in particular. The second half of the 1980s was the period just before the fall of the communist government in Czechoslovakia. This period was also important for developments after 1989. Efforts to change the school system and education were beginning to emerge, but the political and social context was still very complicated.

Cautious reforms of the school system were prepared and partially applied between 1987 and 1989, i.e. during the period of the 'specific Czechoslovak concept

---

[23] In socialist Czechoslovakia, devizový příslib (a foreign currency allowance) was a written permission to draw foreign currency necessary for travel to non-socialist countries (including Yugoslavia). However, this was not the only requirement for the actual travel to Western countries; in addition, a special official permit named výjezdní doložka (an exit permit) had to be issued. The foreign currency allowance was the only official possibility of exchange of a limited amount of Czechoslovak koruna for foreign currency. The exchange of currency was authorized by the State Bank of Czechoslovakia. During the period of normalization, the average waiting time for a foreign currency allowance for non-members of the KSČ could be several years.

of perestroika. These attempts were strongly restricted and limited by ideological dogmas. At the same time, they were accompanied by a disproportion in the political elites' perceptions of the form and scope of reforms. In particular, this concerned the presidium of the ÚV KSČ and the responsible people (party officials, representatives of the administration at the governmental and regional levels), who were directly confronted with the impact of the dysfunctional system on the economy and society (Pullmann, 2011).

On the ideological plane, the intended reforms were limited by the impassibility of the principle of a unified school, which formed an imaginary parallel in the field of education to the impassability of the *Lessons from the Crisis* mentioned above. This was because the KSČ government built its power on unchanging dogmas. The reform proposals also corresponded with the key objective of perestroika: the desire to streamline the state's economy and thus save money.

The need for reforms was also brought about by problems with implementation of the 1984 Education Act. Several analyses of the education system were produced during the 1980s for this reason (Walterová, 2004). The analysis created on the basis of the resolution of the ÚV KSČ on 26 February 1987 was the most visible. *Analysis of the Czechoslovak Education System* (hereafter referred to as the *Analysis*) was finalized in the spring of 1988, and (probably also due to glasnost) a broad public discussion followed. Despite the similarity of its structure, the publicly published version of the *Analysis* is much less critical than the original internal document from February 1988 intended for the government and the KSČ. By the end of July 1988, a total of 5764 comments had been received in the CSR and 2183 in the SSR from institutions and individuals.[24] The final material of the *Analysis* was a background document for the thirteenth session of the ÚV KSČ, held in March 1989 with the school system as its main topic.

The *Analysis* was highly critical of the Czech school system and listed basic ills not unlike those reflected after 1989: excessive bureaucracy, outdated school equipment, low salaries and declining prestige of teachers, overloading students with subject matter, outdated teaching methods, etc. (Z analýzy…, 1988). However, the reaction to the *Analysis* from the political authorities was contradictory, indicating that the document infringed on boundaries that were acceptable from the ideological point of view. The contradiction is indicated by the criticism that the document implies departmental closed-mindedness[25] (K materiálu…, 1990).

---

[24]Archive Fond of the Office of the Government of the SSR 1988–1992 (1988). *Report on the analysis of the Czechoslovak education system.* Slovak National Archives.

[25]By departmental closed-mindedness, it was meant that the *Analysis* did not reflect the problems of the school system in a broader perspective and clung too much to the department of education. The concept of departmentalism was used in other fields as well—it enriched the ideological language during the period of perestroika in Czechoslovakia to allow for criticism, but at the same time to exclude the KSČ government from criticism. The problems were the fault of the component, i.e. the department in which the problems occurred, not the socialist state as such (Pullmann, 2011).

The *Analysis* was referred to by the general assembly of the thirteenth session of the ÚV KSČ in March 1989, which was primarily concerned with the school system. While the background materials and the minutes of the talks accompanying this session do take into consideration the problems of the school system emphasised in the *Analysis*, at the same time, the *Analysis* itself is criticized. Opinions appeared in the internal materials stating that the report based on the *Analysis* was insufficiently political, that it should 'emphasize the issues of worldview education more sharply, demonstrate intransigence from the Leninist principles and strengthen the control of party organizations over the school system,'[26] or 'show the positive results after 1948 and elaborate on the leading role of the party.'[27]

The evaluation of the school system reflected the influence of the growth of discontent in society, which was often associated with young people, and not only in internal materials. In connection with a discussion with the General Secretary of the ÚV KSČ at a teachers' congress held in early September 1989, *Rudé Právo*[28] noted that young people often 'bring various distorted opinions to school—it is then up to the ability of the teacher to influence the youth appropriately' (Větší důvěru..., 1989, p. 2). No less criticism was directed at teachers. In the minutes of an internal talk from the period of the thirteenth session of the KSČ, the psychological instability of teachers, ineffective, incomplete educational actions, and the occurrence of physical punishment of students are mentioned. It was alleged that there were poor relations in the schools, and that school heads and school administrations did not support capable teachers, and, on the contrary, prevented them from advancing in their careers. An inventory of suggestions from discussions with teachers, intended for the highest party authorities, contained harsh criticism[29]:

> The teachers' level of preparedness and their attitude to work is reflected in the nature of the educational process (there is often little creativity, motivation to learn, friendly relationships with students, etc.). There are also non-collegial and suppressive tendencies in teaching staff and school heads aimed towards capable, well-educated, ambitious teachers (p. 29).

---

[26] Archive Fond of the Central Committee of the Communist Party of Slovakia's (ÚV KSS) Committee for Education, Culture and Art 1988–1989 (1989). *Minutes of the session of the Main Working Committee for the Preparation of the Session of the ÚV KSS on the School System—15 February 1989*. Slovak National Archives, p. 2–5.

[27] Archive Fond of the Central Committee of the Communist Party of Slovakia's Committee for Education, Culture and Art 1988–1989 (1989). *Minutes of the session of the Governing Committee for the Preparation of the Session of the ÚV KSS on the School system on 16 February 1989*. Slovak National Archives, p. 3–4.

[28] Red Justice was a daily newspaper and the central press authority of the KSČ, and an important part of party and government propaganda.

[29] Archive Fond of the Central Committee of the Communist Party of Slovakia's Committee for Education, Culture and Art 1988–1989 (1989). *Information on suggestions from discussions with members of the ÚV KSS and workers of the Department of Education and Science of the ÚV KSS with representatives of social practice on the ÚV KSS's session on the school system*. Slovak National Archives.

Further, the problems of the school system resulting from the lagging behind of the centrally planned economy as a whole were criticized, including the overburdening of school heads because of dysfunctional services and the unavailability of goods such as materials for school repairs, which thus had to be dealt with through self-help or personal contacts[30]; poor housing situations; low-quality social and health security; low teacher salaries (Větší důvěru…, 1989); and excessive parental corruption and protectionism (especially in relation to admissions). The previously cited archival material, *Information on Suggestions*, included criticism of widespread parental corruption:

> Many parents are convinced that in order for a child to get into secondary school and university, one must have connections, 'deep pockets'. Although they admit that not every child will get into a school through influence, they consider it necessary to 'insure' and 'arrange' the admission to the school (p. 12).

The unavailability of quality electronics was also criticized in connection to the school systems' computerization programme.[31] The functionality of the school system, even according to contemporary documents, was also limited by the inefficient, authoritarian, and autocratic approach of school unions and school heads and the low proportion of teachers in the administration (Účinné spojení…, 1989a).

Despite its apparent inability to free itself from ideological dogmas, the *Analysis* and its reflection on the party at governmental and professional levels also included a critique of the pedagogical work itself that resembled the post-1989 debates in many ways. Among the most pressing practical problems was the overloading of students with too much subject matter, which was also connected to the reduction of compulsory schooling in primary schools to eight years—a criticism of this approach once again appeared in the list of suggestions made by teachers:

> The orientation of schools and the knowledge and difficulty of the content of teaching causes the children to very soon lose interest in learning and the natural curiosity and joy with which they entered the primary school. How is it possible that in just a few years, the school drives children away and turns learning into something forced and embarrassing? (p. 16).

There was also criticism of the large number of students in classes and the widespread practice of shift teaching.[32] Teachers were burdened by the large amount

---

[30] Archive Fond of the Central Committee of the Communist Party of Slovakia's Committee for Education, Culture and Art 1988–1989 (1989). *Minutes of the session of the Main Working Committee for the Preparation of the Session of the ÚV KSS on the School System—15 February 1989*. Slovak National Archives.

[31] Archive Fond of the Office of the Government of the SSR 1988–1992 (1988). *Political report on the analysis of the Czechoslovak education system: second version: January 1988*. Slovak National Archives, p. 9.

[32] Archive Fond of the Office of the Government of the SSR 1988–1992 (1988). *Working version: Summary report on the analysis of the Czechoslovak education system*. Slovak National Archives. In the postwar period (until the 1970s, rarely until the late 1980s and early 1990s) there was a shortage of schools in some regions or cities, so some children had to attend the 'second shift' (in

of bureaucracy, mandatory meetings, report writing, and training that hindered quality lesson planning:

> The smooth work of schools is also disrupted by the frequent participation of teachers in
> various trainings, in tasks arising from various functions, in meetings and events organized
> not only by the school administration but also by social organizations (Účinné spojení…,
> 1989a, p. 3).

Despite its criticism, the *Analysis* was reflected in the conclusions of the thirteenth
session of the KSČ. It was also reflected in the instructions to individual party members, i.e. indirectly to the government, to the school system workers, and in the
subsequent measures proposed and partly implemented (ÚV KSČ, 1989). Among
the measures considered were those that were in line with decentralization. This can
be seen as one of the perestroika tools that were to lead to increased efficiency in the
economic sphere as well. First and foremost, the district level of administration,[33]
whose rigidity and directive character was widely criticized after 1989, was to be
strengthened (Kalous, 1993). At the same time, school heads were to be given more
powers. The influence of school heads on the filling of teaching posts, which had
hitherto been the mandate of the District National Committees was to be increased
(Účinné spojení…, 1989a). The school heads were to be given the opportunity to
make independent decisions in the secondary school admissions procedure, which
was thus to be streamlined and simplified (Usnesení…, 1989). The admission process to secondary schools and universities during the socialist period is usually
associated with a high emphasis on the reliability of applicants from the perspective
of class and the prevention of access to education to the children from politically
unreliable families. In fact, this possibility was embedded in the Education Act
itself, since it contained the phrase that students were admitted on the basis of a
vaguely defined 'compliance with the needs of socialist society'.[34] In the invitation
to the talks of the ministers of education in Brno in February 1988, a mention of
'new criteria for the application of the social-class perspective in admission to secondary schools and universities' appears without any detailed comment.[35] One can
only speculate on the degree to which the assessment of the political reliability of
applicants and their families was actually abandoned, or whether these were merely
cosmetic adjustments and formal declarations.

---

the afternoon), and in some cases even the third shift. During the day, up to three groups of children
would take turns in one classroom.

[33] Archive Fond of the Office of the Government of the SSR 1988–1992 (1989). *Draft of processed
conclusions of the thirteenth session of the ÚV KSČ by the Ministry of Education, Youth and Sports
of the Czechoslovak Republic.* Slovak National Archives.

[34] Archive Fond of the Office of the Government of the SSR 1981–1987 (1983). *Draft: Principles
of the Act on the system of primary and secondary schools /Education Act/.* Slovak National
Archives, p. 44.

[35] Archive Fond of the Office of the Government of the SSR 1988–1992 (1988). *Problems submitted for decision at the joint meeting of the leadership of both ministries of education in February
1988 in Brno.* Slovak National Archives, p. 2.

The streamlining concerned the entrance examinations as well as the educational process. According to the 1989/90 instructions, teachers and students were to be exempted from side activities and duties beyond education, and supervisors were to reduce the requirement for written reports. School heads were not to require written evaluations of teachers' own work, and meeting activities were to be rationalized and ineffective actions were to be reduced across the board (Účinné spojení…, 1989a; Usnesení…, 1989). This instruction was reflected in a draft of the amendment to the Education Act as well. It contained a section according to which all student and student participation in 'socially responsible work' was to be moved outside of teaching hours.[36] This measure became a subject of controversy during an interdepartmental amendment procedure, as the Ministry of Agriculture and Food of the CSR and CSSR and the Union of Cooperative Farmers of the CSR fundamentally disagreed with the proposal. The farmers predicted impending problems with securing a sufficient labour force, especially during the harvest, during which the students had been actively helping out within the compulsory organized temporary jobs, even in lieu of classes. Following criticism, it was incorporated into the Act that in exceptional cases, if all other options were exhausted and for a limited period of time, the government could grant an exemption.[37]

The introduction of verbal assessment of students in the first year of primary school in 1988 was among the pedagogical measures that were actually implemented. Specifically, according to this measure, students were not to be graded at all in the first half of the first year; at the end of the year, their performance was to be evaluated by teachers only verbally. In this verbal assessment, all the positive aspects of the student's personality were to be emphasized. This was so that the students were motivated by the teacher to learn and the evaluation itself did not discourage the students from continuing further schoolwork (Kopp, 1992; Pedagogicko-organizační opatření…, 1988).

In the guidelines following the thirteenth session of the ÚV KSČ, sub-objectives were also incorporated to respond to some ill-considered decisions of the previous years. For example, the strategy of closing down small schools was to be reconsidered[38] (Trnková, 2006; Usnesení…, 1989), a theme that resonated even in the post-Velvet Revolution period, and a number of 'small schools' were in fact eventually restored (Zprávy, Čerych, 1996).

In 1989, the process of drafting an amendment to Act 29/1984 Coll. on the system of primary and secondary schools (the Education Act) was under way, and a

---

[36] Archive Fond of the Office of the Government of the SSR 1988–1992 (1989). *Draft principles of the amendment to the Act amending and supplementing Act No. 29/1984 Coll. on the system of primary and secondary schools.* Slovak National Archives.

[37] Archive Fond of the Office of the Government of the SSR 1988–1992 (1989). *Minutes from the coordination meeting of ministers of education, youth and sports with the first deputy chairman of the government of the CSSR c. M. Lúčan, held on 16 August 1989.* Slovak National Archives.

[38] A small school is a school with a single class in which children of different ages (different grades) are educated together. In the environment of the Czech school system, these were mainly primary schools with the first stage (i.e. first-fourth grade).

long-term plan for the development of the school system up to 1995 and 2010 was to be drawn up. The Act on State Administration in the School System and the Act on Higher Education were also to be amended by 1990.[39] The amendment to the Education Act was discussed at the level of the republic governments and it underwent an interdepartmental amendment procedure. The federal government was supposed to discuss it in November 1989, but its submission was postponed because of the need for a deeper legal analysis.[40]

The Act introduced only partial modifications and it was intended as a precursor to more fundamental reforms, which were to be ready by 1995 and which were to lead to the establishment of a unified ten-year internally differentiated polytechnic school providing for the full range of compulsory schooling. However, the events of the 'great history' outstripped the amendment process of the Act and led to much more fundamental changes. On the other hand, other changes slowed the process, and the Act 29/1984 eventually remained in force, with many partial modifications, until 2004.

The attempt to streamline the compulsory schooling was the basic and most discussed matter of the draft amendment to the Education Act. This effort was a response to the criticism regarding the overloading of students with subject matter resulting from the *Analysis*, but also to the effort to address the current problems of the economy, and it had two alternative solutions. The victorious alternative allowed the ten-year compulsory schooling to be completed exclusively within primary school. An optional ninth grade followed by a one-year preparatory course was to be introduced so that the students would not have to enrol in secondary school or apply for early completion of compulsory schooling. It is clear that the desire to save on education costs was a key motivation for the proposed measures,[41] as the education at secondary school was more expensive than the education at primary school. It seemed more efficient to keep students in primary school for as long as possible while at the same time not prolong the education process as a whole, which would have been achieved by the general introduction of the ninth grade to the entire school system. This measure was intended to be a precursor to the aforementioned deeper reform of the school system.

The possibility of independent earning activities on part of schools was extended. Previously, schools could only carry out these activities for remuneration (and retain

---

[39] The intention was to introduce more stages of university education. Archive Fond of the Office of the Government of the SSR 1988–1992 (1989). *Draft of processed conclusions of the thirteenth session of the ÚV KSČ by the Ministry of Education, Youth and Sports of the Czechoslovak Republic.* Slovak National Archives.

[40] Archive Fond of the Office of the Government of the SSR 1988–1992 (1989). *Submission report and evaluation of the interdepartmental amendment procedure: draft principles of the amendment to Act No. 29/1984 Coll. on the system of primary and secondary schools.* Slovak National Archives.

[41] Archive Fond of the Central Committee of the Communist Party of Slovakia's Committee for Education, Culture and Art 1988–1989 (1989). *Submission report on the draft principles of the Act amending and supplementing the Act No. 29/1984 Coll. on the system of primary and secondary schools (Education Act).* Slovak National Archives.

their earnings) with the approval of the local national committee, and these had to be activities or services for socialist organizations, such as renting a gym to a sports club.[42] According to the draft of the new Act on State Administration in Education, schools, including primary schools, were to have a direct possibility of independent earning activities with the approval of the local national comitee (Účinné spojení…, 1989b).

Attempts at cautious reforms in the context of perestroika suggest that the immediately successive period of post-socialist transition must be seen in broader contexts. It is a phase of dramatic change, but also of certain continuities. That is why we have presented a comprehensive account of the development of Czechoslovak society and the education system during the period of 'normalization' in this chapter. The effort to 'stabilize' society after the invasion by the Warsaw Pact troops was the leitmotif of this phase. The communist government tried to 'calm down' the population with pro-social and pro-family policies and by tolerating their escape into privacy. The adherence to unchanging power and ideological principles brought increasing stagnation and brought the country to the brink of economic collapse in the late 1980s. All of this affected the school system and the efforts to reform it as well, but these efforts could not go beyond the ideologically conditioned concept of a unified school until November 1989. The fact that the narrative turn in particular was quite sharp after the fall of the communist government will be shown in the following chapter. …

Bibliography

Bálek, A. (2007). Československá ekonomika v osmdesátých letech 20. století [Czechoslovak economy in the 1980s]. *Acta Oeconomica Pragensia, 7*(15), 45–54. https://doi.org/10.18267/j.aop.176

Bašta, J. (2008). Lidové milice: nelegální armáda KSČ [People's Militias: Illegal army of the KSČ]. *Paměť a dějiny, 2*(2), 99–108.

Bolton, J. (2014). *Worlds of Dissent: Charter 77, The Plastic People of the Universe, and Czech Culture under Communism.* Harvard University Press.

Bren, P. (2010). *The greengrocer and his TV: the culture of communism after the 1968 Prague Spring.* Cornell University Press.

Burakowski, A., Gubrynowicz, A., & Ukielski, P. (2021). *1989 – The Autumn of Nations.* Natolin European Centre, European Network Remembrance and Solidarity.

Čerych, L. (1996). *Zprávy o národní politice ve vzdělávání: Česká republika* [Reports on National Educational Policy: The Czech Republic]. Ústav pro informace ve vzdělávání.

Code of Practice for Teaching Staff and Other Staff of Schools and Educational Institutions for which the National Committee Performs Organizational Tasks Resulting from Labour Relations (22 368/85-42). (1985). https://www.epravo.cz/vyhledavani-aspi/?Id=36645&Section=1&IdPara=1&ParaC=2

---

[42] Archive Fond of the Office of the Government of the SSR 1981–1987 (1983). *Principles of the Czech National Council's Act amending and supplementing the ČNR Act on State Administration in Education and the ČNR Act on Educational Institutions.* Slovak National Archives.

Další rozvoj československé výchovně vzdělávací soustavy. Projekt a důvodová zpráva [Further development of the Czechoslovak Education System. Project and Preamble]. (1976). SPN.

Decree of the Minister of the Interior on the Auxiliary Guard of Public Security No. 56/1962 Coll. (1962). https://www.psp.cz/sqw/sbirka.sqw?cz=56&r=1962

Duffková, J. (2003). Česká dovolená na konci 20. století (Obecná charakteristika) [Czechoslovak Vacation at the End of the 20th Century (General Characteristics)]. In *Aktér, instituce, společnost: sborník k 65. narozeninám prof. PhDr. Miloslava Petruska, CSc.* [The Actor, The Institution, The Society: Collection for the 65th Birthday of Prof. Dr. Miloslav Petrusek, CSc.] (pp. 165–189). Univerzita Karlova.

Dumazedier, J. (1966). Volný čas [Free time]. *Sociologický časopis, 2*(3), 443–447.

Green, D. A. (2014). *The Czechoslovak Communist Party's Revolution, 1986–1990*. [Doctoral dissertation, University of Strathclyde]. The University of Strathclyde library: digital collections. http://digitool.lib.strath.ac.uk/R/?func=dbin-jump-full&object_id=24879

Hladílek, M. (1984). *Úvod do didaktiky I. stupně základní školy* [Introduction to didactics of the 1st stage of primary school]. Pedagogická fakulta v Českých Budějovicích.

Hradecká, V., & Koudelka, F. (1998). *Kádrová politika a nomenklatura KSČ 1969–1974* [Cadre Policy and Nomenclature of the KSČ 1969–1974]. Ústav pro soudobé dějiny AV ČR.

Hubatová-Vacková, L., & Říha, C. (Eds.). (2018). *Husákovo 3+1: bytová kultura 70. let* [Husák's 3+1: Housing Culture of the 1970s]. VŠUP.

K materiálu o analýze československé výchovně vzdělávací soustavy [On the material on analysis of Czechoslovak education system]. (1990). *Pedagogika, 40*(3), 315–322.

Kalinová, L. (2007). *Společenské proměny v čase socialistického experimentu: k sociálním dějinám v letech 1945–1969* [Social transformations in the time of the socialist experiment: Towards social history in 1945–1969]. Academia.

Kalinová, L. (2012). *Konec nadějím a novvyá očekávání: k dějinám české společnosti 1969–1993* [The end of hopes and new expectations: On the history of Czech society 1969–1993]. Academia.

Kalous, J. (1993). Školská politika v České republice po roce 1989 [School policy in The Czech Republic after 1989]. *Pedagogika, 43*(3), 235–239.

Kaplan, K. (2004). *Československo v poválečné Evropě* [Czechoslovakia in Postwar Europe]. Karolinum.

Kaplan, K., & Paleček, P. (2008). *Komunistický režim a politické procesy v Československu* [The communist regime and political processes in Czechoslovakia]. Barrister & Principal.

Kluchert, G., & Gruner, P. (2001). Erziehungsabsichten und Sozialisationseffekte. Die Schuleder SBZ und frühen DDR zwischen politischer Instrumentalisierung und institutioneller Eigenlogik. *Zeitschrift für Pädagogik, 47*(6), 859–868. https://www.pedocs.de/frontdoor.php?source_opus=4321

Knapík, J. (2014). *Děti, mládež a socialismus v Československu v 50. a 60. letech* [Children, youth and socialism in Czechoslovakia in the 1950s and 1960s]. Slezská univerzita.

Knapík, J., & Franc, M. (2011). *Průvodce kulturním děním a životním stylem v českých zemích 1948–1967* [A guide to the cultural events and lifestyles in the Czech Lands 1948–1967] (I., [A–O]). Academia.

Knotová, D. (2011). *Pedagogické dimenze volného času* [Pedagogical dimensions of free time]. Paido.

Kohnová, J. (1999). Další vzdělávání učitelů a vzdělávací politika [Further teacher education and education policy]. *Pedagogika, 49*(2), 128–132.

Kopeček, M. (Ed.). (2019). *Architekti dlouhé změny: expertní kořeny postsocialismu v Československu* [Architects of the long change: The expert roots of postsocialism in Czechoslovakia]. Argo.

Kopp, B. (1992). The Eastern European Revolution and Education in Czechoslovakia. *Comparative Education Review, 36*(1), 101–113. https://doi.org/10.1086/447084

Krakovský, R. (2020). *State and society in communist Czechoslovakia: transforming the everyday from World War II to the fall of the Berlin Wall*. Bloomsbury Academic.

Kudláčová, B. (Ed.). (2023). *Two sides of the same coin: Examples of free and unfree education in Slovakia during the period of socialism*. Peter Lang.

Lebeda, M. (1956). Jak ředitel školy zapojuje učitelský kolektiv do spolupráce s pionýrskou organisací [How the school head involves the teaching staff in cooperation with the Pioneer Organization]. *Pedagogika, 6*(3), 726–735.

McDermott, K. (2015). *Communist Czechoslovakia, 1945–89: a political and social history*. Macmillan Education.

Mlčoch, L. (2014). *Ekonomie rodiny v proměnách času, institucí a hodnot* [Family economics in the changes of time, institutions and values]. Karolinum.

Mueller, W., Gehler, M., & Suppan, A. (Eds.). (2015). *The revolutions of 1989: a handbook*. Verlag der Österreichische Akademie der Wissenschaften.

Nosková, J. (2014). *Biografická metoda a metoda orální historie: na příkladu výzkumu každodenního života v socialismu* [The biographical method and the oral history method: An example of research of everyday life under socialism]. Etnologický ústav AV ČR, v.v.i.

Organizační směrnice pro základní devítileté školy [Organizational Guidelines for Nine, Year Primary Schools]. (1972). In *Soubor předpisů pro školy a výchovná zařízení 1. cyklus. 1. část, (Základní devítileté školy)* [Collection of Regulations for Schools and Educational Facilities 1st Cycle, 1st Part (Primary Nine-Year Schools)] (pp. 1–12). SPN.

Pedagogicko-organizační opatření pro základní a střední školy a školská zařízení na školní rok 1988–1989 [Pedagogical and Organisational Measures for Primary and Secondary Schools and Educational Institutions for the 1988–1989 School Year]. (1988). *Učitelské noviny: příloha Obzor* (květen 1988).

Pojetí základní devítileté školy a učební plán této školy [The concept of the nine-year primary school and its curriculum]. (1960). Státní pedagogické nakladatelství.

Poloušek, O., & Zounek, J. (2021). Vzdělávací systém a československá verze přestavby (1987–1989): analýza, kritika a návrhy na reformy v kontextu ideologie a krize [The educational system and the Czechoslovak Version of Perestroika (1987–1989): Analysis, criticism and reform proposals in the context of ideology and crisis]. *Studia Paedagogica, 26*(3), 83–108. https://doi.org/10.5817/SP2021-3-4

Prečan, V. (Ed.). (1990). *Charta 77, 1977–1989: od morální k demokratické revoluci: dokumentace* [Charter 77, 1977–1989: From moral to democratic revolution: Documentation]. Čs. středisko nezávislé litereatury.

Pullmann, M. (2011). *Konec experimentu: přestavba a pád komunismu v Československu* [The end of the experiment: Perestroika and the fall of communism in Czechoslovakia]. Scriptorium.

Pullmann, M. (2012). Eroze diktatury v době přestavby Krize vládnoucích elit a rozpad ideologického konsenzu v Československu (1986–1989) [The erosion of dictatorship in the perestroika years: The crisis of the ruling elites and the disintegration of ideological consensus in Czechoslovakia, 1986–89]. *Soudobé dějiny, 19*(2), 256–274. https://doi.org/10.51134/sod.2012.019

Rezoluce XIV. sjezdu KSČ [Resolution of the 14th Congress of the KSČ]. (1971). *Rudé právo*, 31. 5. 1971, 2–4.

Schindler-Wisten, P. (2017). O chalupách a lidech: chalupářství v českých zemích v období tzv. *normalizace a transformace* [Of Cottages and People: The Cottage Phenomenon in the Czech Lands in the period of normalization and transformation]. Karolinum.

Směrnice o bezplatném poskytování učebnic a školních potřeb čj. 22 552/72-24. ze dne 27. 7. 1972 [Directive on the free provision of textbooks and school supplies no 22 552/72-24 of July 27, 1972]. (1972). *Věstník ministerstva školství a ministerstva kultury, 28*(8), 123.

Štrougal, L., & Jakeš, M. (1987). *Zásady přebudování hospodářského mechanismu ČSSR: schváleno předsednictvem ÚV KSČ a vládou ČSSR. K otázkám přestavby hospodářského mechanismu / Lubomír Štrougal, Miloš Jakeš: projevy na celost. aktivu ÚV KSČ 27. ledna 1987* [On the Principles of Perestroika of the Economic Mechanism / Lubomír Štrougal, Miloš Jakeš: Speeches on the National Meeting of the ÚV KSČ, 27 January 1987]. Svoboda.

Tomek, P. (2019). *Československá armáda v čase sametové revoluce: proměny ozbrojených sil na přelomu osmdesátých a devadesátých let* [Czechoslovak army at the time of velvet revolution: Transformations of the armed forces at the turn of the 1980s and 1990s]. Svět křídel.

Trnková, K. (2006). Vývoj malotřídních škol v druhé polovině 20. století [The development of small schools in the second half of the 20th century]. *Sborník prací Filosofické fakulty brněnské university. C, Řada historická, 54*(11), 133–144.

Účinné spojení školy s praxí neodkladným úkolem: z vystoupení ministra Ľudovíta Kilára [The urgent task of effective connection between school and practice: From an address by Minister Ludovit Kilár]. (1989a). *Rudé právo* (11. září 1989).

Účinné spojení školy s praxí neodkladným úkolem: z vystoupení ministryně Jany Synkové [The urgent task of effective connection between school and practice: From an address by Minister Jana Synková]. (1989b). *Rudé právo* (11. září 1989).

Urban, J. (2010). Několik vět. Posledních pět měsíců komunistické diktatury petiční optikou [A few sentences. The last five months of the communist dictatorship through the Petitioner's Lens]. *Paměť a dějiny, 4*(1), 20–45.

Usnesení 13. Zasedání ÚV KSČ o úkolech československého školství v podmínkách přestavby společnosti [Resolution of the 13th Session of the Central Committee of the Communist Party of Czechoslovakia on the tasks of Czechoslovak education in the conditions of the reconstruction of society]. (1989). *Rudé právo* (1. dubna 1989).

Václavíková-Helšusová, L. (2007). Učitelské sbory z genderové perspektivy [Teaching staffs from the gender perspective]. In I. Smetáčková (Ed.), *Příručka pro genderově citlivé vedení škol* [The Handbook for gender-respectful school leadership] (pp. 37–43). Otevřená společnost, o. p. s.

Větší důvěru a samostatnost učiteli [Greater Confidence and Independence for Teachers]. (1989). *Rudé právo* (9. září).

Vorlíček, Ch. (2004). České školství v letech 1945–2000 [Czech school system between 1945–2000]. In E. Walterová (Ed.), *Česká pedagogika: Proměny a výzvy: Sborník k životnímu jubileu profesora Jiřího Kotáska* [Czech Pedagogy: Transformations and challenges: Collection for the Jubilee of Professor Jiří Kotásek] (pp. 119–176). Pedagogická fakulta Univerzity Karlovy.

Vykoukal, J., Litera, B., & Tejchman, M. (2000). *Východ: vznik, vývoj a rozpad sovětského bloku 1944–1989* [The East: The emergence, development and disintegration of the Soviet Bloc 1944–1989]. Libri.

Walterová, E. (2004). *Úloha školy v rozvoji vzdělanosti. 1. díl* [The role of school in the development of education. Part 1]. Paido.

Yurchak, A. (2006). *Everything was forever, until it was no more: the last Soviet generation.* Princeton University Press.

Z Analýzy československé výchovně vzdělávací soustavy [From the analysis of the Czechoslovak Education System]. (1988). *Učitelské noviny: příloha Obzor (červen 1988).*

Žídek, L. (2019). *Centrally planned economies: theory and practice in socialist Czechoslovakia.* Routledge/Taylor & Francis Group.

Zounek, J., Šimáně, M., & Knotová, D. (2016). Cesta k učitelství v socialistickém Československu pohledem pamětníků [The Journey to teacher profession in socialist Czechoslovakia as seen by eyewitnesses]. *Studia paedagogica, 21*(3), 131–159. https://doi.org/10.5817/SP2016-3-7

Zounek, J. Šimáně, M., & Knotová, D. (2017a). *Normální život v nenormální době. Základní školy a jejich učitelé (nejen) v období normalizace* [Normal life in not so normal times. Primary schools and their teachers (not only) during the so-called normalization period]. Wolters Kluwer.

Zounek, J., Šimáně, M., & Knotová, D. (2017b). *Socialistická základní škola pohledem pamětníků. Sonda do života učitelů v Jihomoravském kraji* [Socialist primary school as seen by eyewitnesses: Probing teachers' life in the South Moravia Region]. Wolters Kluwer.

Part II
Schools and Teachers in the Period of Changes

Chapter 5
Transforming the Education System: A Difficult Return to Democratic Europe

Abstract This chapter introduces the broader contexts of the transformation of the Czech education system after 1989, with an emphasis on primary schools. The political and economic development of Czechoslovakia after the fall of the communist government in 1989 is briefly introduced. The process of transition to a market economy is described, as is the dissolution of Czechoslovakia in 1993 when two separate states were established: the Czech Republic and the Slovak Republic. The chapter focuses primarily on the situation in the Czech Republic by presenting the fundamental reforms to the education system. The actual reforms are explained and the specific legislative changes that formed the background for the changes in the Czech school system are introduced. Attention is then focused on expert discussions and the education system reform proposals that largely remained in the realm of theory and intention. The text describes the fundamental problems of the Czech school system, connected primarily to the complicated economic situation of a country undergoing transformation. The chapter concludes by presenting the developments and reforms of the school systems in neighbouring post-communist countries in comparison to the situation in the Czech Republic.

Keywords Czech Republic · Post-socialist transformation · Economy · Education system · School legislation · Reform proposals · Post-socialist countries

5.1 Broader Contexts of Transformation: Between Ideology, Chaos, and Freedom

The period of post-socialist transformation in Czechoslovakia did not begin with the Velvet Revolution in 1989. Fundamental changes in life in the society only took place after 1989, but in some respects these changes reflected a continuation of efforts that had started in the 1980s. After all, the need for school system reforms was perceived as necessary even before the fall of the communist government. The 1984 amendment to the Education Act was prepared in the context of perestroika. The amendment was supposed to provide more efficiency to the education system

© Masaryk University, Faculty of Arts, Registration no. 00216224,
VAT ID: CZ00216224 2024
J. Zounek et al., *(Post)Socialist Transformation of Primary Schools*,
https://doi.org/10.1007/978-3-031-58768-9_5

and innovations to teaching, and also financial savings in view of the economic stagnation of the state. First, students were to complete the entire compulsory 10 years of education in primary school through the establishment of ninth grades and subsequent preparatory courses. Based on the upcoming Act on State Administration in the School System, schools were also to be allowed to independently earn funds. This allowance was supposed to enable them to raise money for the modernization of outdated equipment and the acquisition of new computer technology, for example. However, other changes remained only in the realm of discussion or 'on the drawing board', for example in the context of contemporary analyses of education. The *Analysis of the Education System* is a good example of this. Until November 1989, the proclaimed efforts to increase the decentralization of school management or to strengthen the responsibility of school heads were not reflected in practice (Polouček & Zounek, 2021).

Presented in the pre-revolution draft of the Education Act, the ninth year of primary schools, which was optional at first and compulsory later, was introduced after the fall of the communist regime. After 1989, decentralization progressed much further than had been planned in the late 1980s. It led to the establishment of school autonomy (self-governance) and to the transfer of school management under the administration of the Ministry of Education. During socialism, the school system had been a part of the state administration's agenda at the district and regional levels,[1] and, of course, under the strong influence of the Communist Party of Czechoslovakia (Komunistická strana Československa, KSČ).

It is possible to study certain continuities between the socialist and post-socialist period in promoting school system transformations, especially in terms of the efforts to decentralize and to make individual schools and the entire school system function more efficiently. However, it was not until the free discussions stemming from democratization and from the enforcement of the basic principles of a functioning civil society that it became possible to go much further in the considerations about reforms of education and of the school system. The new democratic government primarily had to address the urgent problems of the Czech school system, including an underfunded school system and obsolete school equipment and teaching methods. These problems did not automatically disappear after the fall of the communist regime.

Initially, the demonstrators of November 1989 did not call for the dissolution of the state socialist system, but rather for reforms leading to democratization and greater freedom of choice (e.g. in travel or entrepreneurship). However, the question of a transition to the broadest possible market economy model quickly became the order of the day. The idea of a free, unregulated market was inherent to the part of the political representation that eventually came to dominate the political scene. At the same time, it was supported by foreign advisers who drew on the 'Washington

---

[1] This 'central' component of management is actually considered to be a reflection of the directive management of schools during socialism (Kalous, 1993; Čerych, 1996).

Consensus'.[2] As a result, in the first years after the fall of the communist government, the national economy was completely transformed. This transformation included the privatization of both small and large enterprises and allowed the entry of foreign capital.[3]

The attitudes of Czech and Slovak representatives towards transformation continuously diverged, and these divergences were one cause of the dissolution of Czechoslovakia. In the Czech lands, the Civic Democratic Party (Občanská demokratická strana) dominated the political scene as one of the successors of the Civic Forum (Občanské forum), which was founded as a civic initiative during the Velvet Revolution. This right-wing political entity, led by economist Václav Klaus, advocated the broadest economic liberalization possible. The Movement for a Democratic Slovakia (Hnutí za demokratické Slovensko, ruling in Slovakia and led by Vladimír Mečiar, took a more cautious stance and advocated a more gradual transition to the market economy. These divergent views were accompanied by the raising of nationalist issues, reflected, for example, in the 'hyphen war', i.e. in the dispute over the name of the republic.[4] Sociological surveys showed that a large part of the public wanted a joint state with a high degree of autonomy for the individual republics. However, after the second parliamentary elections in June 1992, the election winners Klaus and Mečiar agreed to split the federation.

The Czech and Slovak Federal Republic ceased to exist on 31 December 1992. Two new states were created: the Czech Republic and the Slovak Republic. In Slovakia, privatization was limited; in the Czech Republic, it continued at full speed (Berend, 2009; Ther, 2016). Ideas about neoliberalism were logically also reflected

---

[2] The assertion of the neoliberal free market model in post-communist countries is sometimes referred to as the Washington Consensus, because it was strongly supported by supranational and US institutions (World Bank, International Monetary Fund, US Treasury) (Berend, 2009; Ther, 2016). See more in the Introduction.

[3] In Czechoslovakia, mass privatization was launched in 1991. Small trades were privatized directly within the 'small-scale privatization' and they were often bought out by their previous operators. The 'large-scale privatization' concerned medium-sized and larger enterprises, and the method of 'voucher privatization' was chosen for it. Within this privatization, enterprises were converted into joint-stock companies and citizens could purchase a limited number of shares at a favourable price through voucher books. The basic idea of voucher privatization was for the privatized property to remain in the hands of Czech citizens. Only individuals could buy shares using voucher books. However, investment funds were soon set up to buy out the voucher books from citizens. Although the property was preferably to remain in Czech hands, some strategic enterprises were excluded from the voucher privatization. This was the case of the Škoda automobile company, for example, which was offered for sale abroad because of the need for rapid modernization and import of technologies. While the acquisition of Škoda by the German Volkswagen group is retrospectively evaluated as successful and provided the struggling car maker with a desirable stimulus, the voucher privatization opened the way for numerous speculations and the World Bank now deems it to be an inappropriate privatization method (Ther, 2016; Lieberman et al., 1997).

[4] The dispute over changing the name of the Czechoslovak Socialist Republic was triggered by the 'innocent' need to remove the prefix 'socialist' from the country's name. The Slovaks called for a name that would sufficiently express the equality of the two nations. After the names Czechoslovak Republic and the Czecho-Slovak Republic were rejected, the name Czech and Slovak Federal Republic was finally selected on 23 April 1990 (Rychlík, 2012).

in discussions of possible reforms of the education system; these discussions involved both professional institutions and independent initiatives before and after the dissolution of Czechoslovakia. Their reform proposals were based largely on the rejection of the socialist unified school system. However, the model of a unified school had been cautiously criticized even before 1989 in connection with the need to improve and streamline outdated practices in teaching and in the operation and management of schools (Poloušek & Zounek, 2021). In the proposed amendment to the Education Act, the 'internal differentiation' of the unified school was to be expanded. This practice was already being partially applied before 1989, when schools were being established with expanded teaching of languages, mathematics, and other subjects. The pedagogically problematic division of students into classes according to their abilities can also be regarded as internal differentiation. Therefore, some similar tendencies can be identified in the pre- and post-1989 periods, but the framework of values changed radically.

The key participants promoting a post-communist transformation based on the Washington Consensus were the same people who sought a technocratic innovation of the inefficient and outdated system of state socialism during the period of late socialism (Kopeček, 2019). Before 1989, the ideology limited critiques (not only of the school system); after 1989, the lack of a concept or even outright chaos were the main obstacles to the promotion of change. The differences in viewpoints on reforms, the difficult search for compromise, and the need to quickly deal with urgent everyday problems connected mainly to the underfunding of the school system resulted in no major (pedagogical) reforms taking place in the first years after the Velvet Revolution. Some authors have even spoken of a prevailing feeling that the school system still remained on the sidelines, just as it did during socialism (Kotásek, 1993). Paradoxically, this occurred despite the fact that first-rate education was declared to be one of the pillars of democratization of society in the contemporary discussions (Walterová & Greger, 2006). The economic transformation connected with the privatization of industry and the entry of foreign capital was in fact the key topic of political interest.

It was probably for these reasons that many of the ideas promoted by the professional and teaching public remained on the drawing board. In this chapter, we first present the real changes in the school system. We then take a closer look at the (reform) thoughts and ideas that resonated in discussions about the new form of the school system and education during the 1990s. Next, we focus on the problems of the school system (especially the economic ones) that most hindered the implementation of more fundamental reforms. Finally, we look at the developments in the Czech lands in an international context.

5.2 Legislative Framework of Reforms: (Only) Partial Changes

The first amendments to the Education Acts were passed in the first half of 1990, even before the first free parliamentary elections in June of that year. These were primarily Act No. 171/1990 Coll. On the System of Primary and Secondary Schools (Education Act). This amendment to the Act came into force on 1 June 1990 and its approval garnered huge public interest (Legislativní maratón…, 1990).

Major changes in the Act were connected to the democratization of the country and the constitutional reforms, particularly the state administration reform, which included the need to reform the education system. The amendment therefore introduces autonomy and sectoral management of the school system. This meant that schools were to be governed by the Ministry of Education in matters of education and training (sectoral management), but in legal relations, schools acquired their own responsibility and acted on their own behalf. They thus became the subject of legal relations. This principle, enshrined in Sect. 5.1, has come to be known as 'self-governance'. According to a transitional provision, all primary schools were to acquire self-governance by 31 December 1994 at the latest (Act No 171/1990 Coll.). In accordance with the amendment to the Education Act, it was once again possible to establish private and religious schools at which students could be charged tuition, but the achieved education was to be equivalent to that provided in state schools. Thus, after more than 40 years of Communist rule, the various previous traditional types of non-state or alternative schools returned to the school system.[5] This Act already defined 9 years of primary school. This change was implemented gradually, as the compulsory ninth grades were only introduced from the 1995/1996 school year. The second stage was to be differentiated according to the interests and abilities of the students. In addition, the Act newly allowed (following a First Republic tradition) the establishment of up to 8-year grammar schools (Sucháček, 2014). The first of these opened in September 1990; it was another major change in the school system. In this book, we focus on the new types of grammar schools, including the later impacts of these changes on the primary school system. The lower stage of 8-year grammar schools became a de facto 'competition' for the second stage of primary school.

Act No. 564/1990 Coll. On State Administration and Self-Government in Education, adopted on 13 December 1990, reacted to the changes in the administrative structure. This Act was in the spirit of the general need for decentralization and the simultaneous pedagogical public's call for sectoral management of the school system.[6] The schools were no longer to be supervised by regional state

---

[5] The problems of the emergence of alternative and religious schools go beyond the scope of this book.

[6] Many discussions accompanied the preparation of the Act. After a draft of the Act was published, the pedagogical public feared that schools would be too subordinated to the education authorities and municipalities and that they would once again have 'multiple masters'. They called for the

administration, i.e. specifically by district and regional national committees, but by newly established education authorities that were managed by the Ministry of Education. This was to increase the expertise and quality of school management. The Act led to the separation of school administration from the rest of the state administration. The state administration appointed and dismissed primary school school heads, took action based on the results of school inspections, granted recognition to student certificates issued by foreign schools, and gave approval to municipalities to establish or close down schools. Funding of regional school systems, such as kindergartens and primary schools, was one of the most important functions of the education authorities. The education authorities provided methodological assistance in labour relations and payroll issues to schools that were not self-governed. This assistance was provided at the school's request. The education authorities could also provide these services to self-governed schools on the basis of a contract.

The management of schools was to be simplified. There was to be only one intermediate level between the Ministry and the schools—an education office established in each district. In the end, the municipalities played a greater role in the establishment of schools, and they did so in compliance with democratization and the establishment of local self-governments. The reforms also addressed the issue of school funding. Education-related expenses, i.e. the salaries of staff and education aids, were to be the responsibility of the education authorities and thus of the Ministry of Education. Other expenses (e.g. for the operation or repairs of school buildings) were to be the responsibility of the municipalities. However, soon after these changes, it emerged that the sectorally managed school system was disconnected from other parts of the life of society (Kalous, 1993). A lack of communication between the Ministry of Education and the teaching public was also criticized (Pilař, 1991).

The process of the democratization of society was reflected in the adoption of legal regulations, and the changes also had to be implemented in practice through various organizational measures. Practical matters were mainly regulated Ministry of Education, Youth and Sport (MEYS) decrees. A decree on primary schools, which introduced partial innovations in the organization of teaching, was published by MEYS on 1 January 1991. The decree made it possible to divide classes into smaller groups, for example. Students could also transfer from one school to another with virtually no restrictions, which brought de facto freedom of school choice. This marked a shift from the previous strict catchment system, in which the school a

---

broadest possible powers for school heads (Nad zákonem…, 1990). The role of the municipality probably caused greater concern. We found support for sectoral management in the minutes of meetings of pedagogical councils of one city's schools. Concerns that schools would be too dependent on the discretion and funding of the municipality permeated the *Teacher's Newspaper* (Štefflová, 1991). Criticisms also appeared that the municipality's position was not strong enough. In a draft of the Act, self-government was to be exercised by the school board (which was to include representatives of the municipality as well as of teachers and parents); the final version explicitly stated that self-government was exercised by the municipality (Návrh zákona…, 1990; Act No. 564/1990).

student had to attend was clearly defined and determined by the family's place of residence. This principle greatly influenced the life of some schools. The decree also dealt in detail with the options for recognizing a student's education abroad and the question of transferring students from foreign schools. This was related both to the return of emigrants to Czechoslovakia and to the opening of the borders and the possibility of people moving to or from abroad, which had been significantly restricted before 1989 (MEYS, 1991b).

The Act on Pre-School and School Facilities adopted on 10 September 1991 was also closely connected to the primary school system. Among other things, this Act determined the conditions for the establishment, operation, and funding of facilities that served the needs of primary schools, such as school cafeterias and after-school clubs.[7] These could be established independently and did not have to fall within the competences of the school head within the self-governance of the school (Act No 390/1991 Coll.).

The reforms were disappointing to a large part of both the professional and the lay public. Sharp criticism appeared in the *Pedagogika* (*Pedagogy*) journal, in which the developments were assessed as slow and non-conceptual (Kotásek, 1993; Kalous, 1993). Some authors criticized the mechanical application of market mechanisms to the school system:

> Without preparing any general concept, many new schools of all stages were established, a new inspection system was being created in a rather less than appropriate way, market mechanisms were applied mechanically despite the fact that in the very school system, their positive influence was very problematic, etc. The general relaxation that has been reflected in the school system has taken many teachers by surprise. (…) There is also a lack of good textbooks and the gradually growing dissatisfaction with there being only a few positive changes (Bečvář & Veselý, 1993, p. 134).

The cited authors believed that the reason for the lack of interest in education and the school system was the fact that citizens did not see the actual impact education had on improving their economic situation. At the same time, the increased importance of the financial stimulus must be seen as both a reflection of the neoliberal narrative and a symptom of the poor economic situation of the country, which experienced severe inflation and a (temporary) decline in living standards after 1989.

The idea of a broader and deeper transformation of the school system therefore remained mainly a matter of professional debate. The Ministry put forward its own concepts of changes, including a draft of a constitutional Act on Education, and they did so in connection with the process of drafting a new constitution of the Czech Republic. However, the constitutional Act on Education was not adopted. This meant that no major changes were implemented until 2004, when the new Education Act was adopted. Until then, only slightly amended 'socialist' laws were in force.

Some specific measures reflected a return to tradition or inspiration from history rather than reform. The restoration of multi-year grammar schools can be

---

[7] After-school clubs are school facilities that provide education and training and recreational, sport, and leisure activities for students from one or more primary schools during non-school hours. They are preferentially intended for the youngest students of primary schools.

considered a nod to (First Republic) Czechoslovak traditions. A symbolic 'return' can also be observed in the strengthening of the role of local self-governments in the school system administration. Considering that modernization tendencies—not only in communist countries—are related to efforts to systematically centralize, govern, and control the running of the state from the centre, the inspiration for efforts to decentralize comes from times when public administration was in the hands of traditional communities (including the school system). The neoliberal ideas that provide the basis for decentralization proclaim 'liberation' from artificially created regulations of the centralized state (cf. Ther, 2016). Some Western countries went through a development parallel to that of Czechoslovakia, in which the centralization efforts of the 1960s were followed by a period of decentralization in the late 1970s (Mitter, 1991). It is logical that similar ideas were inherent in debates about education in a country in which a large part of the public and political representation identified with neoliberal ideas.

It was not until after 1995 that the Ministry of Education began to take steps towards the implementation of a more comprehensive school system reform. A rather critical assessment of Czech education by international evaluators from the OECD (Čerych, 1996), the World Bank (Berryman, 2000; Fiszbein, 2001), and the Council of Europe (Bîrzea, 1994) was also an impulse for these steps. The Czech pedagogical public were critical of some of the steps associated with the general consensus concerning the removal of the omnipresent oversight and bureaucracy. For example, the disintegration of the previously relatively well-functioning system of further teacher education when the 'pedagogical centers' managed by the MEYS were closed down was evaluated very negatively (Greger, 2011). Problems with the poor and inefficient funding of the school system over a long period of time as well as the outdated form of the curriculum shaped the political debate of the second half of the 1990s and led to the compilation of the 'White paper' published in 2001 (Kotásek, 2001).[8] Changes were inevitable because of a major reform of the administrative division of the Czech Republic. In 2000, fourteen new regions were created instead of the previous eight, and the regions took over the functions of the former districts.[9] Subsequently, in 2001, education authorities were dissolved and their competences were transferred to municipalities and regional authorities, which were to participate financially in the administration of the school system. Therefore, there was again a transfer of competences from departments to administrations.

---

[8] Although the share of GDP on the funding of the school system kept increasing between 1989 and 1994, this was due to the overall reduction in Czechoslovakia's GDP in the first years of the post-socialist transformation; after 1994 the school system's share of GDP began to decrease (České priority..., 2010).

[9] The new regional establishment was created on the basis of constitutional Act No. 347/1997 Coll. on 1 January 2000. The administrative reform was intended to make the self-government more efficient. This included the administration of infrastructure and the organization of public transport. After the dissolution of the education authorities at the district level, issues related to the school system and education became the responsibility of the regions. Nevertheless, the regions largely left the agenda of primary schools up to municipalities as the founders of these schools.

The need for reforms within the process of the Czech Republic's accession to the European Union was another fundamental impulse (Greger, 2011). The White Paper provided basic frameworks that were partly reflected in the new Education Act adopted on 24 September 2004 (Act 561/2004 Coll.). This was the first 'non-communist' Education Act after 1989. The abolition of the uniform school curricula, to which our narrators also referred at length, is probably the most significant change.[10] The newly created two-stage curriculum was defined by the state education programme, which set out the general frameworks. These were to be further modified at the national level by the Framework Educational Programmes, on the basis of which each school had to develop its own School Education Programme.[11] The intention was for the schools to have as much freedom as possible to adapt their curricula individually, taking into account the needs of students, the interests of parents, and the focus or location of the school.

The discussions on the education system were much more varied and involved various participants. We examine in more detail the most important proposals for school system reforms that significantly affected the discussions about the form of the school system and education during the 1990s. These show what starting points, opinions, thoughts, proposals, and even solutions were discussed at the time, and they also complete the picture of the (theoretical) context of the transformation.

5.3   Expert Discussions on the School System Reforms After 1989

In the first years after the Velvet Revolution, extensive discussions about school system and education reforms were held among experts and teachers, with views ranging from moderate to radical. That is to say, the newly acquired freedom offered unprecedented opportunities to openly discuss the starting points and principles of education reform, which often went well beyond the first amendments to the Education Acts.

The impulse for the discussions came from the Ministry of Education itself. In fact, the ministry's experts (and eventually also the politicians) perceived the amendments to the Acts as temporary steps towards a deeper transformation of the education system. In 1991, the Ministry of Education invited experts and the wider public

---

[10] The curricula were normative documents that set out the aims of teaching of subjects at the given type and stage of school; they defined the subject matter and its sequence and division into the different grades and sections of the school year. Prior to 1989, they were worked out in detail and teachers at all schools had to strictly adhere to them. They were criticized for being normative, but also for their emphasis on the large amount of subject matter they prescribed. This might be one cause of student overload.

[11] It is the responsibility of the school head to ensure that the School Education Programme is consistent with the Framework Education Programme and to ensure that the school actually follows it.

to discuss and also to submit proposals for reform: 'The management of MEYS came to the conclusion that the elaboration of a long-term perspective should be entrusted, at least in the first phase, to a body of experts working principally independently of the Ministry and constituting spontaneously and informally without any special official mandate' (Prokop, 1991, p. 7). This impulse provoked an extraordinary response from the teaching and professional public (at this point, researchers and experts on the school system and education). In the following years, this led to the publication of a number of discussion papers and reform proposals in professional journals, especially in the *Pedagogika* journal.[12]

These contemporary expert (and lay) discussions were dominated by the rejection of the concept of a socialist unified school. Resistance to uniformity and the unity of state socialism significantly permeated the discussions. There was a clear inclination towards individualism under the influence of neoliberal ideas. Taking into account the differences between students was seen as natural according to some experts. The schools were to differ in prestige and difficulty, and the influence of families' economic capital on the availability of education was to be acceptable and natural:

> Democracy, if it is to be viable, must respect the various inequalities among people, e.g. physical, intellectual, psychological, but also economic and social. In a democratic state, equality before the law must be fully respected and an equal opportunity created for everyone as much as possible, knowing that full equality in life cannot be achieved. It is correct that the various talents of a child should be a basic guide and that state support should be given to the poorest of the gifted. However, advantages such as place of residence in a major scientific and cultural center or social origin from the intelligentsia can neither be removed nor compensated for. Plurality and differentiation are the necessary features of the school system in a democratic society and it is well known that formerly, some private schools, and still today in many areas the church schools, are the main vehicles for social equalization in the opportunity to study (Team of Faculty of Education, Charles University, 1992, p. 10).

Resistance to planning, a distinctive characteristic of state socialism, was also symptomatic of the debates on transforming the school system. In fact, some of our narrators identified the general aversion to rules, regulations, and the omnipresent bureaucracy as a characteristic feature of the early 1990s. The rejection of directive management from the centre led to the formulation of utopian visions of a natural self-regulation of schools (competition) in some education reform proposals (NEMES, 1991). The call for introducing or restoring natural order[13] to the school system constituted another leitmotif of the transformation (Čermáková, 1991).

The crucial question was whether to adopt models from abroad or to draw inspiration from the pre-communist past, especially the interwar period. Opinions against adopting foreign models of education as unsuitable for the Czech cultural context began to appear. There were even views that the socialist school system, although

---

[12] At that time, this was one of the most important professional pedagogical journals in the territory of the Czech and Slovak Federal Republic. The journal has been published since the 1950s.

[13] In this case, the natural order stands for the supply and demand mechanisms without larger regulation by the state.

deserving of criticism, 'saved' Czech children from some of the ills faced in the 'West' at that time. The team from the Faculty of Education (1992) led by Jiří Kotásek wrote:

> Not all the developments of democracy and lifestyle in Western countries were positive ones. Therefore, it cannot be ruled out that because of the totalitarian freeze, we find ourselves in a better situation than the Western states in some respects. For example, our distinctly non-democratic school system (change is necessary!!) has prevented some schools from developing to the point of losing discipline. According to the consensus of psychologists, such a loss is a significant cause for the rise in brutality and crime among youth. In addition, we need to learn from Western mistakes and problems with regard to drugs and irresponsible sexuality rather than repeat them as quickly as possible on our way to Europe. (…) In many ways, we can build on the first-rate education of our First Republic; we can also use elements of the Austrian-Hungarian school system that was satisfactory in its time, and we can always reach back to the sources of modern pedagogy in the works of J. A. Comenius. However, in doing so, we must remember that we are always returning to the state of school system that corresponded to the needs of society at least half a century of a rapid development ago. In this context, it is important to know that even in the countries of Western Europe, the school systems are being sharply criticized because their institutional character, established mainly in the interwar period, no longer corresponds to the needs of a highly flexible contemporary society. Although we come from a very different situation, we are not facing the problem of the crisis of the school system and education alone (Team of Faculty of Education, Charles University, 1992, p. 8).

It is interesting to note that the notion of the loss of discipline among young people in the West, presented by critics of the socialist school system, bears a striking resemblance to the portrayal in communist propaganda of a 'decadent' Western society. Other problems, such as the increase in youth brutality, were already inherent in Czechoslovakia at the end of the 1980s and were being cautiously criticized in the press and television of the time.[14]

In addition to discussion papers and partial ideas for reform, several fairly comprehensive proposals for the reform of education were created and published in the *Teacher's Newspaper*[15] in 1991.[16] Four of these proposals were discussed the most. The first was presented by the team from the Faculty of Education at Charles

---

[14]One of the discussants, Alena Nohejlová, who called for radical reform in the *Teacher's Newspaper* in 1991, linked the rise in delinquency in Czechoslovakia to a too-short time in primary school. Too brief an education leads to the overworking of students and the need to choose their profession prematurely at the turbulent adolescent age of 14–15. Therefore, she proposed lengthening primary school education and shortening subsequent studies in secondary school (Nohejlová, 1991).

[15]The *Teacher's Newspaper* (Učitelské noviny) journal is published weekly (except during the holidays) and it provides a full account of events in Czech school system. It contains interviews, cases, controversial topics, reports, analyses, commentaries, expert opinions, advisory boards, information from abroad and direct experiences of schools. The *Teacher's Newspaper* was being published even before 1989; its tradition dates back to the nineteenth century.

[16]Interestingly, in our research, the narrators did not mention these reform discussions in their interviews, and we came across only fleeting references in the archival sources of the schools. For example, in the minutes of meetings of the pedagogical board of a large urban school, we came across a note that a 'very radical' proposal by the NEMES group had been published.

University, the second proposal was prepared by the pedagogical committee of the Union of Czech Mathematicians and Physicists. A proposal was also submitted by the Independent Interdisciplinary Group (Nezávislé mezioborové sdružení, NEMES), which was an initiative formed 'from below', from the ranks of the teaching public. Later, another independent initiative, largely made up of Ministry of Education staff and called Group for Educational Alternatives—IDEA, also presented a proposal of their own.

The proposal by the team from Charles University was published first, and it was a very complex project. Concerning a school teaching organization, it proposed a fundamental revision of the current status, largely based on a return to the First Republic (interwar) Czechoslovak school system. For example, it proposed the introduction of a 5-year primary school and a successive lower secondary school for general education. In the matter of school system management, the proposal advocated decentralization, but emphasized the coordinating role of the Ministry of Education and the state (Kotásek, 1991; Strecková et al., 1991).

The Union of Czech Mathematicians and Physicists put forward a fairly realistic proposal emphasizing that large-scale reforms cannot be implemented without reflecting on the current economic and social situation. This concept corresponded fairly well to the reforms that were subsequently implemented, except that the proposal placed more emphasis on the multi-year grammar school and expected a gradual dissolution of 4-year grammar schools (Koncepce..., 1991).

The proposals of the NEMES and IDEA initiatives were much more radical and suggested the greatest possible independence of schools from the state. At the heart of the NEMES proposal was the idea that the changes were only the beginning of a real reform brought about by the natural self-regulation of the education system through competition. The introduction of market mechanisms was to lead to pluralism in the organization of schools and in education itself. The proposal was based on the consideration of individual needs and goals over the interests of society as a whole. Under socialism, the situation had been the other way around, as individual needs were subordinated to the interests of society. According to the NEMES proposal, the state should only determine basic rights, such as the obligation to educate oneself, but should leave it up to the individual to decide what path in education they would choose (Goulliová, 1991; NEMES, 1991).

The last published IDEA reform project was based on similar, rather radical ideas. However, it was more concerned with issues of school funding and the implementation of market mechanisms into education. It proposed for the school system to be funded directly by the state through the students. Each individual was to receive a subsidy for their education directly from the state (a special account was to be set up for this purpose), and it would then be up to the individual to decide where they would be educated and in which educational institution these resources would then be used. This was to create a natural competitive environment in which schools would directly compete for students (and their parents). According to this proposal, the schools could request varying levels of financial participation from the students over and above the state subsidy (Koucký, 1991a). Although the proposal sounded very utopian, some of the presented ideas were later implemented, albeit in modified form, specifically the funding of schools according to the number of students, a measure that was introduced in 1992. The presenters of the proposal were MEYS employees, including the then Deputy Minister Jan Koucký.

Even before the publication of the IDEA proposal, the Ministry of Education was preparing its own reform proposal, in which it declared that it had been inspired by the earlier proposals. The proposal was presented as a concept anticipating a permeable system responding to the conditions of the market economy and reflecting the different aptitudes of students. The concept published by the Ministry fell far short of the ambitions of the projects presented by the independent initiatives and tended more to reflect the proposals of the teams of the Faculty of Education of the Charles University and the Union of Czech Mathematicians and Physicists. This was shown in the design of the primary school organization, in which MEYS presented two options. The first option was a 9-year primary school with five grades at the first stage and four grades at the second stage. The second option was a 6-year primary school followed by a 3-year lower secondary school. This was a modified version of the proposal of the team from Charles University, inspired by the situation abroad, e.g. in Belgium, Italy, France, and Japan[17] (Krásenský, 1991).

The proposal of the Ministry of Education was elaborated in more detail at the beginning of 1992. In the end, the Ministry decided to implement the first option of the primary school organization, i.e. with five grades in the first stage of primary school, which probably seemed less costly, reflecting the country's economic problems at that time. This change was a part of the extension of the compulsory schooling to 9 years, which students could complete entirely at primary school. These innovations were based on the view that the changes would help overcome many of the problems of the existing education system. In particular, they concerned student overload and students leaving primary schools too early for secondary schools, i.e. deciding on further studies too early, and, to some extent, on the student's future professional careers.

However, the reform was presented 'only' as an experiment to be initially implemented at selected primary schools. This experiment was called General School (Obecná škola), modelled on the interwar Czechoslovak primary school. The general schools were to be set up primarily at existing small and incomplete primary schools, which, because of their low enrolment, had the right conditions for the successful performance of the experiment. The programme was based on having fewer students per classroom and an individual approach to these students. According to the opinions of the time, the demographic situation was also to be helpful in the implementation of the experiment. At that time, fewer children were being born than in the 'normalization' period, so that lower population age groups were gradually entering primary schools (Vopěnka, 1992). In the 1989/90 school year, there were about 1,235,000 students in primary schools, in the 1992/93 school year, there were 1,115,000, and in 1997/98, there were only about 1,092,000 students (*Školství...*, 1998).

---

[17] This organization of nine-year schooling into three-year educational stages (grades 1 to 3, grades 4 to 6, and grades 7 to 9) was experimentally tested at a primary school in Zátor (district Bruntál) (Václavík, 1995; Štefflová, 1995; Transformační projekt, 1995).

Relatively early criticism emerged that the ambitious declarations about transforming education were merely cosmetic reform. Criticism was also voiced amongst MPs in Parliament (Program transformace…, 1993), in which a special Commission for the Transformation of the School System was established in 1993 (Štefflová, 1993a). There were fears that the establishment of general schools would mean a return to the socialist unified school, as the Ministry of Education was once again introducing a reform 'from above' (Dvořák, 1993). The model of the general school was tested in practice on 620 schools in September 1993. At the same time, a proposal for its continuation was presented—a concept of a 4-year second stage called Civic School (Občanská škola)[18] (Štefflová, 1993b).

The extensive discussion on reforms initiated by the Ministry of Education resulted only in the implementation of an educational experiment and the 1995 adoption of the amendment to the Act No. 138/1995, which did not bring about fundamental changes in the principles of the functioning of primary schools.

The introduction of the compulsory ninth grade in primary schools was the most significant change resulting from the reform discussions. It was possible to complete the compulsory 9-year schooling in its entirety at primary school as early as 1990. Between 1990 and 1995, the ninth grades were being opened only for students who did not get into secondary school or who were not interested in further education (of any kind) after completing the compulsory schooling (MEYS, 1991a).

It is not surprising that there was a quite predictable critical and disappointed reaction from the public, as there were in fact no major innovations to the school system at the national level (Václavík, 1995). However, in the first half of the 1990s, teachers were more concerned about the virtually continuous underfunding of the Czech education system.

5.4   Schools and Economic Problems of Transformation

The implementation of a deeper reform of the education system was hampered by the need to address the urgent economic problems connected with the transformation. The deregulation of state-determined prices, leading to high inflation and therefore to a decline in the standard of living, was part of the transformation process.[19] The situation did not change substantially in 1990, but as of 1 January 1991, the government liberalized internal prices and the exchange rate of the Czechoslovak

---

[18] Again, the name used was based on a First Republic school. References to the interwar Czechoslovak school system were thus also made on a symbolic level.

[19] In most post-communist countries, the economic transformation was also accompanied by hyperinflation, mass unemployment, a decline in agricultural production, a reduction in consumption by the population, and social polarization, as former state property was in many cases acquired in various ways by small groups of people. The Czech Republic was relatively less affected by the negative concomitants of the transformation than most transition economies, however, signs of economic revival did not begin to appear until 1994 (Průcha, 2009).

currency. Consumer prices rose by 58% in 1991: 57% in the Czech lands and 61% in Slovakia. This is sometimes referred to as a 'price explosion'. The high inflation of course reflected itself in the living standards of the population; for example, real incomes decreased by up to one third (Průcha, 2009). This situation fundamentally affected the school system, as it led both to an increase in the costs of running schools and to pressure from the teaching public[20] to increase salaries. The tight budget and general lack of funds[21] did not allow for a simple increase in salaries for teachers and other state employees; it required significant salary and funding reforms across the entire education sector. These reforms went hand in hand with the need to streamline funding and to find savings. A World Bank investigation of the Czech school system revealed that it was significantly underfunded and that the funds were being spent very inefficiently (Kalous, 1991).

The search for savings worried the teaching public, who had been hopeful after the Velvet Revolution that the situation would improve. Minister of Education Petr Vopěnka, in his commentary on the 1991 budget proposal, condemned the false hopes given to citizens by the post-revolutionary government:

> The ills of the past years, and the euphoria of the first half of this year, when basically a number of different officials promised things that cannot be fulfilled. Sometimes it gave the impression that after 17 November, we would be living in a communist society. The reality is quite different. We are poor; we must realize this and act accordingly. If the budget is approved at the amount at which it was proposed, and I fear that the school system will probably not get more, I ask the ČNR[22] to take into consideration that I am immediately launching a severe, restrictive cost-saving policy in the school system (Školský rozpočet…, 1991).

Austerity dominated debates on the school system in 1991 and in the years that followed. Under the influence of optimism from the transformation to the market economy, views also appeared that the willingness of private sponsors, especially companies, would help the school system (Štefflová, 1991). In light of subsequent developments, these views proved unrealistic. Even our narrators retrospectively evaluated the interest of entrepreneurs and other sponsors as very limited.

The situation was particularly tense in the summer of 1991. The high inflation meant that without an increase in the school system budget, even the basic operation of schools in the new school year was threatened. In the event of a shortage of money, the Ministry of Education planned to partly or completely cancel payments for textbooks, school supplies, and school meals, for example. It also planned to substantially reduce the number of kindergartens and to charge fees for interest

---

[20]Teachers were mainly represented by the Czech and Moravian Trade Union of Workers in Education (Českomoravský odborový svaz pracovníků školství, ČMOS PŠ).

[21]For example, GDP fell by 14.2% in 1991, industrial production by 22.8%, and average real wage by 24% (Kalinová, 2012).

[22]The Czech National Council (ČNR) was the legislative body of the Czech Socialist Republic and later the Czech Republic from 1969 to the end of 1992. It was the supreme body of state power on the territory of the republic. In 1993, with the independence of the Czech Republic, it was transformed into the Chamber of Deputies of the Czech Republic.

clubs. These expenses had traditionally been covered by the state. However, the greatest 'discord' was over the issue of the valorization of teachers' salaries, without which many teachers would have faced a major existential threat (Neklidné Čelákovice…, 1991). There were even concerns about whether schools would open in September 1991 (Kalous, 1991).

A double financial 'injection' into the school system budget eventually averted the biggest problems, as it allowed for salary valorization and the preservation of the schools' normal operations (Frey, 1991). However, this was a one-off solution; it was clear that without a more fundamental reform, further school funding would remain unsustainable. Criticism of the inefficiency of management reappeared. While the schools struggled with a lack of funding throughout 1991, at the end of the year, they received funding from the remaining resources of the education authorities earmarked for the given year. The schools were forced to spend these funds by the end of the year. They hastily invested into expensive equipment that was not strictly needed, among other things, although they would have spent the same funds through the year on more necessary things related to the running of the school (Štefflová, 1992; Kotásek, 1993).

The Ministry of Education was preparing a reform of the funding of educational institutions, which was to be based on the principle of allocating money to education authorities according to the number of students in the district. This reform was based on the philosophy that money should be distributed at the lowest possible level. The education authorities were to have considerable freedom in the allocation of money to schools, and school heads were to have relative freedom in the remuneration of the teaching staff. The reform represented a more 'realistic' version of the funding proposal from the IDEA school system transformation project (Spravedlivěji…, 1991; Koucký, 1991b). Although these funding principles had been applied already in 1992, the school system faced both a lack of funding and the threat of drastic cost-saving measures even in that year. Once again, it was necessary to increase the budget during the year.

Quite predictably, teacher salaries were the main cause of teachers' protests in 1992. In addition to the school system funding reform, the government was also preparing a salary reform. This reform was adopted by the Federal Assembly on 13 March 1992; it was based on the principle of dividing public employees into salary grades according to their profession, level of expertise, and years of experience (Informace…, 1992). Voices were soon raised that the reform, effective from 1 May 1992, was grossly unfair to the teaching public (Nespravedlivé platové třídy…, 1992).

The Trade Union of Workers in Education reproached the government for not consulting the public on the amendment and because they saw classifying teachers into eight grades as unfair.[23] The path to increasing teachers' salaries, i.e. progress-

---

[23] The reform determined a total of 12 pay grades. The eighth grade started at a salary of 3500 CSK per month and this amount increased after 3 years of experience. After the third year, primary school teachers were to receive 3680 CSK, and, after 27 years of experience, they were to receive 5120 CSK. For the sake of comparison, the average wage in the Czech Republic in 1993 was 5904 CSK (Czech Statistical Office, 2003). According to this proposal, teachers would not a have a

ing to a higher grade, was also the subject of criticism. Successfully passing a 'professional aptitude test', the rules of which were not published in advance, was to be a new condition for promotion. The planned increase of teachers' teaching duties to 27 h per week, presented as a cost-cutting measure, was another reason for the teachers' strike and demonstration (Učitelé…, 1992).

Teachers protested even though the professional aptitude test was replaced by certain requisite criteria in order to be promoted to a higher grade. These criteria were also communicated to the teaching public in advance. On 27 April 1992, a demonstration in Prague's Old Town Square was attended by about 12,500 teachers. At the same time, there was a warning strike in most secondary schools and some primary schools in the form of schools being open but no classes being taught. Instead, the teachers talked to (older) students about the current situation, for example (Stávka…, 1992; Čornejová et al., 2020).

During the demonstration, low teacher salaries were criticized, as was the work of the ministry:

> Sure, it is about money, after all, the money has been allocated to the ministry from the state budget, but the main problem is that incompetent regulations and decrees impair the quality of teaching. (..) Deputy J. Koucký wants to increase the number of children per classroom, to combine lessons that were so difficult to divide, or to dissolve specialized schools. (…) All of this suggests that the Ministry of Education has absolutely no idea what the operation of a school entails (Stávka…, 1992, p. 1).

The protests were partly successful, and the teaching obligations of teachers were not increased (Pokyn ministra…, 1992a).[24] The conditions under which teachers could move up a pay grade were also finally made public. The school head could award a higher salary to up to one-third of the teaching staff of a school who had at least 3 years of experience, had done excellent work, and had published papers or manifested methodological activity (Pokyn ministra…, 1992b).

The ability to increase the salary of no more than one-third of the teaching staff in a school once again caused outrage. The trade unionists considered it unfair that only some of the teachers who had fulfilled the stipulated conditions could receive higher salary (Stanovisko rady ČMOS…, 1992). Pressure from teachers' unions led to the abolition of the set one-third quota, as did the parliamentary elections that were held in June 1992. The new minister, Petr Piťha, abolished the controversial provision on the maximum proportion of teachers who could be given higher salary. The teaching obligation rate was set at 23 h for the first stage of primary school and at 22 h for the second stage (Pokyn ministra…, 1992c).[25]

---

chance to reach even the average wage. However, it should be added that teachers' wages were increased by personal evaluations that could be awarded to teachers, for example, for the quality of their work. The average teacher's earnings were in fact slightly above average.

[24] Protests and strikes by teachers were previously a virtually unused means of coercion.

[25] Although Peter Piťha was responsible for a certain calming of the situation, he did not escape criticism that he was a weak minister who could do little for the school system. One of the commentators in the *Teacher's Newspaper* criticized both the previous and the then minister: 'I believe that both the previous and the current government have thrown the school system overboard. The

The poor financial remuneration of teachers led to protests and to more and more teachers leaving schools, which was criticized in contemporary sources. One rural school chronicle held a critical statement directed at the Minister of Education Petr Vopěnka, signalling significant dissatisfaction:

> The entire school year 1991/1992 was marked on the one hand by efforts to reform the school system, to make the curriculum easier and simpler, to not overburden students, and on the other hand by the hostile attitude of the Minister of Education, P. Vopěnka, towards the teaching public. The poor financial remuneration of teachers' work led to many workers, especially men, leaving for more lucrative fields.

In the following years, the question of savings and the search for possible financial reserves were frequent topics of debates about Czech school system. However, contemporary documents show that the situation had somewhat stabilized and there were no longer situations of such crisis that there would be talk of schools closing because of the lack of funding. The budget was successfully managed with cuts 'only' in matters such as the funding for students' extracurricular activities. This led to more financial participation from parents (Školství a úspory…, 1993).

In 1994 and 1995, the stabilization of public finances and the start of economic growth allowed an increase in the school system budget as well as more significant investments in school buildings and their equipment (Švancar, 1994).[26] Another demonstration of about 10,000 teachers took place in Brno on 29 June 1995, and a readiness to strike was declared during the salary increase negotiations. Teachers' salaries were to be increased by 10% instead of the 20% demanded by the school unions. However, the threat of a strike was subsequently averted thanks to a joint agreement on an increase in funding for the floating component of teachers' salaries in the summer of 1995. Compared to the turbulent situation of 1991 and 1992, such issues are 'classic' disputes, common even in Western European countries (Nový školní rok, 1995; Spokojenost…, 1995). Nevertheless, the remuneration of teachers remained low for university-educated people (in 1997, it was 6% above the average wage). The pay of non-teaching staff, such as school instructors, janitors, and cleaners, was even lower. The teachers' costs of living also varied by region. For example, in the capital city of Prague, where the cost of living is high, teachers received 86% of the local average wage; in some districts, teachers received as much as 130% of the local average wage (Čornejová et al., 2020; see also Školství…, 1998).

Teachers' salaries can be seen from a different point of view: from the perspective of their ratio to the average wage in the Czech Republic. In 1992, the salary of a primary school teacher was 8.7% higher than the average wage in the Czech

---

only thing the ex-minister Vopěnka was able to do was to rename the existing dysfunctional school bureaucracy while responding to all the criticism from the schools by repeating the view that teachers were after all just collaborating with the communists anyway. The present "good" minister does not really annoy the Prime Minister, since from all of his colleagues, he bothers the PM with constant requests for his ministry the least often' (Císař, 1993, p. 10).

[26] In the Czech Republic, GDP grew by 2.2% in 1994 by 6.4% in 1995 (Czech Statistical Office, 2023).

Republic, in 1996, it was 12.1% higher; in 1997, it was 6.9% higher.[27] Despite later disputes and strikes (in 1997 and in 2003), the situation of teachers was gradually improving and, especially after 2010, their salaries kept increasing. This is perhaps one of the main reasons the narrators in our research did not mention or discuss the issue of teachers' financial remuneration very often.

5.5   Comparison of the Transformation of the School System with Neighbouring Post-Socialist Countries

After 1989, Czechoslovakia underwent a major social and economic transformation. The school system also experienced changes in the first decade after the fall of communism, especially in terms of the manner of management and self-governance. On the other hand, some changes were not yet implemented, especially in the fields of teaching and curriculum content.

But what was the situation abroad? Can we look for parallels with countries that underwent a similar neoliberal transformation (Poland), or for comparisons with those that followed a more cautious path (Slovakia, Hungary)?

Walterová and Greger (2006) stated that the processes of post-socialist transformation in the Visegrad Four (V4)[28] countries were quite similar in their basic parameters. In all four countries, either new laws were adopted or the existing ones were amended, the role of self-governments was strengthened, and the autonomy of schools was increased. Primary and lower secondary education disintegrated to varying degrees, and private and religious schools were allowed to be established, although the influence of the church varied from country to country according to the degree of religiosity of the population.

The problems are also common. While the new political representatives declared their interest in education as a democratic value, in practice, it was an area of rather marginal political interest. This may have been due to the idea that education is primarily a cultural value, and it is not associated with social or economic capital (Walterová & Greger, 2006). Thus, while the cultural elites of post-socialist countries may have proclaimed that a higher quality of education would lead to greater economic prosperity for the country, these effects are in fact a long-term matter without a quick and visible impact on salary levels or GDP. Therefore, the link

---

[27] The 1997 pay cut was due to the economic and political crisis in the ČR, among other things. In general, the Czech economy experienced a standard shock, much smaller than the 1991–1992 crisis. The political consequences of this crisis were probably greater, as the crisis eventually led to the fall of the government.

[28] The Visegrád Four consists of the Czech Republic, Hungary, Poland, and Slovakia. It was established in Visegrád, Hungary, in 1991 as a cooperation platform for the purpose of joint advances in the EU and NATO accession process, but also as a space for shaping the common policies and interests of the Central Eastern Europe (CEE) countries.

between the economy and education was not at the forefront of political and public interest.

The Czech Republic is among the Central and Eastern Europe countries that implemented their economic transformation more quickly, more boldly, and at the same time relatively successfully, without serious suffering for most of the society. Nevertheless, Poland was considered even more 'aggressive', as it applied 'shock therapy' in the early 1990s, and it was subjected to drastic deregulation and mass privatization. Unlike the Czech Republic, Poland's liberalization led to hyperinflation and a sharp rise in unemployment, but it was later among the countries with the highest economic growth. While the Czech Republic had its 'moment of glory' in the early 1990s, Poland became a regional 'tiger' only after the harsh lessons of the early phase of its transformation (Ther, 2016).

Of the V4 countries, Poland chose the most decisive path in the field of education. The Polish education reform deviated the most from the original socialist unified school system, disintegrating the first and second stages of primary school. This meant that students moved to a completely different school for the second stage. Similarly to the Czech Republic, the regional self-government of schools was strengthened, with a number of previously closed rural schools being re-established (Walterová & Greger, 2006).

Hungary presented a contrasting example. It had the strongest legal continuity between socialism and post-socialism. In Hungary, it was paradoxically the communist government who started the economic reforms inspired by neoliberalism in the late 1980s. After the transfer of power, the victorious opposition took a more socially sensitive course and somewhat slowed down the reforms. To some extent, the privatization of the economy was forced by the unfavourable economic situation of the early 1990s. However, it should be emphasized that in socialist Hungary and Poland both, the degree of nationalization did not reach the level of Czechoslovakia. For example, small trades remained privately owned in Poland and Hungary (Křen, 2019).

The decentralization reform of the Hungarian school system started in 1985. At that time, the schools had already gained autonomy and local administrations were put in charge of their administration. However, there was no concept of control or support from the responsible participants at the local level, i.e. mayors of municipalities or school heads. For example, there was no concept of any education for them in the field of school administration. Halász (1993, p. 29) wrote: 'While an increasing number of schools benefited from greater freedom, most of them simply felt that the state had abandoned its responsibilities and left them alone to fend for themselves.' In addition, the single central inspectorate was dissolved and the control of schools was left to the responsibility of the founders. On the other hand, Hungary was the only V4 country that did not switch to per-student normative funding of schools (Walterová & Greger, 2006; Halász, 1993).

Slovakia, under the authoritarian government of Prime Minister Vladimír Mečiar, became the 'black sheep' of the V4 countries. After the formation of the independent state, the Slovak government moved away from the neoliberal model of transformation promoted by the government of the dissolved Czechoslovakia. A more cautious path of privatization by a centrally controlled state agency was pursued, but this created a breeding ground for corruption and clientelism. Slovakia as a new independent state suffered from the absence of an established political structure and culture; it was also plagued by economic problems and a decline in GDP. All of this led to an even greater neglect of reforms of the education system than in the Czech Republic.

Prior to the break-up of the federation, Slovakia underwent reforms similar to those in the Czech lands, such as strengthening the role of self-governments. However, in an analysis in 1995, Ladislav Čerych wrote of a tendency to strengthen the state supervision of the school system. More than in the Czech Republic, debates on the school system in Slovakia were dominated by isolationist and traditionalist discourse at the expense of the Europeanization of the school system. The relatively greater influence of the church also cannot be overlooked. As a result, only partial reforms have taken place. Primary schools were extended to 9 years, but the second stage had 5 years instead of the first stage. In Slovakia, this created a situation in which it was possible to obtain a basic education either in 9 years at a primary school or in 8 years because of the possibility to study at an 8-year grammar school, which students could join after the fourth grade of primary school (Kosová & Porubský, 2011; Křen, 2019).

Parallels can be drawn between the broader context of the transformation and the transformation of school systems in the individual countries. The most significant changes were implemented in Poland. A high degree of continuity was inherent in Hungary. Slovakia, in turn, was crippled by the consolidation of its own statehood, which negatively affected the country's integration into Western structures[29] and further delayed the reform of the school system. The Czech Republic remained 'somewhere in between' the Polish and Slovak ways. The search for inspiration in its own democratic past is perhaps the most significant aspect of the Czech transformation.

Although some differences can be identified among the V4 countries as well as in the wider area of Central and Eastern Europe, the period of post-socialist transformation of education was characterized by inspiration from neoliberal values of responsibility, individualization, and autonomy. All the countries faced the inherent dilemma of whether to modernize the school system according to the western model or to draw inspiration from their own traditions. The specific decisions differed according to cultural, economic, and geographical conditions. The transformation processes certainly cannot be interpreted as the 'mere' adoption of Western models (Silova, 2018). While all the countries of the former Soviet Union dealt with the dilemma of whether to draw inspiration from the West, in Central Europe, and especially in the Czech Republic, this question took a different form. Czechs consider themselves Central Europeans, emphasizing their own cultural and democratic traditions with the very strong legacy of the first Czechoslovak Republic (1918–1938).

---

[29] Slovakia joining NATO—the other countries joined in 1999—was postponed until after the change of government and political course in 2004.

From the Czech perspective, the return to Europe was a 'natural' narrative of the transformation, as Czechoslovakia had been part of Europe until it was forcibly removed when it fell into the Soviet sphere of influence (Holý, 1996). Therefore, in the Czech context, the return to democratic school system traditions was essentially in line with its proximity to Western Europe. Unlike the countries of the former USSR, the search for 'one's own path' in Czechoslovakia was not related to space (or geopolitical orientation) but to time. The decision between inspiration from the West and from one's own traditions had a common denominator here—the return to Europe—and the two inspirations are not necessarily contradictory. In fact, a 'return' to democratic traditions was preferred by some commentators as more 'natural' than adopting Western models, including those elements that did not work. But did the school heads and teachers deal with similar decisions? Or were they more concerned with local practices and the problems of everyday life? How and in what fields did schools actually change in the period after 1989, one of the most significant moments in the history of the Czech lands? These and other questions will be addressed in the next chapter of the book.

Bibliography

Act No. 171/1990 Coll. On the System of Primary and Secondary Schools (Education Act). (1990). https://www.psp.cz/sqw/sbirka.sqw?cz=171&r=1990

Act No. 564/1990 Coll. On State Administration and Self-Government in the School System. (1990). https://www.psp.cz/sqw/sbirka.sqw?cz=564&r=1990

Act No. 390/1991 Coll. On Pre-School Institutions and School Facilities. (1991). https://www.psp.cz/sqw/sbirka.sqw?cz=390&r=1991

Act No. 138/1995 Coll. (1995). https://www.psp.cz/sqw/sbirka.sqw?cz=138&r=1995

Bečvář, J., & Veselý, J. (1993). Perspektivy českého školství [Perspectives of Czech school system]. *Pedagogika, 43*(2), 133–136.

Berend, I. T. (2009). *From the Soviet Bloc to the European Union.* Cambridge Unversity Press.

Berryman, S. E. (2000). *Hidden challenges to education systems in transition economies.* The World Bank.

Bîrzea, C. (1994). *Educational policies of countries in transition.* Council of Europe Press.

Čermáková, M. (1991). Formování totalitního školství v poválečném Československu [Formation of totalitarian school system in post-war Czechoslovakia]. *Pedagogika, 41*(3), 323–333.

Čerych, L. (1995). Educational reforms in central and Eastern Europe. *European Journal of Education, 30*(4), 423–435.

Čerych, L. (1996). Zprávy o národní politice ve vzdělávání: Česká republika [Reports on National Educational Policy: The Czech Republic]. Ústav pro informace ve vzdělávání.

České priority pro Evropu [Czech priorities for Europe]. (2010). Ústav pro informace ve vzdělávání.

Czech Statistical Office. (2003). *Vývoj mezd v letech 1993–2003* [Development of salaries in 1993–2003]. https://www.czso.cz/documents/10180/20562725/3111rr01t.pdf/f1bbd31b-aba8-4897-aae1-1b89a260ba91?version=1.0

Czech Statistical Office. (2023). *Česká republika: hlavní ekonomické ukazatele* [Czech Republic: Main economic indicators]. https://www.czso.cz/documents/10180/196622036/chmucr040323.xlsx/f5a961df-f56c-45eb-80e3-475c94fa64fd?version=1.0

Císař, Z. (1993). Pocity pedagoga (nejen nad výplatní páskou) [Feelings of a pedagogue (not only over payslip)]. *Učitelské noviny, 96*(45), 10.

Čornejová, I., Kasper, T., Kasperová, D., Kourová, P., Kratochvíl, P., Lenderová, M., Novotný, M., Pokorný, J., Svatoš, M., Svobodný, P., Šimek, J., & Váňová, R. (2020). *Velké dějiny zemí Koruny české: Tematická řada: Školství a vzdělanost* [Great history of the lands of the bohemian crown: Thematic edition: School system and level of education]. Paseka.

Dvořák, R. (1993). Stanovisko, varování, nebo výkřik do tmy? Aneb jak je to se závazností osnov pro obecné školy? [Statement, warning or a shout in the dark? Or, how binding are the curricula for general schools?]. *Učitelské noviny, 96*(20), 6.

Fiszbein, A. (2001). *Decentralizing education in transition societies: Case studies from central and Eastern Europe*. The World Bank.

Frey, J. (1991). O platech ve školství: Hovoříme s předsedou ČMOS PŠ Jaroslavem Rösslerem [On salaries in school system: An interview with CMOS PS chairman Jaroslav Rössler]. *Učitelské noviny, 94*(43), 2.

Goulliová, K. (1991). Společenské požadavky nově [Social requirements newly]. *Učitelské noviny, 94*(11), 8.

Greger, D. (2011). Dvacet let českého školství optikou teorií změny vzdělávání v post-socialistických zemích [Twenty years of Czech education as viewed through the theory of change of education in post-socialist countries]. *Orbis scholae, 5*(1), 9–22.

Halász, G. (1993). Politika autonomie škol a reformy řízení vzdělávání a výchovy. Změny v Maďarsku v perspektivách východní Evropy [Politics of school autonomy and reforms of management of education and upbringing. Changes in Hungary in perspectives of Eastern Europe]. *Pedagogika, 43*(1), 27–32.

Holý, L. (1996). *The little Czech and the great Czech nation: National identity and the post-communist transformation of society*. Cambridge University Press.

Informace o realizaci nového systému odměňování [Information on implementation of the new system of remuneration]. (1992). *Učitelské noviny, 95*(13), I–IV.

Kalinová, L. (2012). Konec nadějím a nová očekávání: k dějinám české společnosti 1969–1993 [The End of Hopes and New Expectations: On the History of Czech Society 1969–1993]. Academia.

Kalous, J. (1991). Otevřou se v září školy? [Will the schools open in September?]. *Učitelské noviny, 94*(23), 1.

Kalous, J. (1993). Školská politika v České republice po roce 1989 [School policy in The Czech Republic after 1989]. *Pedagogika, 43*(3), 235–239.

Kopeček, M. (Ed.). (2019). *Architekti dlouhé změny: expertní kořeny postsocialismu v Československu* [Architects of the long change: The expert roots of postsocialism in Czechoslovakia].. Argo.

Koncepce vzdělávání v České republice: z návrhu Pedagogické komise Jednoty českých matematiků a fyziků [Concept of education in The Czech Republic: From the proposal of pedagogical commission of Union of Czech mathematicians and physicists]. (1991). *Učitelské noviny, 94*(29), 8.

Kosová, B., & Porubský, Š. (2011). Slovenská cesta transformácie edukačného systému po roku 1989 na príklade primárneho vzdelávania a prípravy jeho učiteľov [Slovakian way of transformation of the educational system after 1989 on the example of primary education and training of its teachers]. *Pedagogická orientace, 21*(1), 35–50.

Kotásek, J. (1991). Návrh organizační struktury vzdělávací soustavy České republiky [Proposal of the organizational structure of the educational system of The Czech Republic]. *Učitelské noviny, 94*(45), 8.

Kotásek, J. (1993). Vize výchovy v postsocialistické éře [Vision of education in the post-socialist era]. *Pedagogika, 43*(1), 9–19.

Kotásek, J. (Ed.). (2001). *Národní program rozvoje vzdělávání v České republice: Bílá kniha* [National programme for the development of education in The Czech Republic. White paper]. Tauris.

Koucký, J. (1991a). Návrh pravidel rozpisu školského rozpočtu na rok 1992 [Proposal of rules of the school system budget for 1992]. *Učitelské noviny, 94*(45), 6.

Koucký, J. (1991b). Snaha najít konkrétní cestu: návrh koncepce rozvoje školství Skupiny pro vzdělávací alternativy IDEA [An effort to find a specific way: School system development concept proposal by the group for educational alternatives IDEA]. *Učitelské noviny, 94*(41) příloha Obzor 1.

Krásenský, M. (1991). Návrh projektu transformace výchovně-vzdělávací soustavy [Project proposal of the educational system transformation]. *Učitelské noviny, 94*(35), 3–10.

Křen, J. (2019). *Čtvrt století střední Evropy: visegrádské země v globálním příběhu let 1992–2017 [A quarter of a century of Central Europe: Visegrad countries in the global story of 1992–2017].* Univerzita Karlova, Nakladatelství Karolinum.

Legislativní maratón: nové školské zákony byly schváleny [Legislative Marathon: New Education Acts Adopted]. (1990). Učitelské noviny, *93*(20), 1.

Mitter, W. (1991). School reforms in international perspective. Trends and problems. *Pedagogika, 41*(1), 7–23.

Lieberman, I. W., Nestor, S. S., & Desai, R. M. (Eds.). (1997). *Between state and market: Mass privatization in transition economies.* The World Bank.

MEYS. (1991a). Plnění povinné devítileté docházky v základní škole [Compulsory nine-year schooling in primary School]. *Učitelské noviny, 94*(5), 15.

MEYS. (1991b). Vyhláška Ministerstva školství, mládeže a tělovýchovy České republiky o základní škole [Decree of the Ministry of Education, Youth and sports on primary schools]. *Učitelské noviny, 94*(27), 8–9.

Nad zákonem [Above the Law]. (1990). *Učitelské noviny, 93*(34), 1.

Návrh zákona o státní správě ve školství [Draft act on state administration in the school system]. (1990). *Učitelské noviny, 93*(28), 1–2.

Neklidné Čelákovice. (1991). Ze setkání předsedů OROS a ředitelů školských úřadů [Restless Čelákovice: From the meeting of OROS chairmen and directors of educational authorities]. *Učitelské noviny, 94*(22), 1.

NEMES. (1991). Svoboda ve vzdělání a česká škola [Freedom in education and Czech School]. *Učitelské noviny, 94*(32) Příloha Obzor 1.

Nespravedlivé platové třídy [Unfair Salary Grades]. (1991). *Učitelské noviny, 94*(16), 7.

Nový školní rok zahájí stávka? [Will the new school year start with a strike?]. (1995). Učitelské noviny, *98*(24), 2.

Nohejlová, A. (1991). Neodkládat řešení [Do not delay the solution]. *Učitelské noviny, 94*(3), 8.

Pilař, J. (1991). V otevřeném dialogu: Je, nebo není pedagogická veřejnost na vedlejší koleji? [In an Open Dialogue: Is pedagogical public being sidelined or not?]. *Učitelské noviny, 94*(10), 7.

Pokyn ministra k nařízení vlády o platových poměrech zaměstnanců rozpočtových a některých příspěvkových organizací v aplikaci na předškolní zařízení, školy a školská zařízení od 1. 5. 1992 [Minister's Instruction on the Government Regulation on Salary Conditions of Employees of Budgetary and Certain Contributory Organisations in Application to Pre-Schools, Schools and Educational Institutions from 1.5.1992]. (1992a). *Učitelské noviny, 95*(22), 7.

Pokyn ministra ke Stanovení kritérií pro zařazení učitelů do vyšší platové třídy [Minister's Instruction on Establishing Criteria for the Classification of Teachers in a Higher Grade]. (1992b). *Učitelské noviny, 95*(22), 7.

Pokyn ministra k zahájení školního roku 1992/93 [Minister's Instruction to Begin the 1992/93 School Year]. (1992c). *Učitelské noviny, 95*(31), 2.

Poloucek, O., & Zounek, J. (2021). Vzdělávací systém a československá verze přestavby (1987–1989): Analýza, kritika a návrhy na reformy v kontextu ideologie a krize [Education and the Czechoslovak form of perestroika (1987–1989): Analysis, criticism, and planned reforms in the context of ideology and crisis]. *Studia paedagogica, 26*(3), 83–108. https://doi.org/10.5817/SP2021-3-4

Program transformace [Transformation Programme]. (1993). *Učitelské noviny, 96*(10), 8–9.

Prokop, J. (1991). Reformní program [Reform Programme]. *Učitelské noviny, 94*(7), 7.

Průcha, V. (2009). Hospodářské a sociální dějiny Československa 1918–1992. *II. díl: Období 1945–1992* [Economic and social history of Czechoslovakia 1918–1992. Part II: The period 1945–1992]. Doplněk.

Rychlík, J. (2012). *Rozdělení Československa: 1989–1992* [Division of Czechoslovakia: 1989–1992]. Vyšehrad.

Stávka v rozvrhu [Strike in Schedule]. (1992). *Učitelské noviny, 95*(18), 1.

Strecková, I., Malach, A., & Motyka, G. (1991). Decentralizační tendence ve správě, řízení a financování školství [Decentralisation tendencies in the administration, management and funding of education]. *Učitelské noviny, 94*(45), 12.

Silova, I. (2018). Comparing post-socialist transformations: Dead ends, new pathways and unexpected opening. In M. Chankseliani & I. Silova (Eds.), *Comparing post-socialist transformations: Purposes, policies, and practices in education* (pp. 193–200). Symposium Books.

Spokojenost s úpravou platů nepedagogů [Satisfaction with Salary adjustment of non-pedagogues]. (1995). *Učitelské noviny, 98*(31), 2.

Spravedlivěji. (1991). Tvoří se nový systém financování školských zařízení [Fairer. A new system of school funding is being developed]. *Učitelské noviny, 94*(26), 2.

Stanovisko rady ČMOS pracovníků školství k pokynům pana ministra školství č. J. 1359/92-2 A 1360/92 [Opinion of the Council of CMOS of Workers in Education on the Instructions of the Minister of Education No. 1359/92–2 A 1360/92]. (1992). *Učitelské noviny, 95*(22), 7.

Sucháček, P. (2014). Spor o víceletá gymnázia: Historický kontext a empirická data [The dispute over multi-year grammar schools: Historical context and empirical data]. *Studia paedagogica, 19*(3), 139–154. https://doi.org/10.5817/SP2014-3-8

Školský rozpočet [School System Budget]. (1991). *Učitelské noviny, 94*(3), 1.

Školství a úspory: Ing. (1993). Ivan Pilip, náměstek ministra školství, mládeže a tělovýchovy ČR [School System and savings: Ing. Ivan Pilip, deputy minister of education, youth and sports of The Czech Republic]. *Učitelské noviny, 96*(4), 1.

Školství na křižovatce: výroční zpráva o stavu a rozvoji výchovně vzdělávací soustavy v letech 1997–1998 [Education at the crossroads: annual report on the state and development of the educational system in 1997–1998]. (1998). Ústav pro informace ve vzdělávání.

Štefflová, J. (1991). Okresní Počítání: dva pohledy na budoucnost rozpočtů škol [District counting: Two perspectives on the future of school budgets]. *Učitelské noviny, 94*(21), 4.

Štefflová, J. (1992). Ředitelské počítání [School head Counting]. *Učitelské noviny, 95*(10), 2.

Štefflová, J. (1993a). Dům se staví od základů: z prvního jednání komise pro otázky transformace základního školství [Building a house from the ground up: From the first meeting of the primary education transformation commission]. *Učitelské noviny, 96*(4), 15.

Štefflová, J. (1993b). Škola budoucích občanů: jak bude vypadat návaznost na školu obecnou [The school of future citizens: What the follow-up to the general school will look like]. *Učitelské noviny, 96*(40), 6.

Štefflová, J. (1995). 3+3+3. *Učitelské noviny, 98*(9), 6.

Švancar, R. (1994). Bude ze tří miliard pět? Ambiciózní projekt na přilákání investic do školství [Will three billion become five? An ambitious project to attract investments to the school system]. *Učitelské noviny, 97*(43), 3.

Ther, P. (2016). *Europe since 1989: A history*. Princeton University Press.

Transformační projekt ZŠ Zátor 3+3+3 [Project of Transformation of Primary School in Zátory 3+3+3]. (1995). Učitelské noviny, 98(9), 15.

Team of Faculty of Education, Charles University. (1992). Rozvaha o školství a vzdělanosti a jejich dalším vývoji v českých zemích [Reflection on the School System and level of education and their further development in Czech lands]. *Pedagogika, 42*(1), 5–18.

Učitelé na staroměstském: Z vystoupení předsedy ČMOS PŠ Jaroslava Rösslera na pražské demonstraci školských pracovníků [Teachers in Old Town: From a Speech by Jaroslav Rössler, chair of the CMOS PS at a Prague demonstration of school workers]. (1992). Učitelské noviny, 95(18), 1.

Václavík, V. (1995). Novela ve starém duchu [An amendment in the old spirit]. *Učitelské noviny,* *98*(31), 12.
Vopěnka, P. (1992). Návrh: Program rozvoje výchovně vzdělávací soustavy v České republice [Proposal: Programme for the development of the educational system in The Czech Republic]. *Učitelské noviny, 95*(6), 6–7.
Walterová, E., & Greger, D. (2006). Transformace vzdělávacích systémů zemí visegrádské skupiny: srovnávací analýza [The transformation of educational Systems of Visegrád Group: Comparative analysis]. *Orbis scholae, 1*(1), 13–29. https://doi.org/10.14712/23363177.2018.132

Chapter 6
Schools: Everyday Life in the Period of Post-Socialist Transformation

Abstract In this chapter, we look in more detail at the everyday life of primary schools and their changes in the post-socialist transformation. The first years after the Velvet Revolution were characterized by vigorous changes, experimentation, and the search for possible ways to reform school management and administration.

Our research shows that the resistance to rules and excessive bureaucracy and the desire for freedom form the dominant images of school in the early 1990s that is present in the memory of teachers. The neoliberal turn brought a high appreciation of responsibility, which was reflected in the self-governance (autonomy) of schools. However, this also brought entirely new responsibilities and rules.

Sensitive topics included changes in school management and the first competitive selections for new school heads; these competitions were initially conducted without clear rules. The chapter concludes with a focus on the relationship between schools and the educational offices that were supposed to manage the schools and that were a part of the school management reforms. Cooperation with municipalities, which became the founders of schools, became a new challenge for schools. The quality of the relationship between the municipality and the school could influence the atmosphere in the school and the conditions for education quite significantly.

Keywords Czech Republic · Velvet Revolution · Schools · Autonomy · Everyday life · School management · Transformation · Changes

6.1 Schools on the Threshold of a New Era

On Friday, 17 November 1989, a student demonstration in Prague was violently suppressed; this event can be seen as the beginning of the Velvet Revolution (Suk, 2003; Krapfl, 2013; Kenney, 2002). In the following days, more and more people decided to participate in the demonstrations in Prague and in regional or district towns across Czechoslovakia. On 27 November, there was even a general strike, an unprecedented phenomenon. The founding of the Civic Forum (Občanské Fórum)

© Masaryk University, Faculty of Arts, Registration no. 00216224,   143
VAT ID: CZ00216224 2024
J. Zounek et al., *(Post)Socialist Transformation of Primary Schools*,
https://doi.org/10.1007/978-3-031-58768-9_6

in Prague as a democratic initiative seeking changes in society prompted the establishment of local Civic Forums in cities, businesses, and schools. This was not a centrally controlled and organized activity, but a spontaneous activity of citizens (Krapfl, 2013).

In citizens' initiatives at the regional level, the revolutionary pro-democratic movement spread gradually. Although mass demonstrations took place in Prague in the first week after 17 November 1989, calm prevailed in the regions. The success of the revolution was still very uncertain, as rumours spread about the suppression of the demonstrations by people's militias, civic patrol units subordinated to the Communist Party of Czechoslovakia (Komunistická strana Československa, KSČ) and even the army.

The mass spread of protest activities throughout the country happened at the end of November 1989. The real effects of the revolution were visible in the first weeks of December: the first staffing changes in political parties took place and changes in other areas of life of society also occurred. By the end of November, the situation was being vigorously debated at some schools, as evidenced by entries in a school chronicle:

> Heated debates about the political situation, which resulted in support for a general student strike on 27 November 1989, were held in the staff room. In classrooms that were still in session at the time of the strike (at 12 o'clock), no classes were taught and the teachers explained the situation to the students; the older students watched television broadcasts of the demonstrations.[1]

The response depended on the atmosphere in the school or in the town. A narrator from a small town recalled that at the end of November, fear of expressing one's own opinion still predominated. This was caused by the school head, who remained a 'loyal' communist, but also by the attitude of the communists in the town management.

> Well, when the general strike was announced, we had a meeting and the school head read the position of the town's national committee in a broken voice. The committee was against participation, of course, and then the school head said in a low voice that whoever wanted to go to the demonstration should tell him so that he could arrange substitutes. Well, four of us went from that quite large school; the others were afraid. (Karolína)

The new government of Czechoslovakia formed on 7 December 1989 after a series of negotiations triggered by strikers' demands and the resignation of the communist chair of the federal government, Ladislav Adamec. Although the communist Marián Čalfa was appointed Prime Minister, the cabinet was composed in part of representatives of the Civic Forum and non-communist political parties. Personnel changes

---

[1] In the text, we refer to school chronicles, minutes of meetings of the pedagogical councils, and other documents from the archival fonds of individual schools. We also work with materials from former District National Committees, such as minutes of meetings of school committees. We anonymize these materials deliberately, as they often contain sensitive information. We do not refer to specific archival fonds when citing them. These materials are stored in the State District Archives (of the Czech Republic) of the Brno-venkov district in Rajhrad, Zlín, and Znojmo, and the Brno Municipal Archive, which serves as the district archive for the Brno-město district.

took place in the Czech government as well, which also included the Minister of Education. On 5 December, Milan Adam, a representative of the democratic movement, became the Minister of Education.

The spontaneity and importance of the grassroots initiative during the Velvet Revolution is clear both from the recollections of the teachers in our research sample and from contemporary documents. The district education administrations also reacted to the new situation with a certain delay. The District National Committees (Okresní národní výbory) and their departments of education were responsible for the management of primary schools.

The minutes of the meeting of the education committee in one Moravian district from 29 November 1989 contained the usual agenda; there was only the addition of a brief note of the need to remain calm and composed.

A more fundamental change did not occur until mid-December. By that time, the first instructions from the Ministry of Education were already coming, albeit in a rather spontaneous manner. It was not unusual for the instructions to be transmitted by telephone.[2] This is evidenced by a unique transcript[3] of a telephone call from a regional school inspector on 15 December 1989, in which the inspector interpreted the current instructions to a member of the department of education of the District National Committee.

In terms of changes in teaching, the instructions mentioned the planned measures only very superficially. One measure concerned a change in the teaching of history for the seventh and eighth grade of primary school (in particular, the teaching of recent history). The instructions included introducing optional instruction in other foreign languages in the sixth to eighth grades. From the 1990/1991 school year, fifth grades were to have a direct choice of several foreign languages other than the compulsory Russian.

The instructions relating to the life and operation of the school had an immediate impact on the life of the school. This concerned the removal of all manifestations of communist ideology and propaganda from schools (e.g. removal of political bulletin boards and portraits of communist movement leaders). The new form of address, Mr. and Mrs., was introduced in both written and oral speech and the form of address of Comrade, which had been used for many years, was abandoned. Furthermore, according to the instructions, preparations were to begin for the rehabilitation of teachers who had been persecuted by the communist regime.

---

[2] The Ministry of Education created a methodological instruction reflecting the fundamental changes in the Constitution from 5 December 1989. That is to say, the article on the leading role of the KSČ in society and the article on education in the spirit of Marxism-Leninism were removed from the Constitution. Information about the instruction was disseminated more or less spontaneously during December 1989. The wider teaching public did not officially learn about the instructions arising from this instruction until January 1990, when the instructions were published in the nationwide *Učitelské noviny* (*Teacher's Newspaper*) periodical (MEYS, 1990a).

[3] The uniqueness of this document lies in the fact that the instructions spread over the telephone were almost never preserved. This transcript is thus one of the few sources of this nature.

The changes were very spontaneous, but understandable in the given situation. The need to act immediately and the absence of clear rules led to situations in which the interpretation and especially the implementation of the (ministerial) instructions depended on the representatives of the state administration at the regional and district level. However, the administration did not change in any way in the first weeks after the Velvet Revolution. Perhaps that is why the situation in schools was ahead of the regulations from central institutions in some respects. During December 1989, even primary school teachers were organizing themselves spontaneously, setting up local organizations of the Civic Forum, and signing statements and declarations advocating political change. For example, the Civic Forum was founded in a rural school (according to the school chronicle) as early as 7 December 1989. However, it should again be noted that the situation may have differed from school to school. It depended on whether the school management also agreed with the Civic Forum. The relations in the school and the position of the school head were also important. Apparently, interpersonal relations and the character of the school head were key to the situation in many schools. For example, school heads from the ranks of the KSČ who remained loyal to the party line and even continued to promote Communist Party policies were generally unpopular. Those school heads who viewed their membership in the Communist Party mainly as a service for the good of their profession and the school (ideology being secondary) could still enjoy the authority and respect of teachers after the Velvet Revolution.

The formation of local organizations of Civic Forums, or simply the formation of collectives of teachers who advocated change in schools, took place in many schools in December 1989. In some places, KSČ members were joining the pro-democracy movement while at the same time renouncing their party membership: 'The first to lay down the KSČ member card was the janitor, and he did it publicly' (Blanka).

The Civic Forum did not consider itself to be a standard political party, but rather a civic initiative striving for change in society. Representatives of the Civic Forum called for the organization of signing events in support of the election of Václav Havel as President of the Republic. Expressing support for the election of a new president illustrated the strong politicization of the revolutionary period in the school system, especially just after the Velvet Revolution. The expressions of professional and political demands were intertwined with the pedagogical public's desire for change. This situation contrasts with further developments. In 1990, an amendment to the Education Act was adopted (Act No. 171/1990 Coll.) that banned the activities of political parties and movements in schools, an apparent reaction to the earlier KSČ practice and its ideological and propaganda activities in institutions and enterprises. In 1991, activities of political organizations in the workplace were banned by the Act on Association in Political Parties and Political Movements (Act No. 424/1991 Coll.).

In her analysis of the transformation in the district city's schools, Dana Moree states that 'the revolution was done by the PE teachers' (2013, p. 41). The teacher initiative was also remembered by the narrators in our research, with several of them also mentioning PE teachers as active agents of change. This may have been because PE teachers were popular for their activities, which motivated them and gave them the courage to apply for the school head's position as well. The active and popular teachers, backed by the teaching staff, were among those who became leaders of the protest movement.

In December 1989, teachers began to organize themselves at the regional level as well. 'District Teachers' Forums' emerged, formulating demands for change, which were then debated in schools. A chronicle of one rural school read: 'Time was devoted to discussions on the political situation and to familiarizing ourselves with the demands made by the District Teachers' Forum.' It is quite understandable that teachers organized themselves at this level as well, thus creating parallel structures to the official ones. The main goal was to negotiate changes with the regional administration and the political representation of the old regime. The management of the Civic Forum in Prague was dealing with a number of fundamental problems related to the transfer of power at the national level and did not have the capacity to deal with individual aspects of the life of society by region, including education or the school system.[4] The Coordination Council for Primary Schools was not established in the Civic Forum until January 1990 (Kitzberger, 1990).

The situation in one South Moravian district serves as an illustrative example. On 20 December 1989, the local Coordination Committee of the Civic Forum of Primary School Teaching Staff sent out a list of demands for change,[5] which was, quite predictably, more radical than the previous instructions coming from the Ministry of Education. Through the demands, the department of education of the District National Committee and all of the schools in the given district were directly addressed. Their list included, for example, the strict removal of all signs of communist propaganda from schools and teaching. It also called for a reorganization of the school management and 'the addition of a majority of non-party membersisans': the majority in school management was to be given to people who were not KSČ members. The authors of the demands claimed that many of the existing school management representatives were beginning to sympathize with the Civic Forum in order to keep their jobs. The Coordination Committee warned of the anarchy in the schools that could be caused by rejecting any cooperation with the existing school management. At the same time, the demands contain specific pieces of advice that were to have an immediate impact on the life of schools. For example, all one-sided ideologically oriented competitions were to be stopped. Many of the demands were motivated by dissatisfaction with the excessive bureaucracy. The demands included the elimination of unnecessary meetings and the shortening of the pedagogical councils. Ideological-political education was not to be replaced by another

---

[4]Although there was a School Commission at the Civic Forum Coordination Centre, it concentrated on dealing with the Ministry of Education regarding general issues of school system and education, not on coordinating the pro-democracy movement in schools. The Civic Forum School Commission was mentioned in the negotiations with the Minister of Education on 11 December 1989 (Suk, 1998).

[5]The fact that Civic Forum representatives from 160 Prague primary schools had already met to coordinate and express their demands on 16 December 1989 serves for a comparison and to illustrate the time lag between the centre of the revolution and the countryside (Hrubá, 2013).

programme. However, nothing prevented teachers from voluntarily meeting to debate the demands for change instead of political education. The school chronicles show that this did indeed happen. The Coordination Committee further advised teachers not to succumb to parental pressure for unprepared and hasty changes. Some parents may have begun to problematize the role and authority of teachers by referring to their subservience to the communist regime; this may have led to tensions in relations with parents. Therefore, the guidelines appealed to teachers to maintain high standards in their teaching.

The District Coordination Committee of the Civic Forum of Teaching Staff criticized the inconsistency and hastiness of the demands and defined itself in comparison to the department of education of the District National Committee:

> Let us be realistic and start where we can achieve change now. The inconsistency and often hasty demands benefit the Department of Education, which puts itself in the role of coordinator of current events in the school system in the district and takes its 'progressive' proposals from our ranks. (…) We reject the unprincipled and alibi-like attitude of the Department of Education of the District National Committee, which has not stood up for the positions of the overwhelming majority of the teaching staff at these serious times and has not itself taken a clear civic stand in support of the legitimate demands of the students. At present, it is run only by KSČ members, which is also unconstitutional. Under these circumstances, it cannot speak of its progressive positions.

The list of demands warns against spreading fear among teachers. There were cases of Russian language teachers being intimidated by suggestions that the political changes would lead to their dismissal. The authors of the demands stressed the need for their retraining.

By the beginning of January 1990, it was definitely clear that the communist rule was over in Czechoslovakia. At this time, the MEYS's instructions on teaching were published in *Učitelské noviny* (*Teacher's Newspaper*). They concerned in particular the teaching of the specific subjects that had been most affected by communist propaganda and ideology before 1989: history, literature, and civics. The instructions stated that certain subjects must be taught without textbooks and that students' initiative rather than their knowledge should be taken into account in their assessments. In history and civics, grading was temporarily abolished in some years. Tips for suitable literature for teaching preparation were published. Specific suggestions were made for modifying the subject matter for teaching history.[6] According to the instructions, the ideological and political training of teachers was officially abolished, effective immediately. The MEYS instructions dealt more extensively with the teaching of foreign languages, which was to be fundamentally modified from the 1990/91 school year (MEYS, 1990a, b).

---

[6] The hectic developments in the school system were evidenced by the minutes of the meetings of pedagogical councils in primary schools. These included calls to collect suitable books for the innovation of history teaching for the eighth and ninth grades. History and literature textbooks from the pre-1989 era contained some distorted information about history and omitted some facts altogether. The first democratic Czechoslovak president, Tomáš Garrigue Masaryk, and the events at the end of World War II are good examples, as students had not previously been taught that some parts of the republic were liberated by the U.S. army in 1945.

In January 1990, the mid-year was nearing. Traditionally, the mid-year evaluation of students was concluded at the meetings of the pedagogical councils (meetings of the teaching staff). These meetings were now an opportunity for school heads to brief teachers on the existing instructions and changes. In January 1990, the pedagogical councils continued to discuss, for example, the removal of the conscription elements from education[7] and the end of preparing students for military service.

The simplification of the documentation kept on students was among the most significant changes. Only information related to education was now to be recorded. Processing complex personal characteristics of students, including the cadre profile of parents or their political views, was abolished. An interesting matter that documents the continuity of certain processes before and after the Velvet Revolution emerges here. The compilation of the personal characteristics of students (e.g. for admission procedures to secondary schools) was already simplified during perestroika, before the fall of the KSČ government. The Ministry of Education referred to the text of the November 1989 decree (published even before the revolution). However, the instruction of January 1990 emphasized that compiling a student's personal characteristics beyond the scope of the decree was completely inadmissible (MEYS, 1990a). However, the socialist school management also kept detailed documentation on teachers. In one school chronicle, we found reference to the fact that teachers were given their own cadre files and their evaluations prepared by the pre-revolutionary school management.[8]

Changes were reflected in the often improvised updates of school work plans. In the archival fonds of some schools, we found updates of the plans in which all ideological topics and tasks that were the product of communist propaganda had been simply crossed out by hand. According to the minutes of their meeting on 22 January 1990, the pedagogical council of one school in a large city stated that the term 'communist education' was to be replaced by 'moral education'.

It is clear from the minutes of the pedagogical councils that the situation calmed down in the first months of 1990 and that the schools again dealt mainly with the regular agenda. However, most issues and problems remained unresolved. The reorganization of language teaching, for example, connected to the retraining of Russian teachers, who constituted quite a large group, resonated very strongly at that time. Even the daily life of the schools reflected that the changes were slow or chaotic. Dissatisfaction was reflected both in comments in the pedagogical press (Sav, 1990) and in the entries in the school chronicles, usually made at the end of the school year. This is documented by an entry in one of the school chronicles: 'Every

---

[7] These were military or civil defence elements in the subjects taught.

[8] In the course of our research, we did not obtain any such evaluation from any of the respondents, although some of them spoke about it. The respondents claimed that they had thrown the evaluations away or did not know where they were, or they did not respond to the question at all. This is a sensitive topic for the respondents even after so many years, and the evaluations may have contained personal or political information, so it is not surprising that the respondents destroyed the documents.

reasonable person wished for and long expected the changes in the stagnant country. And when they came, they seemed to catch everyone unprepared, proceeding in a hurried, even chaotic manner.'

Nevertheless, the desire for greater freedom is the primary leitmotif of the retrospective evaluation of the Velvet Revolution in the contemporary school chronicles. In practice, this may have been reflected in the elimination of everything that teachers considered pointless and unnecessary: 'We have decided to free the school work from formality and bureaucratic approaches.' Other chronicle read: 'An end to the pointless and soulless political trainings, an end to the era of bureaucracy.' Another chronicle described the situation similarly: 'Nervousness, haste and unnecessary paperwork began to be removed from the school.' Resistance to rules and to excessive bureaucracy as well as the desire for freedom form the dominant image of schools in the early 1990s, and they were also present in the memory of the teachers we interviewed.

6.2   Staffing Changes in Schools

The management of schools in the new era was a very sensitive and at the same time hotly debated topic. In some schools, such discussions took place in a tense atmosphere and some conflicts even occurred; in other schools, everything was relatively calm. In some schools, elections to express support for the school heads and their deputies occurred in December. According to the assumptions at the time, the school head was to remain in the job if they had the support of the teaching staff: 'It was determined that if the teachers in the school expressed confidence in the current school head, that such school head would continue in that job' (Radka). Let us just add that this was a completely spontaneous process, neither based on any uniform (legislative) rules nor controlled or directed by anyone. It is an example of the 'revolutionary' processes in the school system.

Confidence votes took place on a large scale in January 1990: 'We formed a counting committee and called a vote in the afternoon and the teachers had their say' (Michal). One village school chronicle described the process in detail: 'On 12 January 1990, the Civic Forum organized a vote of confidence in the school head, the deputy head, and the district school inspector. All the teachers at the school participated in the secret vote except those on maternity leave.' A table of the results followed. No one was given the vote of confidence, with the deputy school head receiving the least confidence: Seventeen participants were against giving confidence, three were in favour, and two abstained. The deputy school head was also the chair of the school's KSČ organization, which had a total of six members. This means that not even all KSČ members supported her in the vote. The school also voted on giving confidence to the district's school inspector. This is another example of revolutionary time in the school system when 'almost anything' was possible. Neither the school nor the teachers could vote confidence in the inspector. Therefore, it was a form of expression of the opinion of the teaching staff on the person of the inspector; this expression could not have a real (legal) influence, for example, on the inspector's remaining in office.

The results of the votes in schools varied. Based on our research, we identified several possible situations[9]:

1. *The school head did not clearly receive the confidence of the teachers, and the teachers elected a new school head.* In such a situation, the superior authority removed the original school head and confirmed the election of a new school head. The removed school heads were often active supporters of the 'old regime' and (at the same time) unpopular with the teaching staff. A school chronicle from a rural town provides an example: 'All the events also had a significant impact on the work of the school. Civic Forums were being formed in the schools. Teachers stopped being afraid to speak up and expressed their distrust of the school head. She always acted in a haughty manner and neuroticized all her colleagues with her behaviour.' The atmosphere in such schools could be tense and unpleasant, as Dana recalled: 'It was so turbulent. The current school head, who was there, I think he sort of sensed that he was going to be replaced and now he was calling upon us and appealing to the fact that he had a family and I don't know, to the point at which it felt a bit embarrassing.'

2. *The teaching staff was divided, and the school head did not receive a vote of confidence.* Michal recalled this situation: 'A vote was taken, which was not as clear-cut, but about two-thirds of the teachers were in favour of the resignation of the school head. And the other third was I would say according to the hand-writing, because we were able to like recognize it a lot, it was mostly the people who were in that party cell.' In schools in which the teaching staff split into multiple camps, the situation could be very tense. In some schools, it was so tense that school inspectors had to help deal with the situation. Naděžda, a school inspector at the time, recalled that two inspectors used to go to such schools to be help handle the situation: '... because they were attacking us, you know: You must do something about it, it can't be like this. We don't want these people here. So fire them! So we were actually kind of—like taming the passions, which was quite difficult (Naděžda).

   Such situations were possible only in the first months after November 1989, because there were no precise rules for replacing school heads or hiring them, but not even the school inspectors had a completely clarified (new) area of activity at that time. Our respondents very often stated that anything was possible then.

3. *The school head, considered a representative of the 'old regime' by the teachers, was given a vote of confidence.* As one narrator suggested, this may have been

---

[9] Some of the narrators in our research worked in schools in which the school heads had been removed by the founder following a vote of no confidence by the teaching staff. Others were part of teaching staff that gave a vote of confidence to the school heads, and therefore the school heads were able to keep their jobs. In our research, we mapped the situation in 25 schools. In this sample, there were 18 schools in which the school head was removed and seven schools in which the school heads were given the confidence of the teaching staff. Our results cannot be generalized in any way; they are just a sample of the situations in the schools.

because there simply was no other suitable successor in the school. 'We finally agreed that because nobody really wanted the job that we would be in favour of him staying in the lead, but the deputy school head had to leave and a new deputy was hired in her place' (Karolína). One of the chronicles from a large city school where there were two consecutive votes also indicated ambiguous support. The first vote took place before Christmas 1989. In it, the school head received the vote of 80% of teachers and the deputy school head received 50%. The second vote was held in January 1990: the school head received the vote of confidence but the deputy school head did not. Note that in these cases, sometimes it was not only the school head but also his deputy whose person could also be quite controversial.

4. *The school head received clear confidence.* In some schools, there was no vote at all. Petra recalled this situation: 'In the end there was no vote, it's not about the party, it's about the people.' Antonín remembered a similar situation: 'Even though he was a communist, of course, the parents said: "We want him there because he was a great guy." Yeah? He was the school head first, then he was a teacher, and he was seen as a communist only in tenth place.' This recollection illustrated a situation in which, especially in rural areas, the interpersonal relations (in and out of school) may have mattered more than membership in the pre-November KSČ. This was also evidenced by the entries in many rural school chronicles in which the school head received full trust.

5. *There was no vote about the job of school head at all.* These cases can be seen as specific, because such a school head was given confidence for a limited period of time or left outright of their own accord: 'The school head was about to retire. So she left on her own' (Blanka). We also came across cases where the replacement was aided by fate. For example, there was a death of a school head who was already seriously ill at the time of the Velvet Revolution.

If the school head was dismissed by the founder, competitive selections were called that did not initially have clear rules, even though this was a very important event that could have affected the operation of the school for several years. Spontaneous competitive selections—or in the terminology of the time, 'auditions'—were already taking place in schools shortly after the fall of communism. The minutes of the meetings of the school commission of the District National Committee show that after successful competitive selections, the district authorities approved the school heads en masse and more or less only formally. At virtually the same time, a recommended process for competitive selections developed by the Ministry of Education was published in the national *Teacher's Newspaper*. The competitive selection was to be publicly announced by the founder and the selection committees were to be composed of representatives of the school, the founder, and experts on the school system. In this committee, representatives of the school were to form a majority, basically confirming the previous practice in which the school head was selected mainly by the school staff (Doporučení MŠMT..., 1990). A sharp criticism of the form of competitive selections, described as 'votes', appeared in *Teacher's Newspaper* as early as the beginning of 1990. The author called for the establishment of a single committee for each district to help recruit school employees 'without totalitarian and normalization dirt under their fingernails' (Nosál, 1990).

The school heads who gained the support of the teaching staff did not have their jobs guaranteed in the long term. They could still be considered representatives of the 'old power'. The question of dealing with the communist past resonated in Czech society for many years after the Velvet Revolution, and has not yet been really resolved. It is logical that the communist past of many people was a strong theme even during the first free parliamentary elections held in June 1990. At that time, dissatisfaction with the situation in society was growing. The quality of life in the free country was not changing for the better. These problems were not blamed on the transformation, but rather on the matter of the insufficient resolution of the 'relics' of communism (Krapfl, 2013).

Dissatisfaction with development was also linked to the issue of the representatives of the 'old regime' remaining in leading positions; this also applied to schools. In this atmosphere, new competitive selections were announced for the positions of even those primary school heads who had received the confidence of the teaching staff at the end of 1989 and beginning of 1990. Again, this was a spontaneous process; the competitive selections were not held on the basis of a specific legislative decree or instructions from the Ministry of Education. There was no (compulsory) mass replacement of all leading workers in the school system, nor did the Ministry of Education order competitive selections to be held in all schools at that time. One motto of the development after the Velvet Revolution was that 'we are not like them'. This motto was a reference to the massive purges carried out by the communists after the seizure of power in 1948 or after the suppression of the reform movement in 1968. The new democratic government, especially President Václav Havel, did not want to stoop to the level of the KSČ and rejected the idea of purges. However, participants at the regional level may have perceived the situation differently and exerted independent activity to remove the communists from the management of schools and higher authorities (Krapfl, 2013).

Regional politics and the local power ambitions of the new political representation gradually began to play a role in the formation of selection committees for new school heads.[10] An employee of a District National Committee recalled the period of competitive selections organized approximately from March 1990:

> (…) these were the repeated competitive selections in '90 and partly '91. And that was an unbelievable shock, because the director of our district authority decided that all primary schools would undergo a repeated competitive selection before the end of '90. And now I was tasked with putting together committees that were then approved by the management. Well and then they added their own people depending on their interest, or the Civic Forum, and I always added the experts. (Václav)

---

[10] We found a description of the composition of the selection committee of 22 March 1990 in the chronicles of a large city school. The selection committee was composed of five teachers from the school, and representatives of the parents, the founder, and another school. The representative of the founder may have been a person representing the political forces or parties that were still being formed at that time.

The same narrator recalled the spontaneous impulse for calling of new competitive selections: a televised speech by the Minister of Education. The speech was not the equivalent of an official directive on competitive selections, based on relevant legal standards. Somewhat surprisingly, however, some people perceived it as such, including high-ranking officials in the regional administration.

> It had no rules. There was only a recommendation, and I think it was Minister Adam at the time, (…) he appeared on television and declared that the Ministry of Education had decided, even though others knew nothing about it, that there would be repeated competitive selections for the jobs of primary school heads. That was on Sunday, the director came to work on Monday and said: "As the minister said on television yesterday, come up with a proposal." So we sat down, we came up with a five-member committee. (Václav)[11]

In one of the districts we researched, all the previous primary school heads were dismissed as of 30 June 1990, and new competitive selections were announced. The next wave of school head dismissals and thus also of competitive selections came at the end of 1991, when the 'Lustration' Act was passed.[12] On the basis of this law, a 'lustration' certificate was needed by people who wanted to hold leading jobs in the state administration, enterprises, and organizations founded by the state, including schools. Every citizen wanting such a job needed a certificate asserting that before 1989, they had not held high positions in the KSČ, cooperated with the Communist State Security, or been members of the People's Militias.[13]

The lustration law was applied in practice, as evidenced by school chronicles. Ludmila recalled that a former employee of the District National Committee won a competitive selection at a small rural school. He had to leave very soon after, because he had not obtained a lustration certificate: 'They said that all leading workers had to have a lustration certificate, and the school head, he was in the People's Militias. Or he was even some commander of the People's Militias—they immediately dismissed him.'

The repeated calls for the dismissal of (former communist) school heads may have appeared as a pretext of ambitious individuals who wanted to take advantage of the opportunity to replace the previous school head: 'A decree came saying that none of the communists would remain in the school. And here in this district, there was only one school head left and all the others were dismissed by an order from the higher authorities (…) Well, then one colleague became the school head, and then we learned in retrospect that she also helped it a little bit' (Olga).

---

[11] For comparison, in the Slovak district of Nitra, all primary school heads were dismissed after pressure from the local Teachers' Forum (Krapfl, 2013).

[12] Act No. 451/1991 Coll., Which Determines Certain Other Prerequisites for the Performance of Certain Functions in State Authorities and Organizations of the Czech and Slovak Federative Republic, the Czech Republic, and the Slovak Republic.

[13] For membership in the security forces, the lustration certificate was issued by the Ministry of the Interior. In other cases (positions in the KSČ, membership in the People's Militias), a statutory declaration of the given citizen sufficed. If there were doubt about the truthfulness of the statutory declaration, citizens could submit a motion for investigation to an independent committee set up by the Ministry of the Interior (Act 451/1991 Coll.).

The competitive selections took place in a number of schools where the school head had passed the vote of confidence. Sometimes, the competitive selection was repeated if it had been won by a former member of the KSČ or a person who had not obtained a lustration certificate. Nevertheless, entries in school chronicles and the recollections of some narrators showed that there were schools in which a previous 'communist' school head won the selection again and remained in office for several years. The practice could vary from district to district, as it largely depended on the initiative of local officials, who were bound by virtually no or very general regulations.

The competitive selections held just after the collapse of the KSČ government or even later did not have clear rules.[14] This raises the question of how they actually took place. Answering this question is not easy, as few sources have survived. The revolutionary and post-revolutionary times did not favour systematic recording and archiving of events. We can rely on entries in school chronicles or other school documents only as an exception to the rule. However, some of our narrators did talk about the competitive selections, stressing the spontaneity and improvisation in their recollections:

> That first competitive selection, if I went to a competitive selection like that today, nobody would even talk to me at all, okay? Because they really didn't have the full picture then, yeah? (…) Basically, it wasn't like we were submitting a written concept at all. It was just verbal, at that time I had no idea how the school worked, (…) just yes, we're going to do it in a general way without ideology, fairly, justly. And I think I succeeded basically because one of my competitors was also some former member of the KSČ. (Barbora)

Another school head who entered the competitive selection in the early 1990s pointed out that he won when he was very young, probably because of his knowledge of English (an exception at that time) and his experience with living abroad in the UK. This particular school head's experience presumably introduced a new era and a new 'generation' of school heads, whose knowledge and skills were assessed in competitive selections quite differently from those before 1989, and ultimately also from those shortly after the Velvet Revolution.

Many of our narrators worked in schools whose management was taken over by a new school head during 1990. Some of these school heads took office in early 1990; others won the competitive selection later. The new school heads varied, of course. Some were successful school heads for a long time or were even still in office in 2022, although these are exceptions. Teaching staffs sometimes had high hopes for their new school heads that were not fulfilled, and the new school heads quit, sometimes quite soon after taking up the job.

One narrator from a large school in a district town gave a positive assessment of a school head who was elected to the job by the school's teaching staff in late 1989

---

[14]The effort to 'purge' schools of the communist era school heads did not die down even after 5 years. In the chronicles of one small rural school, we found a reference to the fact that instructions to hold competitive selections for all school heads who had been in office for more than 6 years were issued by the Minister of Education Ivan Pilip in 1995. It also noted that for the most part only the previous school heads joined the competitive selections in the local district.

and held it until 2010. The narrator suggested that reputation and personal contacts mattered in a small town: 'He was also able to get a lot done for the school, because as he really was into sports and he is such a well-known personality in that town, he was able to negotiate a lot of things' (Jaroslava). A teacher from a school in a small village near the Austrian border gave a similar assessment of the new school head: 'The newer school head, a democratic approach. He was actually local, young, he was adaptable. So it was for the better in our school, of course. Than before '89' (Nina). Many narrators mentioned school heads who had taken up their jobs at a very young age. In fact, the people who were given opportunities in the post-1989 school system would probably not have gotten to their positions so quickly in 'normal times'.

Some headteachers who had lost their jobs for political reasons, most often during the massive purges following the arrival of 'normalization' in the 1970s, returned. The need to rehabilitate previously persecuted school system workers was included in the first statements of the Teachers' Civic Forums in late 1989 and early 1990. Subsequently, rehabilitations took place in 1990. For this purpose, rehabilitation commissions were set up at the district level on the basis of the guidelines of the Ministry of Education of 6 January 1990.[15] Teachers and school heads who received full moral rehabilitation had the option to return to the school system if they had been forced to leave it. A notice of the rehabilitation of a school head dismissed at the beginning of the normalization period was found during archival research:

> Dear Sir, the Rehabilitation Commission of the Department of Education, Youth and Sports of the District National Committee in Znojmo, at its meeting on 9 October 1990, considered your case and came to the following conclusions: In 1971, you were dismissed from the job of school head on the grounds that you were not fit to manage the school politically. Years of bullying followed which damaged your health. Your family was affected along with you. In accordance with the policy of the Ministry of Education of the Czechoslovak Republic No. 10 269/90-19 of 6 January 1990, we apologize to you for the workers of the Ministry of Education of the normalization period who harmed not only individual teachers and students but also contributed to the devastation of our entire school system. At the same time, we express full moral rehabilitation to you. With your honest attitude, you have helped to maintain at least partially the credit of the teaching profession in the eyes of the general public. The hearing of your case will continue after the adoption of the Rehabilitation Act, which we expect already in this year. The undersigned are the representatives of the Rehabilitation Commission.

At the end of 1990, the Act on Judicial Rehabilitation (119/1990 Coll.), which gave the entire process a legal framework and provided for financial compensation for the

---

[15] The guidelines were published in a text signed by the Minister of Education in *Teacher's Newspaper* on 18 January 1990 (Adam, 1990) and they were intended to apply not only to persecuted teachers. The Ministry of Education called on all organizations founding schools to set up working groups to carry out the rehabilitations. These working groups were to consist of impartial and unbiased members. Those rehabilitated, if they expressed an interest, were to be allowed to return to teaching. Although the rehabilitations did not include the possibility of obtaining financial compensation, they did not exclude the possibility of seeking compensation through other legal means.

people affected, was adopted. On the basis of this Act, persecuted persons could, under certain circumstances, return to their original workplaces. Vlasta recalled the return of a rehabilitated school head to his original job:

> Actually, the school head was driven out and a school head who had to leave in '68, over-night, along with his wife, joined our school. (…) And in November there was the coup, so the school head came in and said that he would definitely not drive the dismissed school head out, that he respected her for running the school and that she would stay there normally. (Vlasta)

The new (old) school head treated the former school head with respect and allowed her to continue working at the school. The promotion of a human approach in contrast to the impersonal bureaucracy and pressure of the communist apparatus was a dominant theme of the Velvet Revolution (Krapfl, 2013). Humanity was to prevail in schools as well. Teachers had high hopes for the new school heads who fulfilled this characteristic. In some cases, however, it turned out that while the new school heads had desirable character traits and were a proponent of democratic changes, they lacked some of the necessary competences to lead and/or manage a school. One narrator reluctantly recalled one such school head:

> A member of the Citizens' Forum took over as school head, but because he was such a rather closed, thoughtful person, there was a lack of that spark. I think that the school head needs to take over the communication between the management and the team of teachers and not to lock himself in the school head's office (…) basically I left the school because of the behaviour of this school head. (Michal)

Blanka spoke of a similar school head. In her words, he was a humane, artistic art teacher, but he was gentle and perhaps too liberal because of that. In other words, he lacked the necessary competences to lead a team of teachers and to manage the entire school. After 2 years, this school head left for an art school and a new, more vigorous school head, who promptly dismissed the aforementioned narrator because she had reached retirement age, won a competitive selection. Such stories brought the post-revolutionary period in schools.

Blanka pointed out that some people's careers could be advanced merely because they held views opposing the regime before 1989. She suggested that the fate of an individual may not have been influenced only by political views, but also by their position in the collective. She spoke about an unpopular teacher who was an anti-communist. Even before the Velvet Revolution, the teacher openly declared her support for the first Czechoslovak democratic president, Tomáš Garrigue Masaryk. This was somewhat courageous, because before the Velvet Revolution such views could have led to various sanctions or even punishments. After 1989, the teaching staff suggested her as a suitable candidate for a school inspector. However, the reason was not her expertise or political views, but the other teachers' desire to simply get rid of her.

Interpersonal relations dominated some spirited competitive selections for the school head's job. At the same time, the period of staffing changes offered opportunities to achieve personal ambitions by opening the path to power even for those whose actions showed less desirable character traits. In some stories, the new school head proved to be a poor choice. One narrator recalled the school head of a large city school who was elected by the teaching staff itself to manage the school at the end of 1989 and beginning of 1990. Over time his incompetence to run the school and his tendencies towards clientelism became apparent as he provided advantages for his favourite teachers/friends: 'He joined and said: "I'm the school head here!" We saw that he didn't know a lot of things, how a primary school is supposed to be run, yeah? He was enforcing everything from his position and we could see right away who was his friend and who was not' (Irma).

After a year, a new competitive selection was announced, and despite the disapproval of the teaching staff, this school head won again. As a consequence, a rather unique situation occurred when a large part of the teaching staff left the school. This may also be an example of how a school can lose its good reputation. The situation described in this school and especially the departure of part of the teaching staff to other schools became a matter of public knowledge through the media, and parents and of course the founder knew about the situation. For a relatively long time, there were no efforts to correct this; the school, which originally had an excellent reputation for teaching foreign languages, soon lost its good reputation. The school's reputation was restored in part and only after a long time; and the course to repair the situation was started by the departure of this school head.

On the other hand, some school heads who defended their jobs in the post-1989 competitive selections changed their behaviour in a positive direction. Our narrator recalled a situation in which a feared communist school head was re-elected because no other adequate successor could be found. However, the school head's behaviour towards the teaching staff improved after the Velvet Revolution. 'He started to be quite friendly, and as a person he was not basically bad, but all he cared about was his career' (Karolína). It is possible that the school head changed his behaviour because of the 'relaxation of circumstances' and the emphasis on a human approach during the Velvet Revolution, or the cause of his behaviour towards his subordinates before 1989 may have been the management of the school under pressure from the Communist Party and in a highly bureaucratic management system.

Another important phenomenon connected with the staffing changes and continuities in the post-Velvet Revolution period is related to the effort to keep one's job in the new era. This concerns 'turncoats', which appeared in the school system as well. One narrator spoke of a drastic change of views and attitudes. He recalled a colleague who, despite her pre-1989 KSČ membership, got a job as the school head of a rural school after the Velvet Revolution.

> So we chose this colleague, well, and we had no idea what would become of her the day she would sit in the school head's office, yeah. A complete turn (…) we used to visit each other (before), simply birthdays and so on, and now she started to play the role of a big boss, yeah, (…) [during socialism] she was teaching Russian and socialist history, and she was running an atheist club and driving kids out of religion lessons (…) after the revolution she took a golden cross out of the drawer and started going to church (…) and there was no Russian, so she started teaching German, which she didn't know at all, so she was like one lesson ahead of the kids. (Libor)

The story of this school shows both a change in school management and a change in the new school head's attitudes and behaviour, including a pragmatic change in her view of religious belief. This particular case is an example of how the transformation of a Russian language teacher into a German language teacher might have taken place. In the post-revolutionary era, it was possible for a teacher to start teaching another subject virtually overnight, without any qualifications, any training, or the conditions to complete their qualifications.

The school heads who were removed from their jobs also had to cope with the new situation. Some of them remained as teachers at the school they had previously led. Radka mentioned an unpopular communist school head who began to treat her surroundings better after losing her job: 'She became a normal teacher, a normal woman, and we got along. As unpleasant and mean as she had been before, suddenly she turned into a normal human being. That's why I say the job changed her so much.' It is clear that Radka considered the new face of the former school head to be the more authentic, uncorrupted by the job. The quote shows that she even seemed to consider the former school head her friend, adding in the interview that they still kept in touch. The easing of pressure on the socialist school heads may one reason. In retrospect, however, it is not possible judge the extent to which the change of behaviour was authentic and to which it may have been caused by a desire to save her own pedagogic career.

Other dismissed school heads left the schools, taking their dismissals very hard and viewing them as an injustice. Ludmila added: 'She was spurned. She had been a school head for twenty-five years and left to teach in Brno. A year before she retired, she was teaching as a regular teacher, which must have been a huge disgrace for her. Yeah, and she sort of said how hurt she was and she never went back to that school to visit, no.'

But the staffing changes (not only) in the school system brought various paradoxes and situations that concerned school heads, but of course also concerned teachers. For example, there were cases in which teachers left primary schools 'for something better'. Before 1989, some people who had to leave their original profession for political reasons (for example, university teachers) found refuge in rural schools. This is indicated by an entry in one of the chronicles of a rural school, which mentioned that a teacher who left to work at the university soon after the Velvet Revolution became a representative of the Civic Forum. The available sources did not provide more information about this teacher, but we can assume that this is an example of a person who could not pursue an academic career for political reasons before 1989.

The interviews with the narrators support our thinking in this regard. That is to say, several narrators had experienced rather significant complications during their studies because of their unsuitable cadre profile (parents were religious, etc.). They became primary school teachers after not having planned to do so, because they did not get a job in the field they had studied. As an example, Michal could only study at trade school because of his unsuitable cadre profile:

So I think my career was influenced by the attitude of my dad, who didn't quite have the opinions that the ruling establishment of the time considered the best, so I was warned by my homeroom teacher at the primary school that I shouldn't expect to be applying for grammar school. Even though I had very good grades, I studied to become a car mechanic. (Michal)

After Michal became a car mechanic, he got into a secondary technical school despite the difficulties in getting the approval of the local KSČ cell. Later he even successfully completed a degree at a technical university. Thanks to his talents, he eventually also graduated from the university with a degree in mathematics and was qualified to teach at the grammar school and even perhaps to work in science and research. After graduating from university, he eventually worked as a primary school teacher. After 1989, Michal changed his workplace and became a teacher and later even a deputy school head of a grammar school.

The patchwork of staffing changes was completed by people who came to teach at a primary school after the Velvet Revolution because they lost jobs that were somehow linked to the communist regime. Of course, staffing changes affected not only primary schools, but also other state institutions. Former employees of District National Committees, KSČ officials, and even people who had been dismissed from the army became teachers.[16] Libor described the arrival of former teachers from the military school as an example of the lack of competence of school management by the new school head, because of whom he left the school. 'So she (the school head) hired non-teachers, yeah, and they were just fired politicians, brass-hats from the military university, for example, who were used to teaching in such a way that when they came to the classroom, everyone had to stand at attention.' One reason this school head hired incompetent people as teachers could be that a large part of the teaching staff had left the school (precisely because of the school head's style of work) and qualified teachers were difficult to find. Blanka remembered a teacher who had previously served in the army: 'He came from the military and he gave even Cs in physical education.' Ludmila recalled the arrival of former District National Committees workers:

The people dismissed from the department of education applied for the competitive selection. Some officials, yeah, and he just won the competitive selection. And he became the school head there, so I came in September and there was a new school head and there was his new... and so I didn't know that. I thought that she was a teacher, but she was also some clerk that sat with him at the district. And those old structures, and she went to teach a regular second grade. (Ludmila)

One chronicle had a record of the former director of the district's department of education unsuccessfully running for the job of school head. Although he was supported by the school representatives, another candidate won the competitive

---

[16]The acceptance of this procedure by the Civic Forum was confirmed by the Resolution of the Representatives of the Civic Forum of Primary School Teaching Staff of 20 December 1989 in one district in South Moravia: 'Dismissed workers will be transferred to primary schools or elsewhere as decided.' In this case, it was the dismissed staff of the District National Committee.

selection. Ironically, this was a competitive selection for the place of a school head who had left to work in the same department of education.

The departure of often very good teachers from schools was a pressing problem in the 1990s. People were coming into primary schools from educational institutions, but from clerical jobs, and they often did not have much experience with teaching in a primary school. For a certain time, lack of experience or even qualification did not pose a major problem in hiring new teachers. Teaching at the first stage of primary school requires specific pedagogical competences, so the question remains as to what the quality of such teaching was.[17]

The mosaic of human fates was very varied in the school system in post-revolutionary Czechoslovakia. People's professional careers led in various directions. Teachers who had been dismissed for political reasons during the communist era could return to schools, sometimes after many years of involuntary separation from their profession. Somewhat paradoxically, in schools, those teachers met other people who, by contrast, had to leave higher positions in the school system and in other institutions, even in the KSČ or the army after the Velvet Revolution. There were numerous staffing changes in which schools were used as a kind of exit and entry station in the career path. Our data show that the acceptance of new teachers or school heads by the teaching staff depended more on their character or personal qualities than on whether they were, for example, KSČ members or officials in the communist school system.

6.3   New School Management

A significant number of primary schools had new management in the first years after the Velvet Revolution. In the eyes of many people, this was a satisfying fulfilment of one goal of the Velvet Revolution—to remove incompetent representatives of the communist power from important jobs. In reality, the replacement of school management was only the first step on the road to greater changes. Despite the initial hopes for rapid change, the reforms of the school system dragged on considerably and were both unsystematic and underprepared. The first years after the Velvet Revolution were more in the spirit of experimentation or a search for possible paths to reform. The virtually chronic lack of funding was a significant problem. Theoretical ideas about the (future) shape of education varied (Spilková, 1997).

However, witnesses of the transformation in schools still evaluated this highly chaotic period as the era of the greatest freedom. The need to 'breathe freely' was reflected in the details of everyday school life. One newly elected young school head in a school in a small town recalled, for example, that compulsory walking in

---

[17]At this point, we encounter a certain limitation of our research method. In our sample, we did not have anyone who had ever moved from a clerical job to a primary school and became a teacher. It is generally very difficult to get such individuals to cooperate in research because they may have been intertwined with the communist regime and understandably do not want to talk about it now.

the corridors for students at break ended. Although this was only one partial activity, it represented the strict and rigid rules of the school before 1989 in his eyes:

> First, I fixed the toilets in the whole school because the toilets were terrible. So that was the first thing, and as the second thing, I abolished walking in the corridor during the big break. (Laughs) I hated that both as a student and as a teacher who had to supervise there. It just seemed to me like somewhere in a prison where the prisoners walk around. So that was the first thing I abolished, and I gave freedom to those children to move around during the break according to their abilities and interests. (František)

The new school heads said that they tried to run the school differently—more humanely. One new school head, Zdeněk, emphasized that he still adhered to these principles as a school head: 'But even back then I felt that acting honestly and treating people with empathy was probably what we wanted.' Some school heads contrasted this desire for a sensitive approach with the fear and austerity of normalization. As an example, they cited the strict teacher observations of former school heads. Zdeněk abolished teacher observations altogether: 'For example, I already said back at the time that we would not go to teacher observations and that we would make arrangements with the teachers. That they would keep the door open, that it's the same in Holland, and that we would just say what's going on and that I see it on the basis of trust.'

Zdeněk mentioned inspiration from abroad, specifically the Netherlands. The early 1990s were characterized in part by the establishment of foreign cooperation that started in primary schools. Through these activities, the school heads were able to learn about how schools lived and functioned elsewhere. Understandably, not all schools were involved in such cooperations, only those that were interested. The fall of the Iron Curtain and the opening of national borders made post-communist countries an object of interest for Western experts, foreign language teachers, and ordinary tourists. The management of some foreign schools were willing to cooperate or even offered their cooperation to Czech schools. In their interviews, some school heads recalled establishing contacts with foreign countries, organizing study trips, visiting foreign schools, and developing cooperation. This interest was of course clear in the Czech border region as well. Our research specifically concerns the Czech-Austrian border region. However, as a narrator from a local border school added, interest gradually waned. The attraction of 'unusualness' was replaced by normal relations between two democratic countries. Zdeněk also recalled the acquisition of foreign contacts, describing the warm welcome he received on a school trip to Strasbourg in 1990. The interest of their Western colleagues motivated some of the new school heads to continue their work.

> We went in '90, they welcomed us in Strasbourg. That was absolutely attractive, yeah? We took a bus full of excited kids back. All the kids got chocolates, and cheese for the parents. Of course, it was a very long drive and it was in the summer. The parents came to pick us up at the bus. And they smelled French cheese. Yeah? That was, of course, terribly comical, and beautiful. They even gave us some two crates of wine for the school, so I was eating French cheese and drinking Burgundy wine at school in 1990 and we were feeling like we'd taken over the world… I think the enthusiasm there was terribly important. And I believe

that in all those schools there was that the enthusiasm, that the problems were overcome very quickly by that enthusiasm.[18] (Zdeněk)

The school heads of the time refer especially to the first years after the Velvet Revolution as the period of greatest freedom. Kryštof reported: 'The teachers said: At last, no one is forcing us to do anything.' At this time, the new system of sectoral management of the school system was not yet fully operational. Similarly to the schools, there was an atmosphere of improvisation and a search for optimal functioning at the newly established Educational Offices (Školské úřady), the Czech School Inspectorate (Česká školní inspekce), and the municipalities founding the schools. The Educational Offices were to manage schools methodically and distribute funds to them. However, at least in the beginning, they dealt with the challenges of establishing themselves in the administration of the school system and with the difficulties associated with the start of normal operations of a new institution. The municipalities struggled with a lack of funding, and they had other equally pressing issues to address. For example, possibly due to the neglected municipal infrastructure, the new municipal management itself had to become acquainted with its own tasks and responsibilities. This was one reason that support for schools was significantly uncertain. This was criticized in contemporary records (Kolář, 1991), but our respondents retrospectively evaluated this period of 'chaos' more highly than the period when the schools started to once again be overwhelmed with demands, inspections, and audits.

The perception of legal issues in the school system in the period after the Velvet Revolution is an interesting topic. One of our narrators, a lawyer focused on the school system, added to this: 'In the school system, it was given that the Labour Code did not apply to us because we were following the guidelines of the Ministry of Education, so they still didn't want to sort of like admit that they should start following the Labour Code in schools, nobody just gave a damn' (Eliška). This quote perhaps explains somewhat why this period of time was viewed as free. The perception of the law by many teachers and school heads was probably very simplistic or even naive.

Freedom was an ideal of the Velvet Revolution. The neoliberal turn also brought a high appreciation for responsibility, reflected in the excitement about the possibility of schools becoming self-governed. It also brought entirely new responsibilities. The period when the imposed obligations were few was retrospectively idealized. That is why the first half of the 1990s can be considered the period of 'greatest freedom'. Responsibility in the form of self-governance and the consolidation of school system management (around 1995) may have brought an increase in new

---

[18]The first tourist trips to Western Europe in the 1990s were characterized by a willingness to undergo great discomfort. The opportunity to look beyond the former 'Iron Curtain' for the first time was limited by the exchange rate of Western currencies, which made it almost impossible for Czech tourists to buy anything. The communicative memory of many families still includes memories of sleeping in tents and eating their own poor quality food (canned food, meat spreads). However, according to the recollections of many eyewitnesses, it was well worth the opportunity to see, for example, Vienna or the Mediterranean sea beaches.

responsibilities to school management, including the need for independent and efficient management.[19] In the field of management, accurate records were necessary for many things and processes that were being checked. As one narrator noted, schools began to feel 'reminiscent of those times', by which she meant the bureaucracy and formalism of normalization. One of the school heads in our sample, Helena, perceived the beginning of the increase in responsibilities precisely entwined with the transition to self-governance. When asked how long the freedom lasted, she replied: 'Well, in my opinion, until the self-governing of the schools came into being. Because with self-governance came the fact that you as a school head are actually responsible for everything.'

The increase in the level of responsibilities and administration can lead, at least according to our narrators, to the detachment of the school head from the life of the school, a loss of contact with the teaching staff, and even to distorted perceptions of teacher work, teaching, and students. Barbora saw this as the biggest risk of the school head's job: 'There's already like a certain distortion there, and the person is already detached from the day-to-day functioning among those children, in those classrooms, and I think that it would like help everyone if they would just go back to try the job of a teacher for a little while.'

The new school heads declared the desire for a more 'human' approach to school management. The absence of unnecessary responsibilities in the first half of the 1990s meant that they could afford a personal approach, as they had more time to work with the teaching staff, for example. In contrast to their memories of the later increases in various duties, the narrators' recollections formed an image of a 'golden age' for the very relatively short period after the Velvet Revolution. This was despite the fact that the school heads faced a number of problems related to the lack of funds as well as to the establishment of sectoral management of the school system. The memories of the Educational Office workers painted a very similar picture.

6.4 Educational Offices: The Backbone of Primary Schools

At the end of 1990, the 'sectoral management' of the school system was introduced with the adoption of the Act on State Administration and Self-Government in the School System (Act No. 564/1990 Coll.). Schools were no longer to be directly subjected to the state administration and self-government in the matters of funding and methodological management of education. Newly, they were to be managed by the Educational Offices, which were directly subordinated to the Ministry of Education. The municipalities, as founders, were to be primarily responsible for funding the operation of schools and the maintenance of school buildings.

---

[19] It depended very much on when the school became self-governing. One narrator, Helena, linked the end of 'freedom' or liberty with 1993, when her school became self-governing. In other schools, this change may have come much later.

The establishment of the Educational Offices was a part of a wider reform of self-government. It was preceded by the dissolution of the District National Committees as remnants of the communist state administration and their transformation into district authorities. In January 1991, competitive selections were being held for the posts of directors of the new Educational Offices. Their establishment was supported by a large part of the teaching public, who shared the view that sectoral management would increase both professionalism and management efficiency. In particular, the Educational Offices were to grant municipalities consent to found schools, announce competitive selections for school heads, and appoint and dismiss school heads. Both students and parents could appeal to them against a school's decision (e.g. in relation to a non-admission to secondary school). The Educational Office was to allocate funds to schools for salaries, textbooks, teaching aids and school supplies paid for by the state, even to private and church-managed schools, which were also entitled to contributions. In addition, it was to provide services pertaining to labour law and payroll to schools that were not self-governed, and it was to offer assistance and support to those that were. It was to provide (pedagogical) methodological assistance to schools. After concluding a contract with the school head, the Educational Office could also provide for administrative and technical activities even for self-governed schools, i.e. relatively autonomous schools (Vzorový status…, 1991).[20]

This was to be a fundamental change accompanied by proclamations about ridding schools of the incompetent supervision of officials of the abolished District National Committees and their departments of education. However, in practice, it was often more of a transformation of the departments of education and staffing continuity, as the people from the departments of education just transferred to the Educational Offices. In other cases, new staff joined the departments of education after the staffing changes at the end of 1989 and beginning of 1990. They were not necessarily former 'communist cadres'. The creation of the Educational Offices was intended to bring greater professional competences and to overcome the old, criticized system of school system management.

The staff of the Educational Offices had a lot of work to do in order to be able to solve at least the most urgent problems as soon as they took office. In addition, their directors had to acquire the competence to manage a relatively independent, large, and important institution, something they did not (and could not) have experienced. The directors themselves often had to find suitable premises for their offices first: An Educational Office was established to which the vast majority of people came over from the department of education, and so the former superordinate acted in such a way that he said: "You're a separate legal entity, so get out of the district office. He gave me three months to do it. So I had to find some house" (Václav).

---

[20]The elaboration of the model statute of the Educational Office was intended to help the staff of these newly established institutions, who had the task of drawing up their own by-laws. In doing so, they had to improvise, because they had virtually no available support, which was typical of the precipitous period (of the first phase) of the post-socialist transformation.

The employees of the Educational Office of that time recalled the period of establishment in a similar spirit as school heads and teachers: as a period of humanity, freedom, and improvisation. Václav, the director of the Educational Office in a large city, pointed out that school heads were not used to expressing their opinion and that efforts to democratize school management were met with surprise:

> Until they got used to the new way of doing things, especially the school heads, because previously, they weren't allowed to approach the former director, no opinions were tolerated, they weren't expected, on the contrary, they were being stomped into the ground. Suddenly, they could come up with an opinion, I even called out to them: Come! Tell me! We will discuss it! After all, these very consultations are from the word 'consult' and there won't be any one-sided flow of information. (Václav)

The overall humanization was accompanied by comparisons with the relatively rigid regime during socialism. One of the workers of the time recalled the communist head of the department of education: 'He was a true commie down to the ground, a party member, strict, even when one went to his office, they had to knock. And if he didn't open the door, you just left.' The same narrator then nostalgically recalled the enthusiastic building of the Educational Office because of the very competent director:

> He started building it from scratch and very well. He was my best boss. He gave us freedom. He saw that somebody was working, that it had some parameters, that when we needed to discuss them, that the person would come in and come to a conclusion in advance and he knew that if we came to a conclusion on something and all of a sudden it started to fail or it turned out to be bullshit, you don't get fired. (…) That he was like an amazing person. (Eliška)

A primary school head from the same district also spoke very highly of the first years of the Educational Offices:

> That first phase, those first five years, we really took in everything that maybe today the school heads have to know already at the competitive selections. To know labour law, to know economics. I didn't know any of it and I didn't really need it in that first phase. The Educational Offices played a tremendous role here, and I think a lot of school heads see it that way. And also we were lucky here, the director of the Educational Office was here and he really like knew and was able to map out what we needed and we had some trainings all the time. We were actually constantly learning all of these things, so gradually then when the self-governance came we were ready for it. (Barbora)

In some districts, the school heads felt supported by the Educational Offices; in other districts, the lack of interest and support from the Educational Offices made the schools become self-governed: 'The district actually just forced us to leave them because they stopped doing the accounting, they stopped doing the payroll. So we had to do it ourselves' (František). The differences in the approach between the different Educational Offices were illustrated by an evaluation written by a school head in an unpublished Final Report on the Results of Educational Activities for 1994/95 stored in a district archive: 'The cooperation between the schools and the Educational Office is not completely positive. The office does not carry out its mission as a methodological advisory body to the satisfaction of all school heads.

Rather than being a partner, it carries out inspection, revision, and control activities, and thus actually substitutes for the work of the Czech School Inspection.'

Some Educational Offices were criticized for 'ills' similar to those of the former communist departments of education, reproached for the absence of discussion and for supervision or control instead of support and assistance. But the discontent may have been caused by deeper structural problems of the transforming society as well as by the work of the Ministry of Education. The first years after the revolution in particular were influenced by a lack of funding. Economic problems clearly dominated; issues of pedagogical leadership and school management were not a priority. Václav added: 'In terms of pedagogical leadership, there was nothing from the Ministry.' However, this view cannot be generalized. Retrospectively, the phase of Educational Offices (1991–2000) was viewed rather positively, at least in our sample. This was also evidenced by the recollection of a former employee of the Ministry of Education: 'So that was actually the only decade when the sectoral management worked. And when even the ministry itself actually completely reached out into specific schools' (Valerie). According to a former Educational Office worker, school heads themselves remembered this authority long after their abolition:

> In the decade or so of the operation of the Educational Offices, I think those school heads got used to it. And they took advantage of the services we offered. And when the Educational Offices were actually abolished (…) and I heard for a long time that the school heads remembered how they worked and yet they could turn to them with anything, that they were helped. (Adam)

One of the school heads, evaluating the abolition of the Educational Offices, simultaneously remembered them as a great aid:

> We, who have been in that position for a long time, we remember working with the Educational Office as the best period that there was in the school system. We had legal representation there, we had an economist there. So any time we called them and said we needed something, they never turned us down. They planned a regular meeting of all the school heads once a year. Because we just knew we could rely on them. That they understand, they know us, we know them. (…) And everybody regretted that it was moved to the regional level, because in the beginning it was that at the regional level, the school heads of schools founded by municipalities were invited to the opening meeting. However, the regional administration gradually became interested only in the schools that it founded, and school heads of those primary schools were left to the responsibility of the municipalities. (Helena)

The abolition of the Educational Offices further strengthened the influence of municipalities on the operation of primary schools. However, the municipalities had a strong influence on the operation of schools even in the post-revolutionary period, as they were the founders of these schools.

6.5   Municipality as the Founder of the School

While the establishment of Educational Offices was anticipated with hope by teachers and especially by school heads, the strengthening of the role of municipalities in school administration did not raise as much enthusiasm.[21] The Act on State Administration and Self-Government in the School System (Act No. 564/1990 Coll.) stipulated that the municipality founds the school and participates in its funding, taking care mainly of the building of the school and its operation. The very question of the willingness of the municipal councils to adequately (co-)fund the school was of concern. During the period of the establishment of the Educational Offices, the editor of *Teacher's Newspaper*, Jaroslava Štefflová (1991), interviewed a senior member of the department of education of a district authority: 'I still can't shake the impression that we can't really talk about truly sectoral management yet. The one who distributes the money is in charge. And that will be the municipalities. Now it will depend on who will be in charge and what their opinion of the school will be' (p. 4). This was of course very important, also considering that the municipalities as founders had a major influence on the appointment of the school head.

The form of municipal support for the school varied, for example, according to its size. In the countryside, there was a direct relationship between the often small municipal authority, the municipal council, and the school. The rural environment could offer much more personal and immediate relationships between the school representatives and village representatives than in the city. In cities, departments of education of municipal authorities were being established to serve the needs of the school system. In the largest cities, primary schools were the responsibility of the city district authorities, but with the help of the department of education of the municipal council. Medium-sized cities could found several schools; large cities could found several dozen schools. The cooperation and relations between the founder and the schools thus understandably varied in many ways. The memories of teachers and contemporary records reflected various forms of cooperation.

Professional staff at the departments of education of large cities could offer a wide range of support to school heads: 'Because there was a worker for the kindergartens, for primary schools, for the school catering. That remained the responsibility of that city' (Miroslava). People who promoted reforms and various progressive trends in pedagogy also found their way into important positions within the local administrations of large cities. For example, a municipal Waldorf school was established in a large regional town, representing a major innovation in the school system at the time, as alternative schools could not be established at all before 1989:

> When I think of Brno, there were three city districts that were very progressive. There were also people who had entered the political functions from the pedagogical field as well..., they were connected to the faculties, they had someone who had somehow worked within the alternative pedagogy (…) Montessori pedagogy, or an interest in Waldorf pedagogy, a

---

[21] *Teacher's Newspaper* even carried expressions of concern that the municipality might want to evict the school and use the school building in other ways (Obce…, 1991).

professor from Switzerland came here and introduced Waldorf pedagogy to the teachers here, I went to see it myself, it was amazing, there were a lot of us, we were all hungry for it. (…) But the listening here was very open to these things, and I think that Brno was a bit ahead of its time. (Miroslava)

In this context, it should be noted that municipal support for schools, including support for innovation in teaching, may have varied between whole regions within Czechoslovakia, and, in a way, helped to widen the gaps between the regions.

While the municipal authorities of smaller cities may not have had such an extensive apparatus of support for school system, they may have had the advantage of closer and more personal relationships. František, a former school head of a primary school in a district town, recalled the town's support while confirming that the influence of contacts and acquaintances could have been quite helpful to the development of the school system in the location.

There was good communication with the city, the mayor was in favour of education at that time, so we actually managed to finish construction works on the school building. The gymnasium, it was built there, the IT classroom. A language classroom was created there, a music classroom was created there. And the complete equipment. The surfaces of the playgrounds. Yeah, back them the mayor just told me: 'Yeah, make it what you need it to be.' So I travelled around the country and I looked at what surfaces. (František)

František recalled a situation in which the city gave him a lot of freedom in the 1990s, whereas later[22] it returned to having more control over the financial flows in the school: 'In those nineties we just got a bunch of money and you do what you want with it. We did our own competitive selections, yeah.' Whether the school head was a member of the city council and had the appropriate social capital played an important role:

Well the very relations between the city and the school, the school head was a member of the city council, so you can say basically he made sure he got what he needed yeah? As a result of that then, he could also look after the money because he was deciding on the budget, into which he wanted things to be added, like construction of a gymnasium, or refurbishment of the boiler room, yeah? Because he was a local and knew the people, he had a very good position. (Tomáš)

In smaller towns or villages, the relationship between the school head and the mayor could be even more personal. Stanislava described a situation from a small rural town and illustrated how the situation of the school could have changed. Since the 1990s, the village had a mayor who took little interest in the school. After the municipal elections and the replacement of the school head, the relations improved significantly because of the very good personal relations between the new school head and the new mayoress: 'While I have seen the former mayor come here maybe twice over the decades, the new mayoress is here practically every week, she continuously manages to find some money and the school is gradually being reconstructed' (Stanislava).

---

[22] Here, the narrator spoke about a period, after 2000, that goes beyond the scope of our research.

The changing of political representations at the city hall might have negatively affected the relationship between the school and the municipality even in larger cities. Petra recalled that especially after the victory of a right-wing political party, the town started to save more on the school. 'Once again it depended on the political party, when there was ČSSD,[23] it was kind of easier; when there was ODS,[24] it was kind of a bit tighter, financially it was worse' (Petra).

Funding was a frequent point of contention between the school and the municipality. Especially in rural areas, the municipality could be run by people who did not understand the needs of the school. Mayors of small municipalities often did the job of a mayor in addition to their usual profession, which may have been far removed from the field of education. In this context, Ludmila recalled, for example, the distorted perceptions of the needs of a primary school by the mayor of a small village who was originally a plumber: 'It seemed to me that he saw the first stage as a kindergarten.' People who did not understand much about the school system might have considered it unnecessary to invest in the school. Radka spoke about such a situation. She attributed a share of the funding problems to something other than reluctance on the part of the municipality. According to Radka, part of the blame also lay with the school head and her lack of vigour and negotiating skills. In the long term, the school head was unable to convince the municipality of the need for funding for the school: 'But those twenty years there, I would say it was very unpleasant because there was no money. Well like with any request, the school head just wasn't the type to push for it at all. She just always politely asked if it would be possible, but then she was never successful' (Radka).

Examples of disputes over school funding appeared in contemporary documents, including the periodical press, which carried stories of municipalities in which a dispute over school repairs even led to the dismissal of the school head (Štefflová & Gruša, 1991). One school chronicle had an account of a case in which the school head herself resigned after disagreements with the municipality:

> As of 1 May 1995, I submitted a request to resign as a school head and I requested a transfer at the same time. This deliberate step was prompted by long-standing disagreements and poor cooperation with the municipal authority (…). I am leaving a workplace to which I have devoted my pedagogical skills and a lot of work with bitterness in my heart, because after ten years spent in this environment, which has become my second home, I am leaving with a feeling of futility and uselessness, on the basis of intrigues and inconsistency in opinions. On the basis of hasty decisions made by the municipal council without any understanding of school problems. On the basis of interference with the powers of school head.

The stories of conflict recorded in the school chronicles and in interviews with teachers did not suggest that this was a prevalent practice. There were equally positive examples of cooperation. For example, a narrator who worked as a school head in a small rural town spoke of good relations with the municipality:

---

[23] ČSSD, the Czech Social Democratic Party (Česká strana sociálně demokratická), a left-wing political party, founded in 1893, was restored in its present form after 1989.
[24] ODS, the Civic Democratic Party (Občanská demokratická strana), a right-wing political party, was formed after the break-up of the Civic Forum in 1991.

> I must say that the relations were very good. And especially because the municipality understood that it had a founder obligation, but that the school head was the one who was responsible for the professional and pedagogical part. So I used to come to the town council to give regular reports about the school, always once a year. (…) but I never experienced that the founder would interfere in the school's activities in any fundamental way. Which I consider lucky, because I know, I knew from colleagues, other school heads, how their founders interfered with them. (Helena)

If the problems between the school and the municipality could not be resolved, a 'school council', established in each district, was to be the higher self-governing authority. It was to be composed of one-third representatives of schools, one-third of representatives of parents, and one-third representatives of municipal authorities.[25] We have very little information on the activities of the school councils. Neither teachers nor school heads spoke of them, nor were they mentioned very often in contemporary documents. An article in *Teacher's Newspaper* criticized the chaos and lack of interest during the establishment of school councils and the lack of clarity regarding their competences (Kozel, 1992; Štefflová, 1992). This may be why the narrators did not mention them: they were unlikely to have ever become a functional element of the school system or its management.

The quality of the relationship between the municipality and the school may have influenced the atmosphere in the school and the conditions for education quite substantially. It appears that especially in countryside, municipalities could not always offer competent and professional support to schools. These schools may then have been much more dependent on the work of the Educational Office. This was especially the case when the schools were to become self-governed, i.e. to gain some form of autonomy.

6.6   School Autonomy—Hopes and Disappointments

Paradoxically, many school heads now see self-governance as the end of the greatest freedom in the school system. However, in the 1990s, this form of school autonomy was perceived as the beginning of real freedom. It was in line with the ideals of the time, when everyone wanted to be 'their own boss'. Self-governance was promoted by MEYS workers as the culmination of the schools' journey to freedom. Deputy Minister Jan Koucký said specifically:

> The current changes in state administration and self-government, and among them the self-governance, aim towards independence, profiling and autonomy of schools and opening up of the space that was previously restricted with directive management. It aims to the point that each school gets its own face and character, its own name. It will no longer be possible to hide behind orders 'from above', nor will it be necessary to submit to them (…) Here lies the watershed moment between the former and the present understanding of management and, in fact, the very foundation of the self-governance of schools. It will rid the schools of

---

[25] For example, in one district, the school council had 48 members (Dokoupilová, 1992a).

the excessive administration, including the raised reproachful finger, and the threat that someone will make decisions about schools without schools (Gruša, 1991, p. 2).

In the very early days, some school heads were afraid of the self-governance because of lack of information. This was because the new form of school management also came with new tasks and quite a lot of responsibilities with which they had virtually no experience (Dokoupilová, 1992b; Štefflová, 1993). Other school heads did not hide their enthusiasm for gaining autonomy and attributed their colleagues' fears to the 'old' i.e. socialist thinking. Jaroslav Malíček (1993), a school head, wrote:

> Above all, many see considerably more work and responsibility in it. Yes, they are completely right. I can confirm that since 1 January 1992, when our school became such an entity, I have considerably less time and considerably more responsibility. But I also have considerably more joy and job satisfaction. Therefore, the school has become not for me, but I believe for most of my colleagues, a place where we go to work, but also a place of personal identification. What a role the stamp on the ID card, which specifies the employer, can play! (p. 3)[26]

Malíček mentioned one significant change that self-governance brought to the schools. The teachers were no longer employees of the Educational Office, but rather of the school itself. The school was entitled to enter into labour relationships or to handle finances on its own behalf. In addition, the school could independently apply for subsidies, e.g. for upgrading classroom equipment or acquiring computer technology (Okresní programy…, 1994). All of this represented fundamental changes in the functioning of schools, where it was virtually impossible to draw on any previous experience.

The self-governing of schools was already enshrined in the 1990 amendment to the Education Act. According to this Act, all schools were to acquire their own autonomy by the end of 1994. The mandatory transition to self-governance by the end of 1994 was criticized as inappropriate, in part because of the different conditions of the individual schools. In particular, small rural schools, in which the school head usually also acted as a (homeroom) teacher were mentioned. The obligation to become a self-governing school was eventually abolished. All schools had to gain autonomy less than 10 years later, when a completely new Education Act came into force. A former employee of the Educational Office criticized this practice:

> The year is 2004 and everybody has to get into self-governance. A kindergarten of five people. The school head doesn't know at all what the self-governance concerns! And she still doesn't know to this day. It's just … they don't have all that knowledge. And they don't even have the capacity to do it. (Eliška)

The situation was even more complicated. Although schools were originally supposed to become self-governing by 1994 on a de facto mandatory basis, the

---

[26] ID cards were proof of identity that were given to every citizen who had reached the age of 15 in socialist Czechoslovakia (this is still the case today). Until 1993, the ID card was a small booklet that included a stamp from the employer or school (for students). This was proof that the citizen was working or studying. In socialist Czechoslovakia, because of the general obligation to work, the absence of a stamp on the ID card could lead to police prosecution for 'parasitism' (Adamus, 1992).

transition to school autonomy depended on the consent of the founder as well as the support of the Educational Office. But the approaches were diametrically opposed. In some places, the Educational Offices actively supported self-governance; in others, they were more cautious and carefully considered whether to allow a particular school to become self-governing at all. This was also noticed by the editors of *Teacher's Newspaper* in connection with the upcoming mandatory transition of primary schools to self-governance: 'As time passes, schools are increasingly turning to us asking what will happen from next year with the self-governance of primary schools. In some places, municipalities or Educational Offices are pushing them into it at all costs; in others, they are discouraging or even preventing them' (Štefflová, 1993, p. 3). Our research included a school that, according to the words of the school head, was pushed towards self-governance because it did not feel supported by the Educational Office. The school head wanted to be his own boss in terms of the budget, as he could not rely on the superior authority.

Václav, for example, spoke of the efforts to provide for self-governing for schools, pointing out that the staff of the Educational Office he managed tried to systematically prepare the schools for this fundamental change. The first schools in the district did not become self-governed until 1994:

> We started to do the self-governance from '94. (…) we had enough time to teach the school heads to do it. To teach them how to go around the labour code, economic regulations, BOZP[27] and things like that (…) we took it from the larger ones who had the capacity to do it. (…) The way we went about it was that we always agreed on it with a school head who we had a feeling could do it. The moment we knew that the school head would agree, we both got together, went to the mayor, and we started discussing it. And I have to say that we only went for it in those cases in which the mayor understood and agreed, because he was the one who had to issue the amendment to the deed of foundation. (…) So we had to explain to him what the advantages were, what the disadvantages were, how it would work, especially economically, because he had no experience with it. And now we had three or four test subjects at the beginning that caught on. After a year they saw that A, it can be done. And B, I've always goaded these guys, always: Guys, come on, there's a meeting, you'll stand up here and tell us about your experience with it! What went well, what went wrong, yeah? And then the others went to the schools to watch, basically, and then it went by itself and by the time I left there were only a few small schools left. (Václav)

In another district, the Educational Office acted even more cautiously, and only the larger schools became self-governed there, and not until the end of the 1990s. Adam, a former employee of this Educational Office, states: 'It is true that then in that … '97, '98, the larger primary schools went into that self-governance. But … that was just a few.' He saw the risk in shifting too many important responsibilities to the school head: 'The legal entity had to do everything itself. Yeah? So it was very difficult for many schools. 'However, the approach of the Educational Office may also have been based on the nature of the district. The first example (Václav) concerned a rather industrial district with a larger number of large schools. The second

---

[27] BOZP stands for occupational health and safety. It is a set of rules and regulations to ensure that nothing bad happens to anyone during various activities. In this case, this refers to working at school.

example (Adam) was a purely rural district with a predominance of small village schools. However, Adam also emphasized that they tried to help the schools, especially in the economic aspects of management, at least at the beginning of their autonomy.

After gaining a legal persona, many school heads felt overwhelmed by the responsibilities associated with the economics or management of the school. The uncertainty and the need to improvise in school management did not disappear with the coming of self-governance. In an unpublished Evaluation of the School's Educational Work for 1993/1994, one school head assessed the turn to self-governance as beneficial in the end, but also as the most challenging stage of his career. He criticized the lack of preparedness on part of the municipality:

> After six months, I can say that self-governance has certainly brought many unforeseen problems to the school and that I personally bow to all those who had to survive this period, which was certainly the most critical for the school during my time here, with me. It is only to them that I owe my gratitude for the fact that – without increasing the number of staff – selfless workers were found at the school who, almost overnight, became experts in economic, legal, and payroll problems that – as I have verified for myself – even the experts at the municipality do not understand.

This evaluation concerned a large city school and the school head himself noted in his report that he was able to turn to reliable subordinates. However, smaller rural schools had the same responsibilities, but that they did not have as many non-pedagogical staff (bursar, economist, etc.) to provide for the operation of the school. One such school was run by Barbora, who recalled her normal school day the school became self-governing, when the school head alone (or with the help of a deputy) handled everything:

> It was about working on the organization of the school in some way, so people came in the morning, dealt with the mail, planned substitutions, we went to some teacher observations, did some analysis, plus some administration, … everything was still done on paper. I guess that some usual, I don't know, maintenance had to be done, ordering coal, ordering something for the garden, the material operation of the school, it was done somehow. (Barbora)

The difficult situation of rural schools even smaller than the one managed by Barbora was described in detail and criticized by the Educational Office director Václav. At the same time, he criticized the transfer of responsibility to the school heads of these schools through self-governance, blaming the Ministry of Education:

> To this day, when I have the opportunity to talk about this somewhere, I say that this was the biggest mistake of the Ministry of Education, because – imagine a village. Somewhere where there's a one-room school on the borders of the district. One single teacher, a school head, who could have two hours or three hours of time off [from teaching – authors' note], but who do you get as a second teacher there for two or three hours a week? Well, nobody. So she teaches, but she also has to deal with the operation, so there's one lady who's the cleaner, because in a tiny little school like this it doesn't make sense to cook, so they bring in food from some cafeteria, I'd rather not talk about any kind of adherence to hygienic and nutritional standards, so the cleaner gives the food to the children, cleans it up, and now the school head has to make sure it's done, of course. She's in charge of the economy, labour relations, everything. (…) They do it to the best of their knowledge, but that is not enough. (Václav)

This opinion summarizes several fundamental criticisms of the autonomy of small rural schools. We believe that this topic was very important in the 1990s, but only a few people thought about these implications of autonomy. The revolutionary times demanded quick solutions, but these were often not based on a broader professional framework or analysis. This may be true of other topics as well.

School heads agreed that self-governance further emphasized the economic aspect of school management and led to the neglect of pedagogical work. One school head of a large city school recalled mistakes stemming from ignorance:

> And the self-governance was very interesting in that we as school heads had to create our own structure at that school because we had to take over the whole works. Specifically, the economics, we had to do the payroll. So, for example, I remember that my first economist was a lady who was very nice and she was a mother of one child here and I trusted her and she came to me and started doing the economics. But… I didn't know that she wasn't sending out payments. She was paying people's salaries, but she wasn't sending payments to social security and health insurance. So I had to fire her after maybe three months, and that was my first baptism. Oh, the economic field is actually the primary duty for me. And at that time, all of us school heads also realized that we were actually like losing control over the pedagogical field, because basically the economy was the most important for us, whether the money is coming in, whether the money is being paid, whether the taxes are being paid correctly. (Zdeněk)

After the school became self-governed, the school head became more of a manager/ economist than a pedagogue—or at least that is how some school heads felt. The economic agenda also largely occupied the staff of the Educational Offices who allocated funds to schools. The dominance of dealing with economic issues in contemporary records as well as in memories was due to their own responsibility for the management of the school and to the tight budgets of the schools:

> In that first phase after 1990, we were actually, like I can't say I had the problem of maybe sometimes not having the money to cover the expenses. The fact is that the budget was very tight, yeah? That it just covered our needs, and there was no space for any big spending. (Barbora)

The workers at the Educational Offices agreed that the economic meetings were the most important ones at the Ministry of Education. The dominance of budgetary questions led to a reduction in other important agendas, for example in the field of counselling and support for disadvantaged students. At the same time, there was no space for a deeper reflection on the debates on the reform of the educational system. Discussions on reform proposals conducted at the level of the Ministry of Education and the professional public did not seem to resonate very much in the practice of specific schools. Our narrators did not mention them, and in contemporary written sources (e.g. school chronicles), there are only marginal references to the reform proposals.

Because of economic problems, the schools tried to find resources in cooperation with the private sector. The question of looking for sponsors emerged anew with the self-governance, when schools were able to look for different sources of funding. The narrators reported that sponsors could not be found. 'At that time it was very fashionable, who got the money, who got the sponsor, who got some project, who got any money' (Barbora).

School heads recalled that private companies did not participate in supporting schools to any large degree. Rather, it was common for businesspeople to make a financial contribution because their children had just started attending the school. However, the interest in sponsorship declined immediately after their children graduated from the school. The situation was probably even worse in the countryside than in the larger cities: 'When we received any sponsorships, we were glad, but in the countryside, it was not so significant. Because there are also not so many businessmen there' (Helena).[28]

Self-employment was newly regulated by a decree, a draft of which was published in August 1991 with instructions for immediate application. The draft decree, published in a non-public circular stored in the archives of an Educational Office, stated, inter alia:

> The purpose of the economic activity of schools is the rational use of the available capacities of staff, material equipment and premises of schools and institutions, especially at times when they are not used for main activities. The goal is to raise funds for the improvement of the main activities of schools and institutions. Within the framework of economic activity, schools and institutions may also evaluate the results of their main activities (products, produce, services, etc.), which have a primarily educational purpose, but which will thus not be merely purposeless.

One school head added to this: 'When asked whether entrepreneurship belongs in a primary school, I say: yes! However, it is necessary to maintain a certain degree of such activity, to be resourceful and to give the resources thus obtained back to the children in the first place. To improve the quality of teaching' (Malíček, 1993, p. 3).

Some schools started to earn money for their activities in different, hitherto hardly imaginable ways. One school head in our research sample recalled an earning opportunity that came to the school:

> In 1990, someone brought back from America a truckload of discarded items, such as nail polish that was drying out. Batteries that weren't very usable, yeah? But they could still be used. And we got this stuff here. We got it... for free, and we were supposed to sell it for a price, and to give them back some very low price. So we invited the parents (...), so the mothers here were like painting their nails blue and we were the first ones to sell blue nail polish in Brno, yeah? Stupid, right. But, like, I just want to say that that was the time. It was just the nineties. That it all had this scent of adventure. (Zdeněk)

A time when 'everything had the scent of adventure' is one way to frame the image of the school system in the memory of eyewitnesses in the first years after the fall of communism in Czechoslovakia. However, how and to what extent the unique

---

[28] The school head of a small rural school mentioned in a 1992/93 school chronicle entry that he approached private companies in the area to request sponsorships to upgrade the school equipment. Three companies responded. One donated a video recorder, another donated 6500 CZK for textbooks, and the third donated juice for the Christmas party. According to the records in the chronicle, the school head of this school was a supporter of the transition to a market economy and apparently expected a greater response from the private sector. In a later entry, he criticized the situation in which businesspeople preferred to sponsor sports clubs rather than schools.

opportunities of the post-socialist transformation period could be used by the individual participants depended on the specific conditions of the environment in which they operated. The conditions for education and school system management were influenced by the school's location and by interpersonal relations. In the next chapter, we move from the perspectives of school management to the perspectives of teachers and we focus on the relationships among the individual participants—school heads, teachers, parents, and students. We look in more detail at the different environments in which Czech schools have operated. Although the Czech Republic is a relatively small country, the conditions for education vary considerably from region to region. Finally, we offer a rather unique insight into the specific environment of school inspection and introduce the Czech School Inspectorate.

Bibliography

Act No. 171/1990 Coll. On the System of Primary and Secondary Schools (Education Act). (1990). https://www.psp.cz/sqw/sbirka.sqw?cz=171&r=1990

Act No. 451/1991 Coll., which Determines Certain othe Prerequisites for the Performance of Certain Functions in State Authorities and Organisations of the Czech and Slovak Federative Republic, the Czech Republic and the Slovak Republic. (1991). https://www.psp.cz/sqw/sbirka.sqw?cz=451&r=1991

Act No. 564/1990 Coll. On State Administration and Self-Government in the School System. (1990). https://www.psp.cz/sqw/sbirka.sqw?cz=564&r=1990

Act No. 424/1991 Coll. On Association in Political Parties and Political Movements. (1991). https://www.psp.cz/sqw/sbirka.sqw?r=1991&cz=424

Adam, M. (1990). Rehabilitace učitelů [Teacher rehabilitation]. *Učitelské noviny, 93*(3), 2.

Adamus, V. (1992). Příživnictví – minulost a současnost [Parasitism – The past and the present]. *Správní právo:odborný časopis pro oblast státní správy a správního práva, 25*(3), 30–35.

Dokoupilová, R. (1992a). O vztahu obce a školy: kompromisy jsou někdy nutné, hádky povolené, dohody vítané [On the relationship between the municipality and the school: Compromises are sometimes necessary, disagreements allowed, agreements welcome]. *Učitelské noviny, 95*(19), 5.

Dokoupilová, R. (1992b). Ředitel školy: ekonomem, manažerem nebo právníkem? [School head: Economist, manager or lawyer?]. *Učitelské noviny, 95*(5), 5.

Doporučení MŠMT ČR [Recommendation of MEYS]. (1990). *Učitelské noviny, 93*(6), 9.

Gruša, Z. (1991). O právní subjektivitě [On self-governance]. *Učitelské noviny, 94*(11), 2.

Hrubá, J. (2013). *Občanská fóra pedagogických pracovníků* [Civic forums of pedagogical workers]. http://www.ucitelske-listy.cz/2013/10/jana-hruba-dokumenty-3-obcanska-fora.html

Kenney, P. (2002). *A carnival of revolution: central Europe 1989*. Princeton University Press.

Kitzberger, J. (1990). Názor KC OF [Statement of coordination center of The Civic Forum]. *Učitelské noviny, 93*(13), 1.

Kolář, B. (1991). Mezi školou a úřadem [Between the school and the municipality]. *Učitelské noviny, 91*(38), 5.

Kozel, F. (1992). Školské rady a spol. [School Councils etc.]. *Učitelské noviny, 95*(5), 4.

Krapfl, J. (2013). *Revolution with a human face: Politics, culture, and community in Czechoslovakia, 1989–1992*. Cornell University Press.

Malíček, J. (1993). Žádný strach před právní subjektivitou [No fear of self-governance]. *Učitelské noviny, 96*(4), 3.

MEYS. (1990a). Instrukce Ministerstva mládeže, školství a tělovýchovy ČSR k vyučování na základních školách, školách pro mládež vyžadující zvláštní péči a středních školách [Instruction of the ministry of youth, education and sports of the CSR on teaching in primary schools, schools for young people requiring special care and secondary schools]. *Učitelské noviny, 93*(1), 6.

MEYS. (1990b). Instrukce Ministerstva mládeže, školství a tělovýchovy ČSR k vyučování na základních školách, školách pro mládež vyžadující zvláštní péči a středních školách [Instruction of the ministry of youth, education and sports of the CSR on teaching in primary schools, schools for young people requiring special care and secondary schools]. *Učitelské noviny, 93*(2), 6–7.

Moree, D. (2013). *Učitelé na vlnách transformace: kultura školy před rokem 1989 a po něm* [Teachers on the waves of transformation: School culture before and after 1989]. Karolinum.

Nosál, J. (1990). Znovu o konkursech [Again on competitive selections]. *Učitelské noviny, 93*(13), 2.

Obce a školní budovy [Municipalities and School Buildings]. (1991). *Učitelské noviny, 94*(16), 1.

Okresní programy rozvoje ZŠ a SŠ: pokyn Ministerstva školství, mládeže a tělovýchovy České republiky Č.j. 18 508/94-20 [District Programmes for Development of Primary and Secondary Schools: Instruction of the Ministry of Youth, Education and Sports of The Czech Republic, Ref. No.:18 508/94-20]. (1994). *Učitelské noviny, 97*(46), 15–16.

Sav. (1990). Půl roku nestačí: z tiskové konference o perspektivách našeho školství. [Half a year is not enough: From a press conference on the prospects of our school system]. *Učitelské noviny, 93*(24), 1.

Spilková, V. (1997). *Proměny primární školy a vzdělávání učitelů v historicko–srovnávací perspektivě* [Primary school transformations and teacher education in a historical comparative perspective]. Pedagogická fakulta Univerzity Karlovy.

Štefflová, J. (1991). Okresní Počítání: dva pohledy na budoucnost rozpočtů škol [District counting: Two perspectives on the future of school budgets]. *Učitelské noviny, 94*(21), 4.

Štefflová, J. (1992). Nejasné kontury: Nahlédnutí do praxe školských rad a komisí [Vague contours: Insights into practice of school boards and commissions]. *Učitelské noviny, 95*(8), 4.

Štefflová, J. (1993). Informace od pramene: Co s právní subjektivitou [Information from the source: What to do with self-governance]. *Učitelské noviny, 96*(46), 3.

Štefflová, J., & Gruša, Z. (1991). Havárie: základní škola v Mladých Bukách, školský úřad a starosta [Failure: Primary school in Mladé Buky, educational office and the mayor]. *Učitelské noviny, 94*(26), 4–5.

Suk, J. (1998). *Občanské fórum. Listopad – prosinec 1989: 2. díl: Dokumenty* [Civic Forum. November – December 1989: Part 2: Documents]. Ústav pro soudobé dějiny AV ČR – Doplněk.

Suk, J. (2003). *Labyrintem revoluce: aktéři, zápletky a křižovatky jedné politické krize (od listopadu 1989 do června 1990)* [Through the Labyrinth of Revolution: Participants, plots and crossroads of a political crisis (from November 1989 to June 1990)]. PRO.

Vzorový statut školského úřadu [Model statute of the educational office]. (1991). *Učitelské noviny, 94*(17), 8.

Chapter 7
Schools in a Network of (External) Relationships

Abstract The post-socialist transformation processes of primary schools cannot be fully understood without a deeper insight into the (human) relationships and the environments in which the schools were situated. The introductory part of the chapter focuses on students, parents, and teachers. The narrators' perspectives of the development and transformation of relationships between the different people involved during the post-socialist transformation are the central focus. The text mentions the topic of the (economic) transformations of society based on neoliberalism, the development of private entrepreneurship, and individualism with regard to the changes in parents' behaviour and the transformations of their relationships with teachers. The text touches on the unpreparedness of teachers for the transformation of their position after 1989 and the challenges connected to the perception of parents as partners of the school.

The next part of the chapter focuses on school life in different environments and locations: in small and large cities and in the countryside. Schools that were considered to be of high quality in the 1990s are investigated, as are those that faced a number of challenges. The stories of the schools are connected on two levels—continuities from the socialist period and the need to face new and often unexpected challenges. The competitive relationship between primary schools and the newly established multi-year grammar schools is described. At the end of the chapter, attention is paid to an important external influence in the life of schools: the School Inspectorate.

Keywords Transformation · Schools · Teachers · Students · Parents · Multi-year grammar schools · School inspectorate

© Masaryk University, Faculty of Arts, Registration no. 00216224, VAT ID: CZ00216224 2024

J. Zounek et al., *(Post)Socialist Transformation of Primary Schools*, https://doi.org/10.1007/978-3-031-58768-9_7

7.1 People Involved in School Life and the Transformation of Relationships Between Them

Interpersonal relationships and cooperation between different participants, including those outside the school, play a key role in determining what the atmosphere in the school is like, how the teachers and students feel in school, and whether they like going there (Bitušíková, 2021; Cleveland et al., 2023; Epstein & Sheldon, 2023; Edwards, 2002; Rabušicová, 2004). School is a social institution with the main goal of educating and teaching children. School can be understood as a community of people—adults and adolescents or children. School can also be defined as a specific environment created for learning (Pol, 2007). During our research, we talked to teachers from different schools—rural and urban, small and large, elite and those that faced many challenges. We focus on how the different participants are viewed in teachers' memories as well as in contemporary documents. This allows us to paint a more colourful picture of primary school life in the process of transformation. When talking about the school and the people involved in school life, it is necessary to start with the students, because their learning, or, more generally, their development, is one of the main tasks of a school.

The issue of discipline resonated strongly with the narrators in our interviews. For many of the eyewitnesses, the prevailing idea was that the discipline of students at school had become somewhat 'relaxed' after 1989. In their views, the transformation of post-socialist society was the main cause of these changes. This is illustrated by the viewpoint expressed by Petra, who taught at a large urban school: 'So after '89, I personally started to see how not the children were changing a little bit, but the society in general was changing, and the school system was a kind of mirror of that society. At the time, I saw that a lot of things weren't quite right. Like, my experience was that kids even dared to sneak into the school and spray fire extinguishers all over the place.'

However, some narrators' recollections suggested that the aforementioned 'relaxation of morals' may often be a part of a nostalgic form of reminiscence,[1] evaluating the 'worse' present in relation to the 'better' past. In the context of school, this was illustrated by a sort of a sigh from several narrators: 'The youth of today.' A specific example of the perception of the relaxation of students' morals shortly after the Velvet Revolution was provided by a very critical text entitled 'Work Evaluation' (1993), written by the school head of a larger urban school at the end of the 1992/1993 school year: 'We recognize the difference between our ideas and reality especially at the level of social habits—greetings, showing respect to

---

[1] Nostalgia is defined as an idealized representation of the past based on a view of the present. For example, dissatisfaction with students' current behaviour may lead teachers to believe that students behaved better in the past, regardless of whether this was actually the case. In post-socialist countries, nostalgia often relates to socialism, but nostalgia for the 'free' 1990s is also increasingly common. Depending on the context, both post-socialist nostalgia and nostalgia for the 1990s appeared among our narrators, and even nostalgia for an undefined 'better past', reflected in a longing for better student behaviour in the past (Todorova & Gille, 2010; Pehe, 2020).

adults, occurrences (not rare) of aggression, vulgarity, and carelessness in relations with classmates. (…) Many children lack the awareness of co-responsibility for their environment and relationships'. Interestingly, and to some extent indicative of the early 1990s, the quoted school head considered the students' lack of awareness of personal responsibility to be the cause of the students' unsatisfactory discipline. It is possible that the school head projected his expectations arising from the regime change onto the behaviour of the students, as personal responsibility represented a new key value typical of the neoliberal transformation and of Czech society in general after 1989.

However, as the memories of the teachers in our research showed, the teachers did not see the fault in the students themselves, but rather in the parents of the students (Moree, 2013). Indeed, our narrators linked the reasons for the lack of discipline and the poor student preparation for lessons to the parents' approach to the education of their children. In our interviews, the teachers predominantly associated parental criticism with the changes after 1989. Some teachers did not take kindly to the fact that parents began to complain about teachers' work. 'The worse students, who were maybe even sloppy, I would say that their parents never spoke up (before 1989). And then it turned around and the parents of these students actually started complaining that the school should teach slower, work slower, that the pressure was too much and so on. So I kind of never liked this' (Radka). Radka's quotation revealed something more than her resentment of parental complaints. The parents of students became more emancipated after 1989. During communism, they had avoided open criticism of the school system for various reasons; in the new democratic conditions, they gradually began to come forward with their own more or less realistic ideas and demands, reflecting a completely new situation for many teachers that they had to begin to cope with.

The allegedly excessive individualism of parents was the target of criticism from teachers. In the views of some of our narrators, after 1989, parents began to prioritize their own interests or those of their child without regard for other parents, students, or teachers. In the current perspective of the teachers, the rise of individualism is associated with the ideas of the post-socialist transformation, i.e. the transition to a market economy, the boom of private entrepreneurship, and the excessive adoration of individual personal responsibility. From the narrators' perspectives, the view that everyone was responsible for their own fate predominated among many parents after 1989. This led to an emphasis on one's own diligence, personal success, and competitiveness—values that were relatively new or at least newly conceived in society then. Cooperation and an emphasis on the collective were even criticized by some parents: 'At that time, one of the mothers also said an unforgettable sentence to me in a parental meeting: Ms. Teacher, you are somehow behind the times. There is no collectivism anymore' (Jana). In the eyes of the teachers, the parents who started their own businesses after 1989 were typical representatives of such attitudes. These parents exerted undue pressure on their children to perform, but, because of their own workload, they did not have time to help their children, for example, with preparation for lessons or by creating a suitable learning environment.

The teachers criticized excessive parental pressure, but they also negatively evaluated the opposite problem—parents' lack of interest in their children's education or unwillingness to cooperate with the school. According to the teachers, in the market environment, many parents began to perceive the school more like an institution from which they, as clients, ordered their children's education and demanded that the school deliver an imaginary finished product: a well-behaved and educated child (Rabušicová, 2004). František, who was a school head in a district town after 1989, had a concrete experience with parents' lack of interest in cooperation. Relationships between the school and parents were far from ideal and František wondered how to involve parents more in the life of the school so that relationships would be based on cooperation rather than competition. He was inspired by an approach he saw in Viennese primary schools: 'I tried to involve parents in the school events because I had seen in Vienna that the school library was open during the day. And I said: "Who's manning it, which teacher?" "No, it's the parents, it's the mothers, and they run it."' On the basis of this experience in Austria, František invited parents to run the clubs. However, he said, there was not much interest from parents.

From the perspectives of our teacher narrators, responsibility for the lack of cooperation and for poor cooperation with the school lay with the parents who prioritized their own personal interests. Although the high appreciation of individualism in the transforming Czech society cannot be questioned and has been discussed in the relevant scientific literature (Holý, 2010),[2] in our view, all the negatives in the relationships between teachers and parents resulting from the transformation cannot be blamed solely on the behaviour of parents. It is possible to be critical of this dominant viewpoint of our narrators and to offer other viewpoints of eyewitnesses and experts.

Eliška, who focuses on law in the school system, presented an interesting perspective on the transformation of the parent-teacher relationship. According to her, the attitudes of teachers stem from their lack of preparedness for the transformation of their position after 1989 and their inability to respect the attitudes of parents as partners of the school who have the right to express opinions related to the upbringing and education of their children. In Eliška's view, it was not the parents but the teachers who did not understand the new situation, i.e. to be able to express their views freely in the new democratic conditions and to speak up in case of dissatisfaction with the work of a teacher or the functioning of a school:

> So it occurs to me that the parents have also grown up. After all, who would have dared to open their mouth in the 1980s? (…) When a teacher complained to a parent, the parent

---

[2] In the discussion about the character of Czech society after November 1989, opinions emerged that strong foundations for the adoption of the values of individualism were laid in the period of late socialism, in which a large part of society opted for individual self-fulfilment in private life because of the control and restrictions over public life. Moreover, the inefficient centrally planned economy reduced trust in the functioning of the state and motivated many people to use individual means to raise their living standards through their own social capital and the grey economy (Krakovský, 2020; Možný, 2023).

didn't know to what extent it could have repercussions. So that I (as a student) could continue my studies, I needed good grades, so I needed to have the teacher on my side. So the teachers were used to treating these parents almost as their students. And out of fear, they were obeyed (by the parents). They were respected. So they wouldn't go after the kid later. But then there was a time of freedom. So the parents started to speak up. And the teachers: Shock! He's contradicting us! How can anyone dare to contradict us?! Us? Teachers? We know everything! We have the patent on education! (Eliška)

Rabušicová (2004) observed a somewhat problematic relationship between Czech teachers and parents. This author saw the reason for this problematic relationship in the teachers' feelings that parents were inappropriately interfering with their professional sphere. She also mentioned the frequent situation in which 'it is not clearly stated and confirmed by practice that parents have the right to demand that the school provide information both about their children's progress and about the development of the school as an institution' (p. 39). The author described the situation in 2004; her text suggested that during the first decade after the fall of communist rule, it was often not possible in practice to build a full partnership between the parents and the school that was accepted by all the people involved. In this context, we refer to 'common' disputes or possible misunderstandings between teachers and parents on issues of cooperation within the legal standards of a democratic society. However, there were also extreme examples of parents enforcing their own interests by transgressing the principles of morality and even the law. These included the above-standard or perhaps non-standard treatment of specific students by the school, which some parents expected in the period of post-socialist transition. Teachers connected this problem to the rapid development of private enterprises, in which some people became rich quite quickly and tried to exploit or sometimes even abuse their position. One of our narrators, Zdeněk, mentioned bribery efforts, adding that similar situations no longer occur today. He described a situation in which the son of a businessman was supposed to get a lower grade in conduct and quoted the student's father who came to the school head's office: 'Our František, well, I'll give you a donation of 1000 crowns here, and we won't talk about it anymore, Mr. School head. That won't be a B from conduct.' To this the narrator adds: 'So like completely non-standard procedures that don't exist today. But at the time like this idea was forming, it's in the '90s, right? I've got a big car and I've got a company here. I'm somebody.'

Rather extensive corruption was also typical of the (late) socialist society, including the school system (Šimáně, 2023). One narrator recalled the requirement of a 'special approach' for the son of a communist official in the late 1980s. In principle, this situation is the same as the one mentioned by Zdeněk, only the parent's occupation and the social context have changed:

One had to watch one's mouth, there were students who came from very well situated families, I even got into trouble with one secretary of the district committee of the KSČ, because I taught his son, and he imagined that the grades would be a little bit different, so here this secretary, for example, came from the district to the school, had me summoned directly from the classroom to the school head's office, and there both the school head and the secretary pressured me to change the grades. Which they didn't manage to do, but then you could tell from the relationship with the school head that it wasn't pleasant for him, so he made it a bit unpleasant for me as well. (Tomáš)

The teachers' critical views of the transformation of parents' attitudes towards the school and towards them after 1989 cannot be generalized and considered the only form of this relationship. Although the narrators criticized the parents in the interviews, they also added in many cases that they themselves had and have good relations with many parents: 'When we meet, I am even on a first-name basis with some of the parents, as well as with the children, we write to each other, we visit each other, when they have a reunion they invite me, so I have nice relations with them' (Olga).

Interpersonal relationships within the teaching staff are also an important element in the functioning of schools. A functional teacher collective and good school management have a major impact on the atmosphere in the school and on teacher satisfaction, and therefore on the quality of all the activities that take place in the school. When it comes to the evaluation of the relationships between colleagues on the teaching staff, our narrators' memories are predominantly positive. Antonín specifically recalled: 'Really like what makes up the school is a good teacher collective and a good school head, yeah? So, so I was lucky in that. As far as I've had the opportunity, I've got on with like everybody and it's been good. I like to remember that, too.' Similar memories were shared by most of the narrators.

On the other hand, many references in school chronicles and other records from the Velvet Revolution and early 1990s suggest that relations within the pedagogical collective may have been very strained, not just from the influence of the political events of 1989. Contemporary sources indicate that there were also conflicts among teachers for various reasons, both personal and professional. Some teachers may have completely unprofessionally vented their conflicts in front of their students. This was referenced in a 1993 performance evaluation at one school at which the school head strongly recommended that teachers not try resolve their own disputes in front of students. Relationships within the teaching collectives may not have been nearly as harmonious as many of our narrators depicted them. The teachers may have tried to portray (their own) collective in a better light and more or less idealized the relationships. As an exception, when the narrators talked about bad relations between teachers, they emphasized that those were cases of specific individuals, or they mentioned this in passing in connection with other topics.

For example, one area in which some (professional) conflicts may have occurred, especially between novice teachers and more experienced senior teachers, was the organization of leisure activities for children. This topic served as an example of the relaxed nature and lack of clear rules in the school system in the post-Velvet Revolution era. This period brought the possibility to organize leisure activities without teachers (and parents) being too concerned about possible risks and complications. Matters that are now clearly legally defined by laws, decrees, and school codes, were, according to some of our narrators, 'not cared about' in the early 1990s. The organization of school trips and other activities outside of school at which the teachers were responsible for their students are examples of such approaches. The wide range of possibilities and the freedom of the time that was used especially by younger teachers could prompt disputes with their older colleagues. One of our youngest narrators mentioned that he was not afraid to 'experiment' with a colleague of the same age:

> That period of time, that relaxation also meant that the rules were relaxed a little bit, so that if you went on a trip, you went for two days at most, so my colleague and I went for the entire week, which the children liked very much, we took them to the countryside, there was always something going on. In the winter, when there was ice skating, we would go skating with them, and basically nobody cared because everybody had enough to worry about. It just caused a bit of resentment amongst the (older) colleagues who were set in their ways. But in hindsight, I don't blame them very much because when colleagues were in their 50s, a person often already has a different perspective on the situation. It was such an adventure for us, we were not burdened in terms of work safety, (…) we just didn't let anything get to us. (Michal)

Less openness to change and innovation, as well as a sense of responsibility reinforced by their own experience may have played a role in the negative opinion of the older colleagues. However, in the interview, Michal also spoke very positively about the teacher collective at his school and emphasized that his older colleagues helped him a lot at the beginning of his career. In fact, despite the references to (intergenerational) disputes, it is true that the narrators evaluated the quality of their colleagues mostly positively, regardless of the age or gender of their colleagues. However, it is important to consider a certain degree of idealization in their memories or some nostalgia for the era of freedom in schools in the early 1990s.

7.2 Small-Town Schools and the Founding of Multi-year Grammar Schools

The life of a school is influenced by where the school is located. When the narrators talked about the environment of the school at which they worked, they did make certain generalizations (perhaps unintentionally). For example, there was a simplistic division between urban and rural schools in the interviews. Czech society is largely urbanized, so the urban environment can be perceived as the standard, while the rural environment can be perceived as something specific or different.[3] The specific nature of the school environment was particularly discussed by those narrators who taught in the countryside. Such recollections were dominated by an emphasis on the quality of interpersonal relationships that positively influenced the atmosphere at school: 'I think the advantage of a village school lies in the fact that you are just terribly close, you really know the kids. I really knew almost all the children in that school. I knew them and their parents' (Barbora).

---

[3] According to the demographic data of the Czech Statistical Office, in 1990, 7,044,699 inhabitants, i.e. 68% of the population, lived in cities with more than 5000 inhabitants (Czech Statistical Office, 2023).

However, these simplistic and probably somewhat idealized notions contrasted with the fact that even rural teachers criticized the 'relaxation of morals' of students and the 'higher ambitions' of their parents. Even in the village, according to some teachers, there was anonymization and a loss of parents' interest in the school and the community.[4] These attitudes may be influenced by the experience of a particular teacher throughout their career. Teachers who have taught all their lives in one environment may have a different perspective from those who have switched between several schools, perhaps even in different environments. What a rural teacher might consider a 'relaxation of morals' might be perceived by an urban teacher as a 'rural idyll'. Nina, who had worked at a rural school for her entire time as a teacher, considered the fact that students did not greet teachers and other adults in the village upon meeting them and did not hesitate to use vulgar language in public to be a 'decline in the authority of the teacher'. In contrast, Petra, who taught in a prefabricated housing estate school all her career, recalled her surprise at how calm the atmosphere was at the rural school where she worked for 6 weeks as a substitute for a sick colleague. She noted that she saw 'a completely different approach' at the school, adding that from her perspective 'it's about the people, the school, the group that lives in that particular region.' As an example of the 'decline in conduct' at the school in the large-scale prefabricated housing estate, Petra spoke about the memory of students spraying a fire extinguisher in the school building—she was used to much more serious misdemeanours than the rural teachers.

The environment of each school is unique to some extent. The characteristics of the various locations in which schools are found cannot be simplistically divided into rural and urban areas. The situation in an urban school may differ depending on whether it is located in the city centre or in a large-scale prefabricated housing estate, or whether it is a smaller district town or a metropolis, for example. Rural areas in the Czech Republic are then divided into those that are thriving and those that are rather destitute (Bernard et al., 2018). We look at the specific characteristics of different environments and introduce schools from different parts of South Moravia, one of the most diverse regions of the Czech Republic in this respect.

We start with a small town where there were efforts to establish a multi-year grammar school after 1989. This was a typical and simultaneously important theme of the post-socialist transformation of primary and secondary school system. A specific small-town environment can be notionally found somewhere in the interspace between the city and the countryside. Inhabitants of small towns[5] do not consider themselves to be living in the countryside, but at the same time they are in a non-anonymous environment with strong social control.

---

[4] Some narrators saw the cause of this in the migration of urban residents to the countryside. This accelerated after 1989, when the desire to live in the countryside as well as the social growth of a part of the population and the desire to own real estate led to the construction of 'satellite towns' and catalogue houses, especially in villages near large cities (Pospěch, 2021).

[5] The definition of a small town itself is rather broad. It may be a very small town of 3000 inhabitants, or a district town of 30,000 inhabitants. The identity—how the inhabitants identify themselves—is also important in very small rural towns.

Relatively soon after the Velvet Revolution, voices calling for the restoration of multi-year grammar schools appeared. The efforts were based on the Czechoslovak tradition of the First Republic, i.e. ideas from the 1920s and 1930s. According to the ideas of the 1990s, these grammar schools were supposed to offer education to the most talented students and primarily prepare them for university studies. The possibility of founding multi-year grammar schools was already enshrined in the first amendment to the Education Act of 1990. Indeed, multi-year grammar schools began to be founded in the 1990/1991 school year.

However, multi-year grammar schools were and still are criticized by experts as a tool for the too early selection of students (Greger, 2011; Perry, 2005).[6] A 1996 OECD report even suggested their abolition. The voices for abolishing this type of grammar school became louder at the turn of the millennium when the left-wing Czech Social Democratic Party took over the government. Strengthening the equality of educational opportunities regardless of socioeconomic status or parents' education was the main argument for the abolition (Sucháček, 2014). In addition, some sociologists saw the early selection of students as reproducing social inequalities and dividing society (Matějů & Straková, 2003; Prokop, 2022).[7] Multi-year grammar schools survived the political pressure; this can be attributed to the initiative of a part of the public that fought intensively to save these schools. The parents of children studying at multi-year grammar schools constitute a part of society with the highest economic, social, and cultural capital, and they are both willing and able to engage in the defence of their own interests (Sucháček, 2014).

The existence of natural social differences and the acceptance of different paths to education based on ability and resources was considered legitimate and 'natural' by a part of society during the neoliberal turn in the early 1990s.[8] Small towns then became the ideal place for the local citizens to start working towards the founding

---

[6] In the 1990s, similar criticisms were also voiced by the teaching public. The *Teacher's Newspaper* (Učitelské noviny) featured the opinion that students entering a multi-year grammar school are too young to have a clear idea of what direction they want to take in their studies. Studying at a multi-year grammar school can make it difficult for students to pursue, for example, a technical education (Doubek, 1990).

[7] Because of the early selection, the social capital of the most educated part of the population is not intermingled with contact with artisans and workers. This may mean, for example, that a carpenter knows no lawyer to whom he can turn in a difficult situation. The absence of mutual social ties across different classes of society also helps to create misunderstandings and barriers in opinions, attitudes, values, and political preferences. In his analysis of contemporary Czech society, sociologist Daniel Prokop (2022) wrote: 'A large wave of sorting then takes place when people leave for multi-year grammar schools. Whether you go there depends not only on talent, but also significantly on the aspirations of your parents. Over 40% of students at multi-year grammar schools come from the most educated and wealthiest fifth of families. Equally talented children from poorer or moderately wealthy background are often not motivated by their parents to better education' (p. 70).

[8] Since their founding, multi-year grammar schools have been receiving twice as much money from the state budget per student compared to primary schools (Sucháček, 2014).

of multi-year grammar schools. This happened in one of the small towns[9] in southern Moravia because of the initiative of the local government. Antonín, one of the
teachers at the local primary school at the time, recalled the motivation of the residents, but also the fears at the primary school: 'Why should the kids travel to Brno
to go to grammar schools when we can have a grammar school here too (…) Well,
I know that some of my colleagues didn't like it, that they would take the kids away
from us.' The grammar school was established in the building of the local primary
school in 1993, as another of the resident teachers, Michal, recalled: 'The mayor at
the time, an enlightened one I would say, wanted to found an eight-year grammar
school because he felt it would uplift the small town. And in '93, the first two grades
were established there.' Michal then left the primary school for the grammar school,
along with part of the teaching staff.[10]

Michal, as an expert on the environment of the local primary school and the
multi-year grammar school, emphasized the notion that the grammar school was to
serve mainly local students and that it was to replace the 'best' classes in the local
internally differentiated primary school. In it, a model was applied in which students were divided into classes on the basis of their abilities, and, in particular, their
performance at school. This was a 'division'[11] of students that was already relatively
widespread in late socialist Czechoslovakia: 'The original idea was that the grammar school would function as a part of the primary school, because in the past,
classes "A" and "B" were the classes of prominent students, for which people were
chosen, in quotation marks; the children of prominent citizens were selected for the
class A' (Michal). Local students were more likely to belong to the 'elite' classes;
those who commuted from the surrounding villages tended to be in the 'weaker'
classes. However, it cannot be unequivocally stated that everything was based on the
privileged status of small-town children.[12] It may simply be that their (more educated) parents simply had higher educational aspirations. It should be noted that the
social composition and wealth of the small town in question was also influenced by
its proximity to the large city. It was the very selective classes that were replaced by
the grammar school. Such classes (with extended teaching of, for example, lan-

---

[9] The town had a population of about 9000 in 1990.

[10] The grammar school is still in operation today. In the entries in a chronicle of another school, we
found another example of the founding of a grammar school from the initiative of the local representation in 1993, which was also established directly in the building of a primary school. However,
this grammar school did not survive the 1990s and we were unable to find in the available sources
what the main reason was for its dissolution. And to add to that, it was not in a small town, but in
a neighbourhood of a large city, which has, admittedly, a rather rural character. This shows that not
all multi-year grammar schools that were founded from the initiative of local administrations
survived.

[11] We can provide a general example. In the school, there was a class 'A' with the best students.
Class 'B' consisted of average students, and class 'C' had the worst students.

[12] The suspicion that a part of society will perceive the multi-year grammar schools mainly as a tool
to strengthen their own prestige (their children will be grammar school students, not 'just' primary
school students) also appeared in the *Teacher's Newspaper* (Doubek, 1990).

guages or mathematics) already had a similar function under socialism, because, apart from teaching students, they also fulfilled the need of parents to provide their children with the best possible education. Under socialism, some parents fulfilled this need through corruption or abuse of power to get their children into such classes.

A question arises of whether the newly established grammar school really offered a better quality of teaching. We draw mainly on the recollections of the narrators, as other types of sources could not provide us with an answer. At that time, there were no (national) comparative tests or school inspection reports on the quality of the newly founded schools. Ludmila evaluated the quality of teaching at the grammar school very positively because of the presence of motivated students:

> So into the *prima*, that is the sixth grade, we got the kids who had the potential, yeah. Well especially the girls, but the boys also had distinction. For example, there were thirty-three students in that class and out of those, maybe seventeen had distinction. They were outstanding, they themselves were just coming up to me and like asking questions. … I did really well with them, when it was like a lesson, we did the entire lesson, I also copied the extension materials, and they were really interested. (Ludmila)

Michal also attributes the high quality of teaching to the teaching staff who had previously worked at the local primary school:

> There were great teachers there, in mathematics, there were good foreign language teachers, there were excellent Czech teachers, and as for biology and geography, I think they were among the best in the district, according to the results of the students in various competitions. So the decision [to establish a grammar school—authors' note] has been justified, because the teaching staff did not have to change in any way. (Michal)

The quality of the school and the external image of the school can be judged, for example, from the successes of the students in competitions at that time, as Michal mentioned. Although this is not a completely objective criterion for assessing quality, it serves at least for basic orientation in the differences between schools.

In the first half of the 1990s, the offer of multi-year grammar schools was still relatively limited, so they did not fundamentally distort the composition of primary school students.[13] The boom in multi-year grammar schools (including private ones) can be dated to the period after 1995. In the 1992/1993 school year, there were 220 multi-year grammar schools in the Czech Republic; in 1996/1997, there were already 332. The number then started to stagnate; in 2005/2006, there were 337.

Some primary school teachers and school heads saw the multi-year grammar schools as a threat, as their existence led to the departure of the most talented students. It should be noted that the small-town grammar school we referred to in this chapter absorbed both talented students and first-rate teachers. This is a theme that is not often mentioned in discussions regarding the founding of multi-year grammar schools.

---

[13]The fact that the admission to a multi-year grammar school was not a matter of course is evidenced by an entry in one of the school chronicles from the 1995/1996 school year. It states that 20 children applied and four were admitted.

Teachers at primary schools that were considered to be 'elite' were the most critical of multi-year grammar schools, at least in our sample. These may be, for example, schools with extended language teaching. For these schools, the multi-year grammar schools could represent strong competition: 'For us as a school it was quite bad because they actually took away the best of the school and thus decreased the level of the school' (František). Narrator Jana was even more critical: 'At first it was the eight-year grammar schools. Which robbed us of those fifth graders, yeah? So of course the school went downhill linguistically. But then the six-year grammar schools were founded, so that was another hit below the belt.' Jana pointed out another problem here: six-year grammar schools also poached students from the primary schools. We are now leaving aside the fact that a rather complex and at times almost unclear school system had been created. The efficiency of such a system and the quality of teaching are also issues. However, at the time of the founding of the multi-year grammar schools, these issues were not a priority.

Evidence that the 'elite' primary schools had negative feelings about the founding of multi-year grammar schools can be seen in the criticism presented in an (unpublished) document from 1994 titled 'Evaluation of Educational Work', which was written in a school with extended French language teaching:

> The results of the work at the first stage are considerably better, mainly because after the fifth grade, the best, and sometimes not only the best students leave us for different types of state and private secondary schools, which considerably impairs the work and its organization, especially in specialized classes, such as our French 5.B., from which 10 students are leaving this year and the organization of its continued existence is very complicated.

In 1996, a limit was introduced allowing only 10% of the population year to be admitted to multi-year grammar schools (Sucháček, 2014). The limit was introduced following criticism from the OECD, and it was probably the reason for the slowing or even stopping of the founding of new grammar schools.

The issue of the founding of private primary schools, which could once again be founded after 1989 and thus became part of the school system, is also interesting. This concerned (primarily) church or traditional alternative schools (e.g. Waldorf or Montessori schools). According to the teachers in our sample, their founding had only a marginal impact on state primary schools. The interviews revealed that private schools did not acquire a very good reputation. A former school inspector recalled the problematic beginnings of private schools: 'Private schools were established, well, then they began to dazzle with the equipment ... But the teaching was comparably worse, because they accepted everybody, at least at the beginning the quality of teaching was not worth much in the private schools' (Naděžda).[14] This does not mean that there were not private primary schools of very high quality.[15]

In terms of quantity, church schools were only a marginal phenomenon in the strongly secularized Czech Republic.[16] Only one of our narrators, Dana, mentioned that a church school was established in their small town and enjoyed quite a good reputation at the beginning. However, because of the small number of students admitted, it did not affect life in their large school.

However, large urban schools were still struggling with strained capacity in the early 1990s. The emergence of multi-year grammar schools and private schools may have relieved them to some extent.

7.3 Large Urban Schools and the Reverberations of Late Socialist Building

In the second half of the twentieth century, Czech society faced a number of crises that the communist government was unable to resolve because of its (poorly) centrally planned economic system. An acute shortage of housing, especially in the large cities, constituted one of these crises. The housing problems were longstanding and their origins date back to the work-related migration of people during the nineteenth century Industrial Revolution. Overcrowded and inadequate working-class neighbourhoods served the communist propaganda as proof of the misery of the capitalist First Czechoslovak Republic. But the problem was still relevant and largely unsolved in the second half of the twentieth century. With varying degrees of intensity, the effort to systematically build new neighbourhoods was inherent to the entire period of socialism in Czechoslovakia. In the 1950s, residential blocks in the socialist realist style were built on the Soviet model. In the 'freer' 1960s, the first

---

[14] Similar criticisms also appeared in primary school work evaluations prepared by their school heads. Some used the evaluations as a space to reflect on the current situation in society. The school head of one large urban school of good quality addressed the decline in student numbers as early as 1994, blaming multi-year grammar schools and private schools. The school head was obviously referring especially to the founding of private multi-year grammar schools: 'In this case, the MEYS (Ministry of Education, Youth and Sports) should increase its activity (…) so that students could be readmitted to primary school if their studies at their chosen secondary school would not suit them, and the ČSI (Czech School Inspectorate) should monitor the level and results of work more closely, especially at private schools and newly founded grammar schools, which are allegedly unsatisfactory and mainly pursue the goal of retaining students and the goodwill of their parents.'

[15] The subject of private schools goes beyond the scope of our topic.

[16] In the 1990/91 school year, only one church school was established in the Czech Republic; in 1991/92, there were four, in 1995/1996, there were fifteen church schools, and in 1998/1999, there were twenty. A major breakthrough can be seen after the adoption of the new School Act in 2004. In the 2003/2004 school year, there were forty-two church schools in the Czech Republic. The number then started to decrease (MEYS, 2009).

prefabricated housing estates were built; they are still highly valued both by residents and urban planners, e.g., because of their inspiration in Scandinavia (Kalinová, 2012; Sommer, 2019).

However, these relatively high-quality urban projects did not resolve the lack of affordable housing. Construction accelerated even more after 1969. This was done in line with the government's strategy, in which material abundance was supposed to subdue the population's frustration and dissatisfaction with the political situation in a country occupied by Soviet troops. However, the new large-scale prefabricated housing estates are no rated so highly in terms of the quality of the buildings or public space, as the emphasis was more on quantity.

New school buildings had to be built together with the housing estates as they were needed for the children of the young families moving in, and where there was also a relatively large concentration of inhabitants in a small space. There were other reasons for the need for new housing and school buildings: the period of normalization was characterized by a significant demographic boom, commonly referred to as the era of 'Husák's Children',[17] which was accompanied by a generous pro-family policy including interest-free newlywed loans (Kalinová, 2012) intended to support young families.

However, the efforts to address the housing situation and the construction of new school buildings ran up against the inefficiencies of the centrally planned economy. Although the prefabricated housing estates were built relatively quickly, the pace of handing over new housing units to young families did not go hand in hand with the completion of the proper infrastructure, including primary schools. The housing estate schools often faced problems of limited capacity. The classrooms overcrowded with children born in the 1970s and 1980s did not disappear with the fall of the communist government in 1989; these problems persisted into the 1990s.[18]

Teachers from large housing estate schools recalled the difficulties they faced in the beginning. Until the 1990s, the organization of teaching had to be dealt with by teaching 'in shifts' (Zounek et al., 2017). This consisted of some students attending primary school in the morning and others in the afternoon. Irma, who joined a newly opened primary school at a large urban housing estate in the early 1990s, described the context of the school's foundation and the need to implement shift teaching: 'Well, a huge new housing estate. So there was a heap of kids (…) So I know it was a week when I had the mornings off, but then I had to come here, they would come in at like half past twelve, and they would have classes until like half past four or something.' Irma adds that she was lucky as her own children could be looked after

---

[17] 'Husák's children' was a simplified term for the significant population boom in Czechoslovakia during 'normalization' in the early 1970s, specifically for people born during this period. The designation refers to Gustáv Husák, at that time referred to as the First, later General Secretary of the Central Committee of the Communist Party of Czechoslovakia, and then, from 1975, President of the Czechoslovak Socialist Republic.

[18] The overcrowding of classrooms in the enrolment records of the 1990/91 school year was mentioned in the chronicle of a housing estate school in a district town: 'The planned capacity of the school was once again exceeded by nine classes. All spaces have been used for teaching.'

by their grandparents when she had to be at school in the afternoon. Another narrator, Jana, mentioned that in the first stage, the classes were organized in shifts even at the old and inadequate school in the city centre. The school simply did not have the necessary capacity for all the students. This was not 'only' a problem of newly built housing estates, but also a consequence of neglected investments into the expansion of already inadequate school buildings in the historic development of the city centre.

It is obvious that such an organization of teaching complicated family life for teachers and the parents of students alike. Blanka recalled the 'shifts' in a large housing estate as well:

> Well I experienced it with my own son and myself, it was very unpleasant for those children who had that afternoon shift, that maybe they finished at five or five thirty in the winter! It was dark when we let them go home. Well, I had a lot of experience with that.

However, it was not possible to organize shift teaching at the second stage of primary schools. The reason for this was that the older students had different teachers for each subject, or had lessons divided into groups within the class or even across classes (e.g. in foreign language teaching). If the capacity of schools at the housing estate was exceeded, these students had to travel to other schools in the city. Soňa, who worked at a school in the city centre, remembered: 'Children from Vinohrady,[19] a young new housing estate, used to come to us, lots of children.'[20]

In the 1990s, the situation gradually began to improve. Blanka recalled the gradual decline in the number of students in one of the Brno housing estates: 'And then, not because of politics or anything, but probably because the young people were already moving elsewhere, so suddenly from six first grades we were glad we made two. And, of course, they haven't had to make shifts for a long time now.'

This may have been due to the completion of more primary school buildings in the housing estate, but also by the reduced birth rate and the ageing of the population of the housing estate. This results from the fact that before 1989, mostly young families were moving into the new housing estates, and they all did so at about the same time. Housing estates therefore lacked the diverse generational mix of the population inherent in older developments. This may have introduced fluctuations in the required school capacity. This in turn led to short-sighted school dissolutions and subsequent capacity problems at times when the capacity is needed again because of an increase in the birth rate. For example, the housing estate in which Blanka taught was completed in the early 1970s, and had a reputation as a 'retirement neighbourhood' by the 1990s. Therefore, it was problematic to make up two primary school grades there. However, at the time of the writing of this book, it is

---

[19] A Brno neighbourhood located rather remotely from the city centre.

[20] The phenomenon of students commuting from housing estates to schools elsewhere in the city was documented in school chronicles. The chronicle of a large urban primary school stated in an entry from the 1990/91 school year: fifth grade students are coming to school, commuting from Líšeň (the relatively new housing estate is currently incapable of accommodating all its students with its existing schools). The students are brought and carried away by a school bus.'

once again becoming a neighbourhood of young families and the capacity of schools is again insufficient, not least because of the dissolution of one of three schools in the 1990s (Semrád, 2018). Other housing estates, built later, have yet to go through a generational change. However, the homogeneous character of the population of each individual neighbourhood is one of the current legacies of the centrally planned construction of late socialism.

The newly built housing estates were homogeneous both by virtue of generation and in the character of the population. Before 1989, people from one particular production plant or an entire enterprise were allocated flats in one particular housing estate. Some housing estates therefore also lacked diversity in terms of the level of education of the inhabitants and their cultural capital. This created housing estates with 'better' and 'worse' reputations (Semrád, 2019). Problems with students from some housing estates were captured in materials from the schools to which these students commuted in an organized manner. For example, the Evaluation of the School's Work prepared by the school head of one schools in 1994 stated: 'If I am to evaluate the specific results of the school's work, it should be prefaced by the fact that the clear improvement of the school results was also due to the fact that children from the prefabricated housing estate, whose grades were among the worst and the most problematic, no longer commute to the school.'[21] At the same time, the records showed that before the mid-1990s, authorities were succeeding in completing the construction of the necessary school capacities in the newly built housing estates. However, the number of children was declining at the same time.

In general, the situation with school capacity problems began to gradually improve during the 1990s with the dampening of state-organized socialist construction. On the other hand, the challenges facing schools in socially excluded neighbourhoods and regions became progressively more serious and complex during the 1990s.

---

[21] The commuting of students to more distant schools was also connected to the early 1990s establishment of ninth grades, attended by students who were not admitted to secondary schools from the eighth grade. These may have been students with worse results or sometimes with disciplinary problems. These ninth grades were not established in all schools in the city, only in some, as only a small number of students attended the ninth grade. In an analysis of the work of one urban school for 1989/1990, a statistic appeared: nine out of seventy-seven eighth grade students continued to the ninth grade. According to the national statistics, the number increased: in the 1990/1991 school year it was 7% of students, and in the 1991/1992 school year, it was already 32.5% (Štefflová, 1991). One chronicle, in the minutes for the 1990/1991 school year, mentioned that the newly arrived ninth grade students caused disciplinary problems: 'The biggest educational problems we had were with the ninth graders who came to us for 1 year.'

7.4 Schools and Social Inequalities in Society

The post-socialist transformation brought about the social rise of a certain part of the population and seemingly unlimited opportunities for those who possessed the necessary capital—economic capital and in many cases also social and cultural capital. At the same time, the widening separation between social classes and the deepening problems cannot be overlooked. Sociological research has shown that social mobility was difficult in Czech society. Children from a non-stimulating environment have little chance of being able to achieve success on their own. Neoliberal ideas of personal responsibility and the importance of one's own diligence have not been favourable to the promotion of effective policies addressing the problems of the poorest parts of society (Katrňák, 2004; Prokop, 2022; Pospěch, 2021).

The Roma population, which faced systematic discrimination even during the socialist period, is at the imaginary periphery. The long-ignored problems associated with the culture of poverty and the negative stereotypes of Czech society towards the Roma people were exacerbated by the policies of the communist government. The communists forcibly housed the previously nomadic Roma, especially in unsuitable and dilapidated housing estates that often had been occupied by German or Jewish populations before World War II (Donert, 2017).[22] This created isolated 'ghettos' with bad reputations. The segregation also concerned education to a large extent. The strategy of placing Roma children in special schools[23] regardless of their intelligence was widespread (Henchel, 2020).

The policy of educating the students of Roma descent separately from the majority did not disappear with the fall of the communist government. On the contrary, the introduction of freedom of school choice may have helped to deepen it. If the policy of segregation of Roma students did not take place in a targeted and organized manner, it took place spontaneously because of the gradual loss of parental interest in schools attended by Roma students. We saw a similar example during our research: a school in a neighbourhood inhabited partly by the majority and partly by Roma who had been systematically moved to this neighbourhood into houses that

---

[22] The vast majority of the Jewish population of Czechoslovakia was murdered during the Holocaust in World War II, when the Czech lands were occupied by Nazi Germany (1939–1945). A small portion of Jews managed to emigrate before that (Wein, 2021). The end of World War II was followed by the displacement, removal, or expulsion of Germans from Czechoslovakia (Abschiebung/Vertreibung der Deutschen aus der Tschechoslowakei in German). Between 1945 and 1946, mass deportation of the German population from Czechoslovakia was carried out. To a significant degree, it had the character of ethnic cleansing (Glassheim, 2019). After 1946, only a very small fraction of the pre-war Jewish or German population remained living in the Czech lands.

[23] In socialist Czechoslovakia, special schools were established for children who were unable to meet the requirements of a regular primary school due to deficiencies in their intellectual development. These could include students with mild mental disabilities. Children whose disadvantages stemmed from the social environment in which they grew up or who were neglected in terms of education were not supposed be admitted to these schools. However, this principle was often not followed in practice (Čornejová et al., 2020).

were originally inhabited by the German and Jewish population. Because of the presence of the Roma, after the introduction of the freedom of choice of school, the parents of the students of the majority gradually began to enroll their children in a school in the neighbouring residential area, and the proportion of Roma students in the school gradually increased. This continued to deepen the disinterest of the 'old inhabitants' in the school until it gradually became a segregated school with a bad reputation during the 1990s.[24] Soňa remembers:

> (…) and by them sort of gathering here, the parents from the majority stopped giving us their children. So I go to school in the morning and there are crowds of parents with their children with school bags going the other way [to the school in the adjacent neighbourhood in which the narrator lives—authors' note]. So I say that's wrong. I always say that to the parents who are here. To the ones who are passionate, who used to go to local Sokol, Orel (traditional gymnastics organizations), they also take it hard. I say, why are you giving up? Besides, in no way are there problems between the kids from the majority and those from the minority, absolutely not. They are friends with each other. And I'm even saying that if a kid lives here, and goes to school somewhere else, and those kids don't know him, that there's a greater chance that you're going to have that kid maybe attacked in some way outside or taunted or whatever. But, since we actually go to school together, he's my friend he's from our class, so they won't do anything to him. So I don't think it's practical to put the kid in a different school like that.

The narrator clearly criticized the parents' strategy leading to segregation and emphasized that it led to greater separation between the majority and the Roma minority, when mutual contacts between the students could, on the contrary, help the integration. In addition, she mentioned that despite its bad reputation, the school, in her opinion, provided students with quality teaching and an individual approach. In the interview, she added that the school had a relatively high success rate in the admissions procedure for secondary schools.

In an urban environment, social differences can be clearly visible because of the relative proximity of neighbourhoods with different social compositions and the mutual interaction of their residents. This concerns the ignored problems with the education of the Roma population; in some Czech cities it may also concern the problems caused by the bankruptcy of (large) manufacturing plants as a result of the post-socialist transformation of the economy and the related increase in unemployment.[25]

Social problems in rural areas, including in rural schools, have long remained on the sidelines (Greger, 2011). The Czech countryside does not form a homogenous unit. On the one hand, there is a suburban, developing countryside, which faces

---

[24] Another school in the city centre suffered a similar fate. It was a school that used to have the status of a school (of good quality) with extended foreign language teaching, but gradually, also because of school mergers, its reputation deteriorated: 'And then we got the reputation of a Roma school. Yeah? Those were such sad years' (Jana).

[25] The worsening social situation of part of the population may be a reason for the increase in petty crime. This was evidenced by references in some contemporary materials regarding the need to start locking the school even during school hours because of thefts, and even by references to the fact that the school was burglarized.

problems stemming from urbanization. On the other hand, there is the peripheral countryside located on the borders of regions, far from district towns, often in the borderlands newly settled after World War II. Some areas originally inhabited by the German population still suffer from the absence of functional communities with traditional social ties (Bernard et al., 2018).

These areas have faced depopulation in the post-1989 era as well as problems with the employment of the population. This has led to especially those who are unable to leave staying behind, mainly because of low education, poor economic situation, or the lack of social ties outside their place of residence. Since the Velvet Revolution, a large part of the population of the peripheral countryside has also had less trust in the state and its democratic direction. Many residents do not feel fully part of Czech society because of the impression that politicians and their fellow citizens living in large cities do not care about them and are strangers to their problems. That is why they often nostalgically remember the period of communist rule.

The problems of the peripheral countryside logically concern the school system. Depopulation has led to the closure of schools, and the existing schools have had difficulty in recruiting quality teachers.[26] students have to commute some distance to school, limiting the functioning of the school as a participant forming a part of the community. During our research, we spoke with Nina, who worked in a school near the Austrian border in an area settled by the Czech population after World War II (after the deportation of the German inhabitants). Nina said: 'Children from maybe twenty-three villages come here, it's a big area. Three districts.' This complicates the transportation of students to school.[27] Despite school closures and the wide catchment area that the school has gradually acquired, the number of students is decreasing: 'When I started here in the late 1980s, I had twenty-six students in the first grade, and nowadays I have eight students, for example, by next year we will have thirteen students again, so an average of ten or eleven.'

Nina tended to speak more about the current situation, which may also have been influenced by the fact that the interview took place directly in a school. However, the problems she mentioned are rooted not only in the 1990s, but also in socialism

---

[26] Teachers have been offered various benefits by the founder to accept the job. For example, one of the chronicles of a school located in a peripheral rural area mentioned that in 1993/94, the education office purchased a family house to be able to accommodate a teaching couple.

[27] The availability of public transportation can have a major impact on school life in peripheral regions. Cost-saving measures in the early 1990s also led to the cancellation of bus lines. Particularly the municipalities on the borders of districts or regions faced serious problems. This was evidenced by an entry in a school chronicle from the 1993/1994 school year: 'In December, we were informed that the bus company was planning to cancel the bus line that transports twenty-five children from the surrounding villages. This would have affected the existence of the school considerably, and so negotiations were held that have so far been successful. The fact that students from the neighbouring district might not be able to travel to the school in the future led the education office to considerations about closing the school. (…) the municipality has a strong interest in maintaining operation of the school and it is willing to financially support the school to keep it in operation even with a lower number of students. Thus the closure of the school was averted.' Despite the efforts of the municipality, the school was finally closed in 2005.

and the countryside settlement strategy after World War II. At the same time, in rela-tion to the social composition of the population, Nina emphasized that even with a very small number of students, they as a school can offer an above average and individual approach.

> I would say we don't insult the parents' education in any way; there are, I would say, former secondary school students here, of course there are some starlets who have a college degree, but mostly, the families are socially disadvantaged, so they are happy for anything, if we help them, advise them. You see, it's not anywhere I would say, or anywhere in small schools that the school head would drive a child home. If something hurts them, they will call, we will drive them, help, advise.

The school in which Nina worked since the 1980s is located near the former 'Iron Curtain'. This was the location of the impenetrable border between the Western and Eastern blocs during the Cold War, which was heavily militarily guarded: the border between socialist Czechoslovakia and Austria. Only politically reliable people moved to these areas. Both adults and children were under the influence of specific propaganda. This emphasized that the border guards were heroes and that the defence of the national borders was a guarantee of safety. The propaganda even included information about the risk of the return of the original German inhabitants. The identity and attitudes of the inhabitants, shaped during 40 years of ideological propaganda in the border lands, were not in line with the direction of the country after 1989. One can even speak of a culture of 'memory dissidents' who enclose themselves in an opinion bubble because of their alienation from the pro-Western direction of the country and the absence of visible gains from freedom and democracy (Kreisslová et al., 2019). Because of the distrust in the direction of the country, as well as the remoteness or low education of the population, this region has not been able to fully benefit from the transformation.

This may have been reflected in the matter of cross-border cooperation, for example. Immediately after the Velvet Revolution, the opening of national borders led to the establishment of contacts with neighbouring schools in Austria. However, these contacts did not last. From Nina's point of view, they were hindered by the language barrier, probably caused by the low educational aspirations of both the parents and children. The distrust towards their close Austrian neighbours appar-ently also played a role. This distrust survived from the period of omnipresent com-munist anti-Western (and anti-German) propaganda. The same sense of distrust and alienation may have prevailed on the other side of the border as well, as research conducted among residents in both the Czech and Austrian borderlands showed (Blaive & Molden, 2009).

> Open borders. We participated in various events, joint. We visited the Austrian border school, they in turn came here, so there were mutual visits, which naturally led to the teach-ing of German as a second language.
>
> Interviewer: Well and did the cooperation last?
>
> No, no, it didn't. No. It's hard to establish contacts with others, there's, I would say, a lan-guage barrier rather. Yeah? If the teachers can handle it, then of course the students are not

interested in this cooperation. They're just passive, the students. Even though they have German here, it is passive both from our side and from their side. (Nina)

The language barrier may affect the level of cooperation between schools and the life in the border region as a whole. Currently, some of the residents work in Austria (including graduates of the school in which we conducted the research). However, because of their lack of knowledge of German and their low level of education, they tend to work in less skilled positions. Nina mentioned that former students often regret their lack of interest in German in retrospect:

Well when I meet former students who went to school here and had German. So of course, at that time, as students, they did not prepare for the German classes and now they regret it, because most of the former students work in Austria, so they regret that they did not prepare for the classes more, they just did not prepare at all. But they are making up for it with self-study.

At the moment the school's existence is not threatened, because the vast majority of schools in the area have already been closed. However, the school's position in the already limited community life of the small borderland communities is problematic. This primary school is attended by children from more than twenty villages from a fairly vast area, but this limits the school's abilities to perform as an actor involved in community life. The school's position is also affected by the somewhat atypical fact that it is not located in the largest village in the area, but rather in a very small village. The reason for this is the fact the large school building had been built here already in the period before World War II. That is another reason the school stands somewhat apart from community life. The situation makes it difficult, for example, to organize a school ball:

We usually hold the ball in a nearby larger village. Once in our era, we had it in the gym down here, but since most of the parents had to drive here, so not that they didn't like it, but you know yourself that everybody can drink a little alcohol, so we agreed that it will be in the central village (…) we will bring it there, we will arrange it. (Nina)

The search for a strategy to create and protect a functional community interconnected with the school in the peripheral countryside concerns the whole of Europe. Research from Germany showed that a solution could be providing various decentralized and individualized forms of support for students and parents, such as a rented minibus to drive the children home, even from afternoon children's leisure activities or social events (Jahnke, 2019).

The globally widespread problems of the rural periphery in the post-World War II newly settled borderlands are compounded by the unresolved issues of the lifespan of local communities and the legacy of the politics of memory shaped by the communist government. This manifests itself in the problematic building of trust in the state and in the failure to exploit the potential of cross-border cooperation. The conviction of the inhabitants of the peripheral countryside that the prosperity brought about by the Velvet Revolution will never concern them and that they themselves do not really interest anyone is at the heart of the multiple problems in these areas. However, later we show that even in the countryside, we can find positive cases of functional communities that have led, for example, to the building of a new school.

7.5   The Functional Rural Community and Its Impact on School Life

In the peripheral countryside, the schools rather tended to fade and their sparse network meant that the school was not always an actor involved in co-creating the community life. In those rural areas in which functional and cooperating village communities existed, the situation could be considerably more favourable. The Velvet Revolution brought the possibility of initiative to those communities that had enough of various forms of capital. The availability of resources of different origins is a prerequisite for the sustainability of life in the countryside (Wilson, 2010). One can speak of a functional community in the context of large communities in the traditional fertile areas of the Moravian countryside, villages near large cities, as well as ethnographic regions of southern and southeastern Moravia. This region is associated with a higher degree of religiosity than other areas of the Czech Republic. It is characterized by a strong regional identity, based on the survival of traditional folk culture, including a rich social life, folklore, and festive folk costumes as a marker of local identity.

To some extent, the local community often functioned in the villages even under socialism. For many local officials, being part of the village may have been more important than party loyalty (Polouček, 2020). The village life was described by one of the narrators working in South Moravia. A certain degree of idealization was inherent in the memories:

> This was the chairman of the City National Committee, the parish priest, the school head. Wait, who was the fourth one? And they played tarocks on Sundays after lunch. So they arranged everything, yeah. When the sugar beet had to be dug out, the parish priest mentioned in the sermon that we needed to get on with the sugar beet, so the women started with the sugar beet on Monday, yeah. Something was needed at the school, so they told the chairman of the national committee. He went to the district town and brought the money, yeah. ... Yeah, the fourth was the chairman of the United Agricultural Cooperative. The chairman of the City National Committee, the school head and the parish priest. Those were the tarocks players, yeah. And they had a lot of respect, yeah. They worked for the people, yeah, for the village. The chairman, it wasn't like the mayor that is sitting there today. He took a tractor, he welded the street lights here. Or concreted something, yeah. That, that was a whole different approach. (Libor)

The shift of responsibility for the founding of schools from the district to the municipalities after 1989 provided an opportunity for similarly enterprising local self-government leaders who were interested in maintaining and developing schools in their municipalities. In towns, a similar opportunity could have led to the restoration of the grammar school. In a small village where the existence of the school was threatened, there could be an opportunity to save it. The late socialist period was characterized by the initiative to merge villages. A system of central villages with amenities was created, under which the surrounding smaller villages were to be administratively subordinated. The closing of schools was associated with this system (Valeš, 2014; Kučerová, 2012). A similar fate threatened one of the schools in a village near the regional town. The Velvet Revolution prevented the closure of the school, as an entry in the school chronicle stated: 'Our school, which was actually supposed to be closed this school year, has begun to breathe freely again; the prospect of the school's existence is open again. The reinstated National Committee (since 1 April 1990), promised the school all the help for the next period after the senseless integration of the municipalities.'

Small schools in the smallest villages, in which students from multiple grades were educated together in one classroom were particularly threatened. During late socialism, the prevailing opinion was that this way of educating students was outdated and that it was better to group students in large schools in central villages. However, teachers who worked in these small schools saw the advantages of the local way of teaching. They considered working in a small school to be more challenging for the teachers but in some ways better for the children. Vlasta was able to experience teaching in a small school for a time in the early 1990s and therefore was able to compare it with a regular school:

> But certainly for the teacher there was a lot more preparation if you had those two grades there and it was certainly more demanding for that teacher also in terms of teaching, to be able to attend to one group, then the other group, it's actually group teaching, which was promoted a lot recently. (...) And I think that here in those small schools, the younger children learned from the older ones, the older ones from the younger ones, that they listened and they had to learn such self-discipline, more concentration, because now I work independently, the teacher is working with someone else and I must not disturb them. (Vlasta)

After 1989, some previously closed schools were re-established, which was precisely due to the initiative and interest of local communities (Kučerová, 2012; Čerych, 1996). Thus, in connection with the functioning of rural schools, there was a certain return from the (modernist) centralization to the empowerment of the (traditional) communities. However, this initiative may have gone hand in hand with some of the ideals with which part of society identified after 1989, like the issue of 'natural' competition in a market environment. In some locations, we saw a situation in which the renovation or founding of a new school by the local self-government led to schools competing with each other, a completely new phenomenon both in the school system and for the inhabitants themselves.

While the socialist school system was characterized by a clearly defined catchment area, the Velvet Revolution of 1989 brought freedom of choice to the parents. Some municipalities (on the initiative of parents and/or the municipal self-government) founded their own schools, thus disrupting the relatively even network of schools coordinated at the district level. This may have led to competition for parental interest. Antonín described a situation in which upon the initiative of parents, a second stage was established in a neighbouring municipality in a primary school that previously only had a first stage:

> It was the case there that until the revolution, there was only the first stage. And the second stage was in the neighbouring village, right? And only after the revolution, at the insistence of parents who said, why should the children go to the neighbouring village when we have a new school building built here. The parents forced the opening of the second stage after the revolution. Well, as a result, the local kids started going to their own school and the neighbouring kids now had the option of either one or the other. (Antonín)

The opening of the new school led to a competition between schools located close to each other. Because of the competition, the school in which the narrator taught even started to organize 'Open House' days (after 2000). These were intended to better introduce the school to students and parents and to motivate them to choose the school. Therefore, the competition led to positive things. In this case, it led to the larger openness of the schools to the public, to an effort to communicate better about their work and achievements. 'Open House' days were a relatively new element in the life of schools and their surroundings at that time.

The increase in competition between schools was predictably even more relevant to the urban environment. It was linked not only to the transformation in the post-communist world, but also to the neoliberal decentralization of school systems that was being introduced in Western Europe since the late 1970s (Holger et al., 2019). According to opinions in Czechoslovakia at that time (Team of Faculty of Education, Charles University, 1992), and the opinions of some of our narrators, competition can have a positive effect. There were situations like the openness of the school above, and competition also created pressure to improve the quality of teaching: 'Well, I think that the competition does no harm and that the school will show its value itself by the results of the students, how they assert themselves in secondary schools' (Karolína).[28]

There can be significant differences between rural areas in terms of school competition. In environments without functional communities, there is no competition between schools, so schools gradually close down and students have to commute some distance (Bernard et al., 2018). In contrast, in locations in which communities are active, competition can arise between schools, as both residents and municipal self-governments can generate activity to ensure that a school operates in their place of residence.

Therefore, the decentralization of the school system after 1989 (leading up to competition between schools) may have been more beneficial to participants with more initiative, including representatives of functional rural communities and local parents. The operation of a school in a village benefits the local social life. Parents can meet at social events organized by the school, and students can meet in class and also after school, strengthening their social capital within the community. The friendly relations in the village may motivate some young people to stay in the village and start a family later.[29]

---

[28] The competition stands or falls on the teaching staff, the openness of the school, and the quality of teaching; the school location also has a major impact. Although the parents had the freedom to choose schools since the 1990s, the schools were obliged to give priority to students from their catchment area. However, this particularly disqualifies schools from villages or neighbourhoods with worse reputations from the 'competition' for students.

[29] The connection between the quality of cooperation between parents and the wider public with the school and the existence of a functional local community concerns both rural schools and urban ones, of course. Good cooperation with parents was mentioned in the Evaluation of the Educational Work of a school at the outskirts of Brno, in which the good cooperation with parents was positively evaluated even in 1993. Although the compulsorily established Associations of Parents and Friends of Schools (Svaz rodičů a přátel školy, SRPŠ) were abolished after 1989, in functional

During the socialist period, the social life of the school and the village took place mainly within the compulsory ideological celebrations (e.g. participation in May Day celebrations). These events were compulsory, and schools had to prepare for them. However, as Doušek (2022) showed, in rural communities, people could interpret these communist holidays within their own interests. This was also true because opportunities for gathering, socializing, and presentation were scarce. The limited opportunities to organize celebrations associated with religiosity, which formed a part of the social life of the community before the rise of the KSČ government in 1948 were one reason for this. This was also true of the strongly religious South Moravia in which we conducted our research. Participation in communist festivals was compulsory for all schools. After the Velvet Revolution, a general aversion to such obligations predominated and the schools were freed especially from the excessive meetings, compulsory administration, and trainings as well as participation in ideologically saturated festivities.

The maintenance of social life was in the hands of local (rural) communities after 1989. It depended particularly on them whether the previously obligatory ideological and propaganda events or celebrations were replaced by something else. For example, there could be new events such as Christmas performances/celebrations by students, school balls, and student performances called *academies*. For example, a narrator from a village school recalled the social life after 1989 as follows:

> Classic things at those village schools. Christmas performances, Mother's Day, yeah? I don't know, some kind of fair, yeah? Christmas … classic, well like yeah, I was the music teacher, so I had some school performances, it was quite common every year at least three events like that, yeah? I used to lead the choir there, right, so we'd rehearse, yeah? So before that it was MDŽ (Mezinárodní den žen, International Women's Day), then it was Mother's Day, some Christmas performances, recitation competitions, yeah? So I was also on the panel of judges and stuff like that. It was like a regular part of, like, the presentation of the school. (Antonín)

Antonín stated that the ideologized International Women's Day was replaced by the celebration of Mother's Day. At the same time, as a teacher who tried out various environments, he added that the social life could be rich because the school was located in a large village. It can be more difficult to engage in community life in a school to which children commute from a wider area. Indeed, Antonín spent part of his teaching career in a school at which 'there was nothing like that. Because it was a huge school and there were commuters from about ten surrounding villages' (Antonín).

Where there was no community interest, the social life could disappear from the school altogether. Tomas, who taught in a urban school, noted that school social events 'completely ended, nothing replaced them' after 1989. In contrast, in the village in which Tomáš lived, the school was more involved in social life, possibly because of its cooperation with the local volunteer fire department. However, other urban schools still organized school balls, for example.

---

communities, parents could establish or voluntarily join their own parent organization, which was willing to participate in the organization of school life.

During the Velvet Revolution, a specific situation arose in connection with the compulsory rehearsal of the Spartakiáda—an ideologized nationally organized gymnastics demonstration. Schools and work collectives from all over the country participated in it with their exercise routines (Roubal, 2019). The seventh Czechoslovak Spartakiáda was to take place in the spring of 1990, and everyone had been intensively rehearsing their performances since the autumn of 1989. However, because of the change of the political regime, the Spartakiáda was replaced by Prague Sports Games with a much smaller number of participants, mostly from Prague.

In some schools, the teachers and students stopped rehearsing for the Spartakiáda altogether; in others, the gymnasts decided to participate in various substitute local or district gymnastics festivals.[30] The functioning of the teachers' collective was reflected here. Where there were strong interpersonal relationships of good quality, the motivation to participate and show their skills might have prevailed so that the rehearsals did not go to waste. Elsewhere, where it was merely an annoying 'necessity', they were happy to give up the Spartakiáda.

Whereas under socialism, it was compulsory for people to associate, after 1989, the existence of social life depended on the motivation of the various people involved in working in the school and the community. Interpersonal relationships between parents, teachers, local associations, and the self-government that founded the school could have a significant influence.

7.6   Transformation of School Inspection After 1989

If we examine the school in a 'network of relationships', it is difficult to overlook one institution that could significantly influence the operation of schools: the school inspectorate, which also played an important role in the interviews with our narrators. This role underwent significant changes, especially in the 1990s.

The Czech School Inspectorate[31] and inspection activities that provide an external evaluation of the quality and effectiveness of education underwent a partial transformation similar to that of schools and education offices. Under socialism, it was supervised by local administrations; it became independent after 1989, and in

---

[30] For example, in one of the urban schools, according to the minutes of a meeting of the pedagogical council of 22. January 1990, rehearsals for the Spartakiáda continued, but they were limited so as not to disrupt the classes. On the other hand, according to an analysis of another school's activities in 1990, it ceased rehearsals altogether. Similarly, one of the narrators, Dana, recalled that her urban school stopped rehearsing. On the other hand, one of the village school chronicles mentions participation in local gymnastics festivals.

[31] The Czech School Inspectorate is the national authority for evaluating the quality and effectiveness of education in various types of schools and school facilities (e.g. school counselling centres, leisure centres, school canteens). It is an independent administrative body of the Czech Republic with a nationwide field of action. More information at https://www.csicr.cz/en/Zakladni-informace/Basic-Information

1990, the Czech School Inspectorate (ČŠI) was established by law. In its current form, it is not directly subordinate to the MEYS; it is a separate and independent institution (Bartošová et al., 2019). As was typical in the post-revolutionary period, the rejection of the principles of inspection work for the 'old regime' was particularly declared during its establishment. The first central school inspector of the new ČŠI, Vilibald Knob (1991), announced in the *Teacher's Newspaper*: 'First and foremost, it will be a matter of removing the remnants of the past inspection activity, that is, ridding it of formality, incompetence, directiveness, randomness, lack of concept, and, above all, insidiousness' (p. 2).

This image of communist school inspection presented in 1991 is in some respects consistent with the views of our narrators, who assessed it as strict and directive. This was confirmed by a former school inspector who joined the inspectorate after 1989: 'At first, they did not like to see us. Because they had a bad experience from the previous times, when those inspectors really had to find mistakes, sometimes they probably dressed them down quite badly. Those teachers were afraid of the inspectors, so those experiences stayed in those people' (Naděžda). However, some narrators remembered the strict inspectors differently, and instead criticized the later relaxation and detachment of the inspection from teaching:

> Until the revolution, when the inspector came, he sat in the classroom, we were all like worried about it then. Nothing ever happened, yeah, and he rather advised us on how to deal with the kids. And after the revolution, they fired those inspectors who understood the school system and hired like the rehabilitated people, they didn't understand the school system at all, and since that revolution to this day, the inspection just comes and checks the papers in the school head's office. (Libor)

The narrator shared several dominant images of the Czech School Inspectorate and its development. First, he mentioned the departure of the old inspectors and the arrival of new ones. Staffing changes predictably took place in the ČŠI as well. It is interesting to note here that far from every rehabilitated former teacher or even inspector was an expert their field. This may have been because after being forced to leave the school system, the former teacher/inspector had to work outside the school system and thus lost contact with the field. The inspectorate was unable to recruit qualified staff for a long time.[32] This may have been due to the bad reputation of the socialist inspectorate and the potential applicants' wish not to be unpopular. This was confirmed by one of the narrators:

> Once I also applied to a competitive selection at the inspectorate. When I saw how things worked with that competitive selection, I said, there's no point in going in that direction. It's that matter again when you're just working with papers and you have to tell people the unpleasant things, and that's not the right thing for me. (Petra)

The quoted narrators mentioned another criticized aspect that was typical even in the period shortly after 1989: the school inspector spent more time in the school head's office on administration than in the classroom (Kozel, 1992). On the other

---

[32] In 1992, 1 year after the establishment of the ČŠI, only 60% of the job openings were filled (Kozel, 1992).

hand, the period up to 1995 is portrayed as the freest in the narrators' memories also in relation to inspection activities. The inspectors did not have a clear methodology for inspection and were largely free to exercise their own judgement in evaluating the work of teachers and schools. One narrator emphasized that she found her work as an inspector fulfilling only for a short period of time, when she was able to give advice on how to improve the work even beyond the inspection activity.

> (…) I realized many times that I was a teacher and not an inspector. And I was not comfortable with inspecting to a certain extent. In short, I was probably not acting in accordance with the law, but when I saw the deficiencies, I told them you have to remove them and I will come tomorrow and we will make a report. Which is not in line with the inspection, but it helped the schools. The interest of the Czech school system and its quality was important for me. (Ctirada)

Another inspector at the time, Naděžda, recalled at length the early years of functioning of the Czech School Inspectorate and the intention to 'humanize' it. She also talked about the fact that many of the new inspectors were teachers who had been politically persecuted during the communist rule. In contrast to the example of the incompetence of the new inspectors, the opposite was the case here.

> Dr Vilibald K. was the first central school inspector. And he said that his idea was that … we should be messengers of good news. So actually those first inspectorates began to form, and they followed the district borders because there were the education offices, … then two more colleagues came there, one was for the primary schools, first stage, and one was for the secondary schools. Both of them were rehabilitated, Aleš for political reasons and Pavel had a father who was a political prisoner. So the four of us were the first group of inspectors. There was no methodology, there were no forms, nobody knew how. (Naděžda)

The narrator also suggested that the inspectorate initially dealt mainly with staffing changes in the school system and that there was no space to develop a separate inspection methodology. One narrator who had been a teacher also recalled the early 1990s as a time of freedom:

> In the 1990s, I would say for two years definitely nothing at all. And it wasn't until sometime in 1993 that the first inspection appeared, at that primary school, and I would say it was completely different from the one before, that it was very accommodating Even the analysis was so much simpler, one could even comment on it. Before that, nothing like a comment, before '90, they came and, if I just say so, they just took apart someone, what had he done and what he should have done in addition and what they would have done, they, who did not teach there and could not demonstrate it. (Tomáš)

Inadequate staffing meant that inspectors were also being sent to establishments that did not match their expertise. Ctirada, a former school inspector, was supposed to focus on secondary schools, but she also had to visit primary schools and even kindergartens. However, in a period without clear methodology, it was possible to create one's own initiative and modify the work in one's own way.

> We actually made an agreement on what we were going to do when we come to the school. Are we going to go to a teacher observation? Are we going to talk to the school head? Are we going to talk to the teachers? Are we going to look at this, at this, at this? Because we didn't have any methodology. (…) We told them the shortcomings on the spot and we wrote in the report that it just happened. (Naděžda).

The inspection methodology was not published until 1995 and it identified specific standardized procedures for inspection activities. One of the school inspectors of the time recalled the advent of the methodology:

> The 'School Inspector's Handbook' started to take shape, and in it, they started to come up with uniform procedures on how to evaluate, on what scale, and what the output would be. And because the Act on State Administration and Self-Government stipulated that the Czech School Inspectorate was to evaluate and control, (…), you could say to the teacher during the teacher observation: This is very good, but there are some weak points, but you were not allowed to give advice, because that was not the role of the inspection anymore and they actually expected it, yeah? (Naděžda)

The inability to advise and help teachers also bothered the second narrator who worked as a school inspector. Ctirada was forced to leave the inspectorate by the new methodology with its strictly prescribed formulations for teaching evaluation: 'I quit at the moment at which we received the prescribed formulations that we were supposed to give them. I was saying: I can formulate.'

In the narrators' recollections, the transformation of the school inspection is portrayed as a deviation from freedom towards formalization and separation from the focus on the educational activity. These recollections complement the mosaic with which the development of the school system is portrayed in the participants' memories—from a period of relaxation, improvisation (and chaos) to a return to formalization and bureaucratization. In general terms, the introduction of more precise rules into inspection activities did not necessarily mean a loss of freedom or an increase in bureaucracy. It can also be perceived as providing clear and generally known criteria for evaluating the quality of education. This, in turn, may have helped the schools to know what the priorities or expectations were in various areas of teaching and school operation. At the same time, it brought rules to inspection activities that prevented ambiguity in evaluation. On the other hand, according to Naděžda, after the abolition of the education offices, the inspectorate also assumed the role of the assessor of school management, which increased the importance of verifying the documentation.

The emphasis on verifying documentation by the Czech School Inspectorate was confirmed by another school head who participated in our research. She added to the myriad memories of the renewed emphasis on record-keeping in the school and the associated increase in administrative activities:

> And even from the side of the Czech School Inspectorate, basically those early days of the 1990s were about giving those schools a lot of freedom, as in: Now you don't have to have this plan, you don't have to have this recorded anywhere. Then they figured out that basically when they go in for an inspection, they're going to go over the paperwork. And how the teacher has it worked out, what he's going to be doing there all year. I mean, he has to have a plan for the subject, divided into months. And it started to gradually go back to where it used to be. That is, things that didn't have to be done in the early 1990s started to be done once again during the 1990s. Because just like everything had to be documented somehow. And how are you going to document if not with a paper? But the early nineties were about freedom, like let's not burden these teachers with all this bureaucracy. (Helena)

The story about the inspection[33] fits in with other memories depicting the widely reported relaxed and free period of the early 1990s and the subsequent increase in the level of duties and administrative burden. This was also given by the multitude of activities of the schools and the actors with whom the schools came into contact in a democratic environment. In this chapter, we have set out the variety of these environments and shown that for many schools, the 'starting line' and the array of they issues faced were considerably varied after 1989. The stories of the individual schools were connected on two planes—continuities from the socialist period and the need to face new and often unexpected challenges.

Multi-year grammar schools followed the tradition of selective primary schools, yet they were built under new conditions as 'greenfield projects', mainly because of the enthusiasm of local teachers and the initiative of the community, including the municipal leadership. The large housing estate schools struggled with the legacy of the demographic boom of 'Husák's children', but they had to cope with them during an era of legislative changes including the adoption of school autonomy and the transfer of founder competences to the municipalities. The process of segregating schools in localities inhabited by the Roma population was triggered by a KSČ policy that gave rise to segregated neighbourhoods. The freedom of school choice introduced after 1989 deepened the segregation process. Schools in the borderlands tried to establish foreign cooperation, but 40 years of isolation and the region's remoteness and social problems somewhat predetermined the failure of such activities. Prosperous rural communities with strong local identities were able to reverse the tendency of the communist authorities to close village schools. Resistance to centralization may have made the people involved more motivated to save or restore the schools. However, in doing so, they may have unintentionally upset the equilibrium of the centrally built school system and helped to create a competitive environment in the school system. The Czech School Inspectorate had to fight its bad reputation, which can be considered a kind of a legacy of the communist rule. At the same time, it had to 'calm' the turbulent moods in the transforming schools and deal with the problems arising from the rather extensive and new network of relationships in which schools found themselves after 1989.

Bibliography

Bartošová, J., Šimek, J., & Šustová, M. (2019). *Od školdozorce k inspektorovi: historie školní inspekce* [From a school custodian to an inspector: The history of school inspection]. Česká školní inspekce ve spolupráci s Národním pedagogickým muzeem a knihovnou J.A. Komenského.

Bernard, J., Kostelecký, T., Mikešová, R., Šafr, J., Trlifajová, L., & Hurrle, J. (2018). *Nic se tady neděje…: životní podmínky na periferním venkově* [nothing happens here…: Living conditions in the peripheral countryside]. Sociologické nakladatelství (SLON).

---

[33] Our goal here is not to map and evaluate the development of inspection or the work of inspectors; such a topic is well beyond the scope of this book.

Bitušíková, A. (2021). School and its role in contemporary rural community development. *Národopisný věstník, 80*(1), 73–83.

Blaive, M., & Molden, B. (2009). *Hranice probíhají vodním tokem: Odrazy historie ve vnímání obyavatel Gmündu a Českých Velenic* [The Borders run through the watercourse: Reflections of history in the perceptions of the inhabitants of Gmünd and České Velenice]. Barrister & Principal.

Čerych, L. (1996). *Zprávy o národní politice ve vzdělávání: Česká republika* [Reports on National Educational Policy: The Czech Republic]. Ústav pro informace ve vzdělávání.

Cleveland, B., Backhouse, S., Chandler, P., McShane, I., Clinton, J. M., & Newton, C. (Eds.). (2023). *Schools as community hubs: Building 'more than a school' for community benefit.* Springer Nature. https://doi.org/10.1007/978-981-19-9972-7

Čornejová, I., Kasper, T., Kasperová, D., Kourová, P., Kratochvíl, P., Lenderová, M., Novotný, M., Pokorný, J., Svatoš, M., Svobodný, P., Šimek, J., & Váňová, R. (2020). *Velké dějiny zemí Koruny české: Tematická řada: Školství a vzdělanost* [Great history of the lands of the bohemian crown: Thematic edition: School system and level of education]. Paseka.

Czech Statistical Office. (2023). *Demografické ročenky (pramenná díla) 2009–1990.* [Demographic Yearbooks (Source Works) 2009–1990]. https://www.czso.cz/csu/czso/casova_rada_demografie_2009_1990

Donert, C. (2017). *The rights of the Roma: The struggle for citizenship in postwar Czechoslovakia.* Cambridge University Press.

Doubek, E. (1990). K osmiletým [To the eight-year-olds]. *Učitelské noviny, 93*(30), 2.

Doušek, R. (2022). The village and may day celebrations in 1970s communist Czechoslovakia: Social events between a tool of the regime and a community holiday. *History and Anthropology.*, 1–22. https://doi.org/10.1080/02757206.2022.2132493

Edwards, R. (Ed.). (2002). *Children, home, and school: Autonomy, connection, or regulation?* Routledge Falmer.

Epstein, J. L., & Sheldon, S. B. (2023). *School, family, and community partnerships: Preparing educators and improving schools.* Routledge. https://doi.org/10.4324/9780429494673

Glassheim, E. (2019). *Očista československého pohraničí: migrace, životní prostředí a zdraví v bývalých Sudetech* [Cleansing the Czechoslovak borderlands: Migration, environment and health in the former Sudetenland]. Academia.

Greger, D. (2011). Dvacet let českého školství optikou teorií změny vzdělávání v postsocialistických zemích [Twenty years of Czech education as viewed through the theory of change of education in post-socialist countries]. *Orbis scholae, 5*(1), 9–22.

Henchel, F. (2020). The embodiment of deviance: The biopolitics of the "difficult child" in socialist Czechoslovakia. *East European Politics and Societies, 34*(4), 837–857. https://doi.org/10.1177/0888325419890126

Holger, J., Kramer, C., & Meusburger, P. (Eds.). (2019). *Geographies of schooling.* Springer. https://doi.org/10.1007/978-3-030-18799-6

Holý, L. (2010). *Malý český člověk a skvělý český národ: národní identita a postkomunistická transformace společnosti* [Little Czech Person and the great Czech nation: National identity and post-communist social transformation]. Sociologické nakladatelství (SLON).

Jahnke, H. (2019). Territorial governance of schooling and education in rural areas: Case studies from northern Germany. In H. Jahnke, C. Kramer, & P. Meusburger (Eds.), *Geographies of schooling* (pp. 19–34). Springer. https://doi.org/10.1007/978-3-030-18799-6

Kalinová, L. (2012). *Konec nadějím a nová očekávání: k dějinám české společnosti 1969–1993* [The End of Hopes and New Expectations: On the History of Czech Society 1969–1993]. Academia.

Katrňák, T. (2004). *Odsouzeni k manuální práci: vzdělanostní reprodukce v dělnické rodině* [Condemned to manual labour: Educational reproduction in a working-class family]. Sociologické nakladatelství.

Knob, V. (1991). Několik slov úvodem: O koncepci a struktuře České školní inspekce [A few words of introduction: About the concept and structure of the Czech school inspectorate]. *Učitelské noviny, 94*(24), 2.

Kozel, F. (1992). Školské rady a spol. [School Councils etc.]. *Učitelské noviny, 95*(5), 4.

Krakovský, R. (2020). *State and society in communist Czechoslovakia: Transforming the everyday from world war II to the fall of the Berlin Wall.* Bloomsbury Academic.

Kreisslová, S., Nosková, J., & Pavlásek, M. (2019). *"Takové normální rodinné historky": obrazy migrace a migrující obrazy v rodinné paměti* ["Such normal family stories": Images of migration and migrating images in family memory]. Argo.

Kučerová, S. (2012). *Proměny územní struktury základního školství v Česku* [Transformations in the territorial structure of the primary school system in The Czech Republic]. Česká geografická společnost.

Matějů, P., & Straková, J. (2003). Role rodiny a školy v reprodukci vzdělanostních nerovností. Sociologický pohled na úlohu víceletých gymnázií ve světle výzkumu PISA 2000 [The role of the family and the school in the reproduction of educational inequalities. A sociological look at the role of multi-year grammar schools in the context of the results of the PISA 2000 Study]. *Sociologický časopis / Czech Sociological Review, 39*(5), 625–652. https://doi.org/1 0.13060/00380288.2003.39.5.03

MEYS. (2009). *Zpráva o vývoji českého školství od listopadu 1989 (v oblasti regionálního školství)* [Report on the development of Czech School System since November 1989 (in the Field of Regional School System)].

Moree, D. (2013). *Učitelé na vlnách transformace: kultura školy před rokem 1989 a po něm* [Teachers on the waves of transformation: School culture before and after 1989]. Karolinum.

Možný, I. (2023). *Why so easily …: Some family reasons for the velvet revolution (a sociological essay).* Karolinum press.

Pehe, V. (2020). Velvet retro: Postsocialist nostalgia and the politics of heroism in Czech popular culture. *Beginner books.* https://doi.org/10.3167/9781789206289

Perry, L. (2005). The seeing and the seen: Contrasting perspectives of post-communist Czech schooling. *Compare, 35*(3), 265–283.

Pol, M. (2007). *Škola v proměnách* [School in Transformations]. Masarykova univerzita.

Polouček, O. (2020). *Babičky na bigbítu: společenský život na moravském venkově pozdního socialismu* [Grannies at a big-beat party. The social life in the late socialist Moravian country-side]. Masarykova univerzita.

Pospěch, P. (2021). *Neznámá společnost: pohledy na současné Česko* [The unknown society: Views of Contemporary Czechia]. Host.

Prokop, D. (2022). *Slepé skvrny: o chudobě, vzdělávání, populismu a dalších výzvách české společnosti* (Třetí vydání) [Blind spots. On poverty, education, populism and other challenges of Czech Society (Third Edition)]. Host.

Rabušicová, M. (2004). *Škola a (versus) rodina* [The school and (versus) the family]. Masarykova univerzita.

Roubal, P. (2019). *Spartakiads: Vol. First English edition.* Charles University in Prague, Karolinum Press.

Semrád, J. (2018). *Lesná: život na panelovém sídlišti ve 20. A 21. století* [Lesná: Life in the prefabricated housing estate in the 20th and 21st century]. [Doctoral dissertation, Masaryk University]. Masaryk University digital repository. https://is.muni.cz/th/t033b/

Semrád, J. (2019). Stereotypy spojené se životem na sídlišti optikou etnologickéhovýzkumu. Na příkladu brněnského sídliště Lesná [Stereotypes Associated with the Life in a Housing Estate Through the Eyes of Ethnologic Research. An Example of the Lesná Housing Estate in Brno]. *Národopisný věstník, 78*(2), 36–50.

Šimáně, M. (2023). Socialist egalitarianism in everyday life of secondary technical schools in Czechoslovakia during the normalization period (1969–89). *Communist and Post-Communist Studies, 56*(1), 129–151. https://doi.org/10.1525/cpcs.2023.1798853

Sommer, V. (2019). *Řídit socialismus jako firmu: technokratické vládnutí v Československu, 1956–1989* [Running socialism like a business: Technocratic rule in Czechoslovakia, 1956–1989]. Ústav pro soudobé dějiny AV ČR.

Štefflová, J. (1991). Stále ještě na vodě: vyučujícím v devátém ročníku [Still unsure: Being a ninth grade teacher]. *Učitelské noviny, 94*(41), 5.

Sucháček, P. (2014). Spor o víceletá gymnázia: historický kontext a empirická data [The feud over multi-year grammar schools: Historical context and empirical data]. *Studia paedagogica, 19*(3), 139–154. https://doi.org/10.5817/SP2014-3-8

Team of Faculty of Education, & Charles University. (1992). Rozvaha o školství a vzdělanosti a jejich dalším vývoji v českých zemích. [Reflection on the school system and level of education and their further development in Czech lands]. *Pedagogika, 42*(1), 5–18.

Todorova, M. N., & Gille, Z. (Eds.). (2010). *Post-communist nostalgia*. Berghahn Books.

Valeš, L. (2014). Životní příběhy českých zemědělců v éře komunistického režimu a ekonomické a společenské transformace [Life stories of Czech farmers in the era of the communist regime and economic and social transformation]. In M. Vaněk, & L. Krátká (Eds.), *Příběhy (ne)obyčejných profesí: česká společnost v období tzv. normalizace a transformace* [Stories from (un)common professions: The Czech society in the period of "normalization" and "transformation"] (pp. 461–510). Karolinum.

Wein, M. J. (2021). *Dějiny Židů v českých zemích: od Hilsnera po Slánského* [History of the Jews in the Czech lands: From Hilsner to Slánský]. Univerzita Palackého.

Wilson, G. (2010). Multifunctional "quality" and rural community resilience. *Transactions of the Institute of British Geographers, 35*(3), 364–381. https://doi.org/10.1111/j.1475-5661.2010.00391.x

Zounek, J., Šimáně, M., & Knotová, D. (2017). *Normální život v nenormální době: Základní školy a jejich učitelé (nejen) v období normalizace* [Normal life in not so normal times. Primary schools and their teachers (not only) during the so-called normalization period]. Wolters Kluwer.

Chapter 8
Teachers: Various Life Stories and Perspectives

Abstract In this chapter, we present the life stories of several teachers. Our aim is to get to know the lives of specific teachers, and to contribute to the knowledge about the transformation of the school system with the views and experiences of eyewitnesses. In studying the life stories of teachers, we could not avoid the period before 1989 and the socialist school system, which often had a significant impact on their lives and work.

Although it is not possible to generalize these teachers' stories, they can be used to show how diverse the everyday reality was before 1989 and especially in the period of post-socialist transformation, both in and out of schools. It is important to be aware of the personal lives of teachers and their approaches to life. Teachers' life stories show how complex the paths of post-socialist society and the school system were.

Keywords Teachers · Life Stories · Generations · Memories

8.1 Generations

Teachers who lived through the turbulent period of post-socialist transformation in the former Czechoslovakia and then in the Czech Republic in the 1990s do not, of course, form a homogeneous group. Their experiences may vary considerably based on their teaching qualifications and according to the location and size of the school. Their experiences and feelings are undoubtedly influenced by the stage of their career at the time of the school system transformation. As part of our research, we spoke with some teachers who were close to retirement at the time as well as with teachers who were just starting their careers.

In this chapter, we follow the life stories of teachers of different generations who experienced the period of post-socialist transformation in primary schools at different stages of their teaching careers. We understand the term 'generation', in line with Mannheim and Kecskemeti (1964), as consisting of individuals born at roughly the same time in a particular historical-social space, experiencing the same

J. Zounek et al., *(Post)Socialist Transformation of Primary Schools*,
https://doi.org/10.1007/978-3-031-58768-9_8

contemporary events. Belonging to a particular generation involves a tendency towards certain ways of behaving, feeling, and thinking. At the same time, we are aware that it is difficult to define generational experiences in general terms, as each teacher's life story is unique. It is then particularly problematic to draw boundaries between members of different generations based on the year of birth. Nevertheless, in our research, it is possible to observe characteristic features of the life experiences of teachers who studied or entered into practice at roughly the same time, and it is therefore possible to speak of members of the same generation. A shared experience in youth forms the basis for an individual's natural image of the world (Mannheim & Kecskemeti, 1964), for their concept of their profession, and for the perception of various topics related to education and teaching. It appears that for our eyewitness teachers, the period of their studies and the beginning of their teaching career were particularly important. This is because young people are sensitive; they perceive the world around them intensely and the nature of the times helps to shape their strong and shared life experience (Erikson, 1998). Looking at the history of Czechoslovakia in the second half of the twentieth century, it is possible to see some distinctive characteristics of the individual periods that shaped the teachers who were young during these periods. The 1950s were a complicated stage of history, associated with post-war reconstruction and the building of a new communist society (modelled on the Soviet Union of the time), and at the same time a period of political trials and murders. The 1960s were characterized by a partial relaxation of the regime, with talk of 'socialism with a human face' and efforts to reform the existing regime. Many reform efforts were violently ended by the invasion of the Warsaw Pact troops in 1968, which was also the beginning of the repeated consolidation of the communist regime.[1] For the youngest generation of teachers we interviewed, the fall of the communist regime[2] and the subsequent post-socialist transformation was the key formative period. Some teachers were fundamentally influenced by the political changes after the Velvet Revolution; for others, experiences related to work or family life were more crucial. For example, one of the narrators spent 1989 on maternity leave and her husband died shortly afterwards; as she puts it, there was no time for 'revolutionary enthusiasm'. For another narrator, the staffing changes at the school were particularly significant: she left the school in the early 1990s after the arrival of a new school head and disagreements with him. Her individual life path and experience could have significantly influenced her experience of the events of 'great history', which the fall of the communist regime and the subsequent democratization and transformation of society certainly were. By taking this approach to the study of contemporary history, we seek to undermine the idea that all people were profoundly affected by the great changes after 1989.

Despite the difficulties with defining clear boundaries between the individual generations, and knowing that making any generalizations is difficult, if not

---

[1] This period of Czechoslovak history (of the school system) is discussed in more detail in the Chap. 3 'From Stalinism to the Prague Spring – Education in Complicated Times (1945–1968)'.
[2] The history before 1989 is described in the Chap. 4 'Schools and Teachers Two Decades Before the Fall of the Communist Regime'.

impossible, this chapter introduces representatives of different generations. The image of the post-socialist transformation will acquire greater plasticity as we look in more detail into the lives of specific teachers and their perceptions of important events and processes both in their personal and professional lives.

8.2 Karel's Story

The oldest group of narrators in our research were teachers who were born before the KSČ government came to power in 1948 and remembered the Stalinist 1950s (McDermott, 2015). Some of them were still studying then; others had entered teaching practice. These teachers were shaped by the intense promotion of communist ideology, collectivism, and class conflict. Following the Soviet model, the KSČ government required citizens to actively express support for its policies at that time (Rychlík, 2020). Teachers were to be committed and conscious supporters of communist ideology and they were to take an active part in building a communist society by educating and training the coming generations.

This was a time of major (unprepared) pedagogical reforms and many changes in the school system based on the model of the school system in the Soviet Union. This system was in many ways incompatible with the Czechoslovak system and its traditions, or it was even contradictory. The resulting frequent changes constituted a shared experience for the oldest group of our narrators. These teachers remembered studying before the reform of the education system in 1960, when the Soviet model of the eleven-year secondary school was abolished. They completed compulsory schooling at a time when many schools did not yet have flush toilets and the teachers, especially in the villages, burned logs in the stove during lessons. They also experienced changes in teacher education, in terms of both content and institution. The oldest generations of narrators further experienced drastic changes during their lifetime connected to the transformation of school equipment. They retired when computers were entering the schools and as mobile phones were gradually becoming a part of students' everyday lives.

Our narrators who witnessed the changes of the education system of the 1950s first-hand were a fairly broad group in terms of age. We decided to present two teachers from this group. We studied the life story of Karel in our previous research (Zounek et al., 2017b). However, his fate was somewhat unique in that it shows how the life and work of a teacher could follow a complex path in Czechoslovakia and later in the Czech Republic during the twentieth century.

Karel[3] was born in 1935 into a family of two nationalities originally from the north-east of Czechoslovakia. His father was Czech; his mother was Polish. In

---

[3] This life story is one of the outputs of the previous research project, 'Everyday Life in Primary School During the Normalization Period as Seen by Teachers. Use of Oral History in the Study of Contemporary History of the School System', which was supported by Czech Grants Agency (GAČR) (No. 14-05926S). Karel's life story was published in Czech (Zounek et al., 2017b). For

September 1941, Karel started going to a one-room school, which he attended together with fifty other classmates between the ages of six and fourteen. Karel recalled the teaching style of the school head, who handled the entire large class dispassionately, even during quite demanding activities such as outdoor PE. In the autumn of 1944, the classes were interrupted for a few months because Hungarian soldiers were billeted in the school. At that time, the students went to a municipal office once a week to get their homework. Karel perceived the end of World War II as the symbolic end of his childhood.

In 1953, the school reform that took place together with the abolition of the unified school and the formation of an eleven-year secondary school had an inexorable impact on Karel's life. Students that were one year older still graduated in the normal June term. However, Karel and his classmates were told that their year had to graduate in same year, in August.[4] This was in the summer months; there were 2 months of holidays in Czechoslovakia and the students were supposed to have free time. To accomplish their graduation, they had to undergo 6 weeks of preparation over the holidays, with their class divided into two groups: humanities and science. The contents of the lessons were differentiated accordingly. This memory is an example of how unprepared, non-conceptual and totalitarian system-driven changes were reflected in the lives of individuals. An entire year of study was reduced to a holiday course; after a few weeks, students took the school-leaving Matura exam.

After graduation, Karel chose to become a teacher, so he applied to the newly established University of Pedagogy. As Karel himself stated, he was motivated to choose this profession by his experience from the one-room school and the pedagogical mastery of his teacher (Zounek et al. 2016). The Matura exam was the first step towards getting to university; however, the cadre committee had the decisive say at this time. This committee evaluated each student and their family from a political point of view and also assessed their activities in their place of residence. In Karel's case, there was a problem with the fact that he attended a non-compulsory religion course. This was also the reason the committee initially put a stop to his further studies. However, he was apparently helped by his class teacher who eventually got the committee to change its opinion by skilfully leading the committee meeting.

---

the purposes of this book, the text has been edited and significantly shortened. The cited study also contains methodological notes. Our study is based on the biographical method (Fuchs-Henritz, 2000). We conducted an interview with the narrator and we also communicated in writing via email. We found evidence of his university studies in the university archives. We conducted interviews with several of his colleagues from the school. One of the eyewitnesses read the entire study and provided us with valuable feedback as well as additions and refinements to some of the events from Karel's life. Annual reports of schools and almanacs were used in the research. We even obtained the text of a eulogy that was delivered at his funeral by a former student. We completed the study only after Karel's death.

[4] According to the Copy of the Final Examination Certificate, this change was only published in the Bulletin of the Ministry of Education and Edification in March 1953; the preparatory course was set up by Decree in May 1953. See also Government Decree No. 32/1953 Coll.

Originally, Karel had applied to study teaching the subjects of Czech and Russian, but he could not be admitted, because his grades were too low. Therefore, he pragmatically applied for the combination of English and Czech, where he was eventually admitted. The board stated in its record of his entrance examination: 'He has all the qualifications for his chosen field of study. He is gifted [...]. He will require care in relation to his struggle with some of the relics of an idealistic world view, with which he has the good will to cope.' Karel's father feared that studying English (as the language of the enemies of the communist countries) might cast a bad light on their family, but he accepted it in the end. Karel mentioned nothing in his memories that confirmed his father's fears. As far as studying English was concerned, the misfortune of students in the 1950s was that there was virtually no possibility of travelling or even studying in English-speaking countries.

After graduating in 1957, Karel had to take up a teaching post because the legislation of the time guaranteed the right to work.[5] Karel started his first teaching job in a small village in South Moravia near the border with Austria in 1957. It was a common phenomenon of the time that a teacher with a combination of Czech and a foreign language (other than Russian) had to teach some other subjects as well, as no other foreign languages were taught in primary schools. Teaching subjects without qualifications was common at the time, because of the chronic shortage of teachers in the 1950s and because of the inability of the educational and political authorities of the time to effectively address this long-term shortage. Karel soon learned how easily a school could be drawn into political events and abused by a totalitarian regime. The Unified Agricultural Cooperative (JZD)[6] in the village was unsuccessful and the situation could not be solved. The totalitarian authorities tried to use the local teachers to address the critical situation of the JZD management by sending an inspector (a KSČ member) to the school, who allegedly scolded and even threatened the local teachers in a very indiscriminate manner, saying that the situation in the JZD was their fault because they had not convinced the students of the usefulness of the JZD, and the students in turn had not influenced their parents at home to keep the JZD going. However, according to Karel, this was not a political problem; the problem was that the cooperative's property was being pilfered.

In 1960, Karel's family 'trait' of suspected tuberculosis became apparent. He spent 6 months in hospital. Fortunately, after his (full) recovery he was able to return to school, this time in a village near a regional town. After returning to school, he started an English club (without remuneration), and English was later made an optional subject. He also went on various trips with his students and even tried his hand at theatre. It was a great disappointment for him and the little actors when not even all the parents of all the actors came to see their performance.

---

[5] In his university application form, he had to sign a declaration that after graduating from university, he would work for 3 years at a school designated by the Ministry of Education.

[6] A unified agricultural cooperative (Jednotné zemědělské družstvo, JZD) was a form of farm enterprise organization before 1989. JZDs emerged in Czechoslovakia after 1948 as a result of socialist agricultural policy to create as much arable land as possible, among other things. In many ways, this was an imitation of Soviet kolkhozes.

He started the 1964/1965 school year at the general secondary school in a regional town. He spent nearly 40 years at this school. Immediately after being hired, with almost no previous experience at this type of school, he taught Czech for two graduating classes. Later he became a homeroom teacher, and he was also in charge of the professor's library. Thus, he briefly experienced the more liberal atmosphere of the second half of the 1960s in the school, but also the period of normalization and the screening (political purges) after 1970 (Cuhra, 2009; Černá, 2009). Nevertheless, Karel described this period in the school as tolerable. The expelled colleagues moved to other schools, and new colleagues came to the school where Karel worked. The school head, who tended to soften the edges of conflicts and protect the teachers from the powers in force at the time, apparently played an important role in ensuring that political pressure was not felt too much in the school. Deciding whether to accept new students was also the task of the school leadership. After 1968, it was not only the students' results at primary school that were decisive, but also the political involvement of parents, their attitude to the invasion of the Warsaw Pact troops, membership in a church, membership in the communist youth organization Pionýr, etc. Corrected admission tests only got to the hands of vetted colleagues (KSČ members)—Karel, as a non-partisan, was not among them. As he said himself, he was thus off the hook, but at the same time, he knew that the game was rigged. Nevertheless, relations between the members of the teaching staff were quite proper. Most of them took the obligatory ideological-political work only formally, except for the school leadership. In addition, a group of teachers had formed in the school who had gotten to know each other on various volunteer projects and ski courses to the point where they could fully trust each other, which Karel considered great luck. Karel remembered this difficult period as relatively conflict-free. However, in light of the knowledge of Karel's cooperation with the communist State Security Service (Státní bezpečnost, StB), the described situation appears much more complicated.

According to data from the Security Services Archive,[7] Karel's first contacts with this institution took place in 1975. About a year later, he was transferred to the category of 'agent'.[8] This cooperation could have occurred for many reasons. However, we do not know much about them, because it was a secret cooperation, which Karel himself did not mention to us, and many archival materials of the communist state security were completely destroyed shortly after 17 November 1989. His closest colleagues and friends did not want to talk[9] about this matter, although it was clear

---

[7] The Security Services Archive (Archiv bezpečnostních složek) has existed since 2008. Its main activities include the management of archival materials of the communist state security, military counter-intelligence, and border guards. It provides archival materials to researchers and cooperates with similar institutions abroad. More information at https://www.abscr.cz/en/

[8] An agent was a secret collaborator who was supposed to perform 'tasks related to seeking, elaborating, and documenting anti-state criminal activities and tasks aimed at preventing and inhibiting such crimes'. This characterization applies to the period of 1972–1978. See Gula (1994).

[9] There was one exception among the eyewitnesses. A former colleague spoke openly about Karel's cooperation with the StB only after she learned that all information is being anonymized.

that some of them were informed of it after 1989. According to one eyewitness, the reason for this was clear. They respected their colleague, and by mentioning such information, they feared tarnishing his memory. They believed that Karel could never have told the state security anything that would have subsequently caused problems for them. They were critical of the regime at the time, and such reflections were even the de facto leitmotifs of their private meetings.

We can only speculate about the reasons for the cooperation. Karel's knowledge of English, which the state security wanted to use for various tasks both in the territory of the former Czechoslovakia and possibly also outside of it could have been a reason. This possibility seems likely, as the last trace in the Security Services Archive very vaguely mentioned Karel's activities as an agent at the US Embassy around 1980. The state security may have used Karel's satirical literary work written during the Prague Spring as a means of coercion or blackmail, which may have been the reason for his cooperation. However, other reasons cannot be ruled out. Nor are we able to state, based on the available sources, whether the collaboration was voluntary or forced, or how Karel himself perceived it. This topic has a significant ethical dimension and must be studied very precisely and in a broader context, because it is not a simple problem. The risk of distortion or inaccurate interpretation is great. The lack of source material and the silence of eyewitnesses does not enable a deeper understanding and explanation of this chapter in Karel's life. Karel continued to work at the school even after 1989, when he was able to travel with his students to the United Kingdom for the first time. After his retirement, he continued to teach part-time at the school until 2003, when he left the school for good.

Karel's colleagues who spoke with us during the course of our research agreed that he was highly educated and excelled in speed of thought and encyclopaedic knowledge. He was a very demanding teacher who, for example, used a method of explanation that was close to a university lecture even in the secondary school. In English language and literature, he was very fond of working with the language and plays of Shakespeare. He was strict, but his passion for teaching Czech language and literature motivated many students to study this field at university. Less gifted students did not like him very much because of his demanding nature. Another reason for this lack of popularity among less gifted students was that he could sometimes be ironic towards them and he was particularly fond of talented students, which he often showed openly. Many students and colleagues sometimes found it difficult to get along with Karel because of his emotional volatility.

When asked which period was the most difficult and which was the best in his teaching career, he replied that both applied to the last 14 years he spent at the school, i.e. the period between 1989 and 2003. In his view, there were fewer prohibitions and restrictions, more opportunities but also more responsibilities. Foreign language teachers were helped by lecturers from abroad, albeit of varying quality. According to Karel, older teachers also had to learn the basics of working with computers and other new technologies. The return to an eight-year grammar school reinforced the selective nature of the school, as the first four classes in particular were filled with significantly talented and active students. Working with them was very challenging from Karel's point of view, but it also brought more satisfaction.

Thus, in several sentences, paraphrased here, Karel described his perception of the political transformation, although it largely concerned the transformation of the secondary school.

8.3   František's Story

František[10] is almost a decade younger than Karel. He was born in 1944 in a district town in South Moravia. He followed a family tradition with his choice of profession. 'My mother was a teacher, so I came from a family of teachers.' He was lucky in that he got to choose his profession after the early 1960s, when the regime had relaxed somewhat and the restrictions were not so severe. As an example of such restrictions, it was very difficult (if possible at all) for a candidate whose parents openly professed a religious faith or owned a private farm before 1948 to become a teacher. František's family, like many others, had experienced persecution because of their 'bourgeois' background: 'Dad was persecuted because of his father, who was demoted immediately after the war and driven from his job. He was an educated lawyer but then he worked in working class professions until he retired. And I had that in my records, right? Bourgeois and I don't know what all.' We can see from František's story that the family of a lawyer was regarded as having a 'bourgeois' background, especially if the lawyer had practiced their profession before the advent of communism in Czechoslovakia. The membership of a family member, in this case František's grandfather, in the Czechoslovak army may also have been problematic. Membership in those sections of the army that were formed outside of Czechoslovakia during World War II and were not under the control of the Communist Party (for example, Czechoslovak soldiers or pilots in Great Britain) was considered particularly problematic. Thus, there was not one but two problematic items in František's CV that meant potential difficulties in his life and career, and these records accompanied him practically all his life.

František's studies were associated with several changes that may be considered typical for his generation. He studied at an eleven-year secondary school, which had replaced the division of schools into primary school and grammar school at that time. This system was abolished in 1960 (Čornejová et al., 2020). This occurred when František was sixteen years old, and he was moved to a 'grammar school'.[11] Studying at a general secondary school in the late 1950s included various part-time jobs in production plants; this was related to the political programme that favoured manual work and industry and generally preferred the principles of 'polytechnic'

---

[10] We provide more detailed information about our narrators and former teachers in the Introduction.

[11] The eyewitnesses commonly used the Czech equivalent of 'grammar school' in their interviews, because the term 'general secondary school' was not used much in everyday life. Moreover, there were so many changes in the school system that many of our narrators were unable to say exactly what the school was officially called at the time of their studies.

teaching, even in humanities.[12] The advantage for František was that he obtained an apprenticeship certificate during his studies.

> I am therefore of the generation that has also experienced learning in the local factories. We were going to the factory and we went to the district roads administration, where we learned how to work on a lathe and how to weld and just all the basic things and we ended up with an apprenticeship certificate as a machine fitter.

This quote illustrated the polytechnic education and also showed what the general secondary school curriculum of the time looked like. With some degree of exaggeration, it could be called a hybrid between a grammar school and a vocational school. After graduating from the secondary school, František entered a pedagogical institute: 'Because I gravitated towards sports, I applied to the pedagogical school after graduation and I was accepted.' Studies of teaching at the time were still quite decentralized, and schools preparing future teachers were located in every region. František belonged to one of the years that experienced more chaotic changes in the teacher education system. In 1964, pedagogical institutes were abolished and teachers were once again to be educated at the faculties of education that had themselves been abolished about 10 years earlier. The following quote illustrates the individual experience of a future teacher and how sudden, unprepared, and chaotic the changes were:

> In '62 I was finishing secondary school, in '66 I was finishing the faculty. Actually, in the last year, we were moved from Jihlava to Brno to the Jan Evangelista Purkyně University.[13] and so I finished school in Brno (…) And after completing my qualification in biology, works in the school garden and physical education, I started at a primary school.

The beginning of their teaching careers was a similar experience for the oldest narrators. This may have occurred forcibly away from their original place of residence, as young teachers obtained employment on a 'mandatory placement'. They were usually placed in newly settled borderlands or in industrial areas. This system was intended to ensure a sufficient supply of teachers even in areas where there were (long-term) shortages. František was lucky because after graduating from the Faculty of Education, he was placed in a small town 'only' about 50 km from his home. However, in the 1960s, even this relatively short distance meant that he had to move to his place of work because of the lack of infrastructure and transportation.

---

[12] We discuss this topic in more detail in the Chap. 3 'From Stalinism to the Prague Spring – Education in Complicated Times (1945–1968)'. In this chapter, we describe the transformations of the school system in Czechoslovakia and the preparation of future teachers and its chaotic changes. Polytechnic teaching (also referred to as polytechnic education) was supposed to introduce students to the basic principles of all types of production and to teach them how to use manufacturing tools. Czechoslovak pedagogues adopted most of the ideas about the implementing polytechnic teaching from the Soviet Union. The polytechnic education was supposed to support the introduction of new socialist production.

[13] Masaryk University, named after the first Czechoslovak president Tomáš Garrigue Masaryk (a president in 1918–1935), was renamed Jan Evangelista Purkyně University for ideological reasons after the communists took power in 1960. After 1989, its original name was returned.

Public transport was limited and slow; the roads were obsolete. At that time, cars represented a luxury commodity that was out of reach for many people.

After the first years of a career associated with the 'mandatory placement', our oldest narrators usually obtained a work position in their original place of residence. František also got a job in his hometown.

> After my military service,[14] I came back and ... worked there for another year. I built a play-ing field there and just got very involved. Eventually I wanted to go back to my hometown, so I applied to the district. There wasn't a free spot, but in August 1968, I was approached by an inspector because a free position had opened up for one teacher. I accepted this and got into the school, where I worked for about three quarters of a year. When that teacher came back, I had to leave that job and they offered me a job at a primary school, where I finished that school year, '68/69. I actually experienced the coming of the Warsaw Pact troops there, and in '69, I was asked by my former teacher, who was the school head at the school, to join them. So I joined my school, the one I had been going to since the first grade, and I actually spent my entire pedagogical life there.

František was able to return to his hometown in the difficult period of the ongoing occupation of Czechoslovakia by Warsaw Pact troops. The oldest teachers recalled that they experienced the 'Prague Spring' and the subsequent occupation of the country intensely. However, because of their young age and because they were at the beginning of their teaching careers, they usually avoided the purges at the beginning of 'normalization'. This was because they did not hold any important positions at that time.

The invasion of the Warsaw Pact troops heralded the period of 'normalization', characterized in part by the hardening of conditions. This manifested itself in the restoration of censorship and the limited possibilities to freely express one's opinion or to become involved. The resignation to public involvement, the search for 'escape' areas of interest, and the orientation towards family life constituted the basic characteristics of everyday life during normalization (Vaněk & Mücke, 2016).

František and other narrators of the post-war generation were young and it was a period of natural need for them to create something and self-actualize. At that time, many teachers were trying to find areas of interest that were not outwardly political, but at the same time could meet the requirement of formal political involvement of teachers. These could be activities that entertained the teachers and helped them to find their own self-actualization. In František's case, it was sport. His lifelong hobby provided personal pleasure and offered the 'desirable' positive evaluation of his involvement by both his superior school and party authorities. Indeed, František and his students participated in many sporting competitions, which were then presented

---

[14] Military Service (Základní vojenská služba, ZVS) was the reason for the interruption of male teachers' teaching careers at their very beginning. The military service lasted 2 years in Czechoslovakia in the 1980s. It was compulsory for every male citizen of the Czechoslovak Republic over the age of eighteen who was deemed fit for military service. The length of ZVS for university graduates was 12 months. The students completed a part of the ZVS while studying at the 'military departments' that were part of the universities (Hlaváček, 2021). Since 2005, the Czech army has been fully professional and ZVS was completely abolished by that year.

as achievements of the socialist school or sport. The ideological subtext was often present, as was the case of Spartakiáda[15]:

> So I was very involved in sports, so my day started at 7 o'clock in the morning when I was already in the gym with the kids and actually ended at 4 o'clock, 5 o'clock when I still had these interest groups in the afternoon. I was also involved in the Spartakiáds when I was the district leader for the older students.

In general, the narrators stressed that they tried to avoid politics during the period of 'normalization', or downplayed the political dimension of their activities. František, who describes his qualification as apolitical, also speaks similarly of his political involvement, despite the fact that he also taught geography, which can hardly be said to be apolitical: 'I had apolitical subjects—physical education, biology, and geography.'

Although František lived through normalization actively, the peak of his career did not come until after 1989. Like some of the other narrators from the oldest group, he was offered a management position during this period of staffing changes in schools. Our other narrators also had such experiences, but some turned down the offer to become a managing worker.

František became school head, although he stated that he had no such ambitions. However, during the 'spontaneous' period of the Velvet Revolution, he became the one who was proposed for the post by the teaching staff at the school. He won the subsequent competitive selection for the post of school head and served until 2012. He held the post of school head at the school from which he himself had graduated and which he joined as a teacher in 1968. 'I didn't have any such ambitions, but simply the teaching staff at the various meetings that we did, they just gave me the confidence to go for it, so I went for it. Well and I was lucky enough to win it.'

The changes after the Velvet Revolution are viewed mostly positively by the oldest narrators. František was an example: 'Well, it was a big change, wasn't it? We didn't have to go to various trainings. There was a kind of relaxation. The teacher could create stuff on his own. And I think those were the good years.'

František did not hesitate to highlight the strengths of the school during the socialist period in which he spent a large part of his life. As an avid sports enthusiast, he felt that the conditions for raising athletically gifted students were better under socialism. Moreover, he did not shy away from criticizing the post-1989 development in the context of students' sports education: 'I founded at the school, our school was a sports school since 1977 or 1978, focused on track and field sports. So the kids actually had four hours of physical education and then they had four compulsory trainings. And in the nineties, it ended all of a sudden.' František criticized the loss of systematic support for sports and other specializations in primary schools by the Ministry of Education and the form of education of young athletes as such. He believed that the competition between sports clubs and the pressure on

---

[15] Spartakiáda was the name given to mass public gymnastic performances. Spartakiáds were also held in the Soviet Union (see Roubal, 2020 for more detailed information of Czechoslovak Spartakiáds).

students' performance from parents and coaches led to a 'contest' for talented students and their premature specialization in a particular sport. He attributed this situation to the developments after 1989. At the same time, František added that because of the cooperation with sports clubs in the town, the existence of sports classes in the school was saved.

František ended his career as the school head of an important school in a district town, and he helped to shape the good reputation of an important school in a significant way. He himself evaluated his teaching career positively. He managed to build many things at the school, not just in the field of sports facilities, which was probably his greatest pleasure as a PE teacher. František evaluated his time in the leading position as a phase of 'calm', which did not mean stagnation: 'When I saw that the students were happy and the teachers were happy. It was such a good feeling for the heart. And I was glad that we had peace, calm, cooperation in the workplace, that just nobody was arguing there, yeah. So I was happy.'

František retired in 2012. For the narrators, reaching retirement age and leaving the school did not have to mean the complete end of their teaching careers. Because of the shortage of teachers, many narrators still helped with teaching after they retired. They helped with teaching in the absence or illness of younger colleagues. František was still leading the basketball club at the time of the interview in 2020. Some of the oldest narrators also regularly met with friends from the teaching environment, as well as with former students who invited them to their class reunions. At the time of his interview, František had continuing good relations with students from his first workplace. 'The throwing circle is still there, a throwing place, everything is there and I go there once in a while to look at it because I established a good relationship with those students and we still visit each other.'

František believed that student success depended on the personality and initiative of the teachers and he also evaluated himself and his career in this context. He emphasized that he was one of those who lived with the profession and appreciated this way of life in his subordinates as well: 'In my opinion, it depends on the teachers, it is they who have to fill the children with enthusiasm.'

8.4   Olga's Story

Olga (1953) is a representative of our middle generation of teachers, which includes teachers born in the 1950s, (roughly between 1950 and 1958) who entered the profession during the period of 'normalization'. They experienced the socialist school system only briefly as young teachers and thus have experience with its late socialist form. The greater part of their teaching career was connected to the period of post-socialist transformation.

Olga was from Bohemia, but her career was mainly connected to the south-eastern region of Moravia. Like František, Olga was an avid sports enthusiast since childhood, which led her to teaching.

And there were many opportunities for sports in my hometown, so I was involved in swimming and athletics from a young age. (…) Well, actually, I would say that was what directed my decision of who I was going to be. So I was lucky to have a teacher at primary school who taught us Russian and PE, and she was very modern and progressive for her time, I think. Even though she wasn't the youngest.

The experiences with the Czechoslovak education system differs between František's generation and Olga's. By the second half of the 1960s, the school system was no longer bringing forth unprepared reforms and student teachers did not experience unexpected twists and turns like their predecessors in the 1950s. The occupation of Czechoslovakia by the Warsaw Pact troops in August 1968 was a crucial milestone that could have influenced future teachers. This was then followed by normalization, i.e. a return to a more rigid regime, and by purges in many areas of life, including in enterprises and the school system. The aim was to remove people who disagreed with the invasion or the political situation at the time (Zounek et al., 2017a). The narrators of the middle generation experienced this period as students. Olga attended primary school at the time and experienced the events of August 1968 intensely. She even joined the spontaneous resistance against the invasion. For example, turning signposts on the roads to lead the occupying troops astray can be considered a manifestation of civil discontent or protest.

So we were like fighting against, against the coming of the tanks here, I was just at my grandmother's … and we were turning the signposts there, and the tanks came there, and we kids were like in shock, and the entire week of the holidays we were still like fighting, actually, what are we going to do? What, like, how do we deal with this? Because nobody had any news as to why it happened.

During her studies at the grammar school, Olga heard about the purges from older classmates. Here, the memories diverge from the timeframe, as the purges undoubtedly took place after she had entered grammar school in September 1968. The main wave of purges did not begin until 1969. The narrators sometimes had difficulty with accurately placing their memories in time, but this does not diminish their value:

So then at that grammar school, we came there as novices in '68, and then we experienced, rather more from the narratives of the older students, like from higher classes, that the purge of those professors took place there. It was said that one was excellent and he had to leave, he didn't agree, so I guess the vetting took place there.

Olga went to university after graduating from secondary school in 1972. A large number of the narrators had rather positive memories of their university studies during the 1970s. However, they also pointed out that it was not easy to get into the faculty, and they often had to settle for studying a different field than they originally wanted for reasons related to capacity and politics. The possibility of obtaining a university education was still a relatively elite affair in Czechoslovakia, requiring the political reliability of the applicant and their family.[16] Several narrators empha-

---

[16] In 1980, 8.6% of people ages 25–29, 8.2% of those ages 30–39, 10.1% of those ages 40–49, and 3.8% of those over 50 had a university degree in the Czech part of the ČSSR (Kalinová, 2012). In comparison, according to the 2021 census, 17.6% of the population had a university education (*Census…*, 2021).

sized that they were grateful for the opportunity to study even a field that was not among their priorities. Olga wanted to study chemistry but had to settle for Russian. The memory clearly shows that former teachers of Russian, including Olga, may feel a strong need to 'justify' their role in the socialist school and their choice of field of study:

> I wanted to do chemistry, PE. And in the end, they didn't open chemistry, so the other option was some language and Russian was like a safe bet, like, even though I wasn't any Russophile at the time, still, the foreign language was an option, right, one sixth of the world was Russia and they bragged about it, so I chose the field that was open there, and that was Russian, PE, and that's actually how I got to what I went to study. And to this day I don't regret it.'

From our narrators, we recorded mostly positive evaluations of their study of teaching at the faculties of education in the 1970s, despite the fact that they encountered manifestations of regime consolidation and increased political surveillance in universities. Olga was summoned before the KSČ party organization at the faculty to comment on the alleged anti-socialist activities of a classmate:

> In my second year, I had a classmate, I was invited to the department of physical education once, and it was probably some cell of those communists, and they asked me how this classmate was behaving here, if she was spreading any propaganda and so on. So I was flabbergasted because she was a rather timid girl who came from some village, but somebody from the village sent some letter saying that this girl was from a family that was strongly religious and that it was not in line with her becoming a teacher. Well, it turned out that she graduated normally, and she is still a teacher.

After graduating from university, this generation of narrators no longer had to accept the first job assigned by the school authorities in a mandatory placement. This did not mean that it was easy to get a teaching position directly in the original place of residence or in the school where the young teachers wanted to teach. Olga found her first position in the district of her residence, but not directly in the town where she lived. She taught there for 6 months before going on maternity leave and remembered her beginnings very positively, while simultaneously explaining what was important to her:

> And I remember that six months actually as very good, because you always feel like a scared rabbit when you come into a new environment, and especially as a beginning teacher. And I really had colleagues there who were absolutely incredible. I guess I've been lucky here with the schools and the school heads and the colleagues, … I'm an eternal optimist, and I don't really, at all, I don't really have like negative memories of the whole time I was teaching.

During her maternity leave, she and her husband moved to his hometown in southeastern Moravia. In the interview, she described the process of looking for a teaching position in the 1970s, when everything was planned and managed by the departments of education. In areas with teacher shortages, the departments of education offered a teaching position with an apartment, which could be very enticing, especially for young teachers:

> In those days, the way to do it was to send your CV to the department of education (…) and I was offered a job with an apartment in a village near the district town. Coincidentally,

someone who'd later become a great friend of mine was leaving there, he got a job here at a secondary technical school, so I had chemistry, PE, but because I graduated from chemistry, I didn't mind that I started teaching chemistry.

The quoted recollection shows that even the younger generation of teachers often did not teach the subjects for which they were qualified. Olga was lucky that in her case, there was a need to teach chemistry, the subject she graduated from and had originally wanted to study at university.

Olga had worked for several years in a village near her home and she was happy at the school, but she was still looking for a job directly in the town where she lived with her husband and young children. An opportunity subsequently presented itself, but it was not in the primary school system. Therefore, she was one of the narrators in our sample who left the primary school environment for a time. 'I was approached by a colleague who said that they were starting to build a swimming centre and needed a swimming teacher. Well, at that point I offered myself, since I used to swim competitively, and I got the job, but it wasn't completely satisfying so I went back to school.' This was once again not a school in the town where she lived, but in another village school in the district. She worked here from the mid-1970s until the early 1990s. Olga recalled both working at a rural school and teaching subjects she was not qualified to teach:

'At that time, a colleague offered me that there was a job in the village and some female teacher had gone to America and never returned. So it was by chance that I got there, and I taught there for thirteen years. So the place was like good in that the smaller the school, I say, the more it sort of demands of you, and you have to know more. Yeah? So not only did I teach my subjects, which were PE and Russian, but I taught art, I taught chemistry, and maybe some more. (…) And there I actually verified that even in a village school, you can make such stars out of the kids for example in PE that they envy you and want them to come to a club to compete for them.

Similarly to František, during the period of 'normalization', Olga was involved in activities that were not very much connected to contemporary politics or communist ideology. All her life she was involved in sports, especially gymnastics, but also swimming. The narrators of this generation started their families during the period of the 'normalization'. Therefore, in their memories, many of them emphasized that their working weeks were very busy taking care of the family, raising children, and participating a large number of other leisure time activities. Like Olga, they were mostly involved in sports, but some of them were also involved in the theatre or choir or they spent time building holiday cottages. Some of them considered their interests apolitical. In general, and because of their active lifestyles, they did not have time to think deeply about the authoritarian nature of the times. This may be a typical strategy to 'escape' from the reality of normalization. By emphasizing the apolitical nature of their own activities, many narrators may be helping to retroactively legitimize their work in a profession that was strongly associated with communist power. Even leisure activities could only be carried out under the banner of centrally controlled socialist organizations such as the Czechoslovak Union of Physical Education (Československý svaz tělesné výchovy) or the Socialist Youth Union (Socialistický svaz mládeže).

The degree of consolidation during the normalization period was also influenced by the location and interpersonal relations in the school. Southeast Moravia was generally associated with a higher degree of religiosity than was typical for a Czech region. This was also reflected in the extent to which local communists tolerated religious lessons in the school or students' participation in religious services. Olga mentioned that even the parish priest attended the pedagogical councils. At the same time, she often dealt with the question of how to help a student from a religious family to study at the grammar school.

> So I was always there like especially with the children who were very clever and were entitled to study at those prestigious schools. Whether it was grammar school or I don't know economic or secondary industrial school, there always had to be a kind of a template, what that complex evaluation assessment should look like, and there always had to be that question about religion and political affiliation. And because everybody there went to religion, I had to add a sentence there: Even though he's taking religion classes, he's forming his own world view, which may be different from his parents and grandparents. And that bothered me at the time—that was maybe the only thing that bothered me, that this was a restriction of that human freedom and the division according to who went to religion classes and who didn't.

The atmosphere of the school was largely influenced by the school head. Olga emphasized this when she recalled the atmosphere at a rural school: 'I was really lucky regarding the school head because he was a person who was democratic, even though the system was totalitarian. All those people came together and pulled together as they say.' It should be emphasized that the school head's approach may have been largely made possible by the very nature of a strongly religious region in which the influence of communist ideology was traditionally weaker.

Olga also experienced the Velvet Revolution in this environment. She stressed that the changes in the school were welcomed by the teaching staff, but, at the same time, they expressed support for the existing and popular school head: 'Well, because we were all democrats, we basically accepted that it was good. And there wasn't even any change of school head.' According to Olga, the management of the school in which she worked showed characteristics of a democratic management style even before 1989. She also described her teaching as 'democratic'. She did not teach strictly according to the prescribed curriculum, which was also a product of communist ideology. That in itself was the reason why she did not change her teaching in any fundamental way even during the changes in the school system: 'Otherwise, I taught basically as I was used to and I never accepted this (ideological) dogma here, and basically, fortunately, nobody really asked me to do so.' Her statement that no one was checking her teaching nor demanding adherence to curricula was very interesting, because such demands represented a fundamental characteristic of the school system at the time. The location of the school probably played an important role in this context as well.

A few years after the Velvet Revolution, the school head was dismissed and Olga and several other colleagues left the school for other workplaces. According to Olga, the school head had to leave because of an order from the district authority. At that time, the district dismissed en masse all school heads who had been in office before 1989 and remained in office after the competitive selections. However, a collective of teachers stood up for the popular village school head: 'That was the directive and the decision, and well, we disagreed with that, so basically I don't know if six or seven people left the school then as if in protest. Including the school head.' This example of a change in school management is not entirely typical. A part of the teaching staff stood behind the school head who ran the school even before 1989. Despite this support, the school head had to leave and some of the teachers left with him. Schools went through many changes during this period: sudden and radical changes both of management and of the teaching staff. The reason for the change then remains a question: whether it was the person or the work of the school head, or just the fulfilment of the obligation to replace the 'old' management.

Olga then went to a newly built school near her home. This school was located in a small industrial town that was developing dynamically at that time. Because of the increase in population, a large new school was built there. Therefore, Olga had the opportunity to be involved in the preparation and set up of operation of the new school. She was mainly involved in equipping the new gymnasium.

After 1989, as a Russian language teacher, Olga found herself in a situation in which this particular language was no longer wanted and desired. Very soon after the Velvet Revolution, there were initiatives by parents and later by the new political representation to replace the teaching of Russian with Western languages. In particular, there was an interest in English and also in German. Olga actually started to teach German. She was an example of a forced change in the teaching qualification. At the same time, she was an example of the fact that Russian teachers were not being dismissed en masse after 1989 or even bullied in any way.

Olga presented herself as a pedagogue who had spent her lifetime educating herself on her own initiative and pursuing innovations in education. This approach may have influenced Olga's attitude towards the need for retraining from a Russian language teacher to a German language teacher. While some teachers may have perceived this obligation, stemming from the change in geopolitical orientation after 1989, negatively, for example as unwelcome extra work, for Olga, in her words, retraining was not a burden. She saw it as one of many opportunities for self-education.

Although Olga evaluated the post-revolutionary development of Czech society positively and presented herself as a strong supporter of the democratic development, she was critical of parts of the development of the Czech school system and of society. For example, she evaluated the transformation of the relationship between parents and teachers negatively. Olga worked at the school until her retirement in 2016. She was very active at the school. Before and after 1989, she worked as a methodologist for physical education[17] and thus organized trainings for other teach-

---

[17]The association of teachers into groups according to their field/subject (mathematics, PE) was referred to as methodological association. These associations existed in schools as well as on the district level. Prior to 1989, methodological associations were also advisory bodies to the school head. The activities of the associations included helping the (beginning) teachers, improving the educational practice (exchange of experience, mutual teacher observation), and developing teach-

ers in the district. 'I was the methodologist for physical education, there were train-ings, and it came from faculties, so we had this, that they enriched us regularly.' In addition, Olga was involved in organizing sports competitions. She kept in touch with the school environment, not only because she was still making friends and meeting with colleagues. Until the outbreak of the Covid-19 pandemic, she rehearsed dance performances with ninth-grade students for the school ball every year. In the year in which the interview took place (2021), she declined the offer for the first time.

Although Olga remembered the school vividly, she was already taking stock and evaluating her teaching career from some distance. In doing so, she was shaping her self-image through the feedback of students and colleagues: 'They said I was strict, but friendly, yeah?' She explained her own pedagogical story as a story about a young woman who, despite some handicaps (especially her small stature), managed to find a relationship with her students, reflecting on the fact that a good teacher is born with certain unspecified pedagogical skills or abilities.

> Well and when I came to that first school, because I'm small, tiny, so I was just saying to myself: Now it's going to be terrible. I'm going to be the smallest one in the class. Like in eighth-ninth graders. So I was worried about that, for example. And suddenly, like they say, some personality trait or some fluid that either surrounds a person or not, I walked in and it wasn't a problem. So this is really something between heaven and earth, where maybe the person is sort of predestined for the profession. (…) My daughters always said to me: 'Mom, you have such knowledge, why were you a teacher?' I said: 'Well, because I was so attracted to it, and I enjoyed it so much, so I wouldn't change it even now, girls.' So that's it.

Olga emphasized that for her, the job of a teacher was a calling, and that a good teacher should not pursue the profession only for the purpose of making money: 'I think it's also really in the personality of the teacher. What they want to convey, how they convey it and that it's not just about the money.' Olga only mentioned the finan-cial remuneration after a direct question, which may also indicate that the issue of teacher salary was not important to her, even though low teacher salaries were a pressing problem in the 1990s. Olga's husband was also a teacher, so her family could not rely on any higher income from a better paid profession.

Olga concluded her presentation of her successful career by reminiscing about a very recent time. Just before her retirement, she was nominated by her students for the Golden Amos (Zlatý Ámos) award. This award is given every year on the basis of a poll in which students and the public choose the most popular teacher in the Czech Republic. In the end, Olga made it to the final round of the competition.[18]

Olga was a kind of an illustrative example of the teachers who spoke to us. Indeed, a large part of them were motivated and active people who literally lived for their work. There were those among them who were critical of the current situation in the school system. In our research, we have to take into account the risk of

---

ers' pedagogical creativity. Prior to 1989, the tasks of the methodological associations also included education of students towards a scientific worldview and socialist convictions, as well as supporting teachers in this respect.

[18] The competition has been held since 1993 and is currently organized by the Domino Club and the Dětská tisková agentura (Children's Press Agency) (*Zlatý Ámos…*, 2023).

self-stylization during the interview, in which the narrators try to show themselves in the best possible light. However, the circumstances of our interview also hinted at Olga's popularity. In fact, during the course of the interview, she repeatedly greeted many people in a friendly manner in the café. She herself pointed out that many of them were past or current teachers. As a material proof of her activity (but also of her emphasis on the representation of her achievements), she brought to the interview yearbooks with statistics and photographs of sports competitions she had organized until her retirement.

8.5 Vlasta's Story

Teachers born in the late 1950s and early 1960s form the youngest group of narrators in our research. They experienced the Velvet Revolution as young pedagogues and they were still working in schools at the time of our research. This was probably why they often compared the 1990s with the present in their interviews. Quite predictably, they did not talk much about socialism, because they did not have much experience as teachers with the school system before 1989. Interestingly, of all our narrators, they were the ones who most criticized the development of school system after 1989. At the same time, some of them considered the first years of the post-socialist transformation to be the 'golden era' of the greatest freedom in schools. In this respect, they had similar views to most narrators from other age groups or generations.

Our youngest narrators typically completed their university studies in the early 1980s, but most of them did not enter pedagogical practice until just before the Velvet Revolution. For the women, the reason was maternity leave[19]; for the men, it was military service, which was compulsory at that time. Because of her maternity leave, Vlasta, who was born in 1961 and came from a small town (about 3500 inhabitants) ten kilometres from the Moravian capital of Brno, took up her first teaching job at the age of 28. At the time of the interview, she was still teaching at the primary school there. Vlasta emphasized that she had a childhood ambition to be a teacher, although during her grammar school studies, she dreamed of studying psychology. However, the political profile of those interested in studying the humanities was closely monitored by the Communist Party (e.g. it was necessary to be actively involved in the activities of the Socialist Youth Union). Vlasta did not meet these high demands and therefore could only choose a technical field of study:

> How I got into the profession … I would say completely by accident, because already as a girl we were already playing school… But then I studied at the faculty of engineering, although I wanted to study psychology, I couldn't actually go to that school for political reasons (…) I don't know by what miracle I did it, but I graduated, I enjoyed my studies, I

---

[19] In Czechoslovakia, maternity leave (Mateřská dovolená) was used to care for a newborn child. It was available for women beginning in 1950; the length varied over the years. In the 1980s, maternity leave lasted from the child's birth until 3 years of age.

learned a lot of new things there, (…) and I had a job promised, to go into a manufacturing company. But I was pregnant, so I finished the university while pregnant and actually stayed on maternity leave. Well, while still on maternity leave, I started looking for a place to go to, but nothing much came up. My university classmates were already studying at the Department of Education of the University of Technology, as they wanted to teach after maternity leave. So I applied there, they took me upon appeal, so towards the end of my maternity leave I started studying at the department here and it was for two years. (Vlasta)

The study of pedagogy at the technical university was intended as a preparatory education primarily for future teachers of vocational subjects at secondary technical schools. In this way, Vlasta obtained a teaching qualification, but this was not intended for primary school teachers. Nevertheless, she got a job at a primary school in her hometown. As she herself stated, because of good luck.

> I had finished studies at the Department of Education at Brno University of Technology and I was doing my final thesis, I had to do some research on human personality, and I needed to have the questionnaires filled in by the students so that I could make some output from it. I asked the school head at the primary school here if I could… do the research there and she agreed. So when I had finished the work, I also asked the school head if there was a vacancy there, that I could perhaps join. Well and when my son was three years and two months old, I met the school head by chance and she said: Do you want to take the job? But you'd be a substitute for another teacher on maternity leave, teaching mathematics, geography, eighth graders, seventh graders. Well, I started teaching it. I was thrown completely into the teaching process without any great experience because there was no practical training in that pedagogical programme, so I didn't get to go in front of the students, I just found out how far they were in the subjects, what their subject matter was and where, I went to see one lesson at the primary school and from the first of February '89, I started teaching.

Vlasta began her career as a primary school teacher on 1 February 1989. Therefore, she experienced less than a year of pedagogical work in a socialist school. For Vlasta, the period of socialism was mainly associated with her studies, looking for a job, and her first steps in the teaching profession. If KSČ politics influenced her in any significant way, it was the question of the choice of profession in a situation in which the study of her dreamt-of psychology required a perfect political profile of the candidate. However, just before the fall of the communist government, Vlasta, as a young teacher, was being lured to join KSČ by the deputy school head of the school: 'I had this encounter there, that the deputy school head, she was a communist, so don't you want to join the Communist Party, I said I was too young and I didn't feel like it and I had a family (…).'

In our research, we learned that some of our female narrators used the same or similar tactics to avoid having to join the Communist Party. The main arguments were references to their own youth, inexperience, 'political immaturity', or concern for their families (not only for their own child, but for example for their elderly parents), and thus a lack of time for political work. This tactic seemed to have worked for some; for others it may have only delayed the call to join for a certain period of time, after which the offer to join the Communist Party was repeated and may have been much more urgent.

Very soon after she took up the job of a teacher, Vlasta experienced revolutionary events accompanied by staffing changes. These concerned her as well. There was no room for her at the school where she had been working. However, she was helped out by a new school head who took the place of her communist predecessor who had been dismissed:

> Because I was the last one to start, I was an inexperienced newbie, so there was no job for me, but the school head was good enough to tell me: You will take up something in the next village, there is an excellent school head there, and so you will be in the after-school club for a year, and the next year there will be a vacancy here, so you will come back.

Vlasta went to work in the after-school club at another school in a nearby village. She remembered her year at the small village school very positively: 'It was such a homely, modest school... it was nice, nicely furnished, and the people were nice to each other.' After a year, Vlasta returned to her original school, where at the time of her interview she was still teaching mathematics, science, industrial arts, and PE. She saw the early 1990s as a challenging time because she and her husband moved to a large city nearby and had to commute to school. At the same time, she had to take care of her family and, in her words, had no free time.

> Well, it was hectic because I had a small child and we moved to the city where we lived for five and a half years, so I was up late at night correcting notebooks and I had to get up early in the morning because I had to wake my son up at six, ... and he'd just have breakfast and I'd get him dressed and we'd get on the bus... Then, when he was at school, he'd come to me afterwards and do his homework himself, if I still had classes to teach, and then we'd go to my parents here after school. We would do our homework, I helped my parents with some things in the garden and we went home. That's what my work day was like. But because we were young, we didn't see it as being that demanding at all, even for the child it was demanding.

Vlasta moved back to her hometown after her divorce. She experienced the Velvet Revolution itself with the hope that she would be able to live in a free country. However, she said, disappointment soon came and she was later very critical of the development of society after 1989. This criticism influenced the nature of her memories and her view of the development of the school system as a whole. Two sources can be identified that shaped Vlasta's dissatisfaction: the transformation of her place of residence and the (lack of) environmental protection.

Vlasta's hometown changed fundamentally over 30 years. This was caused by a rapid increase in the number of new inhabitants and the associated growth of the village, which started to take on the character of a large city district.[20] This also had an impact on local interpersonal relations, which became more and more anonymous. A typical example is entrepreneurs who bought (large) family houses near the regional capital without being at all interested in getting involved in the local community, in municipal affairs, or even in the maintenance of public spaces. Perhaps this was also why Vlasta, who remembered the rural character of her home, took this transformation hard.

---

[20] The number of inhabitants in Vlasta's hometown almost doubled. Moreover, the vast majority of these people commute to work in the nearby large city. Therefore, we can speak of a process of suburbanization (Giddens & Sutton, 2013).

> People are not greeting each other here. People don't know each other here. Sure, people die, new people move in here, I guess that's the cycle of life, that's the way it's supposed to be, but I think that those people living an urban lifestyle have no business living here. (…) It bothers them that people burn brushwood here, but that's normal in a village. That the rooster crows. That the bells ring. Whereas before, they used to help each other. Yeah, they cleaned up in front of the house, helped each other shovel snow, yeah? They were interested. What the neighbourhood was like around them.

The strength of the expressed disillusionment seemed related to the fact that Vlasta was long involved in the beautification of public spaces in her city and took an active interest in local events. Vlasta's involvement formed the second pillar that shaped her view of the post-socialist transformation. During the 1990s, when taking care of her young children did not take up so much of her free time as before, Vlasta gradually began to engage in various leisure activities. These were more or less related to her pedagogical practice. To a large extent, she educated herself. For example, she participated in a medical course, which led to her cooperation with the Czech Red Cross. She also attended a course for ski instructors, which enabled her to regularly participate in students' winter ski training stays as an instructor.[21] However, her activities were most influenced by courses in environmental education, which led her to cooperate with a regional environmental educational organization and shaped her world view:

> So I've always had a good relationship towards nature. But not so much that I would be interested in any details, not like that. But back in the nineties I started working with (…), which is an environmental organization. And first I went there as a teacher. But I was really so drawn in by the fact that they were preserving the traditions of those ancestors of ours, so I got to do almost everything I desired. What to work with, and I met a lot of great people there. They are my friends, we understand each other and I learn new things from them again, new experiences and meeting such people always gives me something, advances me somewhere.

First, Vlasta took part in courses organized by an environmental organization, and then she started working with it as a lecturer or sports instructor at their children's camps. Perhaps it was her contact with like-minded people that led her to become interested in improving the environment in her hometown.

> Well, I just don't know where it came from, because at first I was only focused on my family, and then I just felt a need to make a difference. Something broke in me, I don't know what to call it, and a colleague who was teaching here and we were very close, she started organizing the Clean Up the City events. I really liked it, and I didn't like the mess. And the indifference, detachment of the neighbourhood, yeah, of the people in general, so I tried it.

The interest in ecology and dissatisfaction with the quality of public spaces in the municipality motivated Vlasta to start organizing volunteer clean-up works in the town after 2000. She approached the municipal authority and established

---

[21] Ski training was a part of the physical education curriculum of seventh grade in Czechoslovak and then Czech primary schools. The aim was to give students the basic skills and knowledge needed to ski and to teach students how to behave in the mountainous environment, on and off skis. Ski training is still part of the curriculum today.

cooperation with local companies, with whose help she organized the first public clean-up of the town. Subsequently, the event was held every year with the participation of school children. However, it did not stop with the clean-up. During the interview with Vlasta, more and more of her activities came to light, including art activities. She and her students decorated the underpass at the local train station.

Vlasta's personal involvement and breadth of interests were shared by other narrators across generations. At the same time, Vlasta expressed a strong dissatisfaction with the current state of the local community and society. This dissatisfaction seems to be shaped by the values she learned while working with an environmental organization. These included a rejection of the consumerist way of life, care for the environment, an active interest in public space in her surroundings, and a relationship to traditions. However, these qualities were not shared by her neighbours, who, according to Vlasta, tended to care more about themselves. At the same time, she admitted that she was pleased and further motivated by even a little praise from her surroundings.

> Maybe that's why I'm so disillusioned, because sometimes the enthusiasm just wears off, and then when I do something, I see that it has met with success, right. None of us can be liked by everybody. Yeah? That we're gonna please everybody. But then a little praise can make a person feel better, yeah.

Vlasta carried her highly critical attitudes into the school environment. In her view, the relationships between teachers, students, and parents were negatively affected by individualism: 'The very me, me, me -ism. Individuality. That now I just want something, at all costs, and now the teacher has to pay attention to me. And that's also from the parents. After all, the child should have some kind of regime, some, just some boundaries as to how far they can go. And I don't think today's children have that.'

In Vlasta's narrative, the dissatisfaction was strongly linked to expressions of nostalgia for the 'good old days'.[22] Vlasta's idealization of the past may have been partially shaped by working with an environmental organization that, according to Vlasta, emphasized preserving the traditions and proven practices of previous generations. This leitmotif of Vlasta's narrative also related to the 1990s. In her memories, Vlasta often portrayed that period as a 'golden era'. For example in the matter of relations between teachers, who were closer to each other in the 1990s and even spent their free time together:

> Like, I can say that the girls we have in the staff room, most of them are awfully nice, they help others, yeah? (…) But I think it's kind of like that we were probably more … our generation being outdoors more where we experienced those moments together, or going

---

[22] Generally, nostalgia can be defined as the idealization of the past. In the context of Central and Eastern European countries, nostalgia for socialism is often mentioned, but nostalgia for the 1990s is starting to appear more and more. Nostalgia is also mentioned in Chap. 6. Vlasta's narrative contained elements of nostalgia for the 1990s as well as for the undefined 'good old days' of traditional society when people were closer to each other (Boym, 2001; Pehe, 2020; Todorova & Gille, 2010).

tramping,[23] yeah? We were more around that guitar, yeah? And on those camps, yeah? But now they don't sing, they can't sing anything.

The idealization of interpersonal relationships in the past constitutes a frequent motif of nostalgic memories and does not necessarily have to refer to a specific period of time. However, Vlasta's view of the amount of the administrative duties of a teacher was directly linked to the 1990s and the freedom of the time. While after 1989, the amount of compulsory 'paperwork' decreased, at the time of the interview, in Vlasta's view, teachers had to (again) devote more time to administration at the expense of pedagogical work. In her opinion, this was a figuratively return to the school system before 1989: 'I would say that we have somehow moved smoothly from that, from February '89, to the analogy of those times, the period of socialism. (…) I think there's a lot of unnecessary paperwork, that it already occurs even now. (…) It disappeared and then it started to appear again.'

The image of the character of the 1990s as a period without unnecessary obligations is further illustrated by Vlasta's experience with compulsory retraining. Even though Vlasta had voluntarily devoted herself to self-education in the 1990s, a kind of 'sword of Damocles' of insufficient qualifications still hung over her. The need to formally complete her qualifications came only after 2000; in the 1990s, no one had asked her to complete her education. 'Because then I actually had it written in my papers then that I could teach vocational subjects in secondary schools. So anyway, then when I was almost fifty, I had to do this kind of retraining.' The subject of qualification may be an example of why the period of virtually the entire 1990s is seen as a time of freedom, when 'anything was possible'. In the first decade after the revolution, inadequate teacher qualifications did not pose any great problem for school management or, presumably, for the school inspectorate. It was only after a relatively long period of time, with the coming of new school laws and regulations after 2000, when it became necessary to complete the qualifications. This also entailed verifying compliance with the applicable legislation. These matters were perceived rather negatively by some of our narrators.

The criticism of the current situation and the remembering of a 'better' past was also reflected in Vlasta's attitudes towards the organization of the school system. She criticized the novelty of the 1990s—the autonomy of schools. She considered the uniform curricula and the previously compulsorily elaborated detailed learning plans to be better:

> I think that the self-governance was the biggest stupidity that there is, because since then it simply has not been as it should be in the school system. And then the framework education programme, that's another terrible thing, because a child is in one village, they're taught

---

[23] Tramping – in a figurative sense, the narrator was referring to going on multi-day hiking trips into the wild nature, coupled with sleeping in a tent or under the stars. Tramping is also the name of a specifically Czech subculture based on staying outdoors. It originated before World War II and experienced a great increase in popularity during the socialist period, partly because of the limited possibilities of travelling abroad. The tramping subculture was based on stays in the countryside and on the inspiration of the aesthetics of the Wild West taken from popular western stories (Altman, 2023).

something according to the framework curriculum, they come, they have to move to another village, and they're taught completely different things, and they may not even get to some of those things at all, because they have a completely different framework programme.

The 'framework education programmes' and the school education programmes are the result of the new Education Act of 2004.[24] Vlasta's view of the status of the teaching profession in society and her assessment of her own activities in the school system were similarly critical. Vlasta admitted that she considered leaving, and stated that if she were younger, she would have left the school system. At the same time, she was one of the few to speak out about her (inadequate) financial remuneration without being prompted to:

If I were a man, I would definitely not go into teaching. For the money. Yeah? And to get annoyed there all the time. And to bring the work home. So I think he's gonna get the same money somewhere else and he's home with a clear head. But one has got to be a special kind of person, one that enjoys it. That sees it as a calling. That it's not about the money. Only, yeah? A thousand times, I had thoughts about going somewhere else, too, even looked for a job, okay? But I'd always think, I'm home, and then something would give me a jolt, and I'd think, I've just been through a rough patch, and it'll get better. It's just gonna be good again. And now I think I just gotta finish the last five years. But I think if I were young, I wouldn't have lasted as long there. And a lot of my colleagues say they're not going to make it to retirement.

Vlasta was recommended to us as a suitable narrator precisely because she was one of the teachers who participated in the organization of a wide range of activities in and around the school after 1989. Perhaps that was why, when we approached her, we expected another in a line of positive female narrators who enthusiastically talked about their lives. This was suggested by her great willingness to be interviewed. However, in the end, this narrator was among the youngest of our sample and among the most critical. This may be because unlike František and Olga, she was still teaching and encountered the problems of the contemporary Czech school system on a daily basis. To a large extent, however, her attitude was influenced by dissatisfaction with the situation in the location where she lived, worked, and was involved all her life. Therefore, in her memories, she greatly idealized both the past, i.e. life in a traditional rural society, and the 'free' 1990s.

---

[24] In the Czech Republic, the Framework Education Programmes (Rámcový vzdělávací program) form a generally binding framework for the development of school education programmes for all branches of education in pre-school, primary, primary art, language and secondary education. The School Education Programme (Školní vzdělávací program) is a curricular document that is created by the teaching staff of each school in the Czech Republic, it is approved and issued by the director of the relevant establishment and must be publicly accessible. The School Education Programme makes it possible, for example, to profile one's school and thus distinguish it from other schools.

8.6   Life Stories in the Context of Time

In this chapter, we focused on the life stories of several teachers. Our aim was to gain a better understanding of the lives of specific teachers and to add to the knowledge of the transformation of the school system, especially with the opinions and experiences of specific eyewitnesses. When we examine the life stories of teachers, we necessarily include the pre-1989 era and the socialist school system, which often had a significant impact on the lives and work of our narrators.

It is important to realize that narrators may tend to justify their former role or attitude towards life in their memories of socialism, thus coming to terms with the burden of the ideological indebtedness of the teaching profession before 1989 (and thus justifying themselves to themselves). We must also bear in mind that a certain degree of idealization of the past and nostalgia is present in the interviews and memories of the narrators, both for the period before and after 1989. Nostalgia relates to the past, but it can also be shaped by contemporary problems; in our case, these are the problems of the school system and education in the Czech Republic in particular.

The oldest narrators experienced the chaotic period of the 1950s and witnessed many unprepared reforms in the school system. Younger teachers experienced the occupation of the country in 1968 during their studies only to have to adapt to the conditions of a 'normalized' school system early in their careers. The youngest teachers experienced the difficult changes of the 1990s when 'anything was possible' at the beginning of their careers, almost without rules and also without systematic support for innovation and school development. There was no vision in Czechoslovak education at that time towards which the school system reforms could aim. In the first half of the 1990s, no generally accepted (national) concept even emerged of changes in educational goals, contents, or teaching methods.

The youngest narrators entered the period of transformation with a socialist-era education but were no longer bound by many strict (often ideological) regulations and bureaucracy in their work and teaching. They were able to try out new teaching methods, to seek inspiration from outside the field of the school system, and to follow the current trends in education, no longer limiting themselves to socialist countries. At the same time, interestingly, foreign cooperation and studying the experiences of teachers from other countries did not play a very large role in the memories of our teachers. This may be due to the clear orientation towards knowledge of Russian prior to 1989 or due to the need to deal with many domestic topical issues that 'engulfed' the teachers.

The older teachers were able to draw on their experiences and use best practices in their teaching. It was more or less up to them to decide whether and how to approach changes and innovations. For Karel, for example, it was a challenge to incorporate the first computers into teaching and to start working with students who were selected for the school on the basis of merit and aptitude. As an English teacher, he was able to visit the UK and work with native speakers for the first time. František became a school head and used his competences and social networks mainly for the further development of the school. Olga followed trends in education and continued to educate herself, but primarily within traditional and institutionalized paths in the school system—specifically, the Teachers' Methodological Association and further teacher training that took place in collaboration with universities.

Vlasta sought inspiration and resources to enrich her teaching outside the school environment. She began working with an environmental organization whose activities inspired her to become publicly involved within the school and the city.

Despite all the differences, the memories of the narrators of different generations also had some things in common. They were all critical of the socialist period when they mentioned the ideologization of the school system, the directive management of schools, the excessive bureaucracy, and the entrance exams to secondary schools, which were largely controlled by the KSČ. At the same time, some remembered certain characteristics of the socialist school system in positive light. In particular, they mentioned the uniform curricula and textbooks and better support for sports. It is interesting to observe the different perceptions of some similar themes. Centralization is a good example. Our narrators criticized the central and directive management of socialist schools, but they considered the uniform contents of textbooks and centrally prescribed curricula to be a relatively good solution for teaching and its planning. This assessment may reflect the relatively negative experiences with the post-revolutionary non-conceptuality as well as the lack of clarity in pedagogical reforms.

Narrators across generations of teachers evaluated the Velvet Revolution positively, although some were critical of the post-1989 developments. Freedom and liberty were the leitmotif of memories of the first years of the post-socialist transformation. This was manifested in the abolition of many administrative tasks or compulsory (ideological) teacher trainings. On the other hand, there was practically no systematic evaluation of the operation of schools and the perception of legal issues among teachers was quite varied or, in other words, not at an adequate level.

The narrators remembered the 1990s from their current perspective. They were able to compare the free nature of the time with the later return of more rigorous control. New laws and decrees gradually came into force, related to the consolidation of the democratic and legal state. The systematic work of the Czech School Inspectorate also developed gradually. It was perhaps because of their careers beginnings at the time of the greatest 'freedom' that the youngest narrators in particular were very critical of the later 'hardening of conditions'.

By contrast, some of the pressing issues of the 1990s school system were surprisingly absent from the teachers' memories. For example, without a direct question, the teachers did not mention the low salaries in the 1990s and the related protests and many teachers leaving the schools. This may be because teacher salaries have increased significantly in recent years and were not a current political or social issue at the time of our research. After the interviewer directly asked about financial remuneration, Olga and many other narrators then said that they themselves did not do their profession only for money, but perceived it as a calling.

However, this was far from being generally true. The costs of living rose faster than teachers' salaries and the issue of maintaining standards of living was thus very topical (Čornejová et al., 2020; *Školství...*, 1998). Our narrators stressed that they were willing and able to teach despite the low financial remuneration, but many other colleagues left.[25] In this context, we cannot ignore the role of gender. Mainly men left the schools because of the financial evaluation. Vlasta herself admitted that she would have left the school system if she were a man. Men still hold the traditional role of the main breadwinner in Czech society (Vaněk & Mücke, 2016).

One might expect that with the fall of the Iron Curtain, the opportunity to travel abroad or to cooperate with (Western) foreign schools would be reflected in life stories. While this theme did appear in the memories, it was not a particularly prominent one. The narrators mentioned it rather sporadically, depending on the location of the school and personal contacts or the teacher's qualification.

After the Velvet Revolution, our narrators generally preserved their way of life and, for example, pursued their hobbies. Some teachers mentioned that they had almost no free time due to their active lifestyle or their family situation. Indeed, the fact that they were willing to meet with us even more than once showed their attitude towards life. With a certain idealization inherent in their memories, our narrators saw the period of post-socialist transformation as a phase in which the bad things from socialism 'disappeared', and, at the same time, the good things 'still remained'. For many of them, it represented an golden era in their careers. At the same time, some saw the democratization of society as the source of their current problems.

Finally, it should be mentioned that the stories of our narrators cannot be generalized. Through these stories, we have tried to show how diverse the everyday reality was before 1989 and especially during the post-socialist transition, both in and out of school. This breaks down the simplistic 'black and white' notion of a repressive communist regime versus an oppressed society that has become the dominant narrative about communism in the Czech Republic (Pullmann, 2009). At the same time, we show the twisted nature of the paths of post-socialist society and the school system. That is why the perception of the first decade after 1989 was also very varied and the views of our narrators in many ways symbolized or depicted great victories as well as losses and failures or unfulfilled expectations.

Bibliography

Altman, K. (2023). Czech and Slovak tramping movement as a shared cultural heritage. *Slovenský národopis / Slovak Ethnology, 71*(2), 165–179. https://doi.org/10.31577/SN.2023.2.16

Boym, S. (2001). *The future of nostalgia*. Basic Books.

---

[25] Self-esteem and the need for representation usually prevent people from admitting their difficult life situation. Sociological research shows that stories about 'the others' are the dominant way in which respondents thematize the problems of their professional or social group (Vidovićová et al., 2018).

Census 2021: Education. (2021). https://www.scitani.cz/education

Černá, M. (2009). Od školy až do důchodu. V síti kádrových materiálů. [From school till retirement. In the net of cadre materials]. *Dějiny a současnost, 11*, 37–39.

Čornejová, I., Kasper, T., Kasperová, D., Kourová, P., Kratochvíl, P., Lenderová, M.,Novotný, M., Pokorný, J., Svatoš, M., Svobodný, P., Šimek, J., & Váňová, R. (2020). *Velké dějiny zemí Koruny české: Tematická řada: Školství a vzdělanost.* [Great history of the lands of the Bohemian Crown: Thematic Edition: School system and level of education]. Paseka.

Cuhra, J. (2009). Kádrovník nikdy nemůže být se svou prací hotov. Kádrování a komunistické vládnutí [The work of personnel officer is never done. Screening of personnel and communist rule]. *Dějiny a současnost, 11*, 30–33.

Decree No. 32/1953 Coll. Government decree on the transformation of existing schools into schools according to the new Education Act. (1953). https://www.psp.cz/sqw/sbirka. sqw?cz=32&r=1953

Erikson, E. H. (1998). *The life cycle completed* (Extended version). W.W. Norton.

Fuchs-Henritz, W. (2000). *Biographische Forschung. Eine Einführung in Praxis und Methoden.* Westdeutscher Verlag.

Giddens, A., & Sutton, P. W. (2013). *Sociology* (7th ed.). Polity.

Gula, M. (1994). Vývoj typů spolupracovníků kontrarozvědky StB ve směrnicích pro agenturní práci [Development of types of STB counter-intelligence collaborators in directives for agency Work]. *Securitas Imperii, 1*, 12–13.

Hlaváček, J. (2021). *Mezi pakárnou a službou vlasti: základní vojenská služba (1968–2004) v aktérské reflexi* [Between stupidity and service to the homeland: Basic military service (1968–2004) in participants' memory]. Academia.

Kalinová, L. (2012). *Konec nadějím a nová očekávání: k dějinám české společnosti 1969–1993* [The end of hopes and new expectations: On the history of Czech Society 1969–1993]. Academia.

Mannheim, K., & Kecskemeti, P. (Eds.). (1964). *Essays on the sociology of knowledge.* Routledge & Kegan Paul.

McDermott, K. (2015). *Communist Czechoslovakia, 1945–89: a political and social history.* Macmillan Education.

Pehe, V. (2020). *Velvet retro: postsocialist nostalgia and the politics of heroism in Czech popular culture.* Beginner Books. https://doi.org/10.3167/9781789206289

Pullmann, M. (2009). Diktatura, konsensus a společenská změna. K výkladu komunistické diktatury v českých akademických diskusích po roce 1989 [On the Interpretation of Communist Dictatorship in Czech Academic Discussions after 1989]. In L. Storchová & J. Horský (Eds.), *Paralely, průsečíky, mimoběžky. Teorie, koncepty a pojmy v české a světové historiografii 20. století* [Theories, concepts and terms in twentieth Century Czech and World Historiography] (pp. 231–246). Albis International.

Roubal, P. (2020). *Spartakiads. The politics of physical culture in communist Czechoslovakia.* Karolinum press.

Rychlík, J. (2020). *Československo v období socialismu: 1945–1989.* [Czechoslovakia in the period of socialism: 1945–1989]. Vyšehrad.

Školství na křižovatce: výroční zpráva o stavu a rozvoji výchovně vzdělávací soustavy v letech 1997–1998. (1998). [Education at the crossroads: annual report on the state and development of the educational system in 1997–1998]. Ústav pro informace ve vzdělávání.

Todorova, M. N., & Gille, Z. (Eds.). (2010). *Post-communist nostalgia.* Berghahn Books.

Vaněk, M., & Mücke, P. (2016). *Velvet revolutions: an oral history of Czech society.* Oxford University Press.

Vidovićová, L., Petrová Kafková, M., Hubatková, B., & Galčanová Batista, L. (2018). *Stárnutí na venkově: podoby aktivního stárnutí a kvalita života v rurálních oblastech* [Ageing in rural areas: Forms of active ageing and quality of life in rural areas]. Sociologické nakladatelství (SLON).

Zlatý Ámos. (2023). https://cs.wikipedia.org/wiki/Zlat%C3%BD_%C3%81mos

Zounek, J., Šimáně, M., & Knotová, D. (2016). Cesta k učitelství v socialistickém Československu pohledem pamětníků [The Journey to Teacher Profession in Socialist Czechoslovakia as seen by eyewitnesses]. *Studia paedagogica, 21*(3), 131–159. https://doi.org/10.5817/SP2016-3-7

Zounek, J., Šimáně, M., & Knotová, D. (2017a). *Normální život v nenormální době: základní školy a jejich učitelé (nejen) v období normalizace* [Normal life in not so normal times. Primary schools and their teachers (not only) during the so-called normalization period]. Wolters Kluwer.

Zounek, J., Knotová, D., & Šimáně, M. (2017b). Život Karla – příběh učitele v socialistickém Československu [Karel's Life – The story of a teacher in socialist Czechoslovakia]. *Orbis scholae, 11*(1), 31–52. https://doi.org/10.14712/23363177.2018.56

Chapter 9
Learning and Teaching: The Legacy of the Socialist Era and New Challenges

Abstract The chapter maps the teaching and learning in primary schools as well as the level of equipment in schools (including computers) after the fall of the communist regime in broader contexts. Primarily, the text follows the transformations in teaching and in educational contents, the radical changes in foreign language teaching, and the quality of textbooks published before and after 1989 from the viewpoints of teachers and other eyewitnesses. Teachers faced many challenges in these areas. The chapter shows how variedly the teachers perceive the post-1989 period, as they acquired enormous freedom in their teaching practically from 1 day to the next. The range of teaching aids gradually expanded. For many teachers, it was not easy to cope with the challenges brought by the post-socialist transformation. The eyewitnesses evaluated the pre-1989 unified textbooks and unified content positively. The Velvet Revolution represented the end of some established institutions (e.g. in the field of further teacher education), a change that the narrators evaluated negatively. To some extent, the chapter breaks down the often-cited narrative of fundamental and rapid changes in schools and the entirely new opportunities brought about by the post-communist era. Our research has shown that many changes and innovations were introduced slowly and gradually, and that they needed acceptance from teachers themselves and the support of the school head or the school's founder.

Keywords Schools · Teachers · Teacher education · Teaching · Aids · Equipment · Computer · Foreign language

9.1 On Teaching and Learning

In Czechoslovakia (later in the Czech Republic), the transformation of primary schools after the fall of the communist regime represented a rather complex and complicated process with a number of fields and levels. In previous chapters, we dealt with a range of topics within which we noted the matters of teaching and learning, as well as of school facilities, but not in detail.

© Masaryk University, Faculty of Arts, Registration no. 00216224,
VAT ID: CZ00216224 2024
J. Zounek et al., *(Post)Socialist Transformation of Primary Schools*,
https://doi.org/10.1007/978-3-031-58768-9_9

In the following chapter, we focus specifically on the problems of teaching and learning in primary schools. We follow the key processes that take place in schools and in the environment and equipment of schools. These include textbooks, teaching aids, and the first computers in schools. We build mainly on oral history interviews and on the study of contemporary materials. The methodology we chose allowed us to look into the work of teachers through the eyes of the direct participants. In the Czech Republic, this is probably one of the few opportunities to get an eyewitness look at the everyday events in a school or classroom from that time (socialism and post-socialist transformation of primary schools).[1] Especially for the first years of transformation, there are practically no scientific or evaluation studies that seriously and expertly map the teaching and its transformations (Spilková, 1997; Půl roku nestačí, 1990). This is partly understandable, as the institutions of pedagogical research were also undergoing profound changes during the transformation. Independent and modern empirical educational research only gradually began to establish itself in the 1990s after many years during which pedagogy was subjected to ideology and there was minimum contact with 'Western' science (Kalous, 1990; Průcha, 2013).

The methodology we chose has some limitations. In the Chap. 4 'Schools and Teachers Two Decades Before the Fall of the Communist Regime', we mentioned that it is difficult to talk about past routines or everyday life (Nosková, 2014). In the life of a teacher, teaching itself involves completely routine and constantly repeating activities, but there is nothing special about them or anything that sticks in one's memory. This was true in our previous research: the teachers did not talk much about their own teaching (Zounek et al., 2017). For these reasons, we modified the oral history interview scheme to focus more on teaching and learning problems in their course. We gathered large amounts of data, but we cannot expect to obtain comprehensive (expert) accounts of the teacher's own concept of teaching or of the theoretical principles on which the teachers built their teaching. This was especially true for narrators who were retired for a long time, as the period of separation from the end of their teaching career was longer.

We conducted oral history interviews with teachers from several generations as part of our research. For the earlier-born teachers, the problems of everyday teaching were already far removed from their current lives, and some openly said that they no longer felt up to describing teaching and did not remember many things. This is a perfectly normal functioning of human memory, but it is necessary to take this phenomenon into account in teaching research. Teachers (our narrators) who were still working in schools strongly accentuated the current educational issues or problems of their particular schools. They often put these topics in the context of the post-socialist past or compared the 1990s to the present times. In many cases, it was not clear whether they were talking about the present, the period shortly after 1989, or the situation after 2000. The implementation of the first computers to schools, in

---

[1] The number of eyewitnesses is gradually decreasing; therefore, unfortunately, the opportunities to learn more about school and teaching in the period of post-socialist transformation are also decreasing. That is why it is not a good idea to tarry with research of this kind.

relation to which the narrators had difficulties with the timing of their memories (the deviation was sometimes even up to 10 years) was a typical example of such a lack of clarity. Moreover, in 2004, a completely new School Act[2] was adopted that introduced a major curricular reform. This was another theme that kept emerging in the interviews and thus 'covered' or blurred some memories of the period of transformation.

The timing of the recollections was sometimes very problematic (Yow, 2005). We believe that especially in the case of memories of everyday teaching, it is necessary to take these limitations into account and not to overestimate the possibilities of oral history.

Our research took place during the Covid-19 pandemic, which posed an additional challenge for conducting oral history interviews. Quite understandably, many narrators were sensitive to the situation within their own families, in society, and of course in schools. In the Czech Republic, primary schools were closed for several months and 'online' or 'distance' learning took place. This was very problematic in the early days and became a huge challenge for everyone involved in school education, especially in primary schools. This had an impact on the interviews, with narrators very often referring to 'Covid' teaching in connection with teaching and learning in the past.[3] We consider this situation to be a very important aspect of our research, in which a completely unprecedented situation in the lives of both schools and respondents significantly influenced one topic of our research. We deliberately use the term 'unprecedented' because prior to the Covid-19 pandemic, no one had experienced schools being closed for several months with a long-term absence of classroom teaching. Of course, the Covid-19 pandemic affected all fields of school operations, families, and our research, but the topic of teaching was in a somewhat unusual situation because of the 'empty classrooms'.

Despite all the difficulties with conducting the research, we obtained a whole range of unique pieces of information about teaching in primary schools during the period of transformation. In the following pages, we describe and explain the topics that resonated strongly in the interviews, and we anchor them in broader pedagogical contexts. We conclude the chapter by noting which topics emerged less or not at all in the interviews and attempting to explain why.

---

[2] This law is mentioned in more detail in the Chap. 5 'Transforming the Education System: A Difficult Return to Democratic Europe'. This was the first non-communist Education Act; the previous Act had been in force with many amendments since 1984.

[3] We could not interrupt or postpone our research for several months or years, as we were bound by our contract with the grant agency (we were allowed to extend the project time by 6 months, which at least partially compensated for the problems during the spread of Covid-19). We always conducted interviews during the periods in which the spread of disease had subsided and we could meet the narrators in person or visit them at school. We conducted many interviews in the spring or early autumn.

9.2   The Revolution in Schools (That Didn't Happen)

The life of society, as well as the life of schools and other educational institutions, undoubtedly passed a significant turning point in 1989. Vlasta described the 'revolutionary' nature of some of the changes quite aptly:

> Because everything that existed in the past, all the structures, this was also related to the staffing, the functioning systems … what is associated with the past regime, that has to be destroyed, torn down, to give the opportunity to some new forms in education, and I think nobody realized that these were basically methodological matters. That it was not at all maybe with politics, or maybe partially so, that there was some political stuff that it probably interfered with too, but in mathematics, science, well I understand history, or civics, but of course that could be like quite remedied afterwards.

The reference to the past being 'torn down' might not be the only important thing in that quote, but perhaps more important is what the often radical changes involved. Vlasta was referring to methodology, the didactics of each subject, in short 'how and what to teach' in a given subject. The Revolution also 'rejected' many didactic practices that had little to do with ideology or politics and could still have been used, albeit in an innovated or updated form. Furthermore, Vlasta mentioned differences in content between subjects concerning science and those concerning history, civics, geography, and literature. These subjects were indeed 'affected' by ideology in various ways and required different approaches in the post-revolutionary reforms. In social science subjects, the content of the subject matter was often considerably distorted before 1989. In history, for example, the history of the Soviet Union, the international worker, and the communist movements were disproportionately emphasized, while the national history of Czechs and Slovaks was limited, distorted, or even falsified (Průcha, 2015).

Vlasta mentioned another characteristic – the lack of preparedness for most of the changes of the time, as many of the changes 'were not well thought-out by anyone'. Such sudden changes were not foreseen and no one could have been prepared for them. Czechoslovakia, together with the German Democratic Republic, had a virtually unaffected communist school system in 1989, in which, unlike in other socialist countries, there was virtually no relaxation.

Eliška described the changes in the general concept of primary school in a rather unconventional way:

> In the early days, the revolution in fact meant that the school should not interfere in raising of children. Educate. … Leave the raising to the parents. Because you were raising them in the spirit of Marxism-Leninism. That's not allowed. Just educate, don't raise them up. … But after the revolution, they started their own businesses, the kids were growing up unchecked. Nobody was raising them. Parents didn't have time for it and it was forbidden for the school to do it. So then it was discovered that we should also raise them after all, and it wasn't until the law in 2005 … Raising and education, later just education, but understand that you have to raise them too.

The quote captured the thinking shortly after the revolution, which reflected a desire to 'cut off' the primary school from the unified socialist school, which was an ideological tool of the Communist Party. Once again, these reflections show how unprepared some proposals for change were and how difficult it was to predict the subsequent development in the country. At the same time, it is important to note that Eliška saw the school from the position of an expert on legal issues in the school system.

However, it cannot be overlooked that the ideas mentioned are in line with the broader context of the time. The rejection of the 'unified school' was fully in line with the ideas that corresponded to the globally influential neoliberal ideas of the time. Historian Philipp Ther (2022) wrote: 'From the 1980s onwards, not only was the state withdrawing from the economy, but it also kept leaving increasing portions of health care, nutrition, leisure organization, and child-raising to market forces and individuals' (p. 226). However, the processes of education and raising can hardly be separated from each other, especially in primary education.

Naděžda explained why many changes in teaching could not be as rapid or revolutionary as many had wished:

> So they continued doing what they knew ... there were teachers who had gone through that previous era and didn't know any different, because that's how they were taught. They were used to obeying. They were used to following everything that was there. So the notion that all the students would know their multiplication tables in March – that continued. They didn't have anything under control, those teachers. So basically they were still following some syllabi[4] and there was a set learning plan, a set allocation of hours yeah? For each subject. So that was still followed at that time.

Barbora commented:

> From the viewpoint of pedagogy, ... there I think it was perhaps the easiest because the ideology was removed. And like otherwise, nothing was done to the system, the syllabi were followed, we just simply didn't have to include some of that ideological note in every lesson. Which was a great relief...

Zdeněk added more uncertainty with respect to the syllabi: 'We also didn't know how the curriculum was going to continue, because we had the syllabi, they were classically given, everything was clear, and the syllabi were not bad in my opinion, if I leave out the ideological matters.' Ludmila contributed an interesting perspective: 'The textbooks were always the same, the plans were the same, and I would say that it depended very much on the individual teachers, how they presented it, because even in 10 years, for example, nothing changed in the teaching of history in some schools.'

One cannot be too surprised by such a situation. Until 1989, the Ministry of Education as the central state authority managed practically everything that

---

[4] The syllabi were a normative pedagogical document determining the goals of teaching a subject at a given type and stage of school, the contents of the subject matter, its sequence, and its distribution into different sections of teaching. The syllabi also recommended teaching methods and forms. They were developed separately for the individual subjects. It was a sort of a programme of teaching designed for the teacher. Before 1989, they were the strict norm, and they were criticized for oversizing of content and the resulting overloading of students, even in the 1980s, but no changes occurred because the critics were ignored (Průcha et al., 2009). The syllabi were unified and binding for all teachers.

concerned teaching, whether referring to the goals of teaching, its contents, or the organization of the subject matter, and the activities of teachers and students were also planned and organized in detail. Schools and teachers played the role of implementors of central curricular decisions. This 'protected' the teachers from the difficulties or risks of making independent choices about the subject matter and from expressing personal opinions and preferences (Čerych, 1996). For some teachers, the role of an 'executor' of the will of superior authorities could mean fairly comfortable teaching that required little or none of one's own activity or pedagogical invention, both in preparation for teaching and in the classroom itself. At least in the first years after the fall of the communist government, according to some of our narrators, it was quite possible to continue with such an approach to teaching.

However, the situation was more complex in terms of educational content, lesson planning, and especially the syllabi. While the syllabi meant precise planning of teaching and its contents, they contained opportunities to personalize the teaching, at least if the teacher wanted to. Michal said:

> For a long time, we followed the pre-revolutionary syllabi, because I think they were very well worked out… Because there was the basic part and there was the extra subject matter. So the teacher just had space to manoeuvre. It wasn't like everything was restricted, as was said, that wasn't true.

From the 1991/1992 school year, revised syllabi came into force that created some space for teacher creativity and new methods and forms of work. It was possible to adjust the contents of the syllabi for individual subjects, for example by changing the proportions of the subject matter or by adding or omitting it. However, this modification was considered insufficient and was not much used by teachers (Spilková, 1994).

An eyewitness account of teachers' views on the syllabi was provided by one of the few pedagogical research studies focused on primary schools; the study mapped teachers' views on the syllabi (Spilková, 1994). The research worked with a relatively small sample of teachers (questionnaire survey, 125 respondents in total out of 250 interviewed), but it is nevertheless a valuable source of data. The results showed that about 27% of the questioned teachers did not consider the syllabi necessary. The teachers reported that the syllabi were too restrictive and inflexible, and that they completely ignored the skills and attitudes of the students. Nevertheless, 73% considered the syllabi to be justified. The respondents felt that they served as a sort of a guideline for teachers, they ensured continuity and systematicity of the subject matter or its gradual gradation, and they were necessary for defining the core subject matter.

It is clear that the syllabi, and perhaps more generally the topic of the (new) definition of the goals of education, represented a crucial topic for teachers during the post-socialist transformation. Although there were many changes, in most cases these changes were partial and there was no fundamental re-evaluation of the concept of curriculum or teaching. The factor of time played an important role here, because even as late as 1996, an OECD report stated that most schools had not changed the way they taught. The reasons given for this state were the lack of time, external resources, and expert guidance. According to the report, much of the teaching remained 'frontal' and the students were attributed a passive role (Čerych, 1996). This state of affairs was illustrated by Tomáš: 'For those two or three years there really was nothing at all. There really until '95, one could teach whatever one wanted. One wasn't bound by anything … I found out that a lot of people didn't know the methods of teaching, they tended to use frontal teaching and so on…'. The second part of the quote is especially critical. Teaching methods have always been part of teacher training. We can assume that Tomáš meant that teachers mainly used frontal teaching, during which they communicated 'ready-made' knowledge to students who wrote it down. The teachers then expected the students to be able to reproduce this knowledge. Apparently, the teachers did not use different methods and forms of teaching that would correspond with the particular class, students, subject matter, lesson goals, or topic.

During their entire course, attempts to change and innovate teaching were accompanied by reluctance to change, and the reasons for this could vary. Experience or disillusionment from the past – from pre-1989 – played a part in the rejection of anything resembling indoctrination (Čerych, 1996). However, the school head may also have been a cause of resistance to change. Kryštof went on a two-month study stay in Canada in 1996, where he was able to visit a number of schools because he was acquainted with the local school inspector. He commented on his stay:

> A beautiful study stay, so I took advantage of it, I took it all in with all my senses. I flew back, I came to the school here, the school year was just starting, and the first sentence of the school head was: 'And don't introduce any new things here.' … He was basically eight years away from retirement, and he didn't even want to make any more changes. And in fact, he just spent those eight years here, literally: 'And just let me live this out.' … There was no change at all here from 1989 till 2007. That's almost eighteen years.

This is a fairly common story and may have occurred in many schools: teachers went on a study stay where they picked up a lot of new knowledge and experience that they could use to innovate their own teaching or even the work of the entire school. The reactions of the school heads were interesting: they tended to reject change and innovation for an extremely long period of time. However, the interview with Kryštof revealed that in his case, retirement was not the only reason. The school head was also the mayor of the municipality around 1996 (a job he was partly forced into by surrounding circumstances). According to Kryštof, the school head did not want to make changes in the school that would require money, lest he be accused of disproportionately favouring the school over other necessary municipal expenditures. Such relatively complicated relationships could have influenced changes or innovations in teaching.

The life of primary schools was indeed very diverse and it cannot be said that it was unambiguously focused on maintaining the status quo. Many schools and many teachers were trying to make innovations, both within traditional schools and within the emerging alternative schools.

In the interview, Miroslava described the return of alternative schools in a regional city after the fall of communism:

> It was right in '92 … even the people who had joined those political positions, even from the pedagogical field … a Dalton Pedagogy Centre was established in that neighbourhood… Montessori pedagogy, or an interest in Waldorf pedagogy … the Montessori centre actually started here, and the parents were actually rallying around that and looking for opportunities.

But Zdeněk had this to say on the subject:

> Dalton is connected to that in the beginning, whoever brought something new to that environment had a lot of support from parents. Because they immediately sort of gained the support of the parents because those parents wanted to see something different in that teaching … it also might have had a little bit of a negative impact in the sense that whatever those school heads brought in, those teachers and those parents accepted it uncritically. So again, it wasn't just that everything was totally positive, or maybe we didn't know how to grasp it, yeah?

The enthusiasm for change and the inspirations for innovations or for alternatives could, of course, hide various dangers or weaknesses. These included the uncritical acceptance of new things and, perhaps most important, the lack of preparedness of schools and teachers to implement changes based on the principles of alternative schools. Before 1989, the Czechoslovak school system and actually the entire society had only limited opportunities, if any, to get acquainted with the ideas of alternative schools or with the actual functioning of an alternative school system (Lautnerová, 1990; Pol, 1995; Rýdl, 1994). The uncritical acceptance of new things in those circumstances may not have brought the expected improvements, but rather embarrassment or even misunderstandings.

The role of parents and their acceptance of innovations in education should be considered. In particular, any more intensive involvement of parents in the running of schools (the creation of communities) did not seem to have been given proper space in the transforming post-communist country, because the dominant neoliberal ideas tended to favour individual personal success. Therefore, in the Czech environment, the ideas of alternative pedagogy based on community cooperation may have met with misunderstanding and eventually gained less ground.

9.3   Textbooks: New Possibilities and the Free Market

Textbooks are closely related to the topic of syllabi and subject matter, and they were a topic that resonated very strongly in the memory of our narrators. The narrators talked about the quality and the use of textbooks, but also about new textbooks and the advent of the market environment into the production and sales of textbooks.

As with the syllabi, there was quite a strong legacy of communism here and a number of continuities from that period can be observed. Before 1989, the state had a monopoly on the production of textbooks, which were published overwhelmingly by the State Pedagogical Publishing House (Státní pedagogické nakladatelství). This ensured control over both the production and the contents of textbooks. The teachers could not choose; textbooks were allocated to schools according to the number of students, who received textbooks and teaching aids free of charge. Before 1989, textbooks for individual subjects were often created by top experts or scientists, but they usually did not have knowledge of the specific nature of children's learning in primary school. On the other hand, teachers with experience in schools had only a limited influence on the development of syllabi and textbooks (Průcha, 2015). The contents of textbooks were often oversized and had an encyclopaedic character; students could be overwhelmed with information, which was often irrelevant, isolated, too abstract, and not connected to specific ideas.

The unified educational programmes and the only and 'compulsory' school textbooks derived from them ensured uniformity and comparability of teaching in the Czech environment (and elsewhere in Central and Eastern Europe) when there was no standardized measure of student performance or comparison of results between schools (Čerych, 1996).

Stanislava described a common way to use a textbook: 'We were still used from before that the textbook was dogma and that I have to go through a textbook, and here from this page to that page, and these exercises, and I have to go through all of this.' The narrator criticized the manner in which textbooks were used, which was apparently widespread. Considering some of the features of textbooks at the time, it is not surprising that frontal teaching, i.e. handing over ready-made information to students in order to be able to 'go through' everything, prevailed.[5] It is not surprising that some students could not handle the material, were passive, could not apply the knowledge functionally, and might have lost the meaning of learning. Naděžda described the teachers' work with the textbook from the perspective of a school inspector:

> At first, they kept searching for what was in the syllabi. So because they were used to the fact that the textbook was following the syllabi and that the subject matter was in the textbook. And it wasn't in those new textbooks. Or it was arranged differently. And those teachers didn't like it at first because they also really had to learn what to do and how and what to choose. And now, you know, it was such an onslaught, a lot of publishing houses were publishing textbooks, and it was quite expensive, and now which one to choose?

Here, Naděžda captured several legacies or continuities from the pre-1989 era and dilemmas at the same time quite well. The teachers were accustomed to following and proceeding according to a unified plan. The subject matter was contained in the unified syllabi. However, in the new textbooks, the subject matter may have been structured, explained, or processed differently. At the time of the transformation, it was expected that the new textbooks would be used, but sometimes they did not suit the teachers' needs. Although the old textbooks suited the teachers, in many respects, the old textbooks no longer met the requirements of the time, either by being too detailed or by being out of date.

---

[5] This is also shown in the school chronicles, in which, at the end of school years, we often found statements saying that the syllabi 'have been gone through'.

However, the opinions of our narrators were quite diverse. Michal evaluated the textbooks published before 1989 while emphasizing their content from the point of view of pedagogical elaboration in particular:

I don't think that the textbooks that existed before the revolution were all bad. There were a lot of good ideas, and they paid attention to didactics. Which was abandoned a lot after the revolution. Because those who paid attention to didactics were not modern, they were fossilized…I think that not much has changed in terms of the approach to those children, and that those children still need adequacy, consistency…I'm not saying that the examples were bad, but it would be enough to replace the pioneers with the scouts, and the example was again appropriate.

Michal was talking about the mathematics textbook, an example of a subject that was not as influenced by the pre-1989 ideology as history, literature and geography. Records from school chronicles indicated that in some schools, history and civics textbooks were withdrawn from teaching in the last grades as early as December 1989. For example, schools were expected to conclude the teaching of history in eighth grade with 1945 and the results and effects of World War II (Instrukce…, 1990).

However, as Naděžda mentioned, after some time, the teachers were faced with another, completely new challenge. This was the selection of new textbooks. Many were no longer written according to the traditional syllabi, so the content or structure may have been different. Gradually, private publishing houses specializing in textbooks were set up, and the sale of textbooks became a fairly lucrative business, with schools targeted by various marketing campaigns and salespeople coming to schools to offer textbooks and teaching aids. Schools did not have large budgets, and, with the advent of self-governance, the purchase of textbooks was their own responsibility. All of this represented a completely new phenomenon for school heads and teachers.

Barbora explained the situation from the position of a school head:

In those first years, there was only the State Pedagogical Publishing House. They supplied us. And then, when we had the full self-governance, we could choose either to order from them or from the new publishing houses. But in 1995, there weren't that many private publishing houses. I think that started later … and then it took off, it started growing like mushrooms after the rain.

In relation to this situation, the OECD report (Čerych, 1996) commented that political decisions made after 1989 gave schools more freedom in curricular matters and in the choice of textbooks than was usual in many other OECD countries at the time.

With the emergence of the textbook market, the problem of textbook quality emerged; after 1989, the Ministry of Education largely lost control over textbook production and there was no evaluation or regulation of textbooks. For these reasons, an 'approval clause' was introduced for textbooks and other teaching texts.[6]

---

[6]The approval clause was granted by the MEYS based on an assessment of whether the textbooks and teaching texts submitted were compliant with the educational goals set out in the Education Act, curricular documents, and legislation. Its purpose was primarily informational. It provided users of a given textbook or a teaching text with information that the above conditions were met from the point of view of the MEYS. Textbooks went through an evaluation process coordinated

In the 1990s, completely new textbooks were produced and old textbooks were also reissued, 'cleansed' of ideological ballast. For example, 'sir' was used instead of 'comrade' to address people, militant examples disappeared (counting tanks in mathematics), and some paragraphs on the history of the Communist Party were omitted. Some new textbooks were published quite soon after 1989: 'These two reading books were published very quickly... and there they actually very promptly they published all those authors who were once banned. That was published quickly, I don't know, that was maybe in '91' (Barbora). This included Czechoslovak authors who lived in exile during communism and whose works were banned in Czechoslovakia before 1989, and who therefore did not appear in literature text-books. The authors who still lived in socialist Czechoslovakia, but whose (older) books were out of print and not available in shops or libraries because of their views were in a similar position (Janoušek, 2008).

Our narrators also talked about the quality of textbooks and compared the old textbooks with new ones:

> The supply was huge, but one had to be selective to truly find textbooks of good quality. Often, one would rather go back to the 'textbooks' that were published during socialism, that those were the best in terms of content. Even in terms of, for example, practice, exercises, examples ... and there were mistakes in those new textbooks, for example. Yeah? Factual, ... grammatical, the exercises are inconsistent, right? The answer to that question ... is just ambiguous. (Antonín)

This remark proved that some form of textbook verification and evaluation was necessary. In fact, the uneven quality of textbooks was highlighted in a 1996 OECD report that said that 'it is likely that some of the texts published in the past few years are substandard' (p. 129). Perhaps this was also why some narrators remembered the 'socialist' textbooks with nostalgia.

9.4   Aids and Equipment in Schools – A Good Basis of a Socialist School

Jan Průcha (2015), one of the most prominent Czech scholars and experts in the field of pedagogy and schooling, said that the improvement of material and technical equipment of schools and classrooms was among the relatively positive features of the primary school system before 1989. We can agree with this, but we must keep in mind that Czechoslovak schools could only develop within the 'socialist bloc' in this field. In the Chap. 4 'Schools and Teachers Two Decades Before the Fall of the Communist Regime', we described how some teachers created their own teaching aids before 1989, motivated by a desire to improve their teaching and also by the

---

by the Ministry, in the course of which they were assessed by expert reviewers who made recommendations (textbooks may be returned for corrections, etc.). The schools could even use textbooks without this clause as long as they did not contradict the above regulations. The selection and use of textbooks was decided by the school head.

non-existent or very limited offer of teaching aids. In some schools, skilful teachers even made their own furniture.

Barbora commented on school equipment in an interesting way:

> In primary schools, I would say that after '90, it still worked on its own somehow, that we used some of that technology, usually some overhead projectors[7] … I think that the basic classroom equipment, chairs, desks, benches, I don't think there was any major shift. Despite all the complaints I have about the school system before 1989, I think that quite a lot of attention was paid to ergonomics, to healthy development.

To some extent, the opinion of the former school head Barbora confirmed the assertion made by Průcha (2015) about the gradual improvement of school equipment even before 1989. The ergonomics-related matters go beyond the scope of our research, but it was certainly interesting to explore this topic as well. Michal was also satisfied with the school equipment, and additionally explained how the central allocation of equipment to schools worked:

> Because it was a large primary school, there was an institution called the Středisko služeb školám (School Services Centre) that operated before the revolution and supplied aids according to the size of the schools. So, all the aids that were suitable from the point of view of the Ministry of Education were produced by the Comenius cooperative … the aids were distributed to the schools according to the number of students … And other aids were obtained because of the contacts we had at the universities, colleagues helped us a lot there, for example when they were disposing of something …, so we took a lot of things like gauges, transformers from the universities, and this helped us a lot.

Aids were centrally allocated based on student numbers, so some narrators recalled that large schools had an advantage because they could get more equipment and aids than smaller schools with fewer students because of the distribution methodology. Such a system can be considered somewhat unfair. It is interesting to note the cooperation with universities, which provided schools with discarded equipment so that teachers had relatively good equipment even in primary schools, even though it may have been older equipment.

As with textbooks, after 1989, the market for teaching aids opened up; the state monopoly was dissolved and many companies producing new aids were set up. There were similar problems with quality and even with the safety of the aids.

> So from personal experience, for example, from working in a kindergarten. We never really suffered from not having enough things and things of very good quality for the children. We made a lot of stuff ourselves, but that's part of the environment there, but really it was always secure. And after '90, those central supplies were abolished, and companies that offered all sorts of aids started popping up, but those aids were often not tested from the point of view of safety. They were just likeable. So it was all sorts of, like, plastic things that were, like, even dangerous. Because the kids could swallow it, and these companies would go to these schools… (Naděžda)

---

[7]An overhead projector is a simple analogue projector used to project transparent material ('foils' or 'transparencies') onto a wall or a projection screen. The projection could replace the blackboard, and the teacher could prepare materials before class. Markers would be used to write on the foils, and, in the age of laser printers, it was even possible to print on the foils. For more information, see for example: https://en.wikipedia.org/wiki/Overhead_projector

Although the narrator described the situation in kindergartens, it can be assumed that similar situations could have occurred in primary schools (in terms of the safety of some equipment), especially in the first stage.

> In the primary schools, when we were going there, in those years, the teachers' rooms, … were crammed with pictures for teaching, those laboratories for chemistry, for physics and so on. So from the old days I would say there was some basic equipment there, but it needed upgrading, renewal … and from what I remember, the school heads usually complained that they lacked the money to do it. (Naděžda)

Naděžda visited many schools as a school inspector and perceived the equipment as good, but in need of updating. This is of course quite common, but at that time, it was difficult to implement. First, the central supply system had broken down and the free market affected the manufacture of aids, making the situation more complicated. In addition, the schools were not used to company marketing or direct sales in schools. Also, schools often did not have adequate resources to purchase new and often quite expensive aids. However, Naděžda's view may suggest that the equipment in schools was indeed good for the time and the central supply of aids had worked well. Of course, the situation cannot be generalized based on our data. In our previous research focused on primary schools before 1989 (Zounek et al., 2017), some narrators talked about the very poor condition of equipment, for example in small or rural schools. The poorly established system of the central allocation of aids was not necessarily the reason for this state of affairs; another reason could be a school head who did not pay due attention to this field.

9.5 Computers in Primary Schools: The First Shy Steps

Czechoslovakia and all the socialist countries of the 'Eastern bloc' were quite a bit behind the developed countries in terms of the development of computers (Flury & Geiss, 2023[8]), sometimes by as much as 10 years. The situation was made more difficult by the impossibility to import computers or other didactic equipment from 'Western' countries. Despite all the handicaps, Czechoslovakia was virtually the best of the socialist bloc countries. Computers were getting into Czechoslovak schools already before 1989, although their use and the speed of their spread was

---

[8] The book How Computers Entered the Classroom, 1960–2000 (Flury & Geiss, 2023) traces the implementation of computers in several European countries. However, it also follows the activities of international organizations in this direction (OECD, UNESCO). Regarding the focus of our book, the chapters on introducing computers into schools in Hungary (Somogyvári et al., 2023) and Latvia (Kestere & Purina-Bieza, 2023) are interesting. These countries belonged to the Eastern Bloc, and the technology implementation processes in schools showed many similar features. However, the chapters mentioned above cover the period up to the late 1980s and do not focus specifically on primary schools.

not great. After 1989, when the borders and the electronics markets opened, computers permeated primary schools relatively slowly (Zounek et al., 2022).[9]

This state of affairs was evidenced by Adam: 'I think at that time … the 1990s, of course, the information technology was gradually getting into schools, but I think the development of information technology occurred there only after 2000. In that education office, I don't recall having to actually deal with equipping any classrooms with information technology …' Similarly to the situation with educational aids, equipping schools with computers[10] varied. For example, Kryštof looked into his records during the interview and he was able to exactly determine when they had their first computer lab: 'And since the first of September 1995, we have our first computer lab. It was called 'didaktik', the computer, and we even still had the 'IQ 151' here.[11] That was kind of a push-button computer, so that's when we started with the computers, that hard drive had a memory of twenty megabytes. And that was some machine.' Although we do not have any quantitative data on the equipment of schools with computers or computer labs in the mid-1990s for Czechoslovakia, we can estimate that Kryštof's was one of the few primary schools so equipped, at least in the South Moravian Region. Kryštof was the narrator who claimed that nothing changed in the school when he was there for many years because of the school head. Computers were big news, but they did not seem to have made any major impact on teaching at the time, which may be why Kryštof perceived the school as if no major changes had occurred. It is one thing to have a computer lab; it is a different thing to use computers in teaching. The use of computers in teaching was very limited even a few years after the fall of communism. In this case, we are referring here to teaching of subjects such as history, mathematics, and chemistry (Zounek, 2006).

Stanislava added: 'The first computers in school were not for teaching subjects at all, but only for computer science, when it started, so when someone got there, it was the kids in the computer science classes, because none of the other teachers could even operate the technology.' When the narrators talked about the introduction of computers into schools, most of them found it very difficult to determine even approximately when they first encountered computers in school for the first time or when they had their first trainings. This is because the first computers were not in computer labs; they were used for administrative purposes. Stanislava: 'I think so, it was just computers here somewhere in the school head's office, but that

---

[9] Even before 1989, there was a lively discussion in Czechoslovakia about the use of (learning) machines or technology in education, about what roles computers could play in teaching, and what the division of labour between the machine and the teacher could be. These discussions were based on psychological and pedagogical viewpoints (Zounek et al., 2018).

[10] We deliberately use the word 'computer' because these computers were not connected to the Internet. Czechoslovakia was only connected to the Internet in 1992, but schools were connected gradually and later.

[11] The school microcomputer IQ 151 G, Didaktik Alfa, was produced in Czechoslovakia. However, these computers did not reach the parameters of computers produced to the west. More information at: https://en.wikipedia.org/wiki/IQ_151

was about it. That, that not at all … at the beginning, computers were actually not even in the teachers' rooms.'

The same narrator described what she used the computer for in school and how knowing how to use it advanced her career:

> But when we're on the subject of computers here, that was one of the reasons why I actually got to this, to the opportunity to be a deputy school head. Basically, because of my husband, they had computers at work … so I was one of the few, or the first teachers, who knew how to use the computer and could do various things on it, I even dared to do some graphics, because of my husband, and I actually started subtly, at first just as a helper, making various signs for the classrooms, for the bulletin boards, just electronically … We even made a school magazine and by being able to do that, well, someone like that was needed. It wasn't the school head who would be on speaking terms with the technology… (Stanislava)

The knowledge of computer work could be a career boost and it also meant a significant shift in document processing in the school, as well as a completely innovative approach to creation of documents for the purposes of the external presentation of the school. This could have meant a great advantage for the narrator and for the entire school, which could thus be considered very innovative. The mention of a school head who did not know how to use a computer well was significant because school heads determined what money would be allocated to, and therefore whether computers would be purchased for the school. During the 1990s, school heads did not have much support in this area, if any. Moreover, even after 2000, when the national information policy in education gradually took off and schools started to get collectively equipped with computers, school heads did not have an opportunity to receive training or to use specific support in this respect. The trainings were primarily focused on (basic) computer skills and the use of teaching programs (available on CDs or DVDs) (Zounek et al., 2022).

Stanislava expressed herself very eloquently on the topic of using computers in teaching:

> Fundamentally really, with the word fundamentally really fitting there, teaching methods changed a lot with the advent of technology … it actually helps us a lot, neither the children nor we have to copy so much stuff, we don't have to be so dependent on the textbook all the time when we practice, and the interactiveness has one big advantage: the kids have fun with it.

The narrator moved from the past to the present in this statement very quickly, but this quote nevertheless suggests reasons for the involvement of computers in teaching even in the early days. Stanislava returned to the early days of computer use in the next part of the interview:

> It was the time of computers, the computers were beginning and for the students, English was kind of a gateway to that world of computers. To understand the terms, and they enjoyed it. That English at that beginning, when it started in that school, was such a popular subject, and I admit that Czech and history weren't quite what those kids wanted to learn.

9.6   Foreign Language Teaching: Clear Direction, Difficult Implementation

Another important topic in the lives of teachers and one of the key themes of the entire transformation of the school system in Czechoslovakia was undoubtedly the teaching of foreign languages. The compulsory teaching of Russian was replaced by a free choice of one world language, and it was possible to choose English, German, French, or Russian. The number of hours of teaching of these subjects also increased.

Ludmila pointed out an important matter: 'Such a fundamental change, 1989–90, November, so suddenly in January it was already clear that there would be competitive selections for a new school head and that the concept of the individual schools would be different. Especially in terms of foreign language teaching.' Pressure was also exerted by parents for an almost immediate change in the foreign language teaching. In particular, they demanded the end or reduction of Russian language teaching and an introduction of one of the Western languages, predominantly English. This was evidenced by archival documents stored in the National Archives of the Czech Republic as well as by contemporary pedagogical press (K výuce..., 1990). The Ministry of Education allowed schools to replace the teaching of Russian with another world language at the second stage of primary school. The choice of language depended on the staffing of the school; if conditions allowed, schools could implement this change as early as 1 February 1990. The Ministry of Education was apparently already overwhelmed by requests for changes in the foreign language teaching at the end of 1989 and beginning of 1990, because we found a number of requests not only from parents but also from school heads in the National Archives. The Ministry of Education was unable to respond to all of them individually and referred to the instruction it sent to the education departments.[12]

However, the schools encountered several problems in this field. Acquisition of English teachers, who were practically absent from the schools at that time because English was taught only in some schools, usually in schools with extended language teaching, was indeed a major challenge. In addition, our narrators spoke about the fact that those who could speak English after 1989 (including English teachers) did not go work in the school system, but found much better jobs with higher earnings, because there was a huge shortage of such people at that time. This was related to the influx of foreign companies, institutions, and banks to Czechoslovakia, as they were looking for such people with language skills. Hynek added to this: 'With language teachers, another change. We didn't have an English teacher, they all taught Russian. And then, bang, we were among the first here to start with English classes. So what now?! How to get one?' The situation was similar in many schools, as we saw similar information in school chronicles and in inspection reports.

The English language tutors who were coming to Czechoslovakia after the Velvet Revolution to help with language teaching was another big topic. This was a huge

---

[12] Archive fond of the Ministry of Education of the CSR (1990). Carton 819, signature 17A. National Archives of the Czech Republic.

help for the schools, but the potential of this help was not fully utilized for one main reason – many of the tutors had no pedagogical training and therefore their language teaching was quite problematic. Jana described the topic very briefly: 'English tutors, but there the school was just unlucky when it came to the tutors, because they were people of various professions, even students sometimes, yeah? Those were probably more into the adventure of getting to know the country, I guess, but they did not know how to teach.' Irma had a similar experience:

> The school head hired a tutor. The parents were thrilled. For the first month or two. They didn't know how to teach. They just talked to them. Then when the kids took English tests, when they went to language grammar schools, they didn't know anything! They could communicate. But we do grammar tests at school entrance exams...

In the end, Irma taught grammar and other language skills according to the plan, using the textbook and other common tools. The foreign tutor only taught conversation. As Irma added: 'He never opened a textbook in his life. And our school system was definitely not prepared for this and it is not built for this.'

The teacher shortage was addressed by retraining Russian language teachers, which was done very quickly in many respects, so that some retrained teachers admitted to being only one or two lessons ahead of their students. 'It's just been a crazy upheaval I would say, from year to year, well let's say from week to week, they drop Russian and introduce English. So those Russian teachers, to make a living, well, they had to do those courses quickly over the holidays and like that' (Irma).

The school inspectorate tolerated the fact that foreign languages were taught by unqualified teachers in the first years after the fall of communism. However, some inspection reports pointed out this problem as early as in 1990, and the inspectorate even ordered the school head to address the situation. Initially, even a Matura exam from a foreign language or a basic language state examination sufficed. Stanislava described it as follows: 'At first, even having a Matura exam from English was enough. And there was no one else, so the head office had the opportunity to train that person.' During an interview, when we asked how an unqualified teacher could handle teaching, she replied:

> Quite simply. The English textbooks have always been accompanied by methodologies for teachers, and the lessons were practically created by the experts who compile the textbooks, so one actually got a clear idea of the parts of the teaching plan that had to be completed. At that level, what they are supposed to teach these kids ... really the level of English at the primary school can commonly be handled by any skilful grammar school student who knows the language. It's really not that hard there... (Stanislava)

However, the quality of such teaching remained a question, and dealing with disciplinary problems etc. could be problematic. However, at that time, many schools did not have much choice and often had to choose very non-standard solutions or procedures.

Language textbooks constituted the last interesting topic. We have already mentioned textbooks, but language textbooks were somewhat specific. Foreign textbooks began to permeate Czechoslovakia in increasing numbers. According to some of our narrators, the older Czech textbooks lacked audio recordings. These were usually included only with the new textbooks. Teachers had to study the entire textbooks in order to use them in their teaching, to know the texts, the nature of the exercises, the contents of the recordings, etc. They also studied the methodological manuals that were included in the new textbooks. Many of the textbooks were original foreign publications that were completely in English, including methodologies and other supporting materials. This, of course, sometimes caused problems not only for the students but also for those teachers who taught English, for example, shortly after retraining.

9.7   Further Teacher Education: The Old System Has to Be Abolished, But What Next?

Further teacher education was the last major topic that emerged in our data. We found a number of continuities or legacies from communism in the memories of our narrators in this field as well. The narrators who had taken further education courses before 1989 praised many of the training events, both in terms of the topics and the quality of the courses.

Some narrators emphasized that the events were focused on the methodology of teaching of the given subject or they concerned presentations of (scientific) innovations in the field. Tomáš described the further education of history teachers: 'Before the very year '89, he was an ordinary teacher and he did actually those methodological courses through the department of education.[13] These were related to the region, for example, or to certain chapters of history, and it was really worth going and doing that course or that training … And he invited excellent people. From different faculties, he invited archaeologists … So in that way it was very well done. … then in the nineties, those institutions were disbanded.'

Michal shared a similar experience: 'I would say that before the revolution, the quality was good, it was run by good methodologists … as a young teacher, I was sent to these methodological meetings, but I have to say that they were very good, so the training of these teachers was worked on. And in mathematics I must say it was top class.' Our narrators evaluated the further education similarly, for example in music education, where they directly praised the personalities who led the courses in question.

The Velvet Revolution marked the end of the entire system of further education, which was, of course, centrally controlled. The further education also included ideological-political education, which was understandably quickly abolished after 1989. Perhaps even this 'political' part of further education was one of the reasons

---

[13] Before 1989, it was impossible for someone to organize teacher training independently. Such an event always had to be sponsored and approved, for example, by the department of education of the relevant authority.

why the entire system of education was abolished, because it was perceived as a part of ideological education. Vlasta explained what happened then:

> The year '89 absolutely destroyed it, except for five regional centres, which were renamed as pedagogical centres …completely new education agencies or various institutions started to be established 'from scratch', nobody had any idea of how many of them there were, what they actually offered, nobody monitored the quality, didn't even have a basis for it, yeah? So this state of affairs lasted until about the mid-nineties. When basically nobody had an idea of who was teaching what, who was offering what. If it's a high-quality programme, if it's not.

Undoubtedly, this created a very 'interesting' situation, which can be characterized by the word 'chaos' or once again by the motto that accompanied all the chapters mapping the situation in primary schools after 1989 – 'anything was possible'. One of our narrators remarked that after the revolution, nobody really wanted any further education. Vlasta said:

> Those school heads were just thrown into the water, because they were responsible for efficient spending of money… … I remember that quality was a big problem there. Well, and so then sometime in the mid-1990s, there were actually attempts on the part of the ministry to regulate that, so that at least some conditions would be set for drawing money for educational courses for the further education of the teaching staff. So they started addressing what these funds would be spent on, money is always the most important, so it has to go through some kind of check at least in the initial phase. And that was actually the check of the ministry when the accreditations of educational programmes and educational events were introduced.[14]

From today's view, it is remarkable how little experience school heads and other people involved in further teacher education had at the time, and, at the same time, what a positive role the school inspectorate played.

> From an inspection point of view, when I take it back, when we, for example, found during those teacher observations that those new forms and methods of work were not being applied in teaching at all, we usually asked and wanted it documented, because even such education is financed by the state, so we asked how those school heads influence the further teacher education in their school concepts … but they were choosing it without considering the effectiveness and what benefit it would have for that teaching. And we were always convincing those school heads, well if you see that the teachers can't change the approach, can't open up the teaching so that they could just maybe offer some of that project-based learning to those children so that they could participate in it, so that he would know how to do it, okay? Self-reflection. Feedback from students. That was completely lagging. They didn't do that with the kids at all. So we said: Focus the further education in that direction, so that it improves the effectiveness of the teaching. And then the school head usually said: That's right, we didn't think of that. We could do that. (Naděžda)

Further teacher education was developing very dynamically in foreign languages, where there was a range of opportunities. Teachers could participate in training

---

[14] Accreditation refers to an authorization for a certain activity or verification and recognition of such authorization. It can often be synonymous with obtaining a license. Accreditation of a study programme refers to the authorization of an institution, such as an educational institution, to admit students and to teach and issue diplomas in a particular field/course/topic. Its purpose is to ensure an acceptable quality of teaching, teacher qualification, etc.

courses organized directly in Czechoslovakia, and later in the Czech Republic, in which foreign experts in the teaching of a given language (in particular English, French, and German) taught. There were also a number of opportunities to travel abroad to courses and stays of varying lengths, which were, at least by our narrators, evaluated mostly positively. Teachers were not only learning how to teach a foreign language, but they were learning about the culture of the country and meeting colleagues from abroad, which had very positive effects on their teaching and on the development of their personalities and contacts. For some of them, it was the first opportunity to travel to a country in which the language they were teaching was spoken. Czech universities also contributed significantly to further teacher education, and not only in foreign languages.

9.8   Looking Back at the Interviews

We found it very interesting to peek into the teachers' workshops, even though it was a mediated glimpse that could never replace direct observation in a real lesson. However, with regard to our topic, the interviews and the research of contemporary sources provided at least a partial insight into everyday life after the fall of communism. With a certain degree of exaggeration, everything was in motion; at the same time, many things remained unchanged or changed very slowly. Perhaps the everyday reality of the individual schools and teachers remains somewhat hidden behind the narrative of great changes in society and in the structure of the school system. The everyday reality is fading from memory rather quickly. In this chapter, we have tried to show that everyday reality on the basis of the available options of our methodology.

We conclude the chapter with a brief look at what, based on our previous research, we expected to appear in the data but did not actually appear. We have discussed the possible reasons the narrators did not talk much about everyday teaching at the beginning of this chapter. We also described the circumstances (Covid-19) that undoubtedly influenced our research. However, there are still a few 'surprises' from which we cannot draw any generalizing conclusions for the teacher population in Czechoslovakia. On the other hand, many of our findings, for example, complement or partially develop some of the conclusions of the 1996 OECD report (Čerych, 1996).

Looking at the work of teachers, we expected to learn more from our narrators about their preparation for teaching, how the availability of new resources and scientific knowledge changed their preparations, and how the innovative practices permeated lesson planning, as the new impulses for teaching were allowed to spread freely into Czechoslovakia. While the narrators did mention, for example, project-based learning (albeit in passing), a constructivist teaching approach did not appear in the interviews. Likewise, only a few teachers mentioned that they had been involved in any innovative movement or participated in reform activities, even if only at the local level. We noted that the school heads had the role of pedagogical leaders only very rarely, if at all. The narrators tended to talk about competitive selections, replacements of school heads, and increased responsibility, but we rarely registered that the school heads also led the school in the field of education, approaches to learning, and pedagogical innovation. Perhaps this can be explained by the situation in the period of transformation, in which economic and staffing matters prevailed over pedagogical ones. Moreover, school heads did not have any significant support in their role as pedagogical leaders. Thus, for example, there was only 'functional training' after 1989, and it was criticized; more systematic education of school heads was only gradually discussed (Štefflová, 1990). The narrators said relatively little about any teacher education they received. To some extent, it is interesting that in the field of teaching, the interviews focused on syllabi or textbooks, but topics such as the personal development of students appeared in the narrators' memories rather infrequently and very little was said about the development of communication skills, creativity, independence, and responsibility of students. Of course, this may be due to the manner in which the interviews were conducted or because in the 1990s, these topics gradually made their way into further education or everyday practice in schools. The established teaching methods did not change as quickly as, for example, the school equipment.

In addition, any deviation from the established teaching practices or any growth of pedagogical autonomy of schools and of teachers put increased demands on the profession of a teacher. The search for new teaching practices requires the ability to make reasoned choices, well-thought-out textbook selection, often preparation of one's own teaching materials, etc. Teachers work in a social environment and changes in teaching also require collegial communication – joint discussions with colleagues (Purkyně, 1990) and also the ability to explain one's own concept of teaching to parents. These and many other processes are usually not 'revolutionary' in nature, but they require time and gradual change. Perhaps this is why teachers did not talk about them in the interviews. Rather, they talked about individual or incremental changes, or these were processes that were long-term and so much a part of everyday life that they were not part of our narrators' memories. However, we cannot rule out clinging to established practices and resistance to change, as some narrators described themselves as 'conservatives'. Last but not least, the narrators' attitudes themselves may have evolved over time. In the 30 years or so between the period of post-socialist transformation and the time of the interviews, young teachers who were eager to innovate may have become supporters of established and unchanging practices. This may have influenced the nature of the interviews and the form in which they remembered the period we studied. Indeed, some narrators themselves acknowledged an evolution of their attitudes.

We are focusing on a period in which an unreasonable central oversight and ordering or standardizing had been abolished, but a fundamentally new curriculum model had not even been proposed yet, nor had clear ideas about the vision of the school system and education been articulated. This was particularly true in the first half of the 1990s, after which the work on fundamental reform began to intensify considerably.

Bibliography

Čerych, L. (1996). *Zprávy o národní politice ve vzdělávání: Česká republika* [Reports on National Educational Policy: the Czech Republic.]. Ústav pro informace ve vzdělávání. (English version of the OECD report is available at: https://eric.ed.gov/?id=ED420583)

Flury, C., & Geiss, M. (Eds.). (2023). *How computers entered the classroom, 1960–2000*. De Gruyter Oldenbourg. https://doi.org/10.1515/9783110780147

Instrukce [Instructions]. (1990). *Učitelské noviny, 93*(1), 6.

Janoušek, P. (Ed.). (2008). *Dějiny české literatury 1945–1989* [History of Czech literature 1945–1989]. (IV., 1969–1989). Academia.

K výuce cizích jazyků [On the Teaching of Foreign Languages]. (1990). *Učitelské noviny, 93*(5), 2.

Kalous, J. (1990). Pedagogický výzkum [Pedagogical Research]. *Učitelské noviny, 93*(7), 1.

Kestere, I., & Purina-Bieza, K. E. (2023). Computers in the classrooms of an authoritarian country: The case of soviet Latvia (1980s–1991). In *Computers in the classrooms of an authoritarian country: The case of soviet Latvia (1980s–1991)* (pp. 75–98). De Gruyter Oldenbourg. https://doi.org/10.1515/9783110780147-004

Lautnerová, M. (1990). Říkají jim waldorfské [They call them Walldorfian]. *Učitelské noviny, 93*(19), 5.

Nosková, J. (2014). *Biografická metoda a metoda orální historie: na příkladu výzkumu každodenního života v socialismu* [The biographical method and the Oral history method: An example of research on everyday life during socialism]. Etnologický ústav AV ČR, v.v.i.

Pol, M. (1995). *Waldorfské školy: izolovaná alternativa, nebo zajímavý podnět pro jiné školy?* [Waldorf Schools: An Isolated Alternative or an Interesting Incentive for Other Schools?]. Masarykova univerzita.

Průcha, J. (2013). 20 years of the Czech educational research association: History and challenges. *Pedagogická orientace, 23*(6), 848–860. https://doi.org/10.5817/PedOr2013-6-848

Průcha, J. (2015). *Česká vzdělanost: multidisciplinární pohled na fenomén národní kultury* [Czech education: A multidisciplinary view of the phenomenon of National Culture]. Wolters Kluwer.

Průcha, J., Walterová, E., & Mareš, J. (2009). *Pedagogický slovník* [Pedagogical Dictionary]. Portál.

Půl roku nestačí [Half a Year is not Enough]. (1990). *Učitelské noviny, 93*(24), 1.

Purkyně, J. (1990). Tak potřebný team-work [So necessary team-work]. *Učitelské noviny, 93*(17), 3.

Rýdl, K. (1994). *Alternativní pedagogické hnutí v současné společnosti* [The alternative pedagogical movement in contemporary society]. Marek Zeman.

Somogyvári, L., Szabó, M., & Képes, G. (2023). How computers entered the classroom in Hungary: A long journey from the late 1950s into the 1980s. In *How computers entered the classroom in Hungary: A long journey from the late 1950s into the 1980s* (pp. 39–74). De Gruyter Oldenbourg. https://doi.org/10.1515/9783110780147-003

Spilková, V. (1994). *Standardy na 1. stupni ZŠ očima PAU* [Standards at the 1st stage of primary School in the Eyes of PAU]. Agentura Strom.

Spilková, V. (1997). *Proměny primární školy a vzdělávání učitelů v historicko-srovnávací perspektivě* [Transformations of primary school and teacher education in a historical comparative perspective]. Pedagogická fakulta Univerzity Karlovy.

Štefflová, J. (1990). Víme, co chceme? [Do we know what we want?]. *Učitelské noviny, 93*(28), 4.

Ther, P. (2022). *Jiný konec dějin: eseje o velké transformaci po roce 1989* [The other end of history: Essays on the great transformation after 1989]. Univerzita Karlova, nakladatelství Karolinum.

Yow, V. R. (2005). *Recording oral history: A guide for the humanities and social sciences*. AltaMira.

Zounek, J. (2006). *ICT v životě základních škol [ICT in the lives of primary schools]*. Triton.

Zounek, J., Šimáně, M., & Knotová, D. (2017). *Normální život v nenormální době. Základní školy a jejich učitelé (nejen) v období normalizace* [Normal life in not so normal times. Primary schools and their teachers (not only) during the so-called normalization period]. Wolters Kluwer.

Zounek, J., Záleská, K., Juhaňák, L., Bárta, O., & Vlčková, K. (2018). Czech Republic and Norway on their path to digital education. *Studia Paedagogica, 23*(4), 11–48. https://doi.org/10.5817/SP2018-4-2

Zounek, J., Juhaňák, L., & Záleská, K. (2022). *Life and Learning of Digital Teens. Adolescents and digital technology in the Czech Republic.* https://doi.org/10.1007/978-3-030-90040-3

Conclusion

The everyday life and transformations of primary schools in Czechoslovakia (now the Czech Republic) in the period of late socialism and especially during the post-socialist transformation are the main topics of our book. The period between 1989 and 1999 is the centre of our focus. This time span included a largely 'spontaneous' period of transformation for primary schools, and ultimately for the entire school system and education. Of course, the entire society of the time was undergoing a series of changes.

Our book is based on research of the broader historical contexts of the development of education in Czechoslovakia, from the establishment of the Czechoslovak Republic in 1918 to the Velvet Revolution in 1989. That is to say, after 1989, discussions appeared for example about a return to the model of the school system from the First Czechoslovak Republic (1918–1938), which was to become a partial basis for the school reform at that time. Socialism and the socialist school system form an important historical framework. Many teachers and school heads were educated and lived during this period, and a significant portion of them also worked in unified socialist schools. The problems of the school system and the ideas about reforms after 1989 were somewhat connected to the periods of perestroika and glasnost (in Eastern Europe) in the second half of the 1980s. The book therefore also focuses on the period of 'normalization' (1969–1989) with an emphasis on the 1980s and the fall of the communist government.

We have presented the main results of our research, summarized in individual chapters. The chapters differ in their content and in their approach to the research of the given topic, which was determined by the content of the interviews as well as the available source material.

This book represents the completion of one stage of our research efforts over the last decade. In our research, we have focused on understanding the socialist and post-socialist society and school system, drawing mainly on the principles and approaches of microhistory—the history of everyday life, ethnology, and social anthropology.

© Masaryk University, Faculty of Arts, Registration no. 00216224, VAT ID: CZ00216224 2024

J. Zounek et al., *(Post)Socialist Transformation of Primary Schools*, https://doi.org/10.1007/978-3-031-58768-9

In terms of methodology, research has shown that it is useful to use a mixed design when researching the recent history of the school system, i.e. to combine the traditional research of historical sources and archival research with oral history or possibly with research of teachers' life stories. Our research focused on the teachers' everyday life (microhistory) and on the functioning of primary schools during the period of normalization and the period of transformation; it also focused on understanding the general historical context and the general history of the school system (macrohistory). This approach allowed us to get to know the given topic more comprehensively and to understand and interpret the new findings in broader contexts. This can be regarded as one of the contributions of our research: no one else has studied the everyday life of primary schools in the territory of the Czech Republic in the second half of the twentieth century to such an extent and in such a way. Our methodological bases have proven important for the research of the contemporary history of pedagogy and the school system, because they give this rather sensitive topic a solid framework that prevents us from perceiving contemporary history only in black and white, or from simplifying or even vulgarizing some themes.

However, we must also bear in mind the limits of our research and its methodology. Our research was conducted in one region of the Czech Republic. The region is large, diverse, and encompasses environments that vary in terms of economic development and the social composition of the population. It has a large regional city, a number of medium-sized towns, and many rural areas. The region is traditionally characterized by a higher religiosity than many other parts of the Czech Republic. Many of the findings of our research can be quite cautiously considered characteristic of the entire country, but in no way can our results be generalized to the entire Czech Republic. We spoke to many narrators who had worked at various positions in the school system, including teachers and school heads as well as former employees of the Ministry of Education, the school inspectorate, and education offices, so we had a diverse sample of respondents. Every respondent was an eyewitness who was willing to talk to us, share their experiences, or provide us with materials (photos or personal documents) from their archives. It is practically impossible to get the cooperation of, for example, teachers who had to quit the school system for any reason or who were dissatisfied with their profession; we had such respondents in our sample, which we consider a great success. However, this difficulty undoubtedly represents a limitation of the methodology used.

In view of our findings, we believe that a general dislike (or perhaps unwillingness) to talk openly about the period around 1989 played a role for some respondents. This is not surprising, as this was a sensitive period for many people. Nevertheless, our research took place 30 years after the Velvet Revolution and almost 20 years after the end of the first phase of the transformation of the school system, which was completed in 2004 with the first non-socialist Education Act. The predominant view of the communist era at the time the interviews were held may have had a significant influence. The political and economic situation of the time may also have had an influence. During our research, external influences included the refugee crisis in Europe, the Covid-19 pandemic, the Russian aggression in Ukraine, and of course the situation in Czech politics and the economy. The

Covid-19 pandemic in particular influenced the last phase of our research. It would certainly be interesting to repeat the same research in a few years. Another pitfall of research that uses oral history is the respondents themselves, especially with regard to their age. Some of our narrators were in their eighties, and the interviews represented a considerable burden for some of them, although they were happy to talk to us. This type of research clearly cannot be delayed too long. Eyewitnesses pass away and their unique life experiences disappear with them.

To some extent, eyewitnesses who are teachers are a specific group of respondents. On the one hand, they 'know how to talk'—they have no problem with narration. On the other hand, they were very sensitive about the transcripts of their own interviews. They were often surprised by how ungrammatical the transcriptions of the interviews looked, even though they almost always used fairly sophisticated speech. At other times, they were afraid of being recognized in the interviews or of being identified by their colleagues—even though we anonymized everything. Some eyewitnesses did not want to authorize the interviews, or wanted to completely rewrite the interviews so that everything was grammatically and stylistically 'correct'. However, we could not agree to this. From a human point of view, such an approach is quite understandable, but from a scientific point of view, it represents another important methodological observation that will have to be processed, and ways of addressing this complication will have to be found. This is not a completely trivial matter, as it complicates work with oral sources, which constituted one of the cornerstones of our research.

A specific kind of historical source is created through oral history; in some cases, it may be the only source. At the same time, the success of the interview depends on the breadth of the historian's skills, sympathy, expertise, and patience with the respondents. The degree to which the historian's perception is 'attuned' to the narrator's narrative identity then determines the degree to which the unreliability, bias or distortion of the statements is weakened within the oral testimony. Despite these potential limitations, the data obtained should not be seen as a 'distortion' of the past, but rather as a mediation of it. Memory does not necessarily describe the researched event objectively. In particular, we use it to reconstruct and understand a person's actions in a given situation or an event that we would not have otherwise understood. The fundamental contribution of oral history to the learning of contemporary history is that a new historical source is created that can serve in the context of the given research and in other research. Moreover, the interviews have the advantage that the historian can ask the eyewitness about other topics or ask for clarification of certain ambiguities or contradictions. Thus, the informational value of such a source can be greatly enhanced.

Another limitation of our research stems from the unprocessed archival materials. Many archival fonds are still inaccessible because of the archival law, which only allows research of materials older than 30 years. According to the archivists' statements, it may take a long time yet to process the relevant fonds on transformation. Moreover, the 'period of revolution' did not favour the preservation of documents in printed form. Especially shortly after the fall of communism, many decrees and official instructions were disseminated over the phone or via communication in person, so they were not preserved anywhere in print. This is a significant limiting factor for the development of historical-pedagogical research. Contemporary studies (few yet focused on our topic), books, regulations, statistical summaries, and various types of reports that have been published and are available in public libraries can be considered a certain compensation. In some cases, 'detective' work is required to find older publications, but the results are often very interesting and important for the research.

All of our research is based on the conviction that the period of socialism and post-socialism is of key importance to the historical experience of individuals and the entire society of the second half of the twentieth century in the former Czechoslovakia and many European countries. Indeed, even today, we should not underestimate the various forms of the 'heritage' of the difficult period of the second half of the twentieth century in these countries, whether we refer to people's memories or especially to their deliberations about contemporary society, politics, culture, science, education, the school system, or life, but also about the prospects of the near or distant future.

It is not easy for us to conclude this book, because it is the conclusion of many years of extremely interesting research for us, and, with some degree of exaggeration, the end of a project that has been a part of our lives, even in the difficult times of the Covid-19 pandemic. Writing the conclusion is also difficult for us because not even several years is enough time for research of this type, as it can be assumed that the archives, for example, have yet to make many sources on the researched period available.

For these reasons, we have chosen a rather 'open' ending to our book. We do summarize the results so far, while asserting that our research provides only a partial insight into the large and complex topic of the contemporary history of the school system.

When investigating the period of the transformation of primary schools after 1989, it is necessary to remember that—unlike most other socialist countries—Czechoslovakia and the German Democratic Republic had virtually unreformed communist school systems in the late 1980s. Contemporary analyses listed the fundamental ills of the school system, including excessive bureaucracy, uniformity, unified management, outdated school equipment, low teacher salaries, the declining prestige of the teaching profession, students overloaded with subject matter, and teachers using inadequate teaching methods.

On the other hand, cautious reforms of the school system were being prepared and partially applied between 1987 and 1989, i.e. during the period of the 'specific Czechoslovak concept of perestroika'. However, these attempts were strongly limited by ideology, including the belief that it would be impossible to change the unified school system in any way, because the government of the Communist Party of Czechoslovakia (Komunistická strana Československa, KSČ) built its power on unchanging dogmas. Admittedly, the reform proposals of the time corresponded with the key objective of perestroika: streamlining the state's economy. The considered measures thus also included a certain decentralization of the school management and function, which was to lead to increased efficiency. The process of preparing an amendment to the Education Act was also under way in 1989.

Attempts at cautious reforms in the context of perestroika suggest that the immediately successive period of post-socialist transformation must be perceived in broader contexts. The events in the school system after the fall of the communist regime can be described as a stage of many changes and of certain continuities from the previous period, which is an important framework for understanding the school system transformation.

We perceive the term 'transformation' itself as the long-term and complex process of the transformation of society, within which the needs, demands, and expectations associated with the school system and with education in general are changing. Individual schools undergo transformations, of course, and the people involved in school education also change in many ways. The transformation processes therefore reflect the interests of individuals, groups, and the entire society.

The transformation of the education system and the life of schools in Czechoslovakia took place within the context of many structural problems in the changing society. The transition to a market economy affected all aspects of people's lives. The school system also necessarily faced rather significant economic problems; this topic dominated the Ministry of Education and even sidetracked pedagogical issues. In our sample, workers from the education offices mentioned that the economic meetings were the most important ones at the Ministry of Education.

The new political representation declared its interest in education when it emphasized its democratic value. However, education was not a priority in political practice. The economic transformation connected with the privatization of industry and the entry of foreign capital was in fact the key topic of the political sphere. It was even said that the school system was on the sidelines again, as it had been under socialism. This could be caused by the idea that education is mainly a democratic or a cultural value and it is not linked to social and especially economic capital. In other words, the results of reforms in education are not immediately visible (for example, they do not rapidly manifest in salary increases) and they require long-term systematic work to appear in the lives of individuals and the functioning of the entire society.

The contemporary incongruity of opinions on reforms, the difficult search for compromises as well as the need to quickly deal with urgent everyday problems resulted in no major (pedagogical) reforms taking place in the first years after the Velvet Revolution. The period after the Velvet Revolution was one of spontaneous transformation, for which partial changes, experimentation, lack of systems, lack of rules, and, in many respects, chaos, were typical. The situation was aptly described in an entry in a school chronicle: 'Every reasonable person wished for and long expected changes in the stagnant country. And when they came, they seemed to catch everyone unprepared, proceeding in a hurried, even chaotic manner.' The described characteristics also appear in the participant memory of our respondents. However, witnesses of the transformation in schools still consider this period to be the era of the greatest freedom. The need to 'breathe freely' was also reflected in the everyday life of schools. In practice, this may have been reflected in the elimination of everything that teachers considered pointless and unnecessary.

It should be emphasized that changes in the everyday life of schools did not happen overnight. Many of the processes established during the socialist period continued to function due to inertia. Perhaps this is also a reason our narrators had problems remembering the timing of the changes. Of course, many people involved at the local level (school heads, mayors, parents) did not want or even rejected the fundamental changes. This could have simply been a conflict of different interests or priorities, especially in the first years of the 'uncontrolled' transformation. It might not have necessarily been an attempt to maintain the status quo.

The spontaneous character of the transformation contrasted with the need for proper preparation of the political and legislative framework of the transformation. This preparation entailed the formulation of the vision for the future education and school system, which was to lead to gradual and systematic reform steps with clear starting points, areas of change, measures, and implementation steps. This did not happen for a full decade after the fall of communism. The socialist Education Act of 1984 was merely amended multiple times; it was not until the second half of the 1990s that the vision of modern democratic education and school system began to be discussed in the Czech Republic.

Despite the lack of concept and all the ambiguities accompanying the reforms of the school system, the transformation of schools was inspired by neoliberal ideas that were influential in the Western world in the late 1980s and early 1990s. The crucial element of the transformation—the decentralization of the unified school system—was in line with these ideas. Together with decentralization, the adoption of the Law on State Administration and Self-Government in Education at the end of 1990, in which the 'sectoral management of the school system' was introduced, was probably one of the most important events of the school system transformation. Schools were to no longer be directly subjected to the state administration and self-government in matters of funding and methodological management of education. They were to be managed by the education offices, which were directly subordinated to the Ministry of Education. The municipalities, as founders, were to be primarily responsible for funding the operation of schools and the maintenance of school buildings.

The self-governance of schools was a reaction to the strictly directive management of schools before 1989, when 'decisions about schools were made without schools'. The autonomy was intended to enable schools to make independent decisions in all key areas of their operation, to eliminate excessive administration, and to aim towards giving schools individual profiles, in which each school was to have its own 'face' and 'name'. This created a higher level of responsibility for the school management, of course.

That is why the early 1990s can be considered the period of 'the greatest freedom'. Responsibility in the form of self-governance and the consolidation of school system management that occurred around 1995 may have brought increased obligations to the school management. These obligations might have been connected to the need for independent and efficient management of the school. It was in the field of management where accurate records of the many processes that were then being checked was necessary. As one narrator mentioned, the schools began to feel a 'nostalgia for those times'—meaning the directive management and control before 1989. To some extent, these views were based on unrealistic (often even naive) ideas and misunderstanding of the principles of school autonomy on the part of many school heads and teachers, but also on the lack of support for schools and the lack of clarity in the process of transition to self-governance. Even those officials who were supposed to support schools in this reform were not convinced of its positive benefits. This was especially true in relation to small rural schools, which had difficult conditions and for whom the transition to autonomy was a major problem, sometimes because of inexperience and often because of the lack of adequately trained staff to deal with the economics and management of the entire institution. In some small schools, the school did not have the funds for an economist (accountant) and so the school head had to fill this role.

The transition to self-governance can be considered one of the major topics of the primary schools' transformation, but its evaluation by the direct participants varied. We believe that this topic was important in the 1990s and brought huge changes to the schools. All the effects that autonomy would have on various schools were not sufficiently considered and prepared. This can be explained by the fact that the period of revolution demanded quick solutions, but these were often not (and even could not be) based on broader professional frameworks or analyses. Some school heads in our sample remarked that the self-governance further emphasized the economic aspect of school management, which led to a further sidetracking of the pedagogical work of school heads and the pedagogical side of school management.

The eyewitnesses' views of transformation were also affected by repeated and unplanned interventions in the school management system. After about 10 years of operation, the education offices, as regional institutions for the decentralized management of the education system, were abolished. This occurred when these institutions had already established themselves and were able to effectively and efficiently support the schools. Changes in the structure of state administration were usually connected to transformations in regional administration and also to the desire to optimize costs, i.e. to save money. This was one of the main reasons for the abolition of the education offices. The impact of this abolition on the operation of schools and on their support goes beyond the scope of our book. However, according to our narrators, it was not a change in the positive direction, as the support of schools was presumably 'moved away' from the districts to the regional level. The abolition of education offices strengthened the influence of municipalities on the functioning of primary schools, and the schools may have found less professional support than they had from the education offices.

Schools are social institutions with the main objective of training and educating children. A school can be characterized as a specific environment created for learning. In our book, we also understand school as a community of people, adults, adolescents or children, and even participants outside of the school. Especially for (newly) autonomous schools in the period of transformation, relationships within the school and with the school environment gained importance.

Parents had a more significant say in school education after 1989, which in many ways complicated the parent-teacher relationship. The teachers did not always adequately perceive the need to change their attitudes towards parents, seeing the 'emancipation' of parents as an intrusion into their professional field. Conversely, parents sometimes had unreasonable expectations of the school education and upbringing and of the role of teachers. Moreover, the 'heritage' of the socialist school system era, with which the people involved coped in various ways, manifested itself in many respects here. Teachers could even be perceived as the representatives of the old regime, and they had to cope with this burden.

On the one hand, teachers criticized excessive parental pressure; on the other hand, they also negatively evaluated the opposite problem—the parents' lack of interest in their children's education and their unwillingness to cooperate with the school. According to the teachers, in the market environment, many parents began to perceive the school more as an institution from which they, as clients, ordered their children's education, and they demanded that the school deliver an imaginary finished product, i.e. a well-behaved and educated child. From the perspective of our narrators who were teachers, the blame for the lack of or poor cooperation with the school was on the parents who prioritized their own personal interests. However, the high appreciation of individualism was clear and accepted in the transforming Czech society. All the negatives of the transformation of the parent-teacher relationship cannot be blamed on the parents' behaviour. On the contrary, we can be critical of this dominant viewpoint of our narrators and offer other viewpoints from eyewitnesses and experts.

According to our findings and the opinions of some people involved, the attitudes of teachers stemmed from their lack of preparedness for the transformation of their position after 1989 and their lack of respect for the idea of parents as the school's partners with the right to express opinions related to the upbringing and education of their children. This can be understood in connection with another continuity from the socialist school period. The school and the teachers' work were strictly governed, and especially by the Ministry of Education. After the Velvet Revolution, the need to perceive and observe the new legal standards permeated the minds of many people involved only very slowly.

Our results suggest that during the first decade after the fall of the communist rule, in many schools it was not possible in practice to build a full partnership between the parents and the school that was accepted by all the persons involved. However, based on our research the critical view of the parent-school relationship after 1989 cannot be generalized and considered the only form of this relationship. Many narrators have described various forms of good relationships and cooperation with the parents or community in the field of teaching and especially in extracurricular activities.

Interpersonal relationships among the teaching staff were also an important element in the functioning of schools. Functional teacher collectives and good school management have a major effect on the atmosphere in the school and on the satisfaction of the teachers, and therefore on the quality of all the activities that take place in the school. When it comes to evaluating the relationships between colleagues in the teaching staff, our narrators' memories are predominantly positive. On the other hand, many references in school chronicles and other records from the period of Velvet Revolution and later suggest that relations within pedagogical collectives may have been very strained, and not just because of the political events in 1989. Contemporary sources indicate that there were conflicts among teachers for various reasons, both personal and professional. Here, it proved beneficial to combine oral history with the study of archival materials, because it was in the contemporary school materials where we were able to uncover even sensitive topics in the relationships between teachers that did not appear in the interviews. Here, we must not forget the weaknesses of oral history, and bear in mind a certain degree of idealization in the recollections or nostalgia in the interviews with the narrators.

The life of a school is also influenced by its location. When the narrators talk about the environment of the school where they worked, they make certain generalizations (perhaps rather unintentionally). For example, there were simplified divisions into urban and rural schools in the interviews. Czech society is largely urbanized, so the urban environment can be perceived as the standard, while the rural environment can be perceived as something specific or different. In fact, the environment of each school is unique to some extent. The characteristics of the various school locations cannot be simply divided into rural and urban areas. The situation in an urban school may also differ depending on whether it is located in the city centre or in a housing project, or whether it is a smaller district town or a metropolis. The increase in social inequalities in society was also connected to the increase in differences among individual schools. The freedom of school choice brought about competition between schools and led to motivated parents enrolling their children in schools with a 'better' reputation. The character of the higher grades of primary schools was also affected by the outflow of most talented students to multi-year grammar schools.

There were many rapid, albeit sometimes partial or improvised, changes in schools after 1989. At the same time, many teaching practices and approaches to subject matter remained virtually unchanged. The 'heritage' of the socialist school system manifested itself here as well. Teachers and their concepts of teaching do not change from 1 day to the next, nor can they simply be changed with a decree or an Act. Moreover, the experience with the communist regime played a part in the rejection of anything that resembled indoctrination. Resistance to rules and excessive organization formed a dominant image of schools in the early 1990s, an image also present in the memories of teachers.

The transformation brought about a 'destruction of the old' and it is important to take note of what was removed. For example, our narrators spoke about didactics: the 'destruction' affected didactic practices that had little to do with ideology or politics and could still have been used, albeit in an innovated or updated form. Many of the changes were unprepared and did not take into consideration the sometimes multiple impacts or other subtle differences in the reformed areas.

Some subjects had parts of their contents removed due to the ideology they reflected. In some cases, entire textbooks were withdrawn after the revolution. At the same time, the unified form of the previous content was evaluated positively by the teachers. Partial supplementation of the remaining content with topics that had been banned before 1989 and which had thus not been included in the learning curriculum quickly appeared. More fundamental transformations of the subject matter content, for example in completely new textbooks, were not evaluated very positively by the teachers. Once again, the heritage appears in procedures and in the work of teachers who were not prepared for such a change. The degree of their willingness and openness to these changes remains a question. On the other hand, it is clear that at the time of the transformation, many textbooks were published. Some of them were of poor quality, so their rejection by teachers was completely understandable. The gradual formation of the textbook market also played a role, with some publishers apparently having priorities other than quality. The Ministry of Education also stopped directing the publication of textbooks, which can be seen as a positive development. Nevertheless, the loss of control over the quality of textbooks on the developing textbook market was a rather large problem that was only addressed after a certain delay.

We learned relatively little about teaching methods and their possible innovations or transformations, as these routine practices did not represent an important topic for our narrators. Nevertheless, in the interviews and especially from the chronicles, we discovered that changes in this field were quite complex. The practices used in the pre-1989 era of a unified school system, i.e. the prevalence of frontal teaching, the more or less uniform structure of lessons, and the emphasis on getting through the prescribed curriculum regardless of its mastery by the students, played a significant role. The virtually complete freedom shortly after the Velvet Revolution could have been a time of unrestricted pedagogical experimentation, of rejecting unsatisfactory traditional teaching practices, and of using more suitable practices. However, it seems from our data that the status quo was largely maintained and only the biggest negatives, related mainly to ideological ballast, were removed. Understandably, many teachers tried to change their teaching even without any significant support. However, in our sample, we observed only a few innovative teachers and teachers who had participated in training aimed at more fundamental innovations in teaching and learning. There were certainly changes, but these may not have remained in our narrators' memories, because after 1989, there were many simultaneous changes in schools, in personal lives, and in society. Moreover, what was perceived as a change back then may now be considered a standard, so it did not become the topic of our interviews.

The disintegration of further teacher education, during which the original system was practically destroyed, was another important topic of our conversations. One can only speculate on how further teacher education and perhaps even support for innovative teachers would have looked if the original system had been retained and innovated and the content and methods of further teacher education fundamentally changed. In fact, teachers perceived this system positively and also rated many of the pre-1989 courses relatively high. New forms of further teacher education, often on a private basis, with some narrators pointing out the problematic quality of such courses, also played a role.

The equipment of schools with teaching aids was rated relatively highly by the eyewitnesses, although the need arose for innovations of many teaching aids for which there was often no money in the schools. The introduction of computers into schools was gradual and depended more on individual schools, or rather on active individuals who first started to use computers in school administration and then only later in computer science lessons. It was not until 2000 or 2005 that all schools began to be equipped with computers as a part of a national project to introduce digital technologies into schools. At that time, teachers were just beginning to be systematically trained in how to use computers (and the Internet) and how to use them in their teaching. However, this topic goes beyond the scope of our book.

The teaching of foreign languages represents one of the most prominent topics in the interviews, and probably in the entire transformation. During the time of the socialist school system, only Russian was compulsory, and Western languages were taught to a very limited extent and only in selected schools. Russian was replaced by a free choice of one world language, with the choice mainly between English, German, and French. This change took place quickly after the fall of communism, with enormous pressure coming mainly from the parents. This created a whole series of problems because schools were not prepared for such a fundamental change—there were no qualified teachers of these languages, especially English. A temporary solution was sought, including some that seem unusual from today's point of view. Native speakers, whose priorities sometimes lay in getting to know the post-socialist Czechoslovakia rather than in teaching a foreign language, may not have been of much help in schools and often were not even qualified to be teachers. For some time, Western languages were also taught by retrained Russian teachers, with whom the quality of teaching was a big issue, as these teachers were often only 'one lesson ahead' of their students.

Nearly everything was in motion, but at the same time many things remained unchanged or changed very slowly. To put it metaphorically, in the river of change, there were quite a lot of boats led by experienced people who lacked the courage, the desire, and often even the reason to change anything about the boat or the way it was operated. In the same river, there were a few new ships, captained by courageous people, that often crashed into the shore because they were not built very well. However, others navigated the new vessels successfully, and even showed others how. The problem was that no one knew where the river was flowing.

Our research presents a number of challenges for follow-up research that could develop the understanding of the topic of socialist and post-socialist school systems, and not just in the Czech Republic.

Within the Czech Republic, it would be useful to extend the scope of the research to other regions, and especially to the capital city of Prague. It would be interesting to see whether the transformation in schools took place in Prague in advance of other regions, as the capital was the centre of the Velvet Revolution and new information could reach schools quickly. At the same time, it would be interesting to investigate whether and how the transformation processes differed from school to school, given that Prague is one of the most developed regions of the country. It would also be interesting to study the transformation of schools in traditionally disadvantaged regions of the Czech Republic such as North Bohemia. The regions in which the fall of communism meant, for example, the decline of heavy industry or mining and what this change meant for the transformation of schools would also be a challenge for research.

Questions arise about a possible focus on the transformation of special education in the Czech Republic. The transformation of grammar schools or secondary vocational schools would also be interesting. Especially in the case of secondary vocational schools, the situation could have been complex, as many schools were closely linked to large state-owned enterprises that gradually went bankrupt or were privatized. The research of the transformation of further teacher or school head education institutions is a major challenge. The study of transformation through the eyes of other participants, such as the students of the time and their parents, still remains a question. We also do not know much about the transformation of leisure time institutions.

Archival research is a big issue. Many documents will only become available in the coming years, although the main question is when they will be processed and ready for professional research.

Many of the questions concerning school transformation also apply to international comparative research, which could include two or more post-socialist countries and would focus on macrohistory, i.e. on school and education policy in the given countries, and/or on microhistory, in which the research would be directed towards the everyday life of schools, individual participants, or even other school institutions.

Our research led us to questions aimed at comparing the processes of change and innovation in school systems in various regions of Europe, not just in Central and Eastern Europe, where changes and reforms both similar and different have taken place in different periods in the educational policy, in the management or operation of schools, and in teaching. These changes and reforms would sometimes be based in similar theoretical or professional starting points and at other times in different points. All of this information could enrich the knowledge base regarding school systems and education in Europe; it would be valuable to trace the principles of successful and unsuccessful transformations and reforms that have taken place in different parts of Europe.

Index

A
After-school club, 123
Alternative schools, 59, 121, 168, 190,
     249, 250
Archive, 11, 12, 25, 166, 218,
     219, 258
Atheist society, 60

C
Communist Party, 26, 53, 55, 56, 59,
     61, 64, 65, 78, 79, 81, 85, 97,
     118, 144, 146, 158, 220, 231,
     232, 246, 253, 270
Community, 60, 180, 186, 197, 199,
     202–204, 208, 233, 235,
     250, 273, 274
Computer, 118, 172, 215, 219, 238, 244,
     255–257, 277
Curriculum, 65, 95

E
Economic reform, 55, 136
Educational Act, 166
Education policy, 5, 64
Everyday life, xvi, 9, 28, 98

F
Foreign language, 58, 85, 93, 145, 148, 158,
     162, 217, 219, 258, 261, 277

G
German Democratic Republic, 57, 102,
     246, 270
Grammar school, 28, 38, 39, 44, 62, 121, 123,
     128, 187–191, 208, 259, 275

H
Historical research, 8, 12
Hungary, 2, 3, 40–43, 57, 82, 102,
     135–137, 255

I
Iron Curtain, 89, 162, 163, 198, 240

L
Leisure time, 227, 278
Lesson planning, 89, 90, 95, 262

M
Macrohistory, 9
Memory, 2, 8, 14, 21, 22, 28, 91, 93, 94, 98,
     150, 168, 175, 176, 180, 181, 184–186,
     198–200, 206–208, 216, 217, 219,
     225–227, 233, 235–240, 244, 245, 250,
     256, 260, 263, 269, 275
Municipality, 14, 28, 96, 122, 124, 136,
     163–165, 167, 168, 170, 171, 173, 174,
     200, 201, 208, 234, 249, 272

© Masaryk University, Faculty of Arts, Registration no. 00216224,   279
VAT ID: CZ00216224 2024
J. Zounek et al., *(Post)Socialist Transformation of Primary Schools*,
https://doi.org/10.1007/978-3-031-58768-9

O
Oral history, v

P
Parents, 202, 246, 274
Perestroika, 81
Pioneer, 71, 84, 96, 99–101
Poland, 2, 3, 41–43, 57, 60, 82, 135–137
Prague Spring, 66–69, 71, 78, 81, 85, 86,
    219, 222
Prefabricated housing estate, 192

R
Reforms, 1, 4–6, 10, 11, 25–28, 38, 40, 42–45,
    54–57, 62, 63, 65, 67, 68, 78, 79, 81,
    83, 103–110, 117, 118, 120–130, 132,
    134, 136, 137, 153, 161, 165, 168, 175,
    214–216, 225, 238, 239, 245, 246, 262,
    267, 270–272
Religion, 23, 39, 40, 43, 60, 61, 67, 72,
    216, 228
Rural, 186
Rural school, 4, 67, 136, 159, 172, 174, 185,
    196, 201, 255, 273, 275

S
School autonomy, 118, 171, 173, 208, 273
School building, 122, 134, 164, 192, 193, 272
School chronicle, 2, 148, 150, 152, 184,
    252, 276
School head, 1, 9, 13, 14, 28, 61, 118, 122,
    132, 136, 138, 146, 149–159, 162–168,
    171–176, 183, 189, 226, 228, 249, 250,
    252, 255, 257, 258, 261, 262, 267
School Inspectorate, 28, 29, 163,
    204–208, 239
School management, 118, 122, 146, 147, 149,
    159–161, 164, 166, 167, 172, 174, 175,
    184, 207, 229, 236, 270–272, 274
School social events, 203
Soviet Union, 46, 52, 53, 57, 58, 62, 64, 66,
    67, 71, 81, 97, 102, 137, 214, 215, 246

Students, 4, 8, 12, 13, 23, 27, 39, 43, 45, 56,
    58, 61, 62, 64, 71, 80, 82, 84, 86, 90,
    93, 95, 97, 99, 100, 105–108, 118, 120,
    122, 125, 126, 128, 129, 132, 133, 136,
    143, 148, 162, 164, 165, 175, 180, 183,
    184, 187–189, 191, 193, 196, 197,
    199, 201–203, 215, 217, 219, 222,
    223, 225, 228, 230, 232, 234,
    238, 248, 251, 254, 257, 259,
    261, 263, 270, 276
Summer house culture, 103
Syllabi, 88, 248, 251

T
Teacher, 1, 4, 7, 8, 10, 12, 13, 19, 21, 23, 25,
    27, 29, 38, 40, 42, 44, 59, 61, 62, 64,
    66, 67, 69, 71, 83, 85, 86, 88–96,
    98–105, 107, 125, 127, 131, 132, 134,
    138, 144–146, 149–151, 156, 157, 159,
    160, 162, 163, 166, 168, 172, 173, 180,
    182, 184, 186, 188, 189, 192, 193, 197,
    198, 201, 204–206, 208, 213, 215, 218,
    220, 222, 224, 226, 229, 230, 232, 235,
    236, 238, 239, 244, 247, 248, 250,
    252–254, 256–258, 261, 262,
    267, 273, 274
Teacher education, 63, 86, 87, 124, 215, 221,
    260, 261, 276
Textbooks, 62, 91, 93, 250–253, 257, 259,
    263, 276
'Think aloud' technique, 13

U
Uniformity, 29, 88, 90, 126, 251, 270

V
Visegrad Four, 135

W
White paper, 5, 124